# Integrated Multi-Tiered Systems of Support

# The Guilford Practical Intervention in the Schools Series

### Kenneth W. Merrell, Founding Editor
### Sandra M. Chafouleas, Series Editor

*www.guilford.com/practical*

This series presents the most reader-friendly resources available in key areas of evidence-based practice in school settings. Practitioners will find trustworthy guides on effective behavioral, mental health, and academic interventions, and assessment and measurement approaches. Covering all aspects of planning, implementing, and evaluating high-quality services for students, books in the series are carefully crafted for everyday utility. Features include ready-to-use reproducibles, appealing visual elements, and an oversized format. Recent titles have Web pages where purchasers can download and print the reproducible materials.

### *Recent Volumes*

Assessing Intelligence in Children and Adolescents: A Practical Guide
*John H. Kranzler and Randy G. Floyd*

The RTI Approach to Evaluating Learning Disabilities
*Joseph F. Kovaleski, Amanda M. VanDerHeyden, and Edward S. Shapiro*

Resilient Classrooms, Second Edition: Creating Healthy Environments for Learning
*Beth Doll, Katherine Brehm, and Steven Zucker*

The ABCs of Curriculum-Based Evaluation: A Practical Guide to Effective Decision Making
*John L. Hosp, Michelle K. Hosp, Kenneth W. Howell, and Randy Allison*

Curriculum-Based Assessment for Instructional Design:
Using Data to Individualize Instruction
*Matthew K. Burns and David C. Parker*

Dropout Prevention
*C. Lee Goss and Kristina J. Andren*

Stress Management for Teachers: A Proactive Guide
*Keith C. Herman and Wendy M. Reinke*

Interventions for Reading Problems, Second Edition:
Designing and Evaluating Effective Strategies
*Edward J. Daly III, Sabina Neugebauer, Sandra Chafouleas, and Christopher H. Skinner*

Classwide Positive Behavior Interventions and Supports:
A Guide to Proactive Classroom Management
*Brandi Simonsen and Diane Myers*

Promoting Academic Success with English Language Learners: Best Practices for RTI
*Craig A. Albers and Rebecca S. Martinez*

The ABCs of CBM, Second Edition: A Practical Guide to Curriculum-Based Measurement
*Michelle K. Hosp, John L. Hosp, and Kenneth W. Howell*

Integrated Multi-Tiered Systems of Support: Blending RTI and PBIS
*Kent McIntosh and Steve Goodman*

DBT Skills in Schools:
Skills Training for Emotional Problem Solving for Adolescents (DBT STEPS-A)
*James J. Mazza, Elizabeth T. Dexter-Mazza, Alec L. Miller, Jill H. Rathus, and Heather E. Murphy*

# Integrated Multi-Tiered Systems of Support

## Blending RTI and PBIS

**KENT McINTOSH**
**STEVE GOODMAN**

**THE GUILFORD PRESS**
New York    London

**Library of Congress Cataloging-in-Publication Data**

Names: McIntosh, Kent, author. | Goodman, Steve (Steven D.), author.
Title: Integrated multi-tiered systems of support : blending RTI and PBIS /
    by Kent McIntosh and Steve Goodman.
Description: New York : The Guilford Press, 2016. | Series: The Guilford
    practical intervention in the schools series | Includes bibliographical
    references and index.
Identifiers: LCCN 2015036603 | ISBN 9781462524747 (paperback)
Subjects: LCSH: Learning disabled children—Education—United States. |
    Problem children—Education—United States. | Behavior disorder in
    children—United States. | BISAC: PSYCHOLOGY / Psychotherapy / Child &
    Adolescent. | EDUCATION / Educational Psychology. | SOCIAL SCIENCE /
    Social Work.
Classification: LCC LC4705 .M45 2016 | DDC 371.9—dc23
LC record available at *http://lccn.loc.gov/2015036603*

*To my parents, Jennifer and Jim McIntosh,*
*who instilled my love for education from the very start*
—K. M.


*To my wife, Sheila, and my daughters, Stacy and Savannah,*
*who always help me to do better*
—S. G.


*And to Carol Sadler, whose ingenuity and dedication*
*were the inspiration for so many of us in this work*

# About the Authors

**Kent McIntosh, PhD,** is Associate Professor in the College of Education at the University of Oregon and Director of Educational and Community Supports, a research unit at the University of Oregon. In addition, he serves as a coinvestigator for the National Technical Assistance Center on Positive Behavioral Interventions and Supports, funded by the Office of Special Education Programs (OSEP). Dr. McIntosh's current research focuses on the implementation and sustainability of school-based interventions, particularly integrated academic and behavior response-to-intervention systems, and on equity in school discipline. He has disseminated his research results through more than 50 peer-reviewed scientific journal articles, free webinars, workshops, and numerous keynote addresses on the relationship between academic skills and problem behavior, the technical adequacy of functional behavioral assessment, the effects of schoolwide positive behavioral interventions and supports (PBIS) on academic achievement, and the validity of office discipline referrals. This work has been funded through several grants from federal agencies in the United States and Canada. In addition to his active research, Dr. McIntosh serves as a national trainer, consultant, and evaluator of PBIS. He has also worked as a school psychologist, teacher trainer, and teacher in both general and special education classrooms.

**Steve Goodman, PhD,** is Director of Michigan's Integrated Behavior and Learning Support Initiative (MiBLSi) and a partner with the National Technical Assistance Center on Positive Behavioral Interventions and Supports. He was the Michigan grantee principal investigator for the first OSEP-funded model demonstration grant competition utilizing an integrated behavior and reading support model. Dr. Goodman has over 30 years of experience in the field of education as a special education teacher and a teacher consultant, and he has worked as a trainer for Michigan's Positive Behavior Support project. He has coauthored several research articles and book chapters and has presented at numerous national and international conferences. Dr. Goodman is on the board of directors of the Association for Positive Behavior Support, serves on advisory panels for several statewide projects, and has consulted with state- and district-level projects across the United States.

# Contents

**PART I. FOUNDATIONS**     1

**1. Introduction**     3

Multi-Tiered Systems of Support    4
  *Academic and Behavior Response-to-Intervention Systems*    4
  *Integration into MTSS*    5
  *Components of Academic RTI and PBIS*    5
  *Not Just Literacy and PBIS*    8
  *Why Consider Combining Systems?*    9
Conceptual Origins of RTI, Multi-Tiered Systems, and Integrated Models    11
  *Response to Intervention*    11
  *A Tiered Approach to Service Delivery*    13
  *MTSS Misrules*    15
  *A History of Integrated Models*    16
Orientation to This Book    17
  *Purpose and Intended Readership*    17
  *Structure*    20

**2. The Relationship between Academic Skills and Behavior**     21

Research Showing a Connection between Academic Skills and Behavior    21
How Combined Academic and Behavior Challenges Develop over Time    22
  *Pathway 1: Behavior Challenges Reduce Access to Instruction*    22
  *Pathway 2: Underlying Attention Deficits Cause Challenges in Both Areas*    24
  *Pathway 3: Early Academic Challenges Increase Social Rejection*    25
  *Pathway 4: Inadequate Response to Academic Intervention Leads
    to Behavior Challenges*    26
Intervention Research on the Relationship between Academic Skills and Behavior    28
  *Crossover Effects of Academic Interventions on Behavior*    29
  *Crossover Effects of Behavior Interventions on Academic Skills*    30
Some Big Ideas about the Relationship between Academics and Behavior    31

## PART II. CORE COMPONENTS                                             33

### 3. Integrating Data                                                 35

Resistance to Data-Driven Education: Concerns and Solutions    36
  *Common Concerns Regarding Data Collection and Use in Schools
    and Potential Solutions    36*
Categories of Assessment Tools for Data Collection    38
  *Fidelity of Implementation    39*
  *Screening for Additional Support    44*
  *Diagnostic Assessment    47*
  *Progress Monitoring    57*
  *General Outcomes Measurement    59*
Guidance in Selecting Integrated Tools    62
  *Quality of Tools    62*
  *Trustworthy Sources for Selecting Tools    62*
  *Selecting Tools by Identifying Which Data Systems Are Already in Place    63*
Putting It All Together    64
  *Creating an Assessment Plan    64*
  *Creating an Evaluation Plan    64*
Integrating Data Systems    67
  *Necessary Components for Effective Integration    68*
  *Integrated Data Analysis    71*
Team Checklists: Integrating Data    72
APPENDIX 3.1.  Reading Tiered Fidelity Inventory (R-TFI)—Elementary-Level Edition    75
APPENDIX 3.2.  Reading Tiered Fidelity Inventory (R-TFI)—Secondary-Level Edition    78
APPENDIX 3.3.  Reading Tiered Fidelity Inventory—Comprehensive Edition
  (R-TFI-CE)    81
APPENDIX 3.4.  Multi-Tiered Systems of Support Needs Assessment—
  Elementary Version    89
APPENDIX 3.5.  Multi-Tiered Systems of Support Needs Assessment—
  Secondary Version    98
APPENDIX 3.6.  Integrated Academic and Behavior Request for Assistance Form    106
APPENDIX 3.7.  Inventory for Identifying MTSS Assessment Needs    109
APPENDIX 3.8.  Tiers 2 and 3 Intervention Tracking Tool    111

### 4. Integrating Practices                                            113

Smarter Integration    113
Integrated Practices within a Tiered Model    114
  *Tier 1: Universal Supports    114*
  *Tier 2: Secondary Supports    127*
  *Tier 3: Tertiary Supports    133*
Guidance in Selecting Integrated Practices    139
  *Selecting Evidence-Based Practices    139*
  *Selecting Practices by Assessing Practices Already in Place (Resource Mapping)    141*
Team Checklists: Integrating Practices    152
APPENDIX 4.1.  MTSS Quick Audit    155
APPENDIX 4.2.  Tier 2 Function-Based Intervention Resource Mapping Worksheet    156
APPENDIX 4.3.  Integrated Instructional Plan: Literacy and Behavior    157

### 5. Integrating Teaming                                              161

The Team Approach    161
  *Why Is a Team Approach So Important?    162*
Teams in MTSS    162
  *Common MTSS Teams at the School Level    163*
  *Common MTSS Teams at the District Level    167*

Strategic Integration of Teams   169
*Finding the Right Balance   169*
*Alignment of Teams   172*
Strategies for Effective Teaming   172
*Effective Teaming Structures   172*
*Integrated Problem-Solving and Decision-Making Processes   183*
Team Checklists: Integrating Teams   189
APPENDIX 5.1.  School Leadership Team Meeting Agenda   192
APPENDIX 5.2.  Student Support Team Meeting Agenda   195
APPENDIX 5.3.  Grade-Level Team Postbenchmarking Meeting Agenda   199

## 6. Integrating District Support Systems   202

How Districts Can Support Individual Schools in Implementing MTSS   203
*Effective Practices   203*
*Effective Implementation Process   204*
*Effective District Supports   204*
The Drivers of District Support   204
*Leadership Drivers   208*
*Contexture Drivers   210*
*Competency Drivers   211*
*Assessing Implementation Drivers   214*
A Model for Organizing District Support   214
*District Teams and Their Functions   215*
*Coordination across Teams   217*
Variations in District Support   218
*Variations in District Support Based on District Size   218*
*Differentiating Support for Schools Based on Need   220*
Team Checklists: Integrating District Support   224
APPENDIX 6.1.  EBISS Systems Coach Self-Assessment   228
APPENDIX 6.2.  Integrated MTSS Implementation Readiness Application   234

## 7. Integrating Entire Systems   236

Moving to Integrated MTSS Models: How Do We Get There?   237
*Simultaneous Adoption and Implementation   237*
*A Staggered Approach to Integration   238*
*Which Comes First: Academics or Behavior?   239*
Stages of Implementation   240
*Stage 1: Exploration/Adoption   241*
*Stage 2: Installation   246*
*Stage 3: Initial Implementation   249*
*Stage 4: Elaboration   251*
*Stage 5: Continuous Regeneration   252*
Addressing Concerns Regarding Integration   254
*"I Teach Science, Not Behavior."   254*
*"I Just Don't Want to Integrate Practices."   255*
*"I Don't Know How to Do Integration."   256*
*"I Will Not Be Adequately Supported to Integrate."   256*
*"Our Policies and Procedures Don't Allow for Integration."   257*
*"If We Add This New Focus, We May Stop Doing What We Do Well."   257*
*"There Is Not Enough Time to Work on Integration."   258*
Team Checklists: Integrating Entire Systems   259
APPENDIX 7.1.  MTSS Initiative Alignment Worksheet   264

**PART III.  CASE STUDIES OF SUCCESSFUL SYSTEMS**                                    **265**

 8. Oregon's Effective Behavioral and Instructional Support Systems Initiative:          **267**
    Implementation from District- and State-Level Perspectives
    *Erin A. Chaparro, Sally Helton, and Carol Sadler*

    Overview   267
       *District Level   267*
       *State Level   268*
    History of Implementation   268
       *District Level   268*
       *State Level   270*
    Current Status   272
       *District Level   272*
       *State Level   273*
    Unique Features   273
       *District Level   273*
       *State Level   274*
    Evaluation of Outcomes   278
       *District Level   278*
       *State Level   281*
    Lessons Learned   283
       *District Level   283*
       *State Level   284*

 9. Florida's Multi-Tiered Support System for Academics and Behavior                     **287**
    *Don Kincaid and George Batsche*

    Overview   287
    History of Implementation   288
       *Florida Positive Behavior Support Project   288*
       *Problem Solving/Response to Intervention Project   288*
       *RTI and PBIS to MTSS   289*
       *Systems-Level Impact and Collaboration   290*
       *District Action Planning and Problem Solving   293*
    Current Status   299
    Unique Features   299
    Evaluation of Outcomes   301
    Lessons Learned   302

10. Michigan's Integrated Behavior and Learning Support Initiative:                      **305**
    A Statewide System of Support for MTSS
    *Christine Russell and Anna Harms*

    Overview   305
    History of Implementation   306
       *Origins   306*
       *Professional Development Sequence   307*
    Current Status   310
       *Scaling Up a Statewide Project While Continuing to Influence Student Outcomes   310*
       *Structuring MTSS Support   311*
       *Sustainable Infrastructure   314*
    Unique Features   315
       *Investing in Leadership and Existing Structures   315*
       *District Management Structure   316*

    *MTSS Coordination*   *316*
    *Braiding with Current Statewide and District Initiatives*   *317*
    *MiBLSi Project Structure*   *317*
  Evaluation of Outcomes   319
    *Future Directions*   *322*
  Lessons Learned   323
    *Start Small and Use Learning to Scale Up*   *323*
    *Sustainable Change*   *323*
    *Continuous Improvement through Use of Data*   *324*
  Key Points from the Case Studies   324


**PART IV. LOOKING BACK, LOOKING FORWARD**           **325**

**11. Conclusion**           **327**

  Key Lessons in Integrating Systems   327
    *Lesson 1: Integrate Strategically*   *327*
    *Lesson 2: Function Is More Important Than Form*   *328*
    *Lesson 3: Lead with a Team*   *328*
    *Lesson 4: Focus on Doing a Few Things Well*   *328*
    *Lesson 5: Integration Is Hard Work*   *329*
    *Lesson 6: Integration Is Worth the Effort*   *329*
  What We Still Need to Know   329
    *Data*   *329*
    *Practices*   *330*
    *Teaming*   *330*
    *Integration*   *330*
  New Directions for Integrated MTSS Models   331
    *Integrating to Form Comprehensive Educational Systems*   *331*
    *Expanding beyond Educational Systems*   *331*
  Final Thoughts   332


**References**           **333**

**Index**           **352**

# PART I

# FOUNDATIONS

# CHAPTER 1

# Introduction

In a classic article on education reform, the late Glenn Latham (1988) described the state of education as continual change in ideas and practices, in search of continuous improvement. In sincere efforts to improve student outcomes, administrators bring in new educational innovations—initiatives or programs promising to improve instruction or other aspects of schooling—with great fanfare and excitement. The launch of these new initiatives brings equal measures of enthusiasm and new materials, including shiny binders and new buzzwords, with a host of acronyms to be memorized and used to describe how the daily tasks of teaching and learning are to be done differently.

Unfortunately, just as predictably as these educational innovations are installed, last year's promising innovations, regardless of their effects on student outcomes, are abandoned to make room for the new teams, trainings, and practices required for new initiatives. Last year's innovations are relegated to the dusty supply closet, and in a year or 2, today's new initiative, the one that was touted as the answer to every educational problem, will join the others.

The result of this process, one that Latham called "the birth and death cycles of educational innovations," is a predictable pattern of constant surface change, but with no discernible deep change in the way schools work (Coburn, 2003). It is easy to see how this process leads to wasted resources at a time when resources are scarce and quality education is desperately needed. Perhaps the most damaging part of these wasted resources is not the loss of money used to buy new programs or the loss of time spent training school personnel to use new forms and processes, but rather the loss of enthusiasm and willingness to try new approaches in education. The term *initiative fatigue* describes a common problem in education today: the feeling of being overwhelmed by innovation, resistant to new initiatives, and pessimistic about the feasibility of educational change (Greenberg, Weissburg, & O'Brien, 2003). It's easy to become jaded about educational reform when one sees so many promising initiatives come and go, with no end in sight to this cycle. If a teacher is skeptical of a particular new district initiative, he or she can simply ignore it until the next initiative takes its place. And unfortunately, teachers are often the first to be blamed when new initiatives fail to take root, even when such failure is almost certain (Valli & Buese, 2007).

This may seem to be a rather depressing and pessimistic way to open a book about a new educational innovation, one that brings its own new set of acronyms, forms, and processes. However, it is actually this challenging context of implementation—with its threat of poor implementation and abandonment—that makes a new approach so needed. How can adopting a new initiative break the challenge of initiative fatigue? Rather than adding yet another initiative to crowd out the to-do lists of teachers and administrators, what is needed is an approach that can help to connect existing efforts and systems across domains and integrate the support that is already provided to students into a seamless whole. This book attempts to do so by relying on the important connections between academics and behavior (i.e., social–emotional behavior), as opposed to the common approach of treating them as unrelated issues, with separate initiatives. At the same time, we promote a *strategic* approach to the integration of academic and behavior support systems, with careful consideration of where integration best works to improve student outcomes.

## MULTI-TIERED SYSTEMS OF SUPPORT

The term *multi-tiered systems of support*, or *MTSS*, has recently gained prominence in conversations about education reform. Our literature search of the ERIC and PsycINFO databases yielded 24 publications focusing on MTSS, only one of which was published before 2009. Any rapid increase in the popularity of a model should provoke concerns that it is a fad designed to make money for consultants or a poorly conceived media buzzword. But is it an entirely new model to learn, one that is designed to replace current practice, or something else? The answer lies in the widespread adoption of two popular and effective approaches to education.

### Academic and Behavior Response-to-Intervention Systems

Recently, two approaches—academic response to intervention (RTI; Brown-Chidsey & Steege, 2010) and schoolwide positive behavioral interventions and supports (PBIS; Sugai & Horner, 2009a)—have been implemented on a scale of social significance that has evaded many previous attempts at school reform. For example, the National Center on PBIS supports over 21,000 U.S. schools implementing PBIS. Considering that many schools also implement PBIS in the absence of formal support from the center, we conservatively estimate that at least one in five schools in the United States are implementing PBIS.

With respect to academic RTI, a recent survey found that 68% of schools were in some stage of districtwide RTI implementation, with 24% stating that RTI was part of their typical practices (GlobalScholar, 2011). However, most schools reported implementing RTI only for reading and only at the elementary level. In that survey, 51% of elementary schools reported full implementation of RTI for reading, and 20% reported full implementation of RTI for behavior. In secondary schools, 13% reported full implementation in reading, and 8% reported full implementation for behavior. With so many schools implementing one or both of these approaches, it is difficult to identify any other comprehensive school reform initiatives in this day and age that are in use in so many schools.

So why have these approaches been so widely adopted and sustained, when countless other educational practices have been abandoned, sometimes before they were even implemented (Cook & Odom, 2013)? One simple reason is effectiveness: They result in improved student outcomes when implemented by typical school personnel. Regarding PBIS, research from multiple universities, including multiple randomized controlled trials (in which some schools implement and others continue as usual), show reduced disruptive behavior, reduced bullying, increased academic achievement, increased school safety, improved teacher climate and perceived self-efficacy, increased social competence, and increased emotional regulation (Bradshaw, Koth, Thornton, & Leaf, 2009; Bradshaw, Waasdorp, & Leaf, 2012; Horner et al., 2009; Kelm & McIntosh, 2012; Nelson, Martella, & Marchand-Martella, 2002; Waasdorp, Bradshaw, & Leaf, 2012). For academic RTI, there is evidence that implementation, especially in the area of early literacy, can improve academic achievement overall and for struggling learners, improve neurological functioning, and decrease referrals and eligibility for special education services (Gunn, Biglan, Smolkowski, & Ary, 2000; Shaywitz et al., 2004; Simmons et al., 2002; VanDerHeyden, Witt, & Gilbertson, 2007; Vaughn, Linan-Thompson, & Hickman, 2003; Vellutino et al., 1996).

### Integration into MTSS

Given the extensive spread and effectiveness of these two approaches, there has been considerable informal discussion of how these approaches could be integrated into a coherent, unified system, sometimes referred to as *multi-tiered systems of support*, or *MTSS* (Sugai & Horner, 2009b). Some have described MTSS as a comprehensive approach to *one* domain of education (e.g., literacy), incorporating instruction, assessment, and decision making within a tiered model of service delivery, as opposed to a narrow conceptualization of RTI as simply a special education eligibility process (Kansas MTSS Project, 2012). This distinction is helpful in that it focuses attention on the broader context of education, as opposed to a particular educational decision-making process, often completed or led by a school psychologist (Baker, Fien, & Baker, 2010). However, in this book, when we refer to MTSS, we are specifically describing *integration of a number of multiple-tiered systems into one coherent, strategically combined system meant to address multiple domains or content areas in education* (e.g., literacy and social-emotional competence). Table 1.1 provides an overview of academic RTI, PBIS, and integrated MTSS models.

### Components of Academic RTI and PBIS

Both academic RTI and PBIS rely on a few shared, foundational principles that are so important that they govern many aspects of their delivery. These concepts are similar, if not identical, when applied to academic or behavior systems for prevention and optimization of learning. These components are shared briefly here and shown in Figure 1.1.

### Shared Components

It is not a coincidence that academic RTI and PBIS have such similarities. Many of their components are based on elements of quality instruction and effective systems change principles (McIntosh, Goodman, & Bohanon, 2010; Stollar, Poth, Curtis, & Cohen, 2006; Sugai & Horner, 2009b). For example, academic RTI and PBIS have at their core a focus on the prevention of

**TABLE 1.1. Systematic Approaches to Academic and Behavior Support: Definitions**

For clarity, we use the following definitions:

Academic response to intervention (RTI)

Academic RTI is a preventive systems approach to improving schoolwide and individual achievement through high-quality universal instruction and additional tiered supports provided in response to student need. It includes collaborative teaming across general and special education. Decisions in academic RTI are based on data from validated screening and progress monitoring tools. These data may be used as part of the special education eligibility determination process, but academic RTI includes *all* academic instruction systems, including core classroom instruction.

Schoolwide positive behavioral interventions and supports (PBIS)

Schoolwide PBIS is a framework for implementing evidence-based practices, providing a three-tiered continuum of support to students, using systems to support staff in implementation, and using data for decision making. As such, PBIS is considered an RTI approach for social and emotional behavior. PBIS emphasizes an instructional approach to behavior support, prevention through environmental change, adaptation to the local context, and using the science of applied behavior analysis to achieve outcomes that are valued by staff, students, and families.

Integrated multi-tiered systems of support (MTSS)

An integrated MTSS model provides all students with the best opportunities to succeed both academically *and* behaviorally in school. MTSS focuses on providing high-quality instruction and interventions matched to student need across domains and monitoring progress frequently to make decisions about changes in instruction or goals. It is not simply the implementation of both academic RTI and PBIS systems. There is a systematic and careful integration of these systems to enhance the efficiency and effectiveness of all school systems.

student challenges (be they academic or behavioral) that drives the selection and implementation of interventions, as well as the allocation of effort. Both approaches rely on a philosophy that preventing problems is more effective, for more students, than treating them as they arise. In addition, this prevention focus includes intervention for *all students*, regardless of risk, and a continuum of support provided for those who need more assistance to be successful. The goal for both academic and behavior systems is to enhance valued outcomes for students both in school and beyond by providing them with the skills needed to access reinforcement for their actions, be it being able to read content in their interest area, deal with setbacks, or establish and maintain friendships. Prevention and intervention in each system has an instructional focus, and instruction is based on principles of effective instruction, with an emphasis on differentiated instruction as a means of providing that continuum of support. Finally, just as the instructional delivery is based on effective practices, both systems share a commitment to evidence-based practices—that is, to those practices that have been shown to work across a range of classrooms and for more students. These elements of practice are discussed in Chapter 4.

The focus on a systems-based delivery of interventions also looks similar across the two domains. Academic RTI and PBIS are fundamentally *data driven*. Data—such as fidelity of implementation, student screening or benchmarking data, and progress monitoring data—inform both instruction and the implementation of the systems themselves. Data for both types of systems, as well as for integrated systems, are discussed in Chapter 3. Academic RTI and PBIS are also fundamentally *team driven* (Gersten et al., 2008; Sugai & Horner, 2009a). Implementation is undertaken and monitored by teams that use the aforementioned data, as well as formal action planning procedures, to enhance the quality of implementation and student effects over time. Teaming is discussed in Chapter 5. In addition, the team-based approach extends to collaboration across systems in schools. Whole-school initiatives require collaboration across general education, special education, administration, and school- and district-level support staff. As a result, effective academic RTI and PBIS teams include representatives from each of these groups to maximize the extent to which all educators in the school are actively involved in establishing, planning, and sustaining these initiatives.

## Differences in Components

However, despite these strong similarities, there are a number of notable differences that help distinguish academic RTI from PBIS. Some differences are small, such as terminology. In terms of curriculum, Tier 1 support in academic RTI refers to the core curriculum, whereas Tier 1 PBIS describes universal, or schoolwide, instruction. Other differences refer to the drive to implement. Because of legislation, academic RTI is often developed based on a mandate to change the process of special education eligibility determination. PBIS is more likely to be implemented based on concerns regarding overall school climate or levels of disruptive behav-

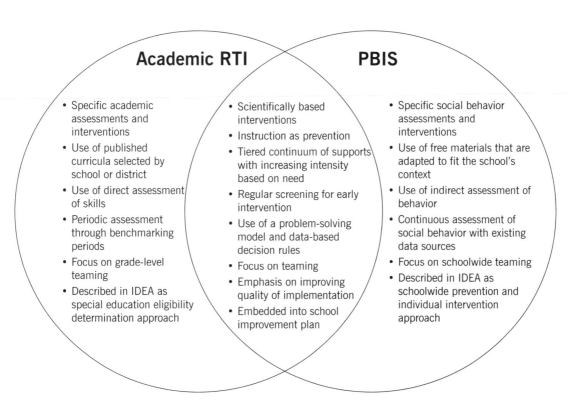

**FIGURE 1.1.** Similarities and differences between academic RTI and PBIS. Based on Sugai and Horner (2009).

ior. As a result, academic RTI may have more of a focus (at least initially) on evaluation and special education support. PBIS implementation generally starts with Tier 1 systems. Hence, the initial focus often occurs at different levels of the support provided. Academic RTI may have initial effects on special education and roles, and PBIS may have an initial, more noticeable effect on schoolwide climate, which can assist in implementation, as initial efforts are reinforced through visible results (Andreou, McIntosh, Ross, & Kahn, 2015). In addition, because of this focus on school climate and culture, PBIS may require more adaptation of practices to fit with the local context, which makes implementation more complex, but also possibly more appealing, as school personnel can modify their systems to meet the needs of their staff, students, and families.

Systems for implementation and delivery can also differ between academic RTI and PBIS. It is obvious that the student performance assessments will differ (e.g., academic skills vs. social competence), but the data systems themselves are fundamentally different. In academic RTI, one of the strengths of assessment is that it relies on direct measurement of skills. PBIS data present challenges because direct measures (i.e., direct observation) are costly, and so teams rely on indirect measures (e.g., office discipline referrals, teacher ratings of behavior). Direct academic measures also benefit from well-established and clear trajectories and benchmarks for skill development, but the same quantitative standards for social and emotional development are not currently available (McIntosh, Frank, & Spaulding, 2010). In addition, the assessment in academic RTI is periodic, whereas PBIS assessment may be periodic (e.g., fidelity assessment, screening) or continuous (e.g., office discipline referrals, suspensions). These differences affect the functioning of teams and the time points for decision making, with decision making happening quarterly more often in academic RTI (to coincide with benchmark data or trimester grades), and monthly more often in PBIS (to react to or prevent patterns of unwanted [i.e., challenging] behavior continually). The teams themselves are also different, with teaming in academic RTI occurring more often at the grade level, and teaming in PBIS more often a schoolwide endeavor. Finally, coaching for implementation may vary. The process of coaching itself may not be different, but the difference in content-area expertise required for coaching in each domain may necessitate different coaches, unless coaches are comfortable providing assistance with both sets of knowledge.

When compared to the similarities, these differences are not monumental, and the divide is easily bridged. It is important to note these differences, nevertheless, for two reasons. First, knowing them can help us avoid making incorrect assumptions about practices. Second, these different perspectives might inform and strengthen efforts in the other domain. In many senses, learning from these differences may help counter weaknesses in a single approach. For example, the quarterly meetings in academic RTI that assess student grouping may be a good opportunity to assess the general effectiveness of Tier 2 behavior support interventions, which may be better assessed periodically rather than briefly in monthly reports or during annual action planning.

## Not Just Literacy and PBIS

It is also important to mention that our conceptualization of MTSS does not simply encompass reading and behavior. Although most current integrated MTSS systems include a focus on early literacy and behavior (and most of our examples are the same), MTSS is not limited to these two domains. Instead, the general MTSS process we describe can be applied to a wide range of domains, including other academic domains (e.g., mathematics) and varying aspects of behavior (e.g., resilience, emotional competence). Moreover, MTSS can incorporate other systems-level approaches that are used in schools or related agencies. For example, school–family partnership initiatives have been integrated into MTSS (McCart, Wolf, Sweeney, & Choi, 2009; Sullivan & Daily, 2013, March). Wraparound support and parenting support have also been conceptualized as components of MTSS (Eber, Hyde, & Suter, 2011; Stormshak, Fosco, & Dishion, 2010). More recently, mental health supports have been linked with PBIS systems in an interconnected systems framework that recognizes the overlap across approaches and views isolated, parallel efforts as less effective than integrated ones (Barrett, Eber, & Weist, 2013). Specific initiatives such as dropout prevention efforts can also be incorporated (Legters & Balfanz, 2010).

Our main point is that any tiered support system or form of interagency collaboration can be integrated into an MTSS. Our primary focus in this book is on integrating academic instruction and RTI systems with PBIS because these are two commonly used systems, and there has been considerable success in doing so. However, this book can be used as a general case example of how to integrate *any* tiered systems related to education.

In addition, even stand-alone academic RTI and PBIS systems are often already integrated approaches of their own. For example, school teams may complete an audit of existing practices to identify which ones are already being implemented to support achievement or behavior (Sugai, Horner, Algozzine, et al., 2010; Sugai, Horner, & Lewis-Palmer, 2001). Within a comprehensive PBIS approach, schools may use a program such as Promoting Alternative Thinking Strategies (PATHS; Kusché & Greenberg, 1994) as a universal (Tier 1) curriculum for enhancing social and emotional learning for all students, the FRIENDS for Life program (Barrett, 2004) as a Tier 2 intervention for supporting students with subclinical (i.e., moderate) levels of anxiety, and restorative practices as alternatives to suspension at Tiers 2 and 3. Likewise, in literacy, schools may adopt different packaged curricula and instructional approaches to provide the most effective continuum of support across each tier.

## Why Consider Combining Systems?

Although it sounds logical to combine existing systems into an integrated approach, one would likely feel daunted by the considerable steps and possible conflicts among passionate and well-intentioned leaders. After all, it is all well and good to think theoretically about combining initiatives, but merging two well-articulated sets of training and technical assistance is not easy. Moreover, the will to collaborate, even among like-minded colleagues, is often tested to the extreme when budgets become shared. In many senses, George Batsche's analogy of a blended family is relevant. One might think aloud, "Why should we consider combining systems if our separate systems are already working well?"

The push for integration of these systems comes primarily from three assumptions. First, there is an established literature base documenting a strong relationship between academic skills and problem behavior, which we describe in detail in Chapter 2. As such, separate systems of intervention for interrelated problems may not be as effective as combined approaches (Stewart, Benner, Martella, & Marchand-Martella, 2007). This combined approach can also provide more seamless support, as opposed to separate systems, wherein a student might slip through the cracks. For example, a student with moderate challenges in both academics and behavior might not receive needed support if no one is looking at both sets of data to see the elevated risk for negative outcomes. In addition, integrating these systems can avoid the common challenge presented by silos of responsibility, in which different departments or teams accept responsibility for parts of the student, and no group takes a shared responsibility for the student as a whole.

Even more important, "siloed" academic and behavior systems themselves may work at cross purposes, because practices that seem effective for students in one system may be detrimental in another. For example, some schools regularly use behavior interventions that remove students from the classroom to reduce problem behaviors (e.g., time-out, cool-down rooms, restorative circles). These interventions are used in behavior systems because they often reduce problem behaviors in the short term. However, overuse of these interventions can reduce access to academic instruction, leading to improved behavior but worse academic achievement (Benner, Nelson, Sanders, & Ralston, 2012; McIntosh, Horner, Chard, Dickey, & Braun, 2008). Similarly, setting rigorous academic standards schoolwide can improve academic achievement (Jussim, 2013), but it may also increase rates of dropout and unwanted behavior. As a result, it is critical to consider both academics and behavior when implementing practices for either domain.

Second, as described above, academic RTI and PBIS share many common features and underlying theories. As a result, implementing practices in one area may make implementing the other practices more efficient. Once school personnel gain knowledge and experience in one area, the concepts, systems, and even intervention skills learned in that one area can build the capacity to make implementation in another area easier. In one sense, an MTSS lens teaches us that effective approaches to service delivery can be used for intervention in any domain of student learning. One need only change the target of intervention to build skills and ameliorate challenges.

Third, integrating academic and behavior support efforts may lead to more efficient use of resources and protection against multiple competing initiatives, enhancing the sustainability of both approaches (McIntosh, Horner, & Sugai, 2009). In an educational system where teachers are continually being asked to do more with less, bringing in new initiatives is more expensive than keeping old ones (Latham, 1988; Tyack & Cuban, 1995). When districts engage in several major initiatives concurrently (e.g., academic RTI and PBIS), the expense of coaching systems and limited time for inservice professional development can threaten both systems. Multi-tiered systems are commonly built as separate but parallel systems. The concept of parallel (or siloed) systems has been around as long as there have been systems, and if you are in education, you are most certainly familiar with the challenges that this parallel work brings, including initiative overload, inefficient use of resources, competition among initiative coordinators for professional development time, confusion among school personnel, and separation of instruction that allows students to fall through the cracks. This situation is even more frustrating considering how similar these initiatives are in both theory and practice.

As an alternative, combining these efforts can save the district in terms of funding, and more important, in capacity-building efforts for school personnel. Explicitly showing how these two initiatives address interrelated challenges (as seen in Chapter 2) can make a strong case for increasing or maintaining funding for an integrated model, whereby efforts in both areas can be sustained (McIntosh, Goodman, et al., 2010). In addition, an integrated model that includes multiple content areas may feel less like "one more thing on the plate" than implementing separate initiatives. Given this point and the previous points, there is considerable interest from implementers, researchers, and policymakers in how these complimentary approaches can be integrated, even when considering the serious challenges that may arise through the integration process.

## CONCEPTUAL ORIGINS OF RTI, MULTI-TIERED SYSTEMS, AND INTEGRATED MODELS

As noted, one of the compelling arguments for integrating academic RTI and PBIS is the shared foundational principles that permeate the daily practices of implementation. These systems are both focused on prevention, with the underlying concepts of assessing response to intervention and a tiered approach for service delivery. Considering how foundational these ideas are for both approaches (and education in general), it may be helpful to examine their origins and evolution, with an eye to how the history of these concepts might inform daily practice in an integrated MTSS model.

### Response to Intervention

With so much discussion regarding RTI, the systems and policies designed to promote it, and a logic that inherently fits with teaching, it is difficult for some to think of the educational system before RTI emerged. Many point to the 2004 U.S. federal reauthorization of the Individuals with Disabilities Education Act (IDEA; 2004) as the birth of RTI as we know it. Although that legislation certainly allowed the practice of RTI to scale up on a national level, the elements of RTI can be traced back many years.

The inclusion of academic RTI into the IDEA legislation had its origins in a workshop held by the National Research Council, which focused on alternatives to identifying specific learning disabilities through the ability–achievement discrepancy (L. S. Fuchs, personal communication, April 9, 2013). As had been noted by a number of researchers at the time (e.g., Reschly, 1988; Reynolds, Wang, & Walberg, 1987), the approach of identifying learning disabilities through comparing cognitive abilities and academic achievement has a number of drawbacks, including methodological, theoretical, and practical challenges. Probably the most salient drawbacks for educators were the lack of treatment validity (the extent to which the assessments indicated specific interventions to use) and having to wait until a significant discrepancy appeared before students became eligible (often until grade 3). This commonly termed *wait-to-fail* approach was viewed as harmful because students could not receive needed services that could potentially prevent their challenges, and the developmental window when remediation is most effective would rapidly be closing, leaving larger gaps and a persistent experience of failure (either academic or behavior) that could cause additional challenges (McIntosh, Horner, et al., 2008).

In place of the ability–achievement discrepancy, leading scholars proposed that special education eligibility decisions could be made through monitoring response to additional intervention (L. S. Fuchs, 1995). This scholarly work was supported by outcomes from districts and regions that had been implementing noncategorical special education delivery, such as the Heartland Area Educational Agency in Iowa (e.g., Reschly, 1995; Tilly, Reschly, & Grimes, 1998), Kansas State Department of Education (Kansas MTSS Project, 2012), and Minneapolis

Public Schools and the St. Croix River Education District in Minnesota (D. Miller, personal communication, June 4, 2013). According to this theory, an adequate RTI would indicate both that (1) a disability was not present and (2) the intervention provided was an effective support for that student's learning. On the other hand, an inadequate RTI would signal (1) the need for more intensive intervention (perhaps specially designed for that individual) and (2) the presence of a disability, based on the lack of growth in response to an intervention that has been shown to be effective for similar students (L. S. Fuchs & Fuchs, 1998). The rise in research in curriculum-based measurement in the previous decade made it possible for educators to assess this growth in a practical manner (Deno, 1989; Deno & Mirkin, 1977). Eventually, the combination of technical and theoretical advances culminated in the Office of Special Education Program's 2001 Learning Disability Summit (Bradley, Danielson, & Hallahan, 2002), leading to policy proposals and changes in federal special education law that instituted RTI as educational policy.

Although RTI currently seems to be firmly rooted in the domain of academic support and eligibility for specific learning disabilities (especially in early literacy), the term was used in the area of behavior and behavior disorders even earlier than for early literacy. In 1991, Gresham proposed the term *resistance to intervention* as a new method of assessing behavior disorders. The methodology was rooted in the applied behavior analysis literature, especially functional behavior assessment. The important foundational notion was that problem behavior could be conceived as adaptive (i.e., a student's best attempt to get his or her needs met), instead of simply maladaptive. As a result, Gresham noted the importance of environmental change (including interactions with adults) as critical to changing behavior. A specific unwanted behavior would be classified as resistant if it persisted even after effective intervention was applied. As an aside, it is interesting to note that the term *response to intervention* is now preferred because it places focus on the success of the support provided, not on individual characteristics, and it carries no implication that a lack of response is due to "willful" resistance by the student.

Some believe that the idea of RTI started even prior to 1991. In 1957, Cronbach proposed an ambitious agenda of merging two disparate bodies of research: the experimental research from behavioral psychology (focusing on intervention effects) and the correlational research from developmental psychology (focusing on individual differences). His thinking was that by examining intervention effects based on individual characteristics, one might uncover aptitude-by-treatment interactions. With knowledge of these interactions, educators could then select interventions based on student characteristics and feel confident that they would be effective. However, after over a decade of intensive research, Cronbach (1975) had found little to no evidence of aptitude-by-treatment interactions that could guide intervention. In reference to the difficulty of matching treatments based on student traits, he famously noted, "once we attend to interactions, we enter a hall of mirrors that extends to infinity" (p. 119). Instead, his research favored a process he called *short-run empiricism*, in which interventions are tested and modified for each individual based on formative assessment. In his words, "one monitors response to the treatment and adjusts it" (p. 126). In essence, he described the process of *response to intervention*.

Yet in reality, the origins of RTI may go back much further, far before the term *RTI*, Cronbach's hall of mirrors, or our modern educational system. In its essence, noting a student's response to an intervention is just a component of good instruction; delivering a lesson that is designed to be effective, identifying whether enough learning occurred for the lesson to be considered successful, and changing instruction as needed to ensure learning. Through this lens,

RTI can be viewed as a very natural way to teach and, in many ways, the complex systems and structures involved in implementing RTI are simply methods of ensuring that all students can learn.

## A Tiered Approach to Service Delivery

Another core concept of multi-tiered systems is right in the name. In fact, if you know anything about multi-tiered systems, chances are that you are familiar with the ubiquitous triangle. There are many variations of the triangle, but it's most commonly shown with three colors (green, yellow, and red), representing not groups of students, but rather levels of prevention (primary, secondary, or tertiary), types of support for students (universal, targeted, or intensive), curricula (core, strategic, individualized), or tiers of instruction (Tier 1, Tier 2, Tier 3). These labels for the tiers are generally interchangeable, in that they all describe the function of multiple tiers. In this book, we use the numbered tiers as our labels.

One of the reasons for the widespread popularity of the triangle, or its "stickiness" (see Gladwell, 2006), is its simple and straightforward presentation of the notion that school personnel can use as a general framework for unifying separate interventions. By using the triangle, teams at the school, district, and state levels can organize their support along a continuum that ranges from support for all students (universal support) to support for some students (targeted support) to support for the few students who require (intensive support). Each of these interventions has a separate target population and purpose, but the triangle allows us to see how these can work together to provide seamless systems of support for all students.

Although there are many stories regarding how the triangle came to be, most education researchers note that the multi-tiered approach came from the field of public health (Walker et al., 1996). Some identify the origin of the three-tiered model as from Caplan and Grunebaum (1967), although Gordon (1983) noted that by then, the model was used so widely in medical textbooks that a single originator is unlikely, and different groups added and subtracted the number of tiers as fit their context. In the same way, the model became widely translated for work in education by many practitioners and researchers. The first major publications describing the application of a multi-tiered model specifically to education (both academics and behavior) came in a text edited by Simeonsson (1994). However, officials from the Ministry of Education in Saskatchewan, Canada, claim that they were using the model as far back as the 1970s (Sanche, 1976; see also McIntosh et al., 2011). In reality, it was most likely a case of the convergent evolution of an idea that may have sprung from, and was elaborated by, many contributors, as was true in the public health field.

Going back to the history of this public health model is actually helpful for us to understand multi-tiered systems work. In the middle of the last century, public health researchers were struggling to support the health of individuals at the population (i.e., large-scale) level. Knowing that some diseases were largely (but not completely) preventable but still affected a sizable population who had to live with and manage their illness, medical researchers and practitioners adopted a theoretical model that could address multiple goals for large groups. As Gordon (1983) described, Tier 1 services are intended to be universal, for all individuals, regardless of their health (i.e., need). The goal of Tier 1 support is to prevent a particular condition from occurring. Tier 2 services (often described as *selected* in the clinical literature) are intended for those who do not have the condition but are at increased risk for contracting it, possibly based on demographics or location. The goal of Tier 2 support is to reduce the chances of individuals contracting the condition. Tier 3 services (*indicated*) are used for individuals who have already contracted the condition. The goal of Tier 3 support is to lessen the effect (or symptoms) of the condition, or cure it, if possible.

Using this public health lens can help us to understand the use of multi-tiered models in education. Let's take influenza, or the flu, as an example with which most of us are familiar. Tier 1 support for flu prevention includes universal hygiene practices. Everyone is encouraged to wash hands regularly and cough or sneeze into one's elbow to avoid transmission of the flu, and you can see signs posted in restrooms, hospitals, and even schools as a universal public health campaign. Adherence to this type of support should prevent most (but not all) people from contracting the flu. Tier 2 support for flu prevention provides additional intervention for those who are more likely than average to contract the flu. Those with compromised immune systems, such as the elderly or children, or those who may have regular contact with those with the flu, such as health care professionals, are strongly recommended to receive a flu vaccine before the start of flu season. This intervention is intended to help those who have more risk factors, and therefore may not receive enough support from universal hygiene practices or general public appeals to get a flu shot. Tier 3 support then addresses those who have already caught influenza and need medical attention to lessen its severity. Interventions include bed rest and fever reducers, possibly under close medical supervision for those with the most intensive needs.

It's easy to see how this model applies to education, but with some helpful alterations. For example, we think of core curricula as universal interventions. In reading, an effective, well-sequenced reading curriculum, delivered effectively, is intended to prevent challenges in learning how to read (and behave, as we discuss in Chapter 2). In the domain of behavior, we teach students expectations and provide them with the skills they need to be successful socially and emotionally to prevent patterns of unwanted behavior or anxiety. Environmental manipulations, such as signs to remind students to use prosocial behavior or routines to manage traffic, help to encourage prosocial behavior, much like signs to wash hands or the sight of hand sanitizer dispensers at convenient locations help with universal hygiene. However, universal interventions can do more than simply prevent problems; we can also view them as opportunities to optimize learning or cultivate students' strengths (Seligman, 2002). For example, we may use academic instruction to expand students' interest areas and develop their curiosity for academic learning, or teach responsibility in a manner that not only discourages problem behavior but also teaches effective skills to intervene with others to promote social justice.

At Tier 2 in schools, we provide additional instruction, structure, or opportunities to practice to avert students from trajectories toward learning or behavior challenges. We may identify students based on demographic risk (e.g., the use of Title I programs in disadvantaged schools) or based on progress monitoring measures. In the medical field, growth charts or blood pressure tests provide quantitative measures of risk by identifying trajectories toward cutoffs for significant challenges (e.g., failure to thrive, hypertension). In schools, we use similar measures that assess trajectories toward healthy academic growth (e.g., curriculum-based measures, unit tests) or negative social outcomes (e.g., office discipline referrals, attendance, behavioral screeners, and high school early warning systems). These tests may tell us that more instruction, more opportunities to experience success, or developing a caring relationship with another adult in the building could help improve the quality of universal support.

Once a student is identified for Tier 3 support, measures have identified that a student is on track toward negative outcomes, and our data may tell us that the generic Tier 2 support (i.e., additional support provided in the same way for all students) has not been enough to prevent significant challenges. At this point, individualized plans (perhaps formally, in the form of an individualized education plan, or IEP, or informally, in the form of general education support plans) are needed to support the student to be successful. It is here that our medical analogy can lose some relevance. Many of the conditions we try to avoid in schools (i.e., learning disabilities, behavior disorders) are socially constructed, in that there is not a clear test for the condition, but rather a point of functioning at which policies declare that a disability exists (Tilly et al., 1998). In this way, Tier 3 support may be alternatively viewed as a treatment to cure the disability (i.e., bring the student's functioning to within typical limits) or as a plan to mitigate the effects of the disability (e.g., teach functional skills, teach Braille, keep the student engaged in school as long as possible). In many support plans, there are elements of both approaches, with the best goals determined through close partnership with families. In either approach, special education services might or might not be part of Tier 3 support.

## MTSS Misrules

A public health lens can also help us consider some of the misrules and myths surrounding multi-tiered systems. Let's return to that analogy of the flu. One misrule of multi-tiered systems is that each tier is a separate system, so that students receive either Tier 1, 2, or 3 support. Instead, each tier of support is *layered on* to the previous tier's support (e.g., Tier 1 *and* Tier 2 support together), so that students receive additional support, not support that replaces or supplants what preceded it. For example, we would never tell elderly patients that when they receive a flu shot, they can stop washing their hands! In the same way, a key aspect of an MTSS approach is that Tier 2 support is more effective when delivered in addition to core classroom instruction, instead of in place of it (Baker et al., 2010). This layering approach is also helpful when removing support when students are successful. For example, aligning expectations in Tier 2 behavior interventions to the Tier 1 (schoolwide) behavior expectations may allow for a more successful transition to only Tier 1 support when Tier 2 support is removed (Campbell & Anderson, 2011).

Similarly, some have noted that a tiered approach implies that students must go through each tier in succession before they can receive the level of support they need (D. Fuchs, Mock, Morgan, & Young, 2003). If a patient already has the flu, there is little reason to provide a flu shot. In the same way, if we were relatively certain that a generic approach is not going to provide the level of academic or behavior support that is needed for a particular student, it would be foolish to insist that the student first fail in order to receive more support. However, in less extreme cases, it may be worthwhile (in terms of resources and the undesirability of providing unnecessary support) to weigh the harms against the possible benefits (i.e., support in the least restrictive environment).

Another misrule is that multi-tiered systems are specific to certain programs or approaches to learning. Multi-tiered systems can be applied as a unifying framework to nearly any approach in education, much in the way that a tiered approach to flu prevention could include both traditional Western medicine (e.g., flu shots) and complementary medicine (e.g., herbal supplements, stress reduction techniques). In the same manner, a universal reading curriculum may include elements of explicit behavioral instruction, cognitive strategy instruction, and student-directed learning. Practices should be selected based on their effectiveness in improving student outcomes, not their philosophy.

A final common misrule regarding multi-tiered systems is that they are just another system used to label students. In contrast, multi-tiered systems are used to describe the level of support that a student requires at that time, not something inherent in that student. Support within multi-tiered systems is intended to be fluid and responsive to student progress, not a label that identifies a "red zone kid." Such thinking leads us to assume that all of a student's needs are intensive (e.g., across all content areas), and it confuses a within-child trait with the need for support at that moment. We don't keep patients on bed rest or in the hospital once they have recovered from the flu!

## A History of Integrated Models

Because this book focuses specifically on integrated systems, it is helpful to examine a brief history of such systems. Like RTI and tiered approaches, it is unlikely that there was one sole originator of integrated systems, but one federal grant competition did serve as a serendipitous pivotal point in the development and proliferation of structures for integrating systems. In 2000, the U.S. Office of Special Education Programs (OSEP) released a request for proposals for model demonstration projects focusing on K–3 behavior and reading intervention models. Although the proposal required a schoolwide focus on behavior *or* reading, four local education agencies applied and received grants for a schoolwide focus on behavior *and* reading. These were the Bethel School District (Oregon), the Lancaster Lebanon Intermediate Unit (Pennsylvania), the Ottawa Area Intermediate School District (Michigan), and the Tigard–Tualatin School District (Oregon). These model demonstration projects were crucial in providing the initial funding and infrastructure for integrating systems, and many of these projects continue to this day (see Part III for case studies).

These successful projects also set the stage for further development: two national OSEP K–3 research centers on reading and behavior in 2001 at the University of Kansas and the University of North Carolina at Charlotte (the University of Oregon was also awarded separate reading and behavior centers). These efforts led to a range of research papers (e.g., Ervin, Schaughency, Goodman, McGlinchey, & Matthews, 2006; McIntosh, Chard, Boland, & Horner, 2006), as well as an influential concept paper describing the logic for an integrated approach to reading and behavior (Sugai, Kame'enui, Horner, & Simmons, 2002). In addition, state professional development grants (SPDGs) became a common funding resource with which some states built capacity for implementing integrated MTSS models. Further, a number of conferences have consistently provided dedicated content on integrated systems (e.g., Goodman, 2005; McGlinchey, Goodman, & Schallmo, 2005; McIntosh, 2007, June; Sadler, 2003), especially the RTI Innovations Conference (see *www.rti-innovations.com*).

Today, over a dozen years after these initial grants, there are a number of exemplar initiatives that demonstrate that integrating both approaches is both possible and sustainable (Ervin et al., 2006; McIntosh et al., 2006; Sadler & Sugai, 2009). However, there remains little research in this area to guide implementers (Stewart et al., 2007), and even fewer resources available for those interested in integrating approaches (McIntosh, Goodman, et al., 2010). This gap can lead to spotty and ineffective integration, in which the logic and intent are strong, but the actual implementation lacks guidance and sufficient articulation.

## ORIENTATION TO THIS BOOK

### *Purpose and Intended Readership*

The purpose of this book is to provide a resource for integrating existing systems in academic RTI and PBIS into a comprehensive MTSS approach or for implementing an integrated system in schools that have neither system in place. Although some background information is provided, we assume that readers have at least some knowledge and experience implementing academic RTI or PBIS (or both) in their settings. As such, the book does not describe academic or behavior systems in detail, but rather the process and systems needed to integrate them. Readers in search of foundational resources for the basics of academic RTI or PBIS are referred to the references in Table 1.2. We recommend that readers follow this book with that background information already in hand so that we can focus on the real purpose here of *providing explicit guidance for integrating existing approaches into a coherent, empirically based process.* This resource is intended to help bridge the gap between integrated MTSS as a good idea in theory and integrated MTSS as an implementable, practical innovation in today's schools.

A key message to which we return throughout this book is that quality integration requires a careful and logical approach. It is important to avoid what we call "parallel play": the simultaneous implementation of two separate systems, one to support academic development and one to support behavior development, with little interaction except to compete for priority and funding. However, it is equally important to avoid integration for integration's sake or integrating components systems that may work better separately. Our goal is not integration—our goals are efficiency and effectiveness. Integration, then, is a means to achieve efficiency and effectiveness, but not an outcome in of itself. We need to let logic guide what to integrate because complete integration may not necessarily be better than separate systems. This book is intended to provide guidance on what aspects of MTSS integration would make both systems more efficient and effective.

The primary intended readers for this book are school-level teams that are integrating academic and behavior systems at the K–12 school level, or district-level teams that are supporting multiple school teams in their implementation. Although these practices are conceived and implemented at the school level and our examples and forms are also school level, it is clear from research that schools require district-level support to function effectively, especially when it comes to sustaining practices over time (McIntosh et al., 2013). Thus, district administrators need to have a deep understanding of how MTSS works at the building level to identify the supports needed for quality implementation, and school team members need to know what kinds of support to request in order to install durable systems that will outlast their involvement as school team leaders. In addition, regional- and state-level administrators may design better policy when they are knowledgeable about what schools need to implement MTSS.

Although district and state support will greatly enhance the ease and durability of MTSS implementation, school teams working on their own will still find the information needed to

**TABLE 1.2. Foundational Resources**

Resources for academic RTI

Websites

*www.rtinetwork.org*

This website provides a range of articles on RTI, its principles, and helpful guidance for implementation by nationally regarded experts in the field. The site also includes some articles on MTSS.

*www.progressmonitoring.org*

This website from the Research Institute on Progress Monitoring provides information on tools for measuring formative growth in academic skills.

*www.interventioncentral.com*

This site provides a wealth of free resources on interventions (primarily academic, but also behavior) for students within a three-tiered model.

*www.fcrr.org*

The website for the Florida Center for Reading Research has a range of resources for teachers, administrators, and researchers on implementing effective literacy instruction.

Books

*The ABCs of CBM, Second Edition: A Practical Guide to Curriculum-Based Measurement* (Hosp, Hosp, & Howell, 2016)

This book is an approachable and informative resource on academic assessment within an RTI model. It provides step-by-step guidance for implementing screening and progress monitoring systems for academic skills across content areas.

*RTI in the Classroom: Guidelines and Recipes for Success* (Brown-Chidsey, Bronaugh, & McGraw, 2009)

This text begins with determining readiness to implement RTI along with background information of the RTI model. Emphasis is placed on evaluating and developing strong Tier 1 systems. Additional chapters provide interventions on content-area interventions (e.g., math, reading, writing, social behavior).

*RTI Applications: Volume 1. Academic and Behavioral Interventions* (Burns, Riley-Tillman, & VanDerHeyden, 2012)

This text begins with an overview of evidence-based interventions and how to match intervention to student need based on stages of learning (acquisition, fluency, generalization, and adaptation). Additional chapters describe academic or behavior interventions based on assessing students' stages of learning.

*RTI Applications, Volume 2. Assessment, Analysis and Decision Making* (Riley-Tillman, Burns, & Gibbons, 2013)

This follow-up companion volume provides guidance in the selection of assessment measures and evaluation of effectiveness of interventions within an RTI model. The book applies a problem-solving approach to help ensure that the educational system is meeting student needs.

*(continued)*

**TABLE 1.2.** *(continued)*

Resources for PBIS

Websites

*www.pbis.org*

The U.S. Office of Special Education Programs Center on Positive Behavioral Interventions and Supports is a comprehensive site featuring introductory articles and videos, practice examples, evaluation briefs, and free tools for training schools, assessing fidelity of implementation, and monitoring student outcomes. The PBIS Implementation Blueprint includes an overview of PBIS systems and common practices, as well as a flexible approach for designing state and district systems to support school-level implementation.

*www.pbismaryland.org*

This site offers an expansive (and ever-growing) set of tools and examples for implementing PBIS at the elementary, middle, and secondary levels.

*miblisi.prg*

This website, from the Michigan Integrated Behavior and Literacy Supports Initiative, provides helpful content for both academic RTI and PBIS.

Books

*Positive Behavior Support in Secondary Schools: A Practical Guide* (Young, Caldarella, Richardson, & Young, 2012)

This text provides guidance for high school leadership teams in implementing PBIS. Background information is provided on the key principles of PBIS and the unique characteristics of the high schools. Information on planning for implementation, addressing Tier 1 support, and using data for effective intervention is provided.

*Responding to Problem Behavior in Schools, Second Edition: The Behavior Education Program* (Crone, Hawken, & Horner, 2010)

This book provides an overview and detailed steps for implementing, monitoring, and troubleshooting a commonly used Tier 2 system called the *behavior education program* (also known as check-in/check-out, or CICO).

*Building Positive Behavior Support Systems in Schools, Second Edition: Functional Behavioral Assessment* (Crone, Hawken, & Horner, 2015)

This book details the steps and tools required to conduct individualized assessments and intervention plans at Tier 3. It walks the reader though the process of identifying the function of problem behavior and aspects of the environment that can be altered to prevent unwanted behavior and teach functional, prosocial skills.

implement MTSS at their schools. In fact, schools may only be able to garner such support *after* showing that MTSS systems can be implemented effectively and improve student outcomes in their schools.

## *Structure*

This book is organized into four parts. In Part I (including this chapter), we provide the context needed to understand the MTSS logic and convince others why integrating separate systems into an MTSS model may be a beneficial pursuit. Chapter 2 reviews the research on how academic skills and behavior are interrelated. This body of evidence provides an empirical rationale for integrating systems. Part II goes into detail regarding the common components of academic and behavior RTI systems and the steps and strategies that comprise implementation. Chapters 3 through 6 provide in-depth descriptions of steps and strategies for implementing the various aspects of an integrated MTSS, including the data structures, practices, teaming, and district systems needed for quality implementation. With this information at hand, Chapter 7 then provides details on the specific processes, structural considerations, and policies needed to achieve a logical integration of entire systems. Each of these chapters concludes with useful, reproducible school- and district-level team checklists to guide implementation. As a complement to the content in Part II, Part III provides three examples of implementation of MTSS. Each of these chapters covers examples and structures from different MTSS initiatives, including descriptions of implementation, outcomes, and lessons learned. Taken as a whole, these case studies demonstrate common themes in MTSS and show how implementation varies according to the specific context, with a key lesson that function is more important than structure. Part IV concludes the book with new directions for research and practice.

## CHAPTER 2

# The Relationship between Academic Skills and Behavior

It should come as no surprise to readers of this book that there is a strong research base—many rigorous studies across many research teams and separate groups of students—showing that academic skills and social and emotional behavior are connected. In this chapter, we provide a review of the research supporting the advantages of an integrated MTSS model, including how academic and behavior skills (and challenges) develop over time, and the effects of intervening in one domain on outcomes in the other domain (e.g., the effects of an academic intervention on social behavior), sometimes termed *crossover effects* (Kellam, Mayer, Rebok, & Hawkins, 1998). It is likely that some or most of this research confirms what you've assumed or seen for yourself in the classroom. Even if you know it, being able to cite studies that back up your points is always helpful; this chapter provides a compact summary of the research findings. However, some of this information may be new to you as well, especially as it pertains to reasons why some of the results are not quite as clear as we might expect, and what that ambiguity means for implementing integrated MTSS models.

## RESEARCH SHOWING A CONNECTION BETWEEN ACADEMIC SKILLS AND BEHAVIOR

Over the past 50 years, solid evidence has accumulated indicating that academic skills and behavior are linked, meaning that students with low academic skills are more likely to exhibit unwanted behavior in schools, and vice versa (Ayllon, Layman, & Burke, 1972; Gray, Carter, Briggs-Gowan, Jones, & Wagmiller, 2014; Merton, 1968). For example, Arnold and colleagues (2005) found that poor readers were significantly more likely than good readers to report symptoms of anxiety and depression, and their parents were significantly more likely to report delinquent behavior. In addition, results from a large twin study (Trzesniewski, Moffitt, Caspi, Taylor, & Maughan, 2006) show the same relation between early challenges in one area and later challenges in the other, especially for boys. The same patterns are also seen for students receiving special education services for emotional and behavioral disorders (Nelson, Benner, Lane, & Smith, 2004; Wanzek, Al Otaiba, & Petscher, 2013). Even though these students were receiving special education services, they were still more likely to fall further behind in academic skill development than to catch up to students without social and emotional challenges.

In addition to establishing the connection between academics and behavior, the evidence base also sheds some light on its nature (McIntosh, Horner, et al., 2008). First, this relation increases in strength throughout a student's schooling, so that students with solely academic or behavior challenges early in school are at much greater risk of facing challenges in the other area through middle and high school (Fleming, Harachi, Cortes, Abbott, & Catalano, 2004; McIntosh, Flannery, Sugai, Braun, & Cochrane, 2008). Second, although the connection has been seen across many areas of academics and behavior (Lin et al., 2013), this connection is strongest between two specific areas: (1) literacy, as opposed to mathematics or other academic content areas and (2) externalizing problem behavior (i.e., "acting out," such as disruption), as opposed to internalizing problem behavior (i.e., "acting in," such as anxiety; Hinshaw, 1992; Nelson et al., 2004). The strong and increasing link between literacy and problem behavior makes intuitive sense, because as students progress through elementary school, they increasingly need to use reading skills across content areas (Heath, 1980). Basically, students with low literacy skills face a more challenging learning environment in which they are continuously asked to use skills that they do not have (McIntosh, Sadler, & Brown, 2012). Third, as would be expected, students facing challenges in both academics and behavior have the worst outcomes, including poor achievement, school dropout, and mental health challenges (e.g., Darney, Reinke, Herman, Stormont, & Ialongo, 2013).

## HOW COMBINED ACADEMIC AND BEHAVIOR CHALLENGES DEVELOP OVER TIME

One of the reasons why the relationship between academics and behavior seems like a given fact is that there are a number of theories that could explain why these two domains are so strongly linked. In addition, they are not necessarily competing theories—many researchers have noted that they could all be operating at once, in multiple pathways to produce both academic and behavior problems for students (e.g., Roeser & Eccles, 2000). In one of the earlier contemporary studies to examine this relation, Coie and Krehbiel (1984) described four distinct pathways to combined problems (see Table 2.1 and Figure 2.1). These pathways and the research supporting each of them are described in the following paragraphs, along with how these pathways can be disrupted.

### *Pathway 1: Behavior Challenges Reduce Access to Instruction*

The first pathway describes students who come to school with behavior problems, either externalizing or internalizing. Without intervention, this problematic behavior reduces access to instruction over time, due to disruption of instruction, removal from the learning environment, or excessive preoccupation with social or emotional challenges (Dishion, French, & Patterson,

**TABLE 2.1. Multiple Pathways to Academic and Behavior Challenges**

Coie and Krehbiel (1984) hypothesized four distinct avenues by which students could develop difficulties in both academics and social or emotional behavior:

1. *Behavior challenges reduce access to instruction.* Initial deficits in social or emotional behavior cause academic skill deficits because behavior interferes with the student's learning.

2. *Underlying attention deficits cause challenges in both areas.* Initial attention deficits are the common cause of both academic and behavior challenges.

3. *Early academic challenges increase social rejection.* Initial academic challenges result in increased rejection by peers and teachers, which in turn causes social or emotional challenges.

4. *Inadequate response to academic intervention leads to behavior challenges.* Initial academic challenges cause social behavior problems (i.e., escape-maintained disruptive behavior) and/ or emotional problems (e.g., anxiety, depression, learned helplessness).

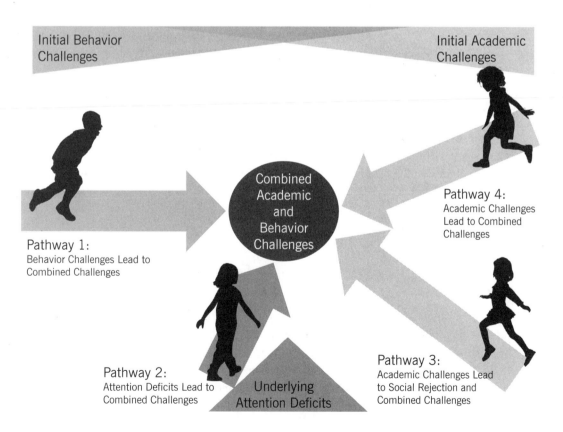

**FIGURE 2.1.** Multiple pathways to academic and behavior challenges.

1995; Levy & Chard, 2001; Wehby, Lane, & Falk, 2003). As a result, students fall behind academically, and during their schooling, consequently acquire academic skill deficits to go along with their existing behavior challenges.

There are a number of studies showing this pathway in effect prior to school entry and extending through high school. Gray and colleagues (2014) found that overactivity at age 1 was a strong predictor of second-grade reading deficits. Spira, Bracken, and Fischel (2005) assessed the reading growth of students from first to fourth grades. They found that although first-grade reading skills were strong predictors of fourth-grade reading skills, those students with serious classroom behavior challenges were significantly more likely to show low achievement in fourth grade. Another example of research supporting this pathway is a study that examined the relation between student academic achievement and office discipline referrals (ODRs) from middle school to high school (McIntosh, Flannery, et al., 2008). In eighth grade, academic achievement and ODRs were negatively correlated (i.e., students with higher achievement had fewer ODRs), and eighth-grade ODRs predicted lower ninth-grade academic grades, but eighth-grade achievement did not predict ninth-grade ODRs. A related analysis of these data showed that by ninth grade, most students had no academic or behavior challenges, some students had academic challenges but no behavior challenges, some students had challenges in both areas, but very few students had challenges only in behavior. In fact, nearly four times as many students had academic challenges alone than behavior challenges alone. Taken together, these data tell us that having behavior challenges put students at much greater risk of developing academic challenges than vice versa.

### Implications for Prevention

It is no surprise that the key to disrupting this pathway is to identify and address social and emotional challenges as early as possible, preferably at school entry. By providing students with the skills that they need to be successful, we can ensure access to instruction, not only for these students, but also for their classmates. Because patterns of negative student–teacher interactions can develop early and become coercive cycles that pervade a student's educational experience (Dishion & Snyder, 2016), reversing this cycle as early as possible can have dramatic effects on both social and academic behavior. Using systems to screen for social and emotional needs (as described in Chapter 3) can be helpful in finding which students need support before their academic progress becomes endangered.

### Pathway 2: Underlying Attention Deficits Cause Challenges in Both Areas

The second pathway is similar in that students come in with behavior challenges, but in this case, the specific problem involves challenges in what is now called *executive function* (Dawson & Guare, 2010)—specifically, a lack of organizational skills and sustained attention to relevant stimuli (i.e., key components of learning from instruction). These challenges then cause both social problems (e.g., inattention to relevant social cues) and academic ones (e.g., inattention to teacher directions). A number of studies have shown that these underlying problems at school entry (or even for toddlers) can lead to both low academic achievement and increased problem behavior (Carroll, Maughan, Goodman, & Meltzer, 2005; Duncan et al., 2007; Fleming et al.,

2004; Gray et al., 2014; Mattison & Blader, 2013; Metcalfe, Harvey, & Laws, 2013; Volpe et al., 2006). This research provides some evidence that the reasons for the connection between academics and behavior may be due primarily to low levels of focused attention on instruction—which, if unaddressed, may cause problems in both areas.

### Implications for Prevention

At first thought, this pathway seems to come from traits within the individual, which might limit how we can prevent attention deficits from leading to combined challenges. Yet we educators know that it is more accurate and useful to consider focused attention to be a teachable skill. Like with phonological awareness, some students grasp it almost immediately, whereas others require explicit instruction and ongoing support or accommodations (Dawson & Guare, 2010). Teaching the key skills and providing cognitive strategies for self-monitoring and maintaining attention can help students attend to instruction and social cues, allowing their other academic and social–emotional skills to grow. Teachers can make it easier for all students to focus their attention by teaching and using classwide attention signals, providing clear directions for tasks, using visual and auditory cues for key behaviors, and removing irrelevant visual and auditory distractions from the classroom (Fisher, Godwin, & Seltman, 2014; Hall, Meyer, & Rose, 2012).

## Pathway 3: Early Academic Challenges Increase Social Rejection

The final two pathways involve academic challenges that lead to social challenges. In the third pathway, when students enter school with academic deficits, they are more likely to fail academically, be rejected by peers (or even teachers), and become the target of bullying. This pattern of social interactions leads to behavior problems as well as to further academic challenges. Over time, these patterns may weaken development in both areas in a transactional pattern (Hinshaw, 1992; Lane, 1999; Morgan, Farkas, Tufis, & Sperling, 2008).

There is somewhat less direct evidence for this pathway. For example, Morgan, Farkas, and Wu (2012) found that poor readers in third grade were twice as likely as strong readers to report social rejection and loneliness in fifth grade. In addition, there is evidence that students with learning disabilities are more likely to be bullied by their peers (Cummings, Pepler, Mishna, & Craig, 2006). Further down this path, Sideridis, Antoniou, Stamovlasis, and Morgan (2013) found that for students with existing learning disabilities, bullying further disrupts academic skill development. In other words, it is difficult for students to focus on academic instruction when they are still recovering from victimization earlier in the day or are worried about bullying that may happen in the hallway or cafeteria (McIntosh, Ty, & Miller, 2014). As another example, a school-level study found that the extent of bullying or harassment in schools was the strongest social predictor of low literacy and math achievement in elementary schools (Gietz & McIntosh, 2014).

### Implications for Prevention

This research points to the possibility of preventing both academic and behavior challenges by reducing bullying and harassment in schools. When we focus on teaching both prosocial behavior and effective responses to bullying behavior (for both recipients and bystanders), we can reduce instances of bullying and increase perceived school safety (Nese, Horner, Dickey, Stiller, & Tomlanovich, 2014; Ross & Horner, 2009). This change in school climate can reduce unwanted behavior and help increase achievement by allowing students greater access to academic instruction (Kelm, McIntosh, & Cooley, 2014).

### Pathway 4: Inadequate Response to Academic Intervention Leads to Behavior Challenges

In the final pathway, students enter school behind their peers in academic skills and increasingly use disruptive behavior when academic instruction becomes frustrating, resulting in removal from instruction and worsening academic deficits in a classic coercive cycle (McIntosh, Horner, et al., 2008). In an even earlier publication than Coie and Krehbiel, Merton (1968) described this final pathway in extensive detail. He wrote about the experience of academic failure and two common (and predictable) responses. When a student is presented with an aversive academic task (i.e., work that is too difficult), he or she may respond with disruptive behavior (e.g., yelling, physical aggression) until the task is removed from the student or the student is removed from the situation (e.g., ODR, time-out). In a different but related scenario, the student responds to the same aversive task with withdrawal. Instead of the disruption, the student shuts down (e.g., puts head on the table). That withdrawal can also lead to removal of the task (e.g., teacher moving on to someone else or not following up on work completion). This situation is challenging because it can lead to what has been labeled *learned helplessness*, a concept described by Seligman (1972) and Dweck (1975). When students encounter repeated academic challenges, this withdrawal response may eventually form a pattern that is difficult to change.

Longitudinal research showing this pathway documents students who start school with academic challenges in the absence of behavior challenges but develop patterns of unwnated behavior over time (Bennett, Brown, Boyle, Racine, & Offord, 2003; Carroll et al., 2005). For example, Morgan and colleagues (2008) found that controlling for problem behavior, low academic skills in first grade predicted both externalizing problem behavior and task avoidance in third grade. In addition, low prereading skills in kindergarten have been shown to lead to increased disruptive problem behavior in fifth grade (McIntosh, Horner, Chard, Boland, & Good, 2006), as well as an increased risk for anxiety (Carroll et al., 2005) and depression (Herman, Lambert, Reinke, & Ialongo, 2008). In an even more sophisticated analysis, Lin and colleagues (2013) showed that both reading and math deficits in third grade strongly predicted both externalizing and internalizing problem behavior in fifth grade, but behavior deficits in third grade were not as predictive of fifth-grade achievement.

One study that clearly shows the RTI pathway examines kindergarten literacy trajectories and behavior challenges at the end of elementary school (McIntosh et al., 2012). In that study, kindergarteners were followed for 6 years, through fifth grade. It is probably not surprising to anyone that students who started kindergarten with low skills in phonemic awareness (the awareness of sound structure in words) were at increased risk of multiple ODRs in fifth grade. What was surprising, however, was that upon further analysis of growth in phonemic awareness skills throughout kindergarten, a curious pattern appeared, as shown in Figure 2.2. Although starting kindergarten without these skills ("at risk") was a strong predictor of negative behavior outcomes, if the students' skills increased throughout the fall to meet phonemic awareness

## Students Starting Kindergarten at *Low Risk* for Literacy Challenges

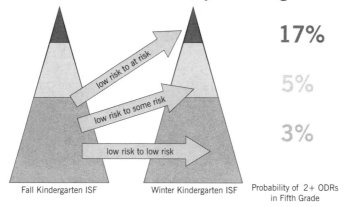

**17%**

5%

3%

Fall Kindergarten ISF    Winter Kindergarten ISF    Probability of 2+ ODRs in Fifth Grade

## Students Starting Kindergarten at *Some Risk* for Literacy Challenges

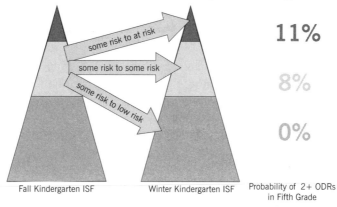

**11%**

8%

0%

Fall Kindergarten ISF    Winter Kindergarten ISF    Probability of 2+ ODRs in Fifth Grade

## Students Starting Kindergarten *at Risk* for Literacy Challenges

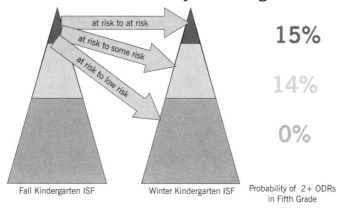

**15%**

14%

0%

Fall Kindergarten ISF    Winter Kindergarten ISF    Probability of 2+ ODRs in Fifth Grade

**FIGURE 2.2.** Change in risk for behavior challenges in fifth grade based on response to literacy instruction in kindergarten. ISF, DIBELS Initial Sound Fluency. Data from McIntosh, Sadler, and Brown (2012).

benchmarks (i.e., they caught up to a positive academic trajectory, or from "some risk" or "at risk" down to "low risk"), their risk for multiple ODRs in fifth grade decreased to zero—not to *nearly* zero, actually to *zero*: No students in the district who acquired these skills had multiple ODRs at the end of elementary school. So who were the students who had the highest risk of behavior challenges in fifth grade? Although students who started at high risk and remained there were at high risk, students who started school on track for positive outcomes but fell far behind their peers had the worst behavior outcomes at the end of elementary school.

## Implications for Prevention

These findings indicate two promising ways to prevent students from moving along the inadequate RTI pathway. First, if early academic deficits can be remedied, students will have no need to use unwanted behavior to escape instruction, and the cycle can be stopped before it begins. We can therefore dramatically reduce unwanted behavior through quality academic instruction for *all students* as early as school entry (or earlier). This pathway results from early academic failure, so it is important not to wait until repeated failure before intervening to improve academic skills. Second, for individual students who have already begun acting out to avoid or escape instruction, it is important to identify and stop the cycle. In these situations, these students are trying their own personal intervention to self-reduce access to instruction and, in many cases, are successful in training their teachers to call on them less often or send them out of the classroom (Wehby, Lane, et al., 2003). It is important to limit the use of exclusionary discipline tactics such as time-out, ODRs, and suspensions, all of which are associated with decreased achievement (Benner et al., 2012; Morrison, Anthony, Storino, & Dillon, 2001). Without intensive academic instruction, their skills are unlikely to improve.

## INTERVENTION RESEARCH ON THE RELATIONSHIP BETWEEN ACADEMIC SKILLS AND BEHAVIOR

Although many of these studies seem compelling, the correlational research reported above has some drawbacks that make it difficult to assess the relationship fully. Correlational research attempts to identify general patterns for large populations of students but cannot always isolate specific causes that are the most promising targets for intervention. For example, perhaps coming to school hungry and parental neglect are the real causes of both academic and behavior problems for these students. Intervention research is important because by changing one aspect at a time, we can be more certain about what makes a difference, and more importantly, how to improve student outcomes. After all, if theory shows us how to avert students from these pathways to combined challenges, we should be able to find research that tests whether we really can do it.

Unfortunately, the evidence for consistent, positive crossover effects (e.g., effects of academic interventions on behavior) is not as promising as we might think. As a whole, the intervention research findings are still somewhat murky, but taking a closer look at the mixed results may identify some helpful trends that can further what we know, plus provide promising implications for integrating academic and behavior support systems.

## Crossover Effects of Academic Interventions on Behavior

### Research Showing Crossover Effects

Based on the pathways described in the preceding material (particularly the fourth pathway, inadequate response to academic intervention), there is strong reason to believe that effective academic interventions would also have social effects as well. There are a number of demonstrations of this very pattern of effects. In two of the first studies, Ayllon and colleagues (Ayllon et al., 1972; Ayllon & Roberts, 1974) showed that simply reinforcing reading performance improved both reading achievement and behavior. Similar effects have been seen for small-group early literacy interventions (Lane, O'Shaughnessy, Lambros, Gresham, & Beebe-Frankenberger, 2001; Lane et al., 2002), academic tutoring, including reciprocal peer tutoring (Coie & Krehbiel, 1984; D. Fuchs, Fuchs, Mathes, & Martinez, 2002; Locke & Fuchs, 1995), and academic interventions tailored to individuals' specific academic deficits (Filter & Horner, 2009; Lee, Sugai, & Horner, 1999; Preciado, Horner, & Baker, 2009; Sanford & Horner, 2013).

### Failures to Find Crossover Effects

However, these positive results cannot be assumed. Even more studies have found a lack of crossover effects from academics to behavior, even when the interventions were effective on academic skills (e.g., Barton-Arwood, Wehby, & Falk, 2005; Lane, 1999; Wehby, Falk, Barton-Arwood, Lane, & Cooley, 2003). In fact, two separate literature syntheses (Nelson, Lane, Benner, & Kim, 2011; Wanzek, Vaughn, Kim, & Cavanaugh, 2006) found few to no (and even sometimes negative) crossover effects of academic interventions on behavior.

### Likely Reasons for Conflicting Findings

So if our theories of pathways to combined problems have such empirical support, what can explain these mixed findings? One important explanation for the lack of consistent crossover effects for academic interventions on behavior may be the function of unwanted behavior. Behavior theory indicates that repeated behaviors continue to be used because they meet a basic need for the individual (Carr, 1977; Crone, Hawken, & Horner, 2015; Skinner, 1953). In schools, research indicates that unwanted behavior is used most commonly by students either to obtain attention (from peers or adults) or to avoid or escape academic tasks (McIntosh, Horner, et al., 2008). If a student's behavior is triggered by an aversive academic task request (as in the inadequate response to academic intervention in the fourth pathway), we can reduce the likelihood of that behavior by teaching the skills needed to make the task easier and therefore less aversive. However, if unwanted behavior is instead maintained by obtaining attention, we should not expect academic interventions to reduce it. In these situations, additional academic intervention (beyond Tier 1 instruction) would simply take time away from providing the needed behavior support. Therefore, when we consider the function of behavior, academic support is deemed either irrelevant or absolutely necessary for behavior change (McIntosh, Horner, et al., 2008).

Some research evidence highlights the role of function in the connection between academics and behavior. First, a study assessing reading fluency of students in fourth, fifth, and sixth grades found that students whose descriptive functional behavior assessments (FBAs) indicated escape-maintained problem behavior had lower scores at the start of the year and slower growth than comparable students with similarly severe attention-maintained problem behavior (McIntosh, Horner, et al., 2008). In addition, a series of intervention studies has shown that academic instruction alone significantly reduces problem behavior when (1) the function of the problem behavior is to escape academic tasks and (2) the targets for academic instruction are the academic tasks that triggered the problem behavior, as identified through the FBA process (Filter & Horner, 2009; Lee et al., 1999; Preciado et al., 2009; Sanford & Horner, 2013). By increasing the student's skills in the deficit academic area, task requests become less aversive, thus making escape or avoidance behaviors unnecessary.

Cook and colleagues (2012) provided a more complete test of this theory. His team studied the effects of a reading-only intervention, a behavior-only intervention, and then both interventions together on reading skills, academic engagement, and problem behavior. Although each intervention was somewhat effective overall and the combined intervention was the most effective, the reading-only intervention was ineffective for students with attention-maintained problem behavior, and the behavior-only intervention was ineffective for students with escape-maintained problem behavior. These results provide further evidence that the function of problem behavior is a critical variable to use when designing effective academic and behavior support plans (McIntosh, Campbell, Carter, & Dickey, 2009), as well as a strong explanation for why academic interventions are only sometimes effective in reducing problem behavior.

## Crossover Effects of Behavior Interventions on Academic Skills

### Research Showing Crossover Effects

As with academic interventions, several studies demonstrate the positive effects of behavior interventions on academic achievement. Recently, a number of studies have examined the academic effects of PBIS (McIntosh, Ty, Horner, & Sugai, 2013). These findings show consistent, positive effects of PBIS on academic achievement for both at-risk students (Nelson, Martella, et al., 2002) and the student body as a whole (Bradshaw, Mitchell, & Leaf, 2010; Horner et al., 2009; Lassen, Steele, & Sailor, 2006; Luiselli, Putnam, Handler, & Feinberg, 2005; Nelson, 1996). Likewise, a recent meta-analysis has shown positive effects of a range of social and emotional learning (SEL) programs on school-level academic achievement (Durlak, Weissburg, Dymnicki, Taylor, & Schellinger, 2011). One important finding of this study was that the strongest effects were seen in programs that consisted of sequenced, active, focused, and explicit skill development activities.

### Failures to Find Crossover Effects

Yet there are also high-quality studies that do not show crossover effects for behavioral interventions on academics, even for some of the same interventions just described. For example, the Social and Character Development Research Consortium (2010) conducted a large randomized controlled trial of eight widely used SEL or character building programs and found almost no positive effects on academic (or behavior) outcomes. Likewise, the Good Behavior Game (Barrish, Saunders, & Wolf, 1969), when implemented alone, has been shown in at least one major study to show positive behavior but not academic effects (Kellam et al., 1998). Coie and Krehbiel

(1984) found initial effects for social skills instruction on academic performance, but the differences had disappeared at follow-up. Finally, some effective behavior interventions have been shown to be detrimental to academic achievement. Think Time (Nelson & Carr, 2000), a structured time-out intervention, was shown to have near-significant negative effects on achievement when compared to control students who did not receive the intervention (Benner et al., 2012).

## Likely Reasons for Conflicting Findings

To understand these mixed results, it is helpful to consider why we might expect behavior interventions to improve academic outcomes. The first three pathways described in this chapter involve reduced access to instruction as the key problematic mechanism; this reduced access stemmed from disruptive behavior interfering with instruction, inadequate academic enabler skills, or preoccupation with rejection and victimization. As such, behavior interventions have been hypothesized to work because they increase access to instruction. For example, improving the social behavior of students through PBIS results in more minutes focusing on academic instruction (Luiselli et al., 2005), less time out of instruction due to exclusionary discipline (Scott & Barrett, 2004), and as a result, higher rates of academic engagement (Algozzine & Algozzine, 2007). Moreover, two studies provide initial evidence that the effects of PBIS on academic achievement may be due to reductions in peer rejection and bullying (Bradshaw et al., 2010; Kelm et al., 2014; Waasdorp et al., 2012). In both of these studies, implementation of PBIS reduced peer rejection and/or bullying, and there was a corresponding increase in academic achievement.

An important consideration when seeking to increase access to instruction is that improvements in achievement are dependent on the quality of that instruction. Put simply, behavior interventions can get students in their seats and attending to instruction without distraction, but if the academic instruction is low quality, we should not expect improved achievement (Algozzine & Algozzine, 2009). Once the behavior intervention has set the best conditions to allow academic instruction, it is still necessary to use the most effective instructional approaches to maximize academic learning.

This theory could help explain why there have been better research findings for the effects of integrated approaches on both types of outcomes. At the student level, Bruhn and Watt (2012) and Cook and colleagues (2012) found combined interventions to be effective on both academic and behavior outcomes. At the classroom level, Ialongo and colleagues (1999) showed strong effects for combined interventions (which included the Good Behavior Game) implemented in first grade. And finally, at the school level, there is some descriptive case study evidence that integrated MTSS models show improved student outcomes in both academics and behavior beyond what is typically seen in schoolwide interventions for either academics or behavior (McIntosh et al., 2006; Sadler & Sugai, 2009; Stewart et al., 2007).

## SOME BIG IDEAS ABOUT THE RELATIONSHIP BETWEEN ACADEMICS AND BEHAVIOR

Although the research findings are not as straightforward as we might think, they do provide support for why integrating systems makes sense, as well as guidance for how to do it well.

There are some big ideas that we can glean as we move forward through the integration process. It can be useful to keep these points in mind while reading the rest of this book and getting deep into the details of integrated MTSS models.

1. ***The best prevention comes from quality Tier 1 support in both academics and behavior.*** When we provide quality academic instruction, students are more successful and more engaged, which in turn can reduce unwanted behavior (Osher, Bear, Sprague, & Doyle, 2010). Likewise, when we create a safe, predictable, and caring learning environment that is free from distraction and bullying, there is more time for instruction, and students can focus on their learning (McIntosh, Ty, et al., 2014). However, the research shows that we can't *expect* strong crossover effects from one domain to the other. We should not assume that having a strong academic system is adequate for supporting behavior, and vice versa. If we want to see improved outcomes in both domains, we need to invest in both (Algozzine & Algozzine, 2009). As a result, when we implement integrated academic and behavior support, outcomes are maximized (Cook et al., 2012; McIntosh, Chard, et al., 2006). Therefore, our best chance of preventing each of the pathways described previously is not by hoping for crossover effects, but rather through quality Tier 1 academic *and* behavior support, delivered before students encounter repeated difficulties.

2. ***The function of behavior is the key to effective integrated support at Tiers 2 and 3.*** A good deal of the conflicting results described in the literature can be explained by the function of unwanted behavior (Cook et al., 2012). Selecting interventions based on the results of an FBA is important because when we don't attend to function, we are as likely to make the problem behavior worse as we are to make it better (Crone et al., 2015). For this reason, exclusionary discipline practices (e.g., time-out, ODRs, suspensions) might momentarily reduce unwanted behavior, but they remove students from instruction, which is likely to increase unwanted behavior in the long run. By paying attention to function, we can stop inadvertently making behavior worse and treat the real causes of escape-maintained behavior.

3. ***The sum is greater than the parts.*** Throughout general and special education, there is a tendency to view students by their within-child deficits. This thinking leads to siloed systems of support, wherein academic and behavior challenges are viewed as different, requiring different skills, different interventions, and different teams. Instead of this narrow focus on each area, the research in this chapter shows that we can both improve student outcomes and save time and resources by considering them as interrelated. Just as we can improve student outcomes by integrating systems, we can improve our instruction by applying the skills we have in one domain to the other. As Darch and Kame'enui (2003) noted, "by thinking about classroom management and classroom instruction as significant parts of the same process, teaching is likely to be clearer, more focused and balanced, more sustaining, and more enriching for both teachers and students over the course of a school year" (p. 5). Adopting an integrated MTSS model can provide synergistic effects that can make our work better across both academics and behavior.

# PART II

# CORE COMPONENTS

This part of the book provides the core content of an integrated MTSS model. Each chapter in this section addresses a different aspect of MTSS, including data and evaluation, practices, teaming, the involvement of district systems to support integration, and the integration process itself. Although the chapters address separate topics, you'll notice that these topics are not as separate as they might appear in this linear presentation. Because they work together as part of an overall system, there is a consistent amount of overlap that is necessary. For example, *teams* at the school and *district* use *data* on fidelity of implementation of *practices* to guide the *integration process*. This typical, ongoing procedure includes all of the major systems that are described separately in this section. As a result, there will also be overlap in how we describe them. This overlap is actually beneficial; although they seem like separate systems at first, the continuity and alignment across all aspects makes it easier to understand both how the systems work together and how knowledge and skills in one system can generalize to the others, much like in academics and behavior.

In addition, a common theme that you will find throughout the chapters in Part II is *strategic integration*. Instead of forcing full integration, it is helpful to look for opportunities where integration is logical and easy. For example, integration can be embedded within a unified school improvement process, as we describe in Chapter 7. When we start with an overall shared goal of improving educational environments to promote successful student outcomes, integration becomes that much easier.

In place of the typical summary of key points, each chapter ends with a pair of team checklists, one for school-level teams and one for district-level teams. These checklists summarize the key points for each system and serve as tools for teams in their efforts to integrate their systems. Taken together, the checklists in Part II can serve as both roadmaps and action planning tools for schools and districts to utilize when integrating their academic and behavior systems more fully.

# CHAPTER 3

# Integrating Data

In this chapter, we discuss the use of data within an integrated academic and behavior MTSS model. Multi-tiered models such as academic RTI and PBIS are strongly dependent on data as foundational for all implementation and decision-making efforts, so data play an even more critical role in integrated MTSS. In fact, it's hard to overestimate the importance of data for optimizing any systems in education, from daily instructional decisions, to special education eligibility decisions, to decisions regarding long-term plans within schools, districts, and states.

As with each of the systems in this section, integrating data systems within MTSS is not often a straightforward task, but there are true benefits. The good news for implementers is that there is very little in the way of new data to collect beyond the data used in parallel academic and behavior systems. The tools themselves (e.g., assessments, measures, tests) are not necessarily integrated because they have often been designed and validated to work as separate units that assess specific academic or behavior skills. Instead, the benefits of integration come from two key aspects of an integrated system: efficiency and effectiveness.

Integrating data systems is more *efficient* because the ideas and principles behind data collection and use for decision making are identical. Once we have the core conceptual understanding of why and how data can improve instruction, which data sources to select, and how to use them for decision making in one content area (e.g., behavior), it becomes much easier to apply this knowledge to another (e.g., mathematics). Strangely enough, the tools themselves—what we often think of as data—become interchangeable. In many cases, the difference in data systems between academics and behavior comes from swapping out tools with the exact same purposes. For example, the diagnostic tests used in intermediate math or behavior may look very different in terms of procedures, but their purpose (to identify how exactly to address a student's needs) and use within a problem-solving model are identical. As such, efficiency increases because school personnel already have the background knowledge in one area to apply to the other. These savings in training costs also come with less resistance to change because we can see that it's not a new concept, it's merely "what we are already doing for [behavior] at this school."

In addition to the benefits to efficiency, there are benefits to integrated data systems in terms of *effectiveness*. Having both kinds of data on the table leads to better decisions in each domain. Being able to look at all of the available academic and behavior data for a school, groups of students, and individual students is much more effective because it both narrows the problems and widens the universe of interventions and strategies. The interactions between academic skills and behavior that were described in the previous chapter allow for a broader, more whole-child perspective, and integrated data systems provide the opportunity to tailor support in a way that a one-dimensional data system cannot. In some cases (as you'll read in Chapter 4), an intervention in one domain or a slight differentiation of instruction may provide enough support for that student or group of students to be successful, with more time for them to learn in the least restrictive environment. In other cases, seeing both sets of data will reveal the need for an individualized intervention that includes both academic and behavior support, and at the same time it will provide more comprehensive data to judge that intervention's effectiveness.

To begin to capitalize on the efficiency and effectiveness of integrated data, we need to build the shared conceptual understanding of data in schools, regardless of the domain of support. Data are used within an integrated MTSS model for five main purposes: (1) to identify what practices are currently in place and how well they are implemented in an ongoing process (e.g., audits of current practices, assessment of fidelity of implementation); (2) to identify students requiring additional support (i.e., screening); (3) to assess what support would be most helpful (e.g., at the school or individual level); (4) to assess continuous student growth on a regular schedule (i.e., formative assessment); and (5) to assess student outcomes on a broader scale (i.e., summative assessment). This chapter describes the data that can be most helpful for integrated MTSS, including data at the schoolwide and individual student levels. The usefulness of certain types of data varies based on these levels. Specific guidance on approaches for using these data for decision making is provided in Chapter 5.

## RESISTANCE TO DATA-DRIVEN EDUCATION: CONCERNS AND SOLUTIONS

What we've just described may sound like a pretty convincing argument for data to play a key role in education. However, for many, *data* is a four-letter word (Horner, Sugai, & Todd, 2001). Actually, there is no denying that statement (in this case, the data are compelling), but aversion to data is a common sentiment in schools. Perhaps you've heard statements such as "I'm not a data person," or worse, "I love everything about PBIS, but I hate the data." If you are reading this book, you're more likely than not to fall into that "data person" category. If so, you may be frustrated with these statements, but just as behavior serves a function to meet basic human needs, there are real, legitimate concerns behind these words. Many educators' regular experiences with data are lousy. As such, it is worth examining these concerns and making plans that reduce these fears.

### Common Concerns Regarding Data Collection and Use in Schools and Potential Solutions

#### Numbers Can Be Scary

For many people, just the mention of numbers or data can bring on anxiety. The level of math phobia in our society, even among educators, compels many people to resist the use of data or start zoning out when data are shown. How many of us, when reading a report or research article, start to get feelings of fear or incompetence when statistics show up? This experience leads many to strongly oppose the use of data—this phenomenon is called *experiential avoidance* (Hayes, Wilson, Gifford, Follette, & Strosahl, 1996). It's a common reaction to avoid uncomfortable experiences, and knowing this information, just as in an FBA, is incredibly important in solving the problem. Providing a flood of numbers or graphs without assisting the audience in understanding the approach or what they mean is likely to result in this reaction. Instead, we can reduce this response any time we bring up data or graphs by being clear and explicit about their purpose and using a "think-aloud" strategy (talking through each step) to guide the group to understanding. Just as with reducing student phobias (Westen & Morrison, 2001), having positive experiences with data use and interpretation will reduce the fear of data.

## Data Can Be Hard to Interpret

Beyond a simple aversion to numbers, even those who value the importance of data or get over their fears can drown in the numbers and what they are supposed to tell us. This response is common because we often collect more data than are needed, and many educators don't have specialized (or any) training in how to use them. Gilbert (1978) distinguished between data and information: *Data* are the raw numbers, and *information* is the data provided in an understandable and actionable format. In education, we are often bombarded by data that we collect—so much, in fact, that to figure out what they all mean becomes inefficient and time-consuming. To address this issue, we need to focus on getting high-quality data (i.e., data that are accurate, relevant, and timely) and then transform the numbers into meaningful and useful information. To make it happen, we need to cut back on the data that we collect and interpret, then provide ongoing training and support in how to use the most important pieces well.

## Data Can Bring Troubling Issues to Light

Once interpreted and understood, an additional concern is that data can sometimes reveal issues that might seem to be easier to ignore than examine further. A common area in which this concern exists is with racial/ethnic disparities in student outcomes, be they academic (the so-called achievement gap) or behavior (discipline disparities). Finding inequities in outcomes is uncomfortable and can lead to questioning the validity of the data or viewing it once and then ignoring it, as opposed to taking action to increase equity (McIntosh, Eliason, Horner, & May, 2014). These problems can be exacerbated by a feeling that there may not be effective school solutions to larger societal problems. However, there is evidence that an academic RTI system and PBIS can reduce these gaps (see Chapter 8; also see Vincent, Swain-Bradway, Tobin, & May, 2011). To address this concern takes courage to act on our values and examine these data regularly; it also takes a systematic problem-solving approach that focuses on addressing the causes of inequities rather than on finding excuses for persistent gaps (McIntosh, Barnes, et al., 2014).

## Data Take Time Away from Instruction

Although this point is technically true, collecting the right kinds of data can make instruction so much more effective that it becomes a true time-saving endeavor. Have you ever sat through an inservice workshop where the content was so basic (or advanced) that you got nothing out of it? A little pretest or initial assessment would have eaten up some time for the workshop content, no doubt, but it would have made the rest of that time so much more valuable. To use an early literacy example, once we know that students have established phonological awareness skills, additional instruction in this area is unlikely to help (Adams, 1990), and so we can be much more effective by assessing these skills briefly and accelerating students who don't need more instruction in it. Likewise, failing to teach students to mastery leaves them with misrules that can be much more difficult to remediate (Wong, Wong, & Seroyer, 1998). Hence, collecting a little data will allow students to progress faster, as long as the data are used to guide instruction.

There are two important guidelines for overcoming this concern. First, we need to be efficient with data collection so as not to interrupt instruction unnecessarily. We have to make sure that any data collected are used to change instruction and not collected just because they could be interesting. We should spend much more of our time acting on data (teaching and providing supports) than collecting them. Our tiered approach to instruction relies on brief, periodic measures (e.g., curriculum-based measurement benchmarks in academics) and existing data (e.g., ODR and suspension information) for all students and increasing intensities of data collection as students move up the tiers of support. This approach is more efficient than adding extensive data collection for all students. Second, any time we ask our staff to collect data, we must share with them (a) a brief, easily understood summary of their information and (b) how it is being used to improve student outcomes. Ideally, this information is shared at the next staff meeting to help strengthen the message that the data they helped collect are leading to changes that will benefit students.

## Data Can Be Misused

Another important concern of educators is that the data they collect are sometimes used to blame them, argue against the effectiveness of public schooling, or label some students as unteachable. With an ever-increasing focus on teacher evaluation and accountability, teachers have, at times, had data used against them to point out what is wrong with them rather than to help them improve instruction. This concern understandably leads to serious skepticism about the value of data in education. It may sometimes be tempting to consider using data to identify educators who are not being effective or refusing to implement interventions with precision. However, in most cases, the tools that are used in education have never been validated for such purposes, and therefore there is rarely a justifiable reason to use them as such. This concern leads to the last recommendation before we get into the details of data: Never use data to punish individuals (Horner et al., 2001). It won't work because they will be tempted to fudge numbers or refuse to participate in data collection—and for good reason!

## CATEGORIES OF ASSESSMENT TOOLS FOR DATA COLLECTION

One issue that contributes to the common feeling of drowning in data just described is the abundance of different assessment tools that are available for educators. With all of the options and all of the data that come from them, the number of choices to implement can be dizzying. However, if we categorize the assessment tools by specific purpose, we can ameliorate the confusion and make the selection process easier. Within an integrated MTSS model, data are collected, analyzed, summarized, and utilized for five main purposes: (1) assessing fidelity of implementation (i.e., Are we doing what we said we'd do?); (2) screening (i.e., Who needs additional support?); (3) diagnostic assessment (i.e., What specific supports are needed?); (4) progress monitoring (i.e., Are the supports changing student trajectories in a positive direction?); and (5) general outcomes measurement (i.e., Are students doing better overall?) (McIntosh, Reinke, & Herman, 2009; Torgesen, 2006). Each purpose is important to ensure that educators are teaching effectively and that students are successful. Although these purposes separate assessment into different categories, some tools may be used for multiple purposes. In this section, we describe each purpose, the common tools used, the typical processes undertaken for data collection, and how each fits within an integrated MTSS model.

## Fidelity of Implementation

Before we can assess whether our practices are effective, it is important to make sure that we are actually doing what we think we are doing. Fidelity measures assess how consistently educators are implementing practices as intended (Gresham, 1989). This form of assessment is often overlooked in education, but it is incredibly important to our work. We often assume that because we purchase a curriculum or provide a series of inservice trainings, practices will be implemented with fidelity. However, that is an incorrect and often dangerous assumption, as research has shown that mere adoption is insufficient to ensure fidelity (Fixsen, Naoom, Blase, Friedman, & Wallace, 2005). It is also unfair to teachers to assume that they can pick up a curriculum or attend a training and deliver it without ongoing support (Joyce & Showers, 2002).

Being able to assess whether practices are implemented with fidelity allows us to rule out inadequate implementation as a reason for poor student performance. If we have data showing that practices are implemented to criteria, we can better assess other reasons for inadequate response (e.g., insufficient intensity, poor match to student need) and change our plans accordingly. Without fidelity data, we can't know whether our plan even has the potential to help support the student to be successful or what aspects we need to change to make it better.

Another potential benefit of measuring fidelity pertains to motivation to sustain the practice. Research has shown that achieving successful student outcomes with an MTSS practice (e.g., PBIS, peer-assisted learning strategies [PALS]) reinforces the staff behavior of implementing the practice with fidelity (Andreou et al., 2015; Baker, Gersten, Dimino, & Griffiths, 2004). In other words, seeing positive change in students motivates us to continue implementing the practice. However, it may take extended time to realize changes in student behavior and academic performance. Fidelity of implementation measures may provide a similar function for school personnel. Before student outcomes are observed, these tools can help staff celebrate successes in terms of adult behavior (i.e., a checklist of progress toward full implementation), as well as identify the next step along this path.

## Common Tools for Assessing Fidelity

Fidelity tools fall into two main types. Fidelity self-assessments are completed by the team or whole school staff, with or without a coach present. External evaluations are conducted by a coach or district team and often include interviews, observations, and permanent product reviews. Self-assessments of fidelity are typically more efficient but also susceptible to over-estimation (Wickstrom, Jones, LaFleur, & Witt, 1996). Generally, self-assessments are more accurate when the self-assessment tool itself is more specific (e.g., a checklist of specific, observable items rather than a global rating of "how well we're doing") and the assessors are more experienced in the practice (Allen & Blackston, 2003; Rasplica, McIntosh, & Hoselton, 2016).

Another consideration is the specificity of the tool. Some tools are tied to specific curricula and are often included as supplementary materials when purchasing a particular published program. These measures typically focus on procedural fidelity (e.g., were all steps in the lesson plan delivered?). Other measures assess critical features of effective instructional practices, based on key variables known in general to improve student outcomes (Horner & McIntosh, 2016). These latter types of assessments are often more useful because they can be used across practices or as systems-level measures of implementation of quality instruction. Table 3.1 provides a list of common fidelity tools used for behavior and literacy. If standardized or valid fidelity assessments are not available, it is helpful for educators to agree on the critical features of the practice being implemented and then spend some time determining whether these features are in place.

## ASSESSMENT OF BEHAVIOR PRACTICES

Within PBIS, there a number of systems-level fidelity assessments that are freely available and can be found on the PBIS assessment website (*www.pbisapps.org*). Research-validated tools for assessing implementation of schoolwide (Tier 1) systems include the *PBIS Self-Assessment Survey* (SAS; Sugai, Horner, & Todd, 2000), *SWPBIS Tiered Fidelity Inventory* (TFI; Algozzine et al., 2014), *School-wide Benchmarks of Quality* (BoQ; Kincaid, Childs, & George, 2005), *School-wide Evaluation Tool* (SET; Sugai, Lewis-Palmer, Todd, & Horner, 2001), and *Team Implementation Checklist* (TIC; Sugai, Horner, & Lewis-Palmer, 2001). Each of these tools has been developed for specific uses. For example, the TIC is useful for initial start-up activities, the BoQ is useful for advanced implementation, and the SET is an external evaluation measure. Fidelity tools are also available for measuring implementation of behavior support systems at Tiers 2 and 3. These include the *Benchmarks for Advanced Tiers* (BAT; Anderson et al., 2012), the *Individual Student Systems Evaluation Tool* (ISSET; Lewis-Palmer, Todd, Horner, Sugai, & Sampson, 2003) and *Monitoring Advanced Tiers Tool* (MATT; Horner, Sampson, Anderson, Todd, & Eliason, 2013). The TFI includes validated subscales for all three tiers (McIntosh, Massar, et al., in press).

## ASSESSMENT OF ACADEMIC PRACTICES

There are fewer fidelity measures available for academic practices, but three tools—all focusing on schoolwide systems for literacy—are worth noting. The *Planning and Evaluation Tool for Effective School-wide Reading Programs* (PET-R; Kame'enui & Simmons, 2002) is a self-assessment tool used to determine to what extent a tiered schoolwide reading improvement model is in place for elementary schools. The PET is used by a school's leadership team to rate the school's current reading program implementation and identify priorities. Another measure, the *Reading Tiered Fidelity Inventory* (R-TFI; St. Martin, Nantais, Harms, & Huth,

2015), is a self-assessment tool designed for a purpose similar to the PET-R, but addressing Tiers 1–3. Scoring is also enhanced through the use of a scoring rubric (see Appendices 3.1 and 3.2 for brief versions of the Elementary and Secondary Level Editions of the R-TFI). The R-TFI is intended to be used by team members to self-monitor their own implementation for action planning purposes. There are two versions of the R-TFI available: one designed for elementary schools and another designed for secondary schools. The R-TFI will soon be available online for free entry and report generation at *www.pbisapps.org*. A more comprehensive version of the R-TFI, the *Reading Tiered Fidelity Inventory Comprehensive Edition* (R-TFI-CE; St. Martin, Huth, & Harms, 2015), is an external evaluation tool for assessing implementation of a school's Tier 1 literacy systems, as well as assessing the behavior support strategies in place to support academic gains. The R-TFI-CE incudes permanent product reviews, interviews, and classroom observations to assess both school-level systems (e.g., scheduling, leadership team actions) and classroom practices (e.g., use of effective instructional principles, student engagement, opportunities to respond). The R-TFI-CE classroom observation form, which includes assessment of teaching strategies, the classroom environment, academic engagement and opportunities to respond, and student–teacher interactions, is included in Appendix 3.3.

## ASSESSMENT OF INDIVIDUAL SUPPORT PLANS

There are also tools available to help assess the fidelity of implementation of individual student support plans at the Tier 3 level. Such measures often take the form of implementation checklists that contain the support plan strategies used or rating scales to assess implementation. As with the plans that they assess, each tool must be tailored to the support plan it assesses. To assist in measure creation, data entry, and analysis, school teams may choose to develop a database (e.g., through Microsoft ACCESS) or adopt a Web-based application such as Individual Student Information System—School Wide Information System (ISIS-SWIS; *www.pbisapps.org*), which provides tools for creating and graphing data for an array of self-created fidelity forms (e.g., implementation checklists, rating scales).

## Typical Processes for Fidelity Assessment

Fidelity assessments are often conducted before implementation begins (i.e., as a baseline or needs assessment to determine what practices are already in place) and periodically to assess progress. During initial implementation, assessment may be more frequent (e.g., quarterly) to ensure that tasks are completed, and once full implementation is achieved, it may move to a yearly assessment to ensure the practice is expanded and sustained. Assessment may take place via team members' self-assessments or external evaluations as part of peer mentoring or the district's formal evaluation processes. Depending on the measure, the scale of assessment may vary from fidelity of schoolwide systems, to classroom systems, to individual support plans. Once completed, teams can use the results to identify strengths and weakness of implementation. Strengths are celebrated, and weaknesses are considered for improvement and next steps when developing action plans.

**TABLE 3.1. Measures for Assessing Fidelity of Implementation of Systems of Support for Behavior and Literacy**

| Measure | Purpose | Typical process | Typical frequency |
|---|---|---|---|
| *Behavior systems* | | | |
| PBIS Team Implementation Checklist (TIC) | Guides school teams to monitor progress and informs action planning in the initial steps needed for Tier 1 PBIS implementation | School leadership team completes one checklist by consensus, with or without external coach (~10 minutes) | Quarterly until 100% (then transition to another measure) |
| PBIS Self-Assessment Survey (SAS) | Provides a needs assessment and obtains staff perspectives on quality of implementation and priorities for improvement for four systems: (1) schoolwide, (2) nonclassroom, (3) classroom, and (4) individual student | Each school staff completes a separate survey, sometimes omitting the individual student systems if the school is new to PBIS (~30 minutes) | Annually or biannually |
| School-wide Evaluation Tool (SET) | Provides an *external evaluation* of Tier 1 PBIS systems through a site visit that includes interviews, observations, and permanent product reviews | Outside observer (e.g., external coach, district coordinator) completes site visit and provides report to team (~2 hours by observer) | Annually |
| School-wide Benchmarks of Quality (BoQ) | Provides an in-depth assessment of Tier 1 PBIS systems to assess and identify areas of strength and weakness to inform action planning | School leadership team and external coach complete measure separately, then meet to find consensus (~45 minutes) | Annually |
| Benchmarks for Advanced Tiers (BAT) | Provides an in-depth assessment of Tiers 2 and 3 PBIS systems to inform action planning | School leadership team completes one measure by consensus, usually with external coach (~1 hour) | Annually |

| Tool | Purpose | Administration | Frequency |
|---|---|---|---|
| Individual Student Systems Evaluation Tool (ISSET) | Provides an *external evaluation* of Tiers 2 and 3 PBIS systems through a site visit that includes interviews and permanent product reviews | Outside observer (e.g., external coach, district coordinator) completes site visit and provides report to team (~2.5 hours by observer) | Annually |
| Monitoring Advanced Tiers Tool (MATT) | Guides school teams to monitor progress and inform action planning in Tiers 2 and 3 PBIS implementation | School leadership team completes one measure by consensus, usually with external coach (~45 minutes) | Quarterly until 80% (then annually) |
| SWPBIS Tiered Fidelity Inventory (TFI) | Provides an efficient assessment of all three tiers of PBIS to assess and identify areas of strength and weakness to inform action planning | School leadership team completes one measure by consensus, usually with external coach (~45 minutes total or ~15 minutes per tier) | Quarterly until 70% (then annually) |
| **Literacy systems** | | | |
| Planning and Evaluation Tool for Effective School-wide Reading Programs—Revised (PET-R) | Guides elementary school teams to monitor progress and informs action planning in implementing seven key elements of a schoolwide reading improvement model | School leadership team completes one measure by consensus, usually with external coach (~1 hour) | Annually |
| Reading Tiered Fidelity Inventory Comprehensive Edition (R-TFI-CE) | Provides an *external evaluation* of Tier 1 literacy systems through a site visit that includes interviews, observations, and permanent product reviews | Outside observer (e.g., external coach, district specialist) completes site visit and provides report to team (~4 hours by observer) | Annually |
| Reading Tiered Fidelity Inventory (R-TFI; Elementary- and Secondary-Level Editions) | Guides school teams to monitor progress and informs action planning in implementing 3-tiered literacy systems | School leadership team completes one measure by consensus, usually with external coach (~1–2 hours) | Annually |

*Note.* Adapted with permission from the Michigan Department of Education.

## Integrated Fidelity Assessment

Fidelity measures that are specific to the implementation of integrated academic and behavioral MTSS are only just beginning to emerge. These interesting measures focus on systems-level implementation of both domains of support in a school or district (e.g., Florida's MTSS, 2013). At this point, there isn't a research base demonstrating the advantages of assessing fidelity of integrated systems instead of using separate fidelity measures for academic RTI and PBIS. Nevertheless, these new measures can be useful in identifying the strengths and next steps for the integration process itself. For example, Furey and Stoner (2015) have developed an electronic self-assessment of integrated MTSS implementation that can serve as a needs assessment and action planning tool (available at *www.sites.google.com/site/mtssneedsassessment*). School teams can complete the measure to assess baseline implementation and track their progress toward full implementation of an integrated model. A paper-and-pencil version of this measure is included in Appendices 3.4 (elementary version) and 3.5 (secondary version). We have also included a general set of school and district checklists for the process of integrating systems at the end of Chapter 7.

## Screening for Additional Support

Screening tools produce data with which to identify students who may be in need of additional supports beyond Tier 1 to be successful. This process is necessary to intervene as early as possible and bring students back on track for positive academic or behavior outcomes. An important consideration in the screening process is to use the results to identify the need for supports and not to label students. With intervention, some students move down tiers of need and may not need additional support at the next benchmarking period. As such, students are not "Tier 2 students," but instead, they are those who currently require Tier 2 support (i.e., practices) for a particular content area. Indeed, by strengthening Tier 1 systems, fewer students would require additional supports. In this way, student needs are not seen as inherent within the individual, but rather dependent on how support is arranged and provided in the school.

It is also important to note that data collected through screening procedures are not intended to indicate the final word on student performance. The screeners are considered to help determine if a student might be having difficulty and may be in need of further support. It is good practice to validate screening results through a combination of other assessments, review of student performance to date, and teacher professional judgment. For example, most schools use a teacher request-for-support form (described on p. 50 and in Appendix 3.6) that can be used throughout the year to identify a student as needing support. A number of studies show that classroom teachers can be highly accurate in identifying which students need additional support (Lane & Menzies, 2005; Layne, Bernstein, & March, 2006).

## Common Tools for Screening

Because they are used either with all students or all students at Tier 1, screening tools must be brief, efficient, and assess the most important indicators of skill development. As such, they are often incomplete assessments, but they provide the information needed to assess whether more assessment or support is warranted.

## SCREENING FOR BEHAVIOR NEEDS

There are two major types of screening tools for behavior. First, given the inefficiency of direct observation of behavior and the fact that behavior varies across settings based on the situation, school teams often use existing data to assess behavior (McIntosh, Reinke, et al., 2009). These data include attendance, suspensions, and ODRs. ODRs are forms used to document events of unwanted behavior that require teacher or administrator intervention. Although the use of informal referrals (i.e., incident reports) can vary across school personnel and lack reliability (Nelson, Benner, Reid, Epstein, & Currin, 2002), standardizing referrals into ODRs (e.g., standard forms with checklists and definitions, regular training and discussion about correct use, standard procedure for entry and analysis) greatly enhances their accuracy and use for decision making (McIntosh, Campbell, Carter, & Zumbo, 2009). Therefore, if schools are required to collect data on behavior incidents, we recommend standardizing the ODR form and process for using it. Part of being able to use ODR data for decision making includes entry and analysis through an electronic database that allows for easy data entry and instantaneous graphing of data by student, location, type of problem behavior, time of day, and month. Options for schools and districts involve developing their own district database or warehouse (e.g., through Microsoft ACCESS) or using existing products designed especially for these tasks. One example is the *School-Wide Information System* (SWIS; *www.pbisapps.org*). SWIS includes guidance on standardization and allows for use of ODRs and other behavior data at all three tiers of MTSS.

Once standardized, screening with ODRs is relatively efficient. ODRs should be entered continually into the data system, which allows for instant analysis of trends in the data. Identifying a student's needed level of support can be based on local patterns or the commonly used guidelines of 0 to 1 ODRs indicating that Tier 1 support is adequate, 2 to 5 ODRs indicating that Tier 2 support may be needed, and 6 or more ODRs indicating that Tier 3 support may be needed (McIntosh, Campbell, Carter, & Zumbo, 2009; Sugai, Sprague, Horner, & Walker, 2000). However, these totals are based on end-of-year tallies, which do not allow for early identification and intervention. A series of studies has examined what numbers of ODRs received during early months predict these needs for support. In elementary school, receiving 2 or more ODRs by the end of October or 1 or more ODRs for disrespect or physical aggression is a strong indicator that the student requires Tier 3 support (McIntosh, Frank, et al., 2010). In middle school, receiving 2 or more ODRs by the end of September or a single ODR for defiance indicates the need for Tier 3 support (Predy, McIntosh, & Frank, 2014). It is important to note, however, that ODRs are strongly related to externalizing (e.g., aggression, conduct problems) behavior needs, but only weakly related to internalizing (e.g., anxiety, depression) needs. As a result, screening only with ODRs will not identify students with internalizing needs as requiring behavior support.

Another type of screening for behavior needs is the systematic behavior screener. These measures are completed by teachers for all students as a proactive way to detect a range of behavior support needs (Severson, Walker, Hope-Doolittle, Kratochwill, & Gresham, 2007). There are a number of different measures available, including brief screeners in which teachers rate each student on critical predictors of behavior needs, such as the *Behavioral and Emotional Screening System* (BESS; Kamphaus & Reynolds, 2007) or the *Student Risk Screening Scale* (SRSS; Drummond, 1994). Others are known as multiple-gate screening systems, such as *Systematic Screening for Behavior Disorders* (SSBD; Walker & Severson, 1992), in which students pass through multiple gates of increasing intensity of assessment, including rankings, rating scales, and direct observations. For those who are interested in systematic behavior screeners, Lane, Menzies, Oakes, and Kalberg (2012) provide an excellent resource for school teams. Lane recommends implementing systematic behavior screeners only after solid practices at Tiers 1, 2, and 3 are in place with adequate fidelity. Otherwise, school personnel will expend a good deal of energy identifying students in need without having options to provide support.

## SCREENING FOR ACADEMIC NEEDS

Although class grades can provide an efficient means of screening, they can be more subjective and conflated with behavior needs (i.e., truancy) than more direct measures. Direct measures for academic screening procedures often involve the use of curriculum-based measurement (CBM; Shinn, 2008). First developed by Deno and Mirkin (1977), CBMs are brief, repeatable, timed assessments of core academic skills. For example, in measures of oral reading fluency, students read grade-level passages for 1-minute assessment periods. The assessor then records a score (e.g., the number of words read correctly per minute and, optionally, any errors made). This score is then compared to local or national norms to determine whether additional support is needed. Another common example of CBM is Dynamic Indicators of Basic Early Literacy Skills (DIBELS; Good & Kaminski, 2010). Hosp, Hosp, and Howell (2016) provide an excellent resource for administering and interpreting CBMs within an MTSS approach. As with behavior measures, it is most efficient and effective to enter academic screening data into an electronic database for quick graphing and analysis in screening decisions. Options include a locally developed database (e.g., ACCESS) or some of the commercially available systems, including AIM-Sweb (*www.aimsweb.com*), the DIBELS Data System (*www.dibels.uoregon.edu*), DIBELSnet (*www.dibels.net*), and Easy CBM (*www.easycbm.com*).

## Typical Processes for Screening

Although screening for behavior support is often continuous (e.g., with ODRs), specific universal screening tools and academic screeners take place at set periods during the year. For academics, all students within the school are screened through an academic benchmarking process that usually takes place three times per school year. The first screening is conducted at the beginning of the school year, generally 2 weeks after students start the school year. Waiting a few weeks for screening provides students time to become comfortable or reacquainted with school routines, instructional content, and teachers. The second screening typically occurs in January, during the second week back from the holiday break. The final screening process occurs several weeks prior to the end of school, usually in the beginning of May. Additionally, screening can take place each time new students join the school.

There are two common options for conducting academic benchmarking. In one approach, a district team blitzes each school one at a time so that all students are assessed by experts in accurate and efficient administration. In the other, classroom teachers conduct their own screenings, perhaps with less experienced teachers working alongside reading specialists. Given these two options, we believe that there are distinct advantages for classroom teachers to take an active role in conducting the screening. First, it helps improve understanding and skills in the assessment process, which is helpful in understanding academic skill development and the larger MTSS process, as well as building skills that may be needed for progress monitoring. Second, screening assessment becomes more informative for instruction when the instructor does the assessing. For example, although error analysis is usually not part of the screening score, an experienced teacher will take note of error patterns observed during the assessment and use this information to improve instruction. If a district team were to conduct this assessment, this information might be lost, either because it wasn't collected or it wasn't communicated to the teacher.

## Integrated Screening

Examining screening data from both academic and behavior assessments can provide additional advantages above making screening decisions separately (Kalberg, Lane, & Menzies, 2010). Some districts utilize academic screening data as part of their behavior screening decision making (Sadler & Sugai, 2009). For example, the low rates of ODRs in kindergarten make them less likely to identify students in need, whereas low prereading scores may indicate the need to ask the teacher about possible needs for behavior support (McIntosh, Horner, et al., 2006). In general, however, it is usually more accurate in elementary schools to screen for academic needs with academic data and screen for behavior needs with behavior data (Algozzine, Wang, & Violette, 2011). For the most part, screening with both academic and behavior data is less important for identifying students in need but more important for selecting Tier 2 or 3 interventions (as described next in diagnostic assessment). One exception is screening for student needs in high school, where a combination of academic (course failure) and behavior data (attendance and ODRs) is more effective in screening students for dropout prevention (Jerald, 2006).

If a school is adopting benchmark behavior screeners or periods of time for assessing number of ODRs, we recommend aligning the screening periods with existing academic benchmarking periods. For example, if screenings take place at the start of the year, they can be aligned with the fall academic screening, or in middle or high schools, they can be aligned with the school's semester or trimester schedule to align with grades. By aligning the academic and behavior benchmark periods, both types of the data will be available for decisions regarding support, which in turn allows for integrated decisions regarding screening.

When screening periods are aligned, the process can be further simplified by using a single form for academic and behavior data (Lane et al., 2012). Although the screening data sources are separate, using one form for integrated screening simplifies the process and reduces the effort involved in data collection. Even though multiple data sources are needed, efficiency is maximized because integrated screening involves one process with one set of paperwork.

## Diagnostic Assessment

After screening data identify students as needing academic or behavior support beyond the support provided at Tier 1, diagnostic assessment provides additional information on students' current skill levels and specific needs for intervention. Although it is tempting to jump directly into providing intervention, diagnostic assessment helps to tell us just what Tier 2 or 3 interventions will be most effective.

It is important to identify students' error patterns (whether they are in academics or behavior) and the reasons for them, while using a developmental lens that accounts for skill development. Success in school often depends on using a hierarchy of skills that build upon one another to allow the student to respond with the appropriate answer or behavior. For example, completing mathematics story problems may require reading decoding and comprehension, problem conceptualization, and complex and basic computation skills (Jitendra, 2002). Skill deficits in any of these areas can lead to incorrect responses, and identifying which prerequisite skills need remediation helps immensely in developing effective interventions. The same approach can be used in behavior. Disruptive work refusal may result from an academic skill deficit in the subject, a lack of fluency in requesting help, lack of clarity in the request, failing to see value in the task, lack of sleep, or an incorrect social attribution (e.g., perception that the teacher is trying to embarrass the student). Diagnostic assessment provides information to identify the most effective support to build success.

In place of using specific diagnostic assessment tools, screening tools often provide useful diagnostic information. In academics, school teams may go to the original test booklet or protocol to assess error patterns for intervention (e.g., trouble decoding multisyllabic words, handling remainders in long division). In behavior, the team may analyze ODRs received to determine the contextual conditions that predict the problem. Beyond the type of behavior itself, potentially useful conditions include location, time of day, day of the week, others involved, and any perceived motivation (i.e., behavioral function) for the behavior. This information provides clues for why the behavior may be happening and what support can increase social competence. Utilizing screening data is obviously very efficient because the team may learn enough information to match interventions to student needs and then select appropriate Tier 2 interventions. However, there are circumstances—especially for Tier 3 support planning—where screening data will not provide the full picture and more specific diagnostic assessment tools are needed.

## Common Tools for Diagnostic Assessment

Specialized measures used to gather more information often vary based on the domains of concern. Some may be completed with little additional support, but others may require specialized skills or training to ensure that the data are collected accurately and interpreted correctly.

### DIAGNOSTIC ASSESSMENT OF BEHAVIOR

Effective diagnostic assessment of behavior rarely involves additional individual testing of students, but rather a detailed analysis of the unwanted behavior (i.e., FBA) displayed and the context in which the behavior occurs (identifying the antecedents and consequences to the problem behavior (Crone et al., 2015; Loman, Strickland-Cohen, Borgmeier, & Horner, 2013; O'Neill, Albin, Storey, Horner, & Sprague, 2015). An FBA can identify variables that occur before and after the behavior, leading to a hypothesis regarding the function of the behavior, or how the behavior is used to meet basic human needs. An FBA attempts to determine whether an uunwanted behavior serves the function of obtaining access to desired outcomes (e.g., activities, attention, items) or escaping or avoiding aversive outcomes (see left side of Figure 3.1). Interventions then link to these assessment results by modifying antecedents and consequences to change the environment and thereby increase prosocial behavior and prevent unwanted behavior (described in more detail in Chapter 4).

FBAs are particularly important to an integrated MTSS model. As described in Chapter 2, identifying behavioral function becomes critical when we move to integrate support at Tiers

2 and 3. Without knowing the function of the problem behavior, we do not know whether academic support is a crucial or irrelevant component of potential behavior support. When a student shows unwanted behavior in response to academic demands (the antecedent), the behavior may serve the function of escape or avoidance of these academic tasks (the consequence). As a result, an integrated FBA process can uncover academic deficits that require intervention to improve behavior.

There are a number of existing resources for using the FBA process to identify how academic and behavior needs may be related (Daly, Neugebauer, Chafouleas, & Skinner, 2015; Witt, Daly, & Noell, 2000). These texts often focus on diagnostic assessments to determine whether a student has skill deficits—a "can't do" problem—or is not motivated—a "won't do" problem (VanDerHeyden & Witt, 2008). The right side of Figure 3.1 shows how this distinction fits within the FBA process. *Can't do* academic problems result from deficits in the specific academic skill, deficits in prerequisite skills, improper application of strategies, or lack of fluency. These reasons all indicate specific academic instruction as necessary to support behavior. *Won't do* problems arise when the student has the needed skills to perform the academic task adequately, but is not motivated to do so. In these situations, unwanted behavior may be due to the effort involved in performing the task or undesirable outcomes (e.g., teasing by other students for answering correctly). These concerns indicate the need to change the environment (e.g., the nature of the request, natural or artificial reinforcement systems).

| **Functional Behavior Assessment** | **Functional Academic Assessment** |
|---|---|
| **1. Identify function of unwanted behavior:** | **1. Identify nature of the academic problem:** |
| **To Avoid or Escape:**<br>• Tasks or activities<br>   ○ Difficult academic tasks<br>   ○ Nonpreferred activities<br>• Attention<br>   ○ Adults (e.g., correction, specific individuals)<br>   ○ Peers (e.g., harassment, specific individuals)<br>• Sensory stimulation<br><br>**To Obtain or Retain:**<br>• Activities or tangible objects<br>   ○ Preferred activities<br>   ○ Preferred items<br>• Attention<br>   ○ Adults<br>   ○ Peers<br>• Sensory stimulation | **"Can't Do" Problem (i.e., unable to do):**<br>• Acquisition (accuracy) deficit<br>   ○ Deficit in target skills<br>   ○ Deficit in prerequisite academic skills<br>   ○ Application of misrules<br>• Fluency (automaticity) deficit<br>• Generalization deficit<br>• Mismatch between skill level and task difficulty (tasks too hard)<br>• Problems due to missing prerequisite skills (e.g., organization, focusing attention)<br><br>**"Won't Do" Problem (i.e., unwilling to do):**<br>• Motivational deficit |
| **2. If function of unwanted behavior is to avoid or escape academic task demands:**<br>Complete functional academic assessment to identify academic tasks that trigger behavior and academic skills to teach (integrated assessment) | **2. If student is repeatedly removed from instruction or student's unwanted behavior repeatedly interrupts instruction:**<br>Complete functional behavior assessment to identify triggers of unwanted behavior and social skills to teach (integrated assessment) |

**FIGURE 3.1.** Diagnostic assessment process for behavior, academic, or integrated assessments.

Common tools used in this FBA process of diagnostic assessment include request-for-support forms, interview tools, and direct observation measures. Appendix 3.6 includes a sample teacher request-for-support (i.e., referral) form that integrates academic and behavior support needs into a form that can provide initial information to identify academic skill deficits, specific problem behaviors, antecedents, and possible functions as part of the referral process. FBAs also often include interviews of individuals who know the student and can describe the problem behavior. These forms can range from streamlined school-based tools such as the *Functional Assessment Checklist for Teachers and Staff* (FACTS; March et al., 2000), which is freely available at *www.pbis.org* and research validated (McIntosh, Borgmeier et al., 2008), to more extensive tools such as the *Functional Assessment Interview* and the *Student-Directed Functional Assessment Interview* (O'Neill et al., 2015). Observation tools to confirm referral and interview information are also available (O'Neill et al., 2015). There are many resources for conducting FBAs and linking the results to behavior support plans, including a freely available training manual developed by the Center on PBIS (Loman et al., 2013).

## DIAGNOSTIC ASSESSMENT FOR ACADEMICS

Although some approaches involve using extensive test batteries for diagnostic assessment in academics, one of the most common approaches in an MTSS model is a survey-level assessment. This approach originated in the efforts to determine the appropriate level of reading passages for instruction, but it can be used across academic content areas as well, such as identifying prereading skills or component skills within a mathematics curriculum. Shapiro (2010) provides detailed directions for how to complete survey-level assessments in literacy (with grade-level reading passages) and mathematics (with single-skill probes mapped onto the math curriculum). These results can then be used to identify skills that have been mastered and require teaching, as well as identify appropriate levels (i.e., those that will maximize learning but minimize escape-maintained problem behavior) for teacher-led instruction, independent work, and progress monitoring.

## Typical Processes for Diagnostic Assessment

The steps involved in diagnostic assessment often occur directly after a screening meeting or review of a request-for-support form. First, the screening data or request form can be assessed to examine whether the student can be assigned to intervention based on this information. If the data are clear regarding strengths and needs and the intervention options straightforward, additional diagnostic assessment is not required. For example, screening data in written expression may indicate that fine motor intervention is needed. Likewise, if the student has nonsevere challenges in working with others and there is an existing social skills intervention in place, or there is one standard Tier 2 intervention used as a standard protocol (e.g., check-in/ check-out), more data will not necessarily enhance intervention selection. However, where needs are unclear or Tier 3 support is required, a school team may add more assessment to the plan in order to tailor support. The team may conduct FBA interviews directly within the initial request for assistance meeting or schedule assessments and reconvene to view results and build the support plan.

## Integrated Diagnostic Assessment

Integrating diagnostic assessment does not involve using new or different tools, but instead involves examining both academic and behavior data at the same time for team decisions. This *integrated analysis* can be incredibly useful for diagnostic purposes. For example, when a student is referred for behavior challenges, it is helpful to examine academic screening data to assess whether the student's academic skills may be contributing to the problems. If the student's academic skills are strong (i.e., at benchmark or above), it indicates that a behavior-only intervention could be sufficient. However, academic skill deficits, particularly in the subjects when unwanted behavior occurs, indicate the need for either an academic and behavior or academic-only intervention. Having both sets of data at the table allows for more efficient FBAs, which reduces the need to collect additional diagnostic assessment data.

---

### VIGNETTE 3.1. Diagnostic Assessment

To understand diagnostic assessment within an integrated MTSS model, let's consider a student named Eddie. The school's integrated Tier 2/3 support team members review their ODR data (through the SWIS application) as a screening tool to identify students requiring additional behavioral support, and Eddie, who has quickly received 15 ODRs (both minor and major) since their midyear meeting, has been identified. Before moving forward with additional diagnostic assessment, the team gathers some diagnostic information from its screening data, in the form of three graphs, to determine which factors might be contributing to Eddie's unwanted behavior. The first graph the team examines is his ODRs by problem behavior (see Figure 3V.1). The data show referrals for eight different types of behavior, most commonly inappropriate language and disrespect. The second graph is ODRs by time of day, noting that his ODRs happen throughout the day, but with spikes at 8:30 and 1:15 (see Figure 3V.2). The third graph is location of problem behavior, finding that most of his ODRs have come from the classroom (see Figure 3V.3).

Eddie's ODR data suggest that the team should focus on the classroom and what the ODRs from that location can tell them. Using the SWIS Drill Down function, the team data coordinator quickly generates and shows three more graphs of ODRs only from the classroom: type of behavior, time of day, and possible motivation. In the classroom, the team members see that the most prevalent behaviors were inappropriate language (see Figure 3V.4). They also note that all of his classroom ODRs came at either 8:30 A.M. or 1:15 P.M. (see Figure 3V.5). A quick look at his schedule shows that language arts takes place from 8:00 to 9:30 A.M., and silent sustained reading takes place from 1:15 to 1:30 P.M. They also examine perceived motivation, a rating of function or "why" the behavior keeps happening (see Figure 3V.6). Problem behavior seems to be maintained by avoiding the task or avoiding adult attention. So far, simply by viewing existing ODR data, the team has found that Eddie's unwanted behaviors most often take place in the classroom during reading. The behavior problems seemed to be motivated by avoidance of work. They start to wonder whether there might be a connection between his problem behavior and academics.

This pattern of behavior indicates that the team should also check his reading benchmark scores to see whether skill deficits are contributing to the problem. The team uses the DIBELS Data System (*http://dibels.uoregon.edu*) to enter and analyze Eddie's DIBELS reading data. When reviewing Eddie's Oral Reading Fluency performance, the team members see that he is in the lower third of the class in this skill (see Figure 3V.7). They also notice that Eddie has made no progress from fall to winter (i.e., beginning to middle assessment periods) on this reading indicator. Taken

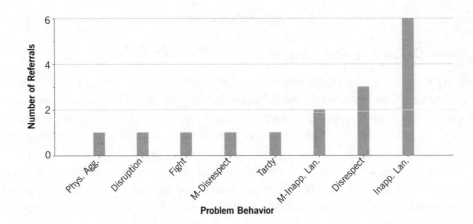

**FIGURE 3V.1.** Eddie's referrals by problem behavior. From SWIS. Reprinted with permission from Rob Horner.

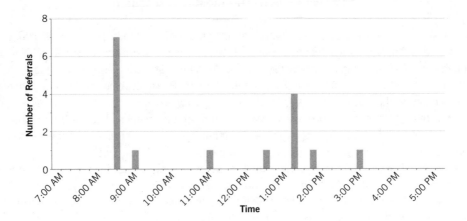

**FIGURE 3V.2.** Eddie's referrals by time of day. From SWIS. Reprinted with permission from Rob Horner.

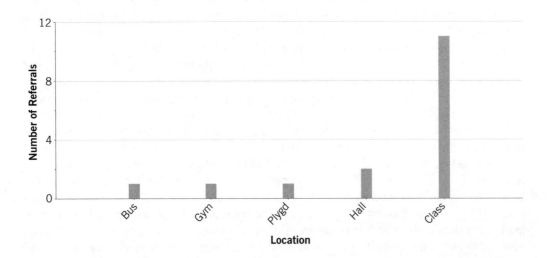

**FIGURE 3V.3.** Eddie's referrals by location. From SWIS. Reprinted with permission from Rob Horner.

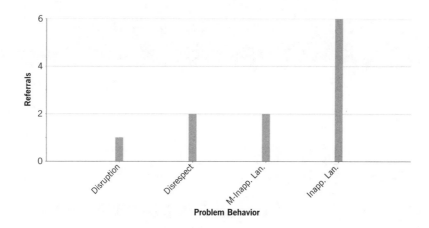

**FIGURE 3V.4.** Eddie's referrals by problem behavior—classroom only. From SWIS. Reprinted with permission from Rob Horner.

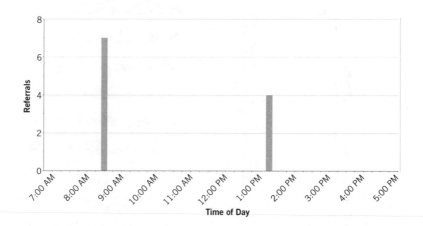

**FIGURE 3V.5.** Eddie's referrals by time of day—classroom only. From SWIS. Reprinted with permission from Rob Horner.

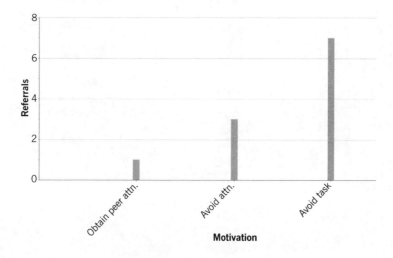

**FIGURE 3V.6.** Eddie's referrals by perceived motivation—classroom only. From SWIS. Reprinted with permission from Rob Horner.

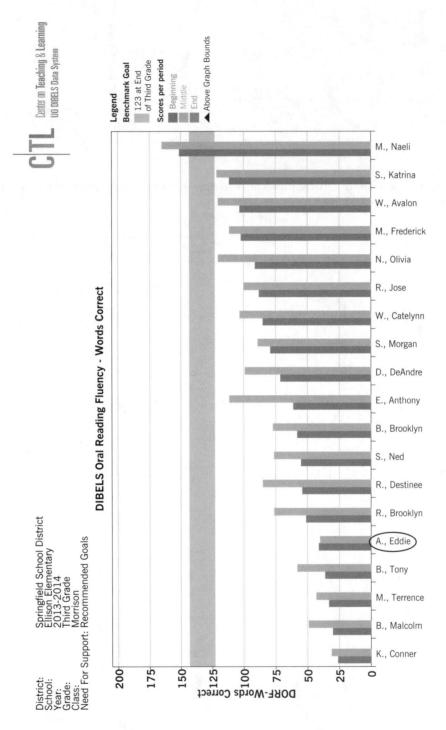

**FIGURE 3V.7.** Class reading progress graph. From DIBELS Data System. Reprinted with permission from Hank Fein.

together with the ODR data, this information suggests that Eddie's problem behavior stems from difficulty in reading.

To gather even more specific information, team members review Eddie's winter benchmark DIBELS Next Oral Reading Fluency protocol (see Figure 3V.8). They notice that he showed low fluency and low accuracy for his grade level. Because his teacher recorded his specific errors (an option in assessment), the team members see that during Eddie's errors, he often substituted incorrect words with the same initial letter sounds. This pattern of errors suggests that he may need remediation in decoding skills. To test this hypothesis, the team examines his past benchmark performance on early literacy measures (see Figure 3V.9) and finds that he has mastered phonemic awareness but never successfully mastered the alphabetic principle. Additionally, his reading fluency has been consistently below the benchmark goal for his grade level.

This process of using existing screening data for diagnostic assessment represents an efficient way for teams to understand challenges without more resource-intensive diagnostic assessment. Using only information that is already available, the team forms a strong idea of the setting (classroom), the activity (reading), the function of behavior (Eddie uses inappropriate language to avoid or escape reading tasks), and an indicated intervention (instruction in reading decoding to make reading less aversive). The team has gained valuable insight into why Eddie has challenges and what needs to be done to intervene, leaving them more time and resources to implement than if they had requested additional diagnostic testing from specialists. However, these benefits came primarily from being able to examine both academic *and* behavior data *at the same time*. Without both types of data at the table, the team may have come to the wrong conclusion or wasted resources on additional diagnostic assessment to learn the same information.

**2** **DIBELS® Oral Reading Fluency**
Grade 3/Benchmark 2.2

▶ *Now read this story to me.*
*Please do your best reading.*
*Ready, begin.*

| | |
|---|---|
| Total words: | 57 |
| Errors (include skipped words): – | 16 |
| Words correct: = | 41 |

**Raising a Calf**

| | | |
|---|---|---|
| 0 | Some of your friends probably have pet dogs or cats. Others might | 12 |
| 12 | have gerbils or goldfish. But do you know anyone who has a baby | 25 |
| 25 | cow? It might astonish you to know that many children do! Every year, | 38 |
| 38 | thousands of young people raise baby cows, or calves, to compete in | 50 |
| 50 | livestock shows. | 52 |
| 52 | Imagine that you are going to raise a calf for a livestock competition. | 65 |
| 65 | Get ready to work hard! First, you must prepare a place for your calf. It | 80 |
| 80 | needs a clean, dry pen that is roomy enough to run around. The enclosure | 94 |
| 94 | should have a good fence so the calf can't escape and get injured or lost. | 109 |
| 109 | Before you put the calf in its new home, check to make sure there is | 124 |
| 124 | nothing sharp or dangerous. Calves like to explore and put everything in | 136 |
| 136 | their mouth. It is your responsibility to watch out for them and protect | 149 |
| 149 | them. | 150 |

**FIGURE 3V.8.** Eddie's DIBELS Oral Reading Fluency benchmark passage. Reprinted with permission from the Dynamic Measurement Group.

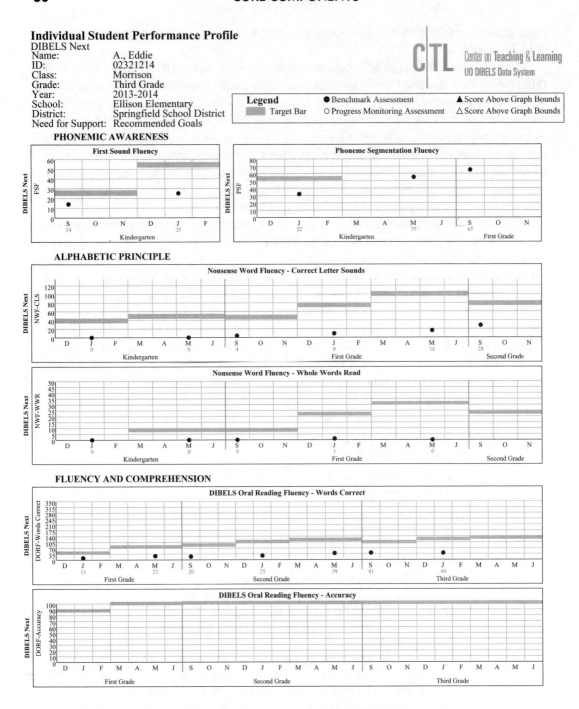

**Individual Student Performance Profile**
DIBELS Next

| | |
|---|---|
| Name: | A., Eddie |
| ID: | 02321214 |
| Class: | Morrison |
| Grade: | Third Grade |
| Year: | 2013-2014 |
| School: | Ellison Elementary |
| District: | Springfield School District |
| Need for Support: | Recommended Goals |

CTL — Center on Teaching & Learning — UO DIBELS Data System

**Legend**
- ● Benchmark Assessment
- ○ Progress Monitoring Assessment
- Target Bar
- ▲ Score Above Graph Bounds
- △ Score Above Graph Bounds

**PHONEMIC AWARENESS**

First Sound Fluency

Phoneme Segmentation Fluency

**ALPHABETIC PRINCIPLE**

Nonsense Word Fluency - Correct Letter Sounds

Nonsense Word Fluency - Whole Words Read

**FLUENCY AND COMPREHENSION**

DIBELS Oral Reading Fluency - Words Correct

DIBELS Oral Reading Fluency - Accuracy

**FIGURE 3V.9.** Eddie's benchmark reading growth. From DIBELS Data System. Reprinted with permission from Hank Fein.

## Progress Monitoring

After screening identifies students who require targeted or intensive support, and diagnostic assessment is used to select interventions, progress monitoring plans are used to assess whether students are making adequate growth. Progress monitoring measures are similar to screening measures but are used and analyzed more frequently (e.g., monthly, weekly, daily), with more frequent assessments conducted when challenges are more intense. In a sense, these measures serve the same function as screening data but fill in the gaps between the regular screening benchmark periods (e.g., fall, winter, spring).

Progress monitoring needs to occur more frequently than screening because the data are used to make instructional decisions that cannot wait until the next benchmark period. For Tier 1 instruction, it can be sufficient to make corrections only a few times per year (e.g., in response to fall or winter screening data), but for students requiring Tier 2 or 3 support, we need to know right away if things are not working so that we do not lose opportunities to intervene most effectively (Archer & Hughes, 2011). The data tell us whether the student is making adequate progress with the current support. If not, we can change our plan (e.g., change interventions, move from Tier 2 to Tier 3 support). In addition, these data can tell us when students are being consistently successful and may be ready to move down the tiers.

### Common Tools for Progress Monitoring

Progress monitoring tools are often the same as those used in screening, but because students have been previously identified in need of additional supports, progress monitoring usually targets one or two specific skills that are the best indicators of growth, as opposed to all indicators of growth. This less intensive, less time-consuming approach allows assessments to be conducted more frequently.

#### PROGRESS MONITORING FOR BEHAVIOR NEEDS

For behavior, school teams may continue to use ODRs to monitor levels of serious problem behavior, but ODRs—even those for minor incidents—may not be sensitive enough to show change on a daily or weekly basis (McIntosh, Frank, et al., 2010). In addition to monitoring ODRs at monthly meetings, teams often monitor progress with daily behavior report cards (Volpe & Fabiano, 2013). These cards are commonly used as part of check-in/check-out, a Tier 2 intervention to support behavior (Crone et al., 2010; see Chapter 4).

Daily behavior report cards divide the student's day into smaller periods, which correspond with subject changes or other natural transitions. At the end of each of these periods, the teacher rates the student behavior on a predefined set of behaviors (e.g., a 1 to 3 rating of a few prosocial behaviors). To enhance linkages across the tiers and allow for fading of Tier 2 support (Campbell & Anderson, 2011), it is helpful to use the schoolwide PBIS expectations (e.g., Respect Self, Respect Others, Respect the Environment) as the behaviors to be rated. These behaviors allow the schoolwide systems to support Tier 2, because the language is familiar to students and staff, schoolwide lessons are available for use, and the expectations are already posted around the school for additional support. When a student transitions off the card, the schoolwide expectations are still in place for consistency. For Tier 2, we recommend using the same exact card for all students (i.e., no individualization of behaviors to be rated) to maximize efficiency and reduce disruptions to instruction. Cards can be individualized at Tier 3, where more intensive progress monitoring may be needed.

   Daily behavior report card data are often graphed by percent of possible points earned per day. When entered and graphed in an electronic system, it is easy to use card points to assess student progress and see whether changes need to be made. Systems for graphing include simple Microsoft Excel spreadsheets (see the online supplement for a downloadable, basic point card graph at *www.guilford.com/mcintosh-materials*) or specialized programs, such as CICO-SWIS, an application within the SWIS suite (*www.pbisapps.org*). Figure 3.2 shows a daily point graph developed from the Excel spreadsheet. In the graph, it is easy to see that although there was initial success for the student, the student's daily points have decreased each week, with a decreasing trend within each week and Fridays as particular challenges. The team can use this information to change the intervention, with a particular focus on more support on Fridays.

## PROGRESS MONITORING FOR ACADEMIC NEEDS

In the academic realm, CBM has been used for both screening and progress monitoring purposes. However, whereas screening with CBM often includes a short battery of measures per domain (i.e., measures of different components), progress monitoring typically focuses on only one skill component area. Options include one measure within the CBM screening materials that is most reflective of that level of development (e.g., oral reading fluency in grade 2) or sometimes specific single skills (e.g., single-digit addition with regrouping; Shapiro, 2010). In addition, it is best to monitor progress at the skill level that will show the most growth. For example, a student in grade 6 reading grade 4 passages accurately but slowly might be monitored for progress in grade 5 reading passages. Progress monitoring at the student's grade level may not be sensitive to change because of the difficulty of the reading passages for this student.

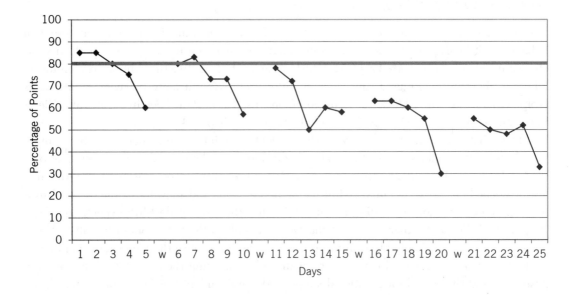

**FIGURE 3.2.** Daily behavior report card graph (from a student enrolled in check-in/check-out).

## Typical Processes for Progress Monitoring

As with screening, progress monitoring is most effective when completed by the student's instructor as opposed to a specialist who does not teach the student. Within the classroom, it can be most efficient to fit in individual progress monitoring sessions (daily behavior report card ratings or CBM probes) when students are completing independent work. This situation allows the instructor to work briefly with a small number of students without detracting from teacher-led instruction. It is also useful to be somewhat judicious in selecting which students need progress monitoring. Although it would be helpful to assess growth for almost all students in the school, it is important to remember that screening benchmark periods provide at least minimal assessment for all students. Our guidance regarding these decisions is to assess risks for negative outcomes. Greater concern about lack of progress translates into a need to progress monitor on a more frequent basis.

## Integrated Progress Monitoring

In an integrated MTSS model, knowledge about the interaction between academics and behavior can sometimes provide efficiencies in progress monitoring. In some cases, it may be possible to monitor progress in the area of greatest concern and wait for screening benchmark periods for the other. For example, if there are concerns regarding low academic skills that result in nondisruptive off-task behavior and the team determines that only an academic intervention is needed, the team may choose to monitor progress only in academic skills and not use a daily behavior report card. However, if the behavior needs are more severe, monitoring in behavior is also recommended.

## General Outcomes Measurement

Data regarding general student outcomes are intended to give a global view of student academic or social development that is broader and more holistic than the specific skills that are assessed with progress monitoring measures. Measures at this level look at the overall academic and behavior "health" of the school, as well as health at the grade, class, and individual student levels. This type of summative assessment provides an indication of the overall effectiveness of the educational program, including the effectiveness of an integrated MTSS model.

## Common Measures for Assessing General Outcomes

The general outcome measures that are most familiar to educators are state high-stakes achievement tests. Given that these tests are often mandatory, summarized for schools, and of interest to stakeholders (e.g., school board, the general public), it makes sense to use them in decision making, particularly if they are valid and reliable measures. In the minds of some stakeholders, these assessments are the only measures that matter.

However, the data collected for other purposes described above can also be utilized to assess general outcomes. For example, data collected for screening (i.e., benchmarking) can also be used to measure general outcomes as well (Sadler & Sugai, 2009). Instead of identifying students for support, the data can be examined to determine how successful Tier 1 support is in meeting the needs of students. For example, if a significant proportion (e.g., over 20%) of students need support beyond Tier 1 to achieve academic and behavior goals, then the Tier 1 program is not sufficient as implemented. These data would indicate a need to focus on delivering Tier 1 practices with fidelity, or if fidelity is adequate, intensifying the universal support provided at Tier 1 by adding more or stronger practices. Without this different lens to view student outcomes, the school team may devote too much energy to systems at Tiers 2 and 3 without shoring up Tier 1 support to prevent an overload of students requiring additional supports.

## GENERAL OUTCOMES MEASUREMENT OF BEHAVIOR

Student outcomes measurement for behavior may include a monthly or yearly review of ODRs, suspensions, and attendance in a format that allows accurate month-to-month, year-to-year, or school-to-school (with similar demographics) comparisons. To do so, it is important to standardize counts so they do not fluctuate for reasons other than changes in student behavior (Horner et al., 2001; Todd, Sampson, & Horner, 2005). Common standardizations include dividing by the number of days per month (so that months can be compared without needing to account for differing school days, including midmonth reports) and by number of students (so that changes in enrollment are controlled and schools can be compared more readily). Schools may also use their discipline data to assess the percent of students with different numbers of ODRs (e.g., 0 to 1, 2 to 5, 6 or more) to indicate effectiveness at each tier. In addition, many schools use surveys of school climate, school engagement, or school safety as a method of getting student perceptions on important social aspects of schooling (Bear, Gaskins, Blank, & Chen, 2011; Christenson et al., 2008; Sprague, Colvin, & Irvin, 2002). School districts or states may use any or all of these data to compare schools that are implementing a specific approach (e.g., PBIS, integrated MTSS) with fidelity to those that are not, as a way to assess differential effectiveness.

## GENERAL OUTCOMES MEASUREMENT OF ACADEMICS

Academic outcomes measurement often focus on state achievement test results and benchmark screening data to assess overall effectiveness of Tier 1 support in academic areas. As with behavior data, these scores can be compared within and across schools to assess effectiveness of academic practices (e.g., use of a particular Tier 1 curriculum) in comparison to previous years or schools using different practices. Additional measures that are commonly used to assess outcomes include district-required assessments, unit or placement tests from specific curricula, course credit accrual (especially in high schools), and the CBMs used in screening and progress monitoring.

## GENERAL OUTCOMES MEASUREMENT OF RACIAL/ETHNIC DISPROPORTIONALITY

An important general outcome that cuts across both behavior and academics is the issue of racial/ethnic disproportionality in educational outcomes. Disproportionality is a pervasive and persistent challenge in, school discipline (e.g., students of color receiving higher rates of ODRs and suspensions; Skiba et al., 2011), academics (e.g., the achievement gap; Lee, 2002), and special education (e.g., students of color with higher rates of placement; Harry & Klingner, 2014; Skiba et al., 2008). Just as with the overall relation between academics and behavior, disproportionality in academics and behavior are most likely linked (Gregory, Skiba, & Noguera, 2010), with initial disproportionality in one area leading to the other. For example, there is consistent evidence that black males receive significantly higher rates of ODRs and suspensions, with the discipline gap increasing consistently over the years (Losen, Hodson, Keith, Morrison, & Belway, 2015). This pattern seriously reduces access to instruction, widening the achievement gap as well. The increased achievement gap then understandably leads to increased escape-maintained problem behavior, further reducing access to both academic and behavior instruction (McIntosh, Horner, et al., 2008). However, implementing PBIS (Vincent et al., 2011) or an integrated MTSS (see Chapter 8) has been shown to decrease discipline and achievement disparities.

An important first step in closing the discipline and achievement gaps requires examining student outcomes that are disaggregated by race/ethnicity and monitoring these outcomes consistently over time to document improvement (McIntosh, Girvan, Horner, & Smolkowski, 2014). Examining disproportionality for behavior involves calculating risk indices or ratios for ODRs or suspensions by racial/ethnic group (Boneshefski & Runge, 2014). The Center on PBIS has released a free guide (McIntosh, Barnes, et al., 2014) that walks teams through the process of selecting and calculating outcomes measures for discipline disproportionality. For academics, it includes calculating and graphing separate lines for the percent of students meeting or exceeding expectations (state achievement tests) or benchmarks (CBMs). For an example, see Figure 8.5 in Chapter 8 (p. 280).

## Typical Processes for General Outcomes Measurement

Outcomes are often considered either formatively (e.g., monthly or quarterly progress) by grade level or school teams or summatively (e.g., yearly outcomes) by teams, district administrators, the school board, the community, and the state. To facilitate data-based decision making, formative data results should be available instantaneously and graphically. Summative data are often compiled in a report that describes how outcomes are related to the school improvement process through the school improvement plan's goals.

## Integrated General Outcomes Measurement

Using both academic and behavior data as components of general outcomes measurement is important for stakeholders who understand the connection between academics and behavior but even more so for those who do not. Simply including goals and outcome data for behavior in the school improvement plan elevates social competence to an equal level of importance as academics. The old adage that "What gets counted, counts" has relevance here—without accountability for measuring behavior outcomes, it is easy to disregard them. In addition, reporting behavior outcome data can illuminate the connection. For example, research that students score higher on state math and reading comprehension assessments when teachers' expectations for student behavior are clear (Gietz & McIntosh, 2014) shows how schools can improve achievement *through* behavior support. School reports that show both academic and behavior data on the same graph help draw the links and increase priority for behavior support, even if the only ultimate goal for some stakeholders is increasing academic achievement. For an example, see Figure 10.5 in Chapter 10 (p. 321).

## GUIDANCE IN SELECTING INTEGRATED TOOLS

One of the primary challenges regarding integrated MTSS models is collecting and making sense of all the data. Although it is tempting to try to be completely comprehensive, the sheer number of measures and the data they produce can easily overwhelm even schools with high-performing systems. With MTSS data, more is not necessarily better. We need not only the right information but also information at the right time and in the right amounts. Although it is a common mistake not to collect enough data to make better decisions, it is just as common to collect so much data that less time is available to understand and act upon them. Just as with intervention, a sound approach to assessment within MTSS is to adjust the intensity of data collection to match student need. Instead of collecting as much data as we can, it is better to consider our confidence in understanding a given student's academic and behavior status and how much risk comes from not understanding enough. With more risk for adverse consequences (e.g., academic failure, dropout) comes more need to collect data. If we can make good decisions with more modest data collection, we will have more time for intervention. However, with too little data collection, we risk making the wrong decision. The right balance is needed.

### Quality of Tools

As described previously, we need good data to make good decisions, and unfortunately, not all tools produce good data. Tools that are more likely to provide helpful information have the qualities of being valid, reliable, efficient, and useful for decision making (Horner et al., 2001). *Validity* refers to whether the assessment measures what is intended. *Reliability* means that the measures are consistent in producing similar outcomes during each measurement, so that data points are comparable in measuring growth. Reliability is not inherent in the tool, but a product of both the tool and the training and coaching on its use. It would be like buying an expensive guitar and expecting it to make beautiful music without learning how to play it. The guitar itself is necessary but insufficient to make good music. In the same way, the tools themselves are necessary but insufficient to make useful data—regular training and periodic observation of assessors may be needed to ensure that the assessments are conducted reliably. Additionally, measures should be *efficient*—easy to use by individuals with basic educational training (as opposed to specialists). This aspect is critical because teachers need to spend as much time as possible engaged in providing instruction for students. Finally, measures must be *useful* for decision making. Data from assessments should be readily available when decisions must be made, and these data must indicate which interventions would be more or less effective.

### Trustworthy Sources for Selecting Tools

The task of finding tools is much easier when we can rely on others' work in describing the uses, strengths, and drawbacks of the various tools for adoption consideration. There are a number of sources for tool review, including trusted books (e.g., Rathvon, 2004) and independent (i.e., nondeveloper) websites (e.g., *www.rti4success.org*). When considering integrated MTSS models, the general considerations for all tools apply, but given the added load of assessments across academic and behavior content areas, it can be easier on educators to select measures that are administered and interpreted similarly. For example, using brief 1-minute CBMs across academic content areas (e.g., math, literacy, written expression) produce raw data that can make interpretation easier. Likewise, using a check-in/check-out daily behavior report card with schoolwide expectations as the social competencies for universal screening and progress monitoring students at Tiers 2 and 3 will make both assessment and collection of long-term progress monitoring data (for team data and IEP progress) easier to understand for teachers, students, and families alike (Burke et al., 2012). However, greater complexity in academic or behavior needs indicates that more individualized assessment may be necessary to create effective support plans. In these situations, assessment of single skills (e.g., long division, taking a break when frustrated) may be more sensitive measures.

## Selecting Tools by Identifying Which Data Systems Are Already in Place

Another approach to building a comprehensive set of tools that remains relatively efficient is to use a two-step process for identifying assessment needs (McIntosh, Reinke, et al., 2009). The first step is to examine which tools are already being used. It can be effective to generate an inventory of all tools currently used in the school or district (see Appendix 3.7 for a blank inventory form). For each of the tools listed, ask three questions: (1) Is it required (i.e., by the district or state)?; (2) Are the data high-quality (i.e., valid, reliable, efficient, and useful for decision making)?; and (3) What modifications could improve data quality (e.g., ongoing coaching in administration or interpretation)? If tools are neither required nor of high quality, it is worth considering replacing them with better tools. If tools are required, it is worth examining whether they produce useful information or could be improved. For example, the district may require the use of generic incident reports, but developing a standardized behavior incident report form that includes checklists with operationally defined terms would improve their reliability and efficiency (McIntosh, Campbell, Carter, & Zumbo, 2009). Alternatively, the tool may be valid and reliable, but not readily available for decision making, such as attendance data that must be reported but are not readily accessible by school teams. However, some tools, even though required, may not be worth the effort to modify, especially if there are serious questions about their validity or usefulness for decision making. The second step in the process is to identify whether additional measures are needed to fulfill these purposes. It is also helpful to consider whether existing tools in one content area can fulfill purposes for another content area. For example, academic screening tools may also be useful for behavior screening (McIntosh, Horner, et al., 2006), as long as they are available for the teams that make screening decisions.

Once these additional measures are selected, it is wise to consider the order of implementation. Although the ultimate goal is to have an MTSS model with all assessment purposes filled for all content areas, trying to implement a full complement of new tools all at once is more likely to overwhelm the system and make the tools inefficient and underused for decision making. Instead, it is useful to ascertain which assessment needs are strongest and start there, with a multiyear plan to get all of the pieces in place. Some measures (e.g., screening in academics, fidelity of implementation in behavior) are more essential than others. One clear example of a need with less priority is systematic behavior screening. Kathleen Lane recommends adding such tools only after behavior support practices for Tiers 1 and 2 are in place with high fidelity of implementation. Otherwise, the screening tools will overidentify students for no available programs. These situations rightly cause concern for educators and families alike.

## PUTTING IT ALL TOGETHER

Once a comprehensive set of measures is identified, it is all too easy to become overwhelmed with the logistics of assessment and interpretation. Two separate but related types of plans allow school and district teams to make sense of it all: assessment plans and evaluation plans.

### Creating an Assessment Plan

An *assessment plan* is a roadmap for completing all of the school or district's assessments for the school year. Assessment plans are generally laid out by month and include not only data collection (i.e., testing) but also training, analysis, and sharing with staff. By including all of the assessments and related activities in one document, it is easier to map out a schedule that avoids overloading the system at certain times of the year and to ensure that all components of using data are completed. These main components include (1) training staff in accurate data collection, (2) coordinating data collection, (3) analyzing data, and (4) using results for decision making (e.g., action planning, guiding instruction). Without all of these components in place, the data that are collected are less likely to be accurate, to be useful for decision making, and actually to be *used* for decision making.

Figure 3.3 provides a sample schoolwide assessment plan for a school implementing an integrated MTSS model. This comprehensive assessment plan includes all necessary data but no more than can be handled by school personnel. It is designed to distribute the load across the year as much as possible, but certain times of the year are likely to have more assessment-related tasks, and it is helpful to be able to anticipate points when school personnel may feel overwhelmed with assessments (e.g., September, January, and May). This plan highlights times when staff may need additional supports for collecting and using assessment data.

### Creating an Evaluation Plan

One of the core activities of an assessment plan is developing an evaluation plan (Algozzine et al., 2010). Evaluation plans have two main functions. First, they provide a summative annual analysis of achievements and areas for action planning for the school or district team and staff. Second, they help teams to report results of their efforts to the broader staff, the school board, families, and other stakeholders. Instead of collecting new data for evaluation, a more efficient method is to sample some of the data already collected and answer a short list of important questions, with an emphasis on a few graphs that best answer them. A simple but effective structure for an evaluation plan answers the following questions:

1. What are we doing to improve student outcomes (process)?
2. How well are we doing it (fidelity)?
3. Are our actions actually improving student performance (outcomes)?

Evaluation plans also include steps for presenting reports to stakeholders. Common elements of evaluation plans, as well as data associated with the plans, are described separately, as they relate to school and district applications, in the following sections.

| Month | Activities |
|---|---|
| August | • Review assessment plan for the upcoming year.<br>• Communicate schedule to school personnel.<br>• Order assessment materials.<br>• Coordinate training on conducting assessment.<br>• Coordinate training on data entry into academic RTI and PBIS databases. |
| September | • Train/review benchmark assessment procedures.<br>• Train/review discipline referral data collection process (e.g., ODR definitions, procedures, office vs. staff-managed behaviors).<br>• Conduct fall benchmarking for academic RTI.<br>• Summarize data and disseminate results to grade-level teams and all staff.<br>• Use benchmark and ODR data to screen for students in need of additional supports.<br>• Conduct fidelity of implementation assessment for academic RTI and PBIS.<br>• Use benchmark, ODR, and fidelity data for action planning. |
| October | • Train/review progress monitoring assessment procedures.<br>• Conduct progress monitoring.<br>• Conduct fidelity checks for academic RTI and PBIS practices. |
| November | • Conduct progress monitoring. |
| December | • Conduct progress monitoring.<br>• Prepare for winter benchmark assessment (organize assessment materials, schedule assessments in classrooms).<br>• Conduct fidelity of implementation assessment for academic RTI and PBIS. |
| January | • Conduct winter benchmarking for academic RTI.<br>• Summarize data and disseminate results.<br>• Use benchmark and ODR data to screen for students in need of additional supports.<br>• Use benchmark, ODR, and fidelity data for action planning. |
| February | • Conduct progress monitoring. |
| March | • Conduct progress monitoring.<br>• Conduct fidelity of implementation assessment for academic RTI and PBIS. |
| April | • Conduct progress monitoring.<br>• Prepare for spring benchmark assessment (organize assessment materials, schedule assessments in classrooms). |
| May | • Conduct spring benchmarking for academic RTI.<br>• Summarize data and disseminate results.<br>• Use benchmark and ODR data to screen for students in need of additional supports.<br>• Use benchmark, ODR, and fidelity data for action planning. |
| June | • Review/revise assessment plan for next year.<br>• Conduct fidelity of implementation assessment for academic RTI and PBIS.<br>• Complete annual evaluation report for sharing with staff, district, and families. |

**FIGURE 3.3.** Sample schoolwide assessment plan.

## School Evaluation Plans

For schools, evaluation plans often concentrate more on the first function (summarizing information for action planning) than the second (reporting to a broader audience). Data for answering process questions include the leadership team's list of action plan items and which were accomplished. Data for fidelity questions include results from fidelity of implementation assessments. The focus of evaluation plans is generally on schoolwide fidelity, as opposed to classroom-specific results. For outcomes questions, schools will generally report their overall outcome results, academic benchmarks, or ODR data, often in the form of percentages of the student body scoring at low risk, moderate risk, and high risk in academics and behavior (as described previously in the section on general outcomes measurement). This information (often presented visually in a triangular form) primarily indicates the effectiveness of the Tier 1 support provided to all students. When outcomes are combined with fidelity data (as is shown in Figure 3.4), evaluation reports can show a clear link between quality of implementation and student outcomes over time.

An additional form that is helpful for school evaluation plans and decision making is an intervention tracking tool (a blank form is included in Appendix 3.8) for Tiers 2 and 3. This tool displays four kinds of important information. First (down the left column), it shows what academic and behavior interventions are in place in the school. Second, for each intervention, the tool depicts its level of use (i.e., how many and what percentage of students are receiving the intervention). This information is important because an effective intervention that is not accessed by students has diminished value. Third, it indicates what proportion of students receiving the intervention is performing successfully (indicated either by existing screening or progress monitoring data). Finally, it provides a quick glance at fidelity of implementation. This information helps to indicate what changes may be needed, including modifying an intervention to make it more effective, replacing it, or providing more support to ensure that it is implemented adequately in the first place.

## District Evaluation Plans

Although evaluation plans are similar at the district level, there is a stronger emphasis placed on evaluating specific practices, with an eye to how the district can enhance implementation of effective practices across schools. Process data often document use across schools, such as (1) what practices are being implemented in schools in the district, (2) how many schools are implementing these practices, and (3) what steps the district is taking to support the use of effective practices and systems in their schools (as described in Chapter 6). Fidelity data show not only what percent of schools is implementing to criterion, but also the effectiveness of current district supports on improving fidelity. The team may use this information to revise its plans of support

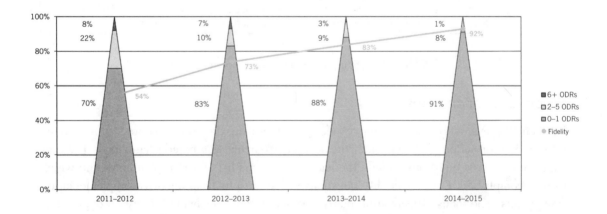

**FIGURE 3.4.** Sample evaluation report graph showing PBIS fidelity and discipline data by year.

or differentiate support for individual schools to enhance their fidelity. Outcome data overlay implementation and student outcome data to indicate the importance of implementing practices with fidelity. One example of this type of evaluation is to compare student outcomes from schools implementing practices with fidelity to those not implementing the practices. Figure 3.5 shows such a graph, comparing literacy benchmark scores between schools implementing PBIS to criterion and those not implementing PBIS. The graph shows improved student literacy outcomes for schools implementing PBIS with fidelity, clearly documenting crossover effects of behavior practices on academic outcomes. This aspect of integrated MTSS data is discussed in the next section.

## INTEGRATING DATA SYSTEMS

Unfortunately, simply collecting both kinds of data is necessary but insufficient. As we've described, the advantages of an integrated academic and behavior model do not come from implementing two separate, parallel systems, and this point is just as true for data. We need to be able to analyze the data in an integrated fashion to maximize the benefits of treating academics and behavior as interrelated. For example, teams can make better decisions about how much and what kinds of support to provide when they have both types of data at the table. Academic screening data can flag students who may also need behavior support. FBAs, in particular, are more effective and efficient when teams can check academic skills against levels of problem behavior in particular content areas. Integrated assessments can point to the need to intervene across content areas or focus only on one. In addition, monitoring RTI more broadly ensures that support plans are effective beyond simply remediating skill deficits or reducing problem behavior. It is also helpful to keep in mind that integration becomes increasingly more impor-

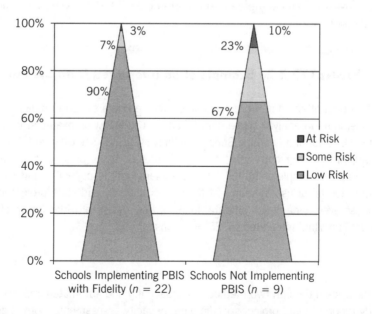

**FIGURE 3.5.** Sample evaluation report graph showing end-of-year literacy benchmark scores by school PBIS implementation fidelity.

tant as students move up the triangle. Yet none of this can happen efficiently without finding ways to bridge data systems.

## Necessary Components for Effective Integration

Although integrating data is conceptually straightforward, it can be difficult to accomplish in terms of technology. There are a number of prerequisites that must be met before data systems can be integrated. Although some existing Web-based programs allow for the entry and use of some forms of both academic and behavior data, such as AIMSweb (*www.aimsweb.com*) and SWIS (*www.pbisapps.org*), more commonly there is a need to integrate a broader range of tools and data than are entered into just one application. The most basic prerequisites for integrating data systems are using electronic data entry and storage and common student identification numbers across all data systems in the school or district (most often a district or state ID number). In the absence of this information, individual student data cannot be linked without a level of effort that would make integration incredibly inefficient (e.g., manual linking, matching cases based on student names). Many computer applications allow users to enter a common ID number when student data are first entered into the system. It is best to avoid using data systems that do not have this feature. Another basic prerequisite is the use of database software to manage and connect the data. District teams often use a relational database program (e.g., Microsoft ACCESS) for creating datasets for graphing and decision making. Creating data systems that allow for easy importing of student and school data into a central database is known as *data warehousing*. Finally, any integrated data systems should be easy to use for educators. Ideally, district information technology teams can build systems that make integrated data graphs appear instantaneously, with no sign of the linking of databases that takes place behind the scene. If data can only go into the data warehouse but don't come out in useful visual formats, all of the effort is wasted. An example of an integrated MTSS data system and how it was built is included in Vignette 3.2.

---

### VIGNETTE 3.2. Example of an Integrated Data System

Integrated MTSS data often come from multiple sources and are stored in multiple data systems, making it cumbersome to analyze these data together. The following example, created by Michigan's Integrated Behavior and Learning Support Initiative (MiBLSi; see Chapter 10 for a description of the initiative), provides for entry and storage of different types of data (e.g., student reading and behavior outcomes, implementation fidelity, implementation capacity) and summarizes this information into reports for use by teams at the school, district, and state project levels. It is not intended to house every type of school data. Instead, this system provides for an efficient way to answer the most important integrated MTSS questions.

#### Data Entry

Data go into the system through two methods: manual entry and automated imports. For data that are not already reported (e.g., project-specific data, capacity assessments, some fidelity of implementation measures), the system allows for easy user data entry at each level (i.e., school, district, state). However, to enhance efficiency, data that are already required to be input and submitted to the state department of education (e.g., state achievement scores, student information) or through another system (e.g., AIMSweb, DIBELSnet, PBIS Assessment, SWIS) are imported either through batch import or an automated process. These data are automatically updated as new data come into the other data systems. Automating these processes (as opposed to double entry) provides incredible time savings and allows for personnel to focus their efforts on analysis and instruction.

## Reporting

The data system allows for instantaneous production of a range of reports, each designed for the needs of different audiences (e.g., school teams, district teams, state departments of education). The school-level reports are organized to provide information for teams to make common decisions. For example, these reports show whether threshold cut scores (either for fidelity or student outcomes) were met. Embedded within these reports are narrative explanations of why each analysis is important and how to interpret scores. School teams bring their reports to trainings so that they can learn how to analyze the data and use it for action planning. The teams also use the information to evaluate the effectiveness of their systems and determine areas for improvement. District-level reports aggregate data across schools. These reports focus on assessing project effectiveness and professional development needs, as well as providing information to report on school improvement requirements. State-level reports aggregate the data at each level for initiative-level decisions and for communicating the status and impact of the initiative to key project stakeholders.

## Data Dashboards

In addition to reports, the data system makes extensive use of data dashboards. *Data dashboards* are tools to display data instantaneously and in a comprehensible format, focusing on key metrics that are instrumental to educational success. When users log in, they see a specific data dashboard that summarizes key data for their level of analysis. The school-level dashboard focuses users on fidelity of implementation and student outcomes. The district-level dashboard, in addition to school-level information, displays the initiative's reach (number of schools implementing within the district), as well as the district's capacity to support integrated MTSS work. For example, Figure 3V.10 shows a district-level data dashboard displaying the reach of implementation across the district. District teams use this information to evaluate how many schools within the district are implementing, what tiers of support are being developed within the implementing schools, and their stage of implementation. The second district-level data dashboard example (see Figure 3V.11) displays fidelity of implementation of behavior support using the *School-wide Benchmarks of Quality* and the *Benchmarks for Advanced Tiers* across implementing schools over time. The targets in the graph on the upper right can be toggled to show either criterion goals or district averages. This information can then be used to assess quality of implementation, implementation trajectories, and needs for support at the school and district levels.

## Technical Specifications

Creating an integrated data system requires technical expertise in project evaluation, data visualization, and Web-based database development. A team of project staff and Web-based technologists worked on the project. Database development included the use of a SQL Server database with SQL server reporting services. The system uses a .NET platform (version 4.5) with an IIS 7 Hosting Service. A MVC website development tool was used for website design. Importing data from other systems requires several steps. First, data are exported from the original systems as comma separated files (CSVs) with column headings that exactly match the integrated data system file layout. Data are matched and imported based on the column headings to assure that data integrity remains intact dur-

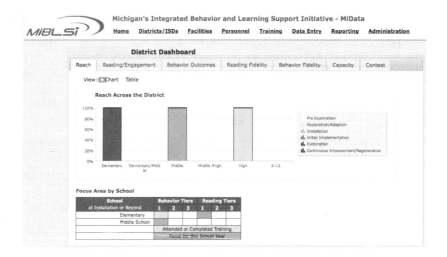

**FIGURE 3V.10.** District dashboard showing reach across the district. Reprinted with permission from the Michigan Department of Education.

ing the import process. Specific column headings are identified for each type of data to be imported (e.g., AIMSweb, DIBELSnet, PBIS Assessment, school enrollment, student information, SWIS).

### Continuous Improvement

As with any other technological innovation, the integrated data system must improve and evolve over time to remain useful. Users can click on a prominent link to report system error messages or other problems. This information is sent to the technology consultant to address. There is also a separate link to submit a suggestion or feature request. This information is then reviewed by the team for priority and feasibility determination.

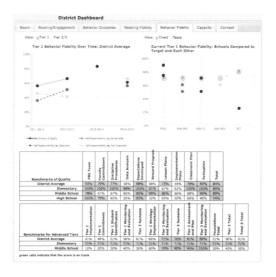

**FIGURE 3V.11.** District dashboard showing PBIS fidelity. Reprinted with permission from the Michigan Department of Education.

## Integrated Data Analysis

Although integrated data analysis (i.e., examining and using data for ongoing decision making) is powerful, it can also be overwhelming without the right tools or plan. These tasks become vastly easier when one has access to the right pictures for making sense of it. Only the most skilled of data analysts can look at tables of integrated data and identify problems and solutions. Because of the complexity of integrated data, it is critical to have charts and graphs that can show us quickly what is happening and what to do about it. Here are a few figures showing integrated data in ways that enhance decision making. Figure 3.6 (based on work by Scott Baker, Hank Fien, and Rob Horner) shows an integrated screening scatterplot for a grade 3 classroom (generated from Microsoft Excel) in which each student is represented by a data point that shows screening results in both academics (in this case, literacy) and behavior. Students in the upper right region (low risk in literacy and behavior) are experiencing success with the current level of academic and behavior support. Students in the lower right region (high risk in literacy, low risk in behavior) require academic support, and students in the lower left region require intensive support that addresses both areas. The graph provides a clear way to assess student needs and assign students to different practices or student groups based on these needs (covered in Chapter 4).

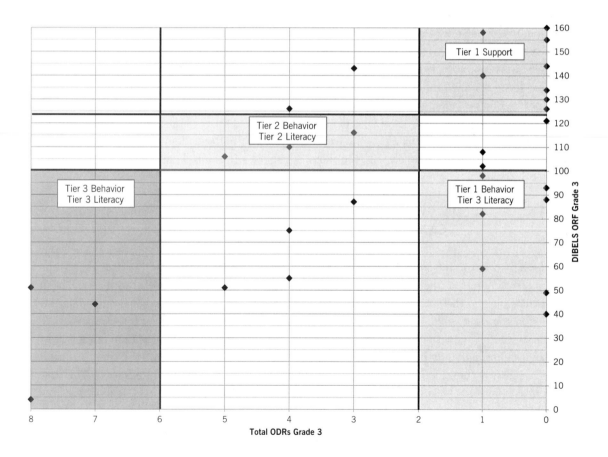

**FIGURE 3.6.** Integrated screening scatterplot for a grade 3 classroom.

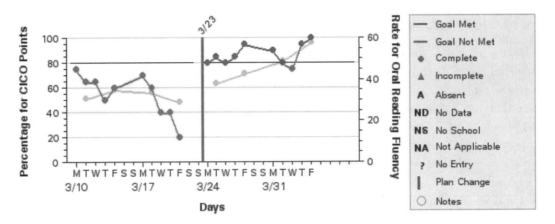

**FIGURE 3.7.** Integrated individual progress monitoring graph showing check-in/check-out points and oral reading fluency for a student. From ISIS-SWIS. Reprinted with permission from Rob Horner.

It is also beneficial to see both types of data on the same picture for individual students at Tiers 2 and 3. Figure 3.7 shows an integrated individual progress monitoring graph (generated from ISIS-SWIS, *www.pbisapps.org*). In this line graph, progress monitoring data from academic and behavior domains can be shown in the same picture to assess student success across content areas. Data regarding problem behavior here (check-in/check-out daily behavior report card ratings) appear as a dark line, noted on the left-side *y*-axis. Data regarding literacy (oral reading fluency probes, twice weekly) appear as a light line, noted on the right. Changes in intervention are seen as solid vertical lines. As seen, before the change, student success is low (i.e., no days above the goal of 80% of check-in/check-out daily points, flat slope in reading). When the intervention is changed, one can see effects on both academics and behavior. This integrated graph shows how easy it is to monitor progress in multiple areas simply by placing both types of data on the same picture.

## TEAM CHECKLISTS: INTEGRATING DATA

As described in the introduction to Part II, the team checklists in this section provide a summary of key points in the chapter but in a format that is more readily useful to teams. These checklists include the core activities of integration on the left, and a rating for implementation status on the right, much like the TIC (Sugai, Horner, et al., 2001) or the PET (Kame'enui & Simmons, 2002). As with the TIC, the first activity is to self-assess implementation of each item as *not in place*, *partially in place*, or *in place*. Once completed, teams can track their progress (and successes), then identify and prioritize a short list of next steps for integration. The first checklist is for school-level teams, such as a building-level leadership team (e.g., school improvement team), schoolwide systems team, or grade-level teams. The second checklist is for district-level teams that are supporting schools in their integration process. The checklists in this chapter include common steps for integrating academic and behavior data efficiently and effectively.

# SCHOOL-LEVEL TEAM CHECKLIST FOR INTEGRATING DATA

| Implementation Step | Implementation Status | | |
|---|---|---|---|
| | Not in place | Partially in place | In place |
| 1. A school team (or teams) meets at least once per month with the purpose of improving both academic and behavior outcomes for all students within the entire school. | | | |
| 2. The team collects and summarizes fidelity of implementation data (i.e., quality or integrity of implementation) in both academics and behavior. | | | |
| 3. The team conducts regular screening for early identification of students whose performance is not responsive to instruction in (a) academics, (b) behavior, or (c) both. | | | |
| 4. The team has skills in basic functional behavior assessment and function-based support. | | | |
| 5. The team has access to expertise in more complex functional behavior assessment and function-based support. | | | |
| 6. The team oversees progress monitoring for students whose performance is not responsive to instruction. | | | |
| 7. The team collects and summarizes student outcomes data in both academics and behavior. | | | |
| 8. The team completes an inventory of all tools currently used and identifies (a) tools that can be eliminated, (b) tools that may need modification, and (c) needs for new tools. | | | |
| 9. The team conducts trainings and reliability checks to ensure that data collection is accurate. | | | |
| 10. The team regularly analyzes both (a) implementation and (b) outcomes data for assessing goals and next steps. | | | |
| 11. The team develops and maintains an ongoing action plan for improving both (a) implementation and (b) outcomes. | | | |
| 12. The team shares implementation and outcomes data at least quarterly with (a) the entire staff, (b) the district, and (c) other stakeholders (e.g., PTA, community groups). | | | |

| Priority for Action Planning (the three most important items from above) | Who is responsible? | By when? | How will we know when it is accomplished? |
|---|---|---|---|
| 1. | | | |
| 2. | | | |
| 3. | | | |

# DISTRICT-LEVEL TEAM CHECKLIST FOR INTEGRATING DATA

| Implementation Step | Implementation Status | | |
|---|---|---|---|
| | Not in place | Partially in place | In place |
| 1. A district team meets at least once per month with the purpose of supporting schools in their systems-level integration efforts. | | | |
| 2. The district team completes an inventory of all tools currently used in the district and identifies (a) tools that can be eliminated, (b) tools that may need modification, and (c) needs for new tools. | | | |
| 3. The district team builds and maintains district data systems that allow for easy entry and instantaneous graphical display of academic and behavior data. | | | |
| 4. The district data system includes efficient capabilities (e.g., integrated applications, data warehouse) that allows for integrated data analysis of academic and behavior data. | | | |
| 5. The district team creates annual district evaluations, including (a) level of use, (b) fidelity of implementation, and (c) student outcomes in both academics and behavior. | | | |
| 6. The district team develops and maintains an ongoing action plan for improving both (a) implementation and (b) outcomes. | | | |
| 7. The district team maintains a list of integrated MTSS exemplar schools (i.e., with strong fidelity of implementation) for other schools and agencies to tour. | | | |
| 8. The district team shares implementation and outcomes data at least annually with (a) the school board, (b) the state department of education, and (c) other stakeholders (e.g., PTA, community groups). | | | |

| Priority for Action Planning (the three most important items from above) | Who is responsible? | By when? | How will we know when it is accomplished? |
|---|---|---|---|
| 1. | | | |
| 2. | | | |
| 3. | | | |

# Reading Tiered Fidelity Inventory (R-TFI)—Elementary-Level Edition

**Scoring Form**

School: _____ District: _____ Date: _____

School Leadership Team Members:

Facilitator:

Note Taker:

Directions: The **School Leadership Team** completes the R-TFI together by using the *R-TFI Scoring Guide* to discuss each item and come to **consensus** on the final score for each item. Scores are recorded on this *Scoring Form* below and then entered into *http://webapps.miblsimtss.org/midata* for schools in Michigan.

| | Tier 1 School-Wide Reading Model Features | | | |
|---|---|---|---|---|
| **Tier 1: Teams** | | | | |
| **Item Number** | **Item Description** | | **Score** | |
| 1.1 | A **School Leadership Team** is established to support the implementation of a **Tier 1** reading system. | 2 | 1 | 0 |
| 1.2 | The School Leadership Team uses an effective team meeting process. | 2 | 1 | 0 |
| 1.3 | The School Leadership Team's work is coordinated with other school teams. | 2 | 1 | 0 |
| 1.4 | **Grade-Level Teams** are established to support the implementation of a Tier 1 reading system. | 2 | 1 | 0 |
| 1.5 | Grade-Level Teams use an effective team meeting process. | 2 | 1 | 0 |
| **Tier 1: Implementation** | | | | |
| 1.6 | The school uses a formal procedure for selecting programs and materials to provide Tier 1 reading instruction. | 2 | 1 | 0 |
| 1.7 | The school allocates **adequate time** for core reading instruction. | 2 | 1 | 0 |
| 1.8 | The school has a **School-Wide Reading Plan**. | 2 | 1 | 0 |
| 1.9 | Grade-level **Instructional Plans** include an emphasis on Tier 1 instruction. | 2 | 1 | 0 |
| 1.10 | **Class-wide expectations** for student behavior are established and taught. | 2 | 1 | 0 |
| 1.11 | **Procedures** are implemented for common reading activities. | 2 | 1 | 0 |
| **Tier 1: Resources** | | | | |
| 1.12 | Written guidelines are available for teaching the **core reading program**. | 2 | 1 | 0 |

*(continued)*

| Item Number | Item Description | Score | | |
|---|---|---|---|---|
| 1.13 | A **school-wide reading universal screening assessment schedule** is available for the current school year. | 2 | 1 | 0 |
| 1.14 | The school has identified an individual(s) to assist in data coordination for **school-wide reading assessments**. | 2 | 1 | 0 |
| 1.15 | **Professional learning** is purposely selected for supporting the implementation of a **School-Wide Reading Model.** | 2 | 1 | 0 |
| 1.16 | The School Leadership Team uses **system-level coaching**. | 2 | 1 | 0 |
| 1.17 | All staff have access to **instructional coaching**. | 2 | 1 | 0 |
| **Tier 1: Evaluation** | | | | |
| 1.18 | **Universal screening** assessments have been purposely selected. | 2 | 1 | 0 |
| 1.19 | The school uses a data system that allows access to universal screening assessment reports. | 2 | 1 | 0 |
| 1.20 | Staff collect reading universal screening data with **fidelity**. | 2 | | 0 |
| 1.21 | The **School Leadership Team** collects Tier 1 **system fidelity data**. | 2 | 1 | 0 |
| 1.22 | The School Leadership Team uses data to monitor the health of the **School-Wide Reading Model**. | 2 | 1 | 0 |
| 1.23 | The School Leadership Team uses a process for **data-based decision making**. | 2 | 1 | 0 |
| 1.24 | **Grade-Level Teams** use a process for data-based decision-making. | 2 | 1 | 0 |
| 1.25 | The School Leadership Team monitors implementation of the **School-Wide Reading Plan**. | 2 | 1 | 0 |
| 1.26 | Grade-Level Teams monitor implementation of the grade-level **Instructional Plans**. | 2 | 1 | 0 |
| 1.27 | The School Leadership Team provides a status report on student reading performance to stakeholders. | 2 | 1 | 0 |
| **Tier 2 School-Wide Reading Model Features** | | | | |
| **Tier 2: Teams** | | | | |
| 2.1 | The **School Leadership Team** defines a process to be used by Grade-Level Teams for supporting students with reading skill deficits. | 2 | 1 | 0 |
| 2.2 | Grade-Level Teams work to support students who are not making adequate progress in the **Tier 1** core reading curriculum. | 2 | 1 | 0 |
| **Tier 2: Intervention Implementation** | | | | |
| 2.3 | The school uses a formal process for selecting **evidence-based** reading interventions. | 2 | 1 | 0 |
| 2.4 | The school uses a data-based process for matching student needs to specific reading interventions. | 2 | 1 | 0 |
| 2.5 | Intervention groups are appropriate for students receiving reading intervention. | 2 | 1 | 0 |
| 2.6 | The school notifies parents/guardians of intervention plans for their child. | 2 | 1 | 0 |

*(continued)*

| Item Number | Item Description | Score | | |
|---|---|---|---|---|
| **Tier 2: Resources** | | | | |
| 2.7 | The scheduling of reading interventions is coordinated with Tier 1 reading instruction. | 2 | 1 | 0 |
| 2.8 | All staff providing reading interventions receive implementation supports. | 2 | 1 | 0 |
| **Tier 2: Evaluation** | | | | |
| 2.9 | The school monitors data on student access to reading intervention supports. | 2 | 1 | 0 |
| 2.10 | Staff collect **progress monitoring** data with fidelity. | 2 | 1 | 0 |
| 2.11 | The school uses a data system to display student progress. | 2 | 1 | 0 |
| 2.12 | The school monitors the **fidelity** of **Tier 2** interventions. | 2 | 1 | 0 |
| 2.13 | **Grade-Level Teams** monitor the percentage of students who are responding to Tier 2 supports. | 2 | | 0 |
| 2.14 | Grade-Level Teams adjust reading intervention supports based on individual student progress. | 2 | 1 | 0 |
| **Tier 3 School-Wide Reading Model Features** | | | | |
| **Tier 3: Teams** | | | | |
| 3.1 | Grade-Level Teams support students with intensive reading needs. | 2 | 1 | 0 |
| 3.2 | **Student Support Teams** are established to improve students' reading performance. | 2 | 1 | 0 |
| 3.3 | Grade-level teachers access the assistance of the Student Support Teams. | 2 | 1 | 0 |
| 3.4 | Student Support Teams use an effective team meeting process. | 2 | 1 | 0 |
| **Tier 3: Intervention Implementation** | | | | |
| 3.5 | The school uses a variety of data sources to design intensive reading intervention plans. | 2 | 1 | 0 |
| 3.6 | The school alters **intervention variables** to intensify reading intervention supports. | 2 | 1 | 0 |
| 3.7 | The school invites parents/guardians to collaborate on intervention plans for their child. | 2 | 1 | 0 |
| **Tier 3: Resources** | | | | |
| 3.8 | All staff supporting students with an **intensive reading intervention plan** receive implementation supports. | 2 | 1 | 0 |
| **Tier 3: Evaluation** | | | | |
| 3.9 | Staff collect **diagnostic assessment** data with fidelity. | 2 | 1 | 0 |
| 3.10 | The school monitors the percentage of students who are responding to **Tier 3** supports. | 2 | 1 | 0 |
| 3.11 | There is a protocol to monitor the fidelity of Tier 3 interventions. | 2 | 1 | 0 |
| 3.12 | Intensive reading intervention plans are adjusted based on **decision rules**. | 2 | 1 | 0 |

# Reading Tiered Fidelity Inventory (R-TFI)—Secondary-Level Edition

**Scoring Form**

School: _____    District: _____    Date: _____

School Leadership Team Members:

Facilitator:

Note Taker:

Directions: The **School Leadership Team** completes the Reading Tiered Fidelity Inventory (R-TFI) together by using the *R-TFI Scoring Guide* to discuss each item and come to **consensus** on the final score for each item. Scores are recorded on this *Scoring Form* below and then entered at *http://webapps.miblsimtss.org/midata*.

| Tier 1 School-Wide Content Area Reading Model Features | | | | |
|---|---|---|---|---|
| **Tier 1: Teams** | | | | |
| **Item Number** | **Item Description** | | **Score** | |
| 1.1 | A School Leadership Team is established to support implementation of the **School-Wide Content Area Reading Model**. | 2 | 1 | 0 |
| 1.2 | The School Leadership Team uses an effective team meeting process. | 2 | 1 | 0 |
| 1.3 | The School Leadership Team's work is coordinated with other school teams. | 2 | 1 | 0 |
| 1.4 | **Department Teams** are established to support the implementation of **Tier 1** content area reading instruction. | 2 | 1 | 0 |
| 1.5 | Department Teams use an effective team meeting process. | 2 | 1 | 0 |
| **Tier 1: Implementation** | | | | |
| 1.6 | The school uses a formal procedure for selecting **Content Area Reading Strategies** to provide content area reading instruction. | 2 | 1 | 0 |
| 1.7 | An **Instructional Routine** is available for each content area reading strategy that has been adopted for use school-wide. | 2 | 1 | 0 |
| 1.8 | The school has a **School-Wide Content Area Reading Plan**. | 2 | 1 | 0 |
| 1.9 | Department Teams develop **Instructional Plans** to improve students' understanding of the content area. | 2 | 1 | 0 |
| 1.10 | **Class-wide expectations** for student behavior are established and taught. | 2 | 1 | 0 |
| 1.11 | **Procedures** are implemented for common classroom activities. | 2 | 1 | 0 |

*(continued)*

Reprinted with permission from the Michigan Department of Education.

| Item Number | Item Description | Score | | |
|---|---|---|---|---|
| **Tier 1: Resources** | | | | |
| 1.12 | The school has identified an individual(s) to assist in data coordination for the **Early Warning System**. | 2 | | 0 |
| 1.13 | An **Early Warning Indicator (EWI) Assessment Schedule** is available for the current school year. | 2 | 1 | 0 |
| 1.14 | **Professional learning** is purposely selected for supporting the implementation of a School-wide Content Area Reading. Model. | 2 | 1 | 0 |
| 1.15 | The **School Leadership Team** uses **system-level coaching**. | 2 | 1 | 0 |
| 1.16 | All staff have access to **instructional coaching** for the **Content Area Reading Strategies**. | 2 | 1 | 0 |
| **Tier 1: Evaluation** | | | | |
| 1.17 | The school uses a data system that provides access to **Early Warning Indicator** data. | 2 | 1 | 0 |
| 1.18 | **Historical data** are gathered to inform school personnel of student needs. | 2 | | 0 |
| 1.19 | The School Leadership Team collects **Tier 1 system fidelity data**. | 2 | 1 | 0 |
| 1.20 | The School Leadership Team uses data to monitor the health of the **School-Wide Content Area Reading Model**. | 2 | 1 | 0 |
| 1.21 | The School Leadership Team uses a process for **data-based decision-making**. | 2 | 1 | 0 |
| 1.22 | **Department Teams** use a process for data-based decision-making. | 2 | 1 | 0 |
| 1.23 | The School Leadership Team monitors implementation of the **School-Wide Content Area Reading Plan**. | 2 | 1 | 0 |
| 1.24 | Department Teams monitor implementation of **Instructional Plans**. | 2 | 1 | 0 |
| 1.25 | The School Leadership Team provides a status report or presentation on student reading performance to stakeholders. | 2 | 1 | 0 |
| **Tiers 2 & 3 School-Wide Content Area Reading Model Features** | | | | |
| **Tiers 2 & 3: Teams** | | | | |
| 2.1 | The School Leadership Team defines a process to be used by **Cross-Department Teams** for supporting students with reading skill deficits. | 2 | 1 | 0 |
| 2.2 | Cross-Department Teams work to support students who are not making adequate progress. | 2 | | 0 |
| 2.3 | **Student Support Teams** are established to improve students' reading performance. | 2 | 1 | 0 |
| 2.4 | Teachers access the assistance of Student Support Teams. | 2 | 1 | 0 |
| 2.5 | Student Support Teams use an effective team meeting process. | 2 | 1 | 0 |

*(continued)*

| Item Number | Item Description | Score | | |
|---|---|---|---|---|
| **Tiers 2 & 3: Intervention Implementation** | | | | |
| 2.6 | The school uses a formal process for selecting **evidence-based** reading interventions. | 2 | 1 | 0 |
| 2.7 | The school uses a variety of data sources to design **Reading Intervention Plans**. | 2 | 1 | 0 |
| 2.8 | Intervention group size is appropriate for students receiving reading intervention. | 2 | 1 | 0 |
| 2.9 | The school alters **intervention variables** to intensify reading intervention supports. | 2 | 1 | 0 |
| 2.10 | The school invites parents/guardians to collaborate on intervention plans for their child. | 2 | 1 | 0 |
| **Tiers 2 & 3: Resources** | | | | |
| 2.11 | The school has identified an individual(s) to support the use of reading assessments for students with reading deficits. | 2 | 1 | 0 |
| 2.12 | All staff providing reading interventions receive implementation supports. | 2 | 1 | 0 |
| **Tiers 2 & 3: Evaluation** | | | | |
| 2.13 | The school monitors data on student access to reading intervention supports. | 2 | 1 | 0 |
| 2.14 | The school uses a data system to display student reading progress. | 2 | 1 | 0 |
| 2.15 | Staff collect **progress monitoring** data with **fidelity**. | 2 | 1 | 0 |
| 2.16 | Staff collect **diagnostic assessment** data with fidelity. | 2 | 1 | 0 |
| 2.17 | The school monitors the percent of students who are responding to reading intervention. | 2 | | 0 |
| 2.18 | There is a protocol to monitor the fidelity of Tier 3 reading interventions. | 2 | 1 | 0 |
| 2.19 | Reading Intervention Plans are adjusted based on **decision rules**. | 2 | 1 | 0 |

# Reading Tiered Fidelity Inventory—Comprehensive Edition (R-TFI-CE)

## CLASSROOM OBSERVATION DIRECTIONS

### Materials Needed

- Stopwatch or a watch with a second hand to record accurate observation times for the "Opportunities to Respond" and "On-Task/Off-Task Behavior" portions of the observation.
- Calculator: useful for determining the various rates on the Scoring Guidelines document.
- Clipboard
- Pencil

### Part 1: Explicit Teaching and Classroom Environment Checklists

*Explicit Teaching Strategies Checklist*

1. Check any of the following features that you observed during the reading lesson.
2. Items that you did not observe or were not appropriate to observe given the scope of the lesson should be reflected by placing a checkmark in the "No opportunity/inappropriate given activity" column.
3. Check items as "Not observed" when you see both examples and nonexamples of the descriptor. For example, if the teacher used clear and concise language in one explanation of a concept but did not use clear and concise language in another explanation (e.g., allowing the possibility of a student misinterpreting the concept), then mark that item as "Not observed."

*Classroom Environment Checklist*

1. Check any of the following features that you observed while in the classroom.
2. Items that you did not observe or were not appropriate to observe given the scope of the lesson should be reflected by placing a checkmark in the "No opportunity/inappropriate given activity" column.
3. Check items as "Not observed" when you see both examples and nonexamples of the descriptor. For example, if it appeared there was a routine established for gaining the students' attention at the beginning of a task but not for collecting assignments, you would mark the item as "Not observed."

### Part 2: Academic Engagement

*A. On-Task/Off-Task Behaviors—10 minutes*

1. Observe the students in the classroom for a total of 10 minutes using a 10-second momentary time sampling of each student.
2. It is recommended that you observe students by rows during an all-class activity or by group if they are divided for different activities.

*(continued)*

Reprinted with permission from the Michigan Department of Education.

3. At the beginning of the observation, start the timer and after each 10-second interval, observe a student momentarily (e.g., <1 second) and decide if the student is on task or off task at that specific point in time. (If using a timer, it is important to make sure the timer either vibrates or omits a very quiet tone so as to not disrupt the students.)
4. In box "1" mark a "+" at the end of the 10-second interval if a student appears to be on task or mark a "−" if a student appears to be off task. (See examples below.)
   a. On-task behavior ("+") = The student meets the behavioral expectations for the task or situation. Examples include making an oral academic response when asked, looking at the teacher when the teacher is talking, writing in a workbook, raising a hand, looking at an academic book or worksheet, following a behavioral instruction, or looking at a peer as he or she responds to a question.
   b. Off-task behavior ("−") = A motor activity or audible verbalization that is not directly associated with the assigned academic task and/or that is not permitted. Also, when a student is passively not attending to an assigned academic activity. Examples include a student's being out of his or her seat without permission during an in-seat assignment, making unauthorized comments or remarks, staring out the window, or showing noncompliance to a behavioral instruction.
5. After you have recorded a "+" or "−" for the first student, momentarily observe the second student and then record a "+" or "−" in box "2."
6. Continue this pattern until you have observed all of the students in the classroom.
7. Cycle back to the first student and continue observing in 10-second intervals until you have filled the entire grid below. That means, if there are 20 students in the class, you will need to cycle through the students three times until all 60 boxes on the On-Task/Off-Task Behaviors chart are filled.

### B. Opportunities to Respond—10 minutes

1. Look at your watch and record the time you started observing this portion of the observation form. You will collect data for at least 10 minutes.
2. Mark one (1) tally in the appropriate response box for every individual student or group academic response (i.e., oral or action) made during the observation of reading instruction.
3. Correct academic response = The student completely fulfills the requirements of the direction/question asked of the students (e.g., if sounding out the name *Sam*, "/sss/-/aaa/-/mmm/" counts as one response, not three; reading a sentence, defining a word, or answering a comprehension question is one response, as is showing a facial expression to indicate understanding of a word, or raising one or two fingers to choose from two possible answers.
4. If the response is given by a group of students, *every* student must respond correctly (see examples of correct academic responses in the previous bullet).
5. An incorrect response = Tallied when *any* student gives the incorrect response (e.g., does not respond when requested or responds well after the rest of the students during a group response).
6. When you stop observing this portion of the observation, look at your watch and record the "end time." Calculate the total number of minutes you observed "Opportunities to Respond" in the space provided.

### C. Student–Teacher Interactions—10 minutes

1. Mark one (1) tally in the "Responses to Appropriate Behaviors" box any time the teacher makes a response to an appropriate student behavior (e.g., meets the behavioral expectations for the task, is conducive to student's/classmates' learning).

*(continued)*

2. The teacher's response may be vocal, physical, or gestural and directed to the entire class, a small group of students, or individual students.

3. Indicate if the teacher's praise was specific (i.e., the teacher names the appropriate behavior when praising) or general (e.g., the teacher gives a "thumbs up" signal but does not name the behavior) by placing the tally within either the "Specific" or "General" columns within the "Responses to Appropriate Behaviors" box.

4. Mark a tally in the "Responses to Inappropriate Behaviors" box any time the teacher makes a response to an inappropriate student response (e.g., the teacher's response may be a redirection or a showing of disapproval through words, physical prompts, or gestures). The teacher's response may be directed to the entire class, a small group of students, or individual students.

5. **Do *not* tally teacher responses that indicate correctness or incorrectness of a student academic response** (e.g., "That's right, the word is *peninsula*" or "No, the correct word is *woman*, not *women*").

## CLASSROOM OBSERVATION FORM

School: _____     District: _____

Observer: _____     Date: _____

### Part 1: Explicit Teaching and Classroom Environment Checklists

*The Explicit Teaching Strategies and Classroom Environment Checklists can be completed while you are collecting data for the other parts of the observation.*

| A. Explicit Teaching Strategies | Observed | Not observed | No opportunity/ inappropriate given activity |
|---|---|---|---|
| 1. Began lesson with a clear statement of the lesson's goals and the teacher's expectations. | | | |
| 2. Reviewed prior skills and knowledge before beginning new instruction. | | | |
| 3. Clearly demonstrated (modeled) a new skill or strategy *and* provided guided/supported practice. | | | |
| 4. Used clear and concise language throughout lesson. | | | |
| 5. When practicing previously taught skill, provided sufficient practice opportunities until students mastered the examples presented. | | | |
| 6. Students were provided with opportunities to respond both chorally (or with partners) *and* individually. | | | |
| 7. Walked around the room to monitor student responses. | | | |
| 8. Immediately corrected almost all (≈90%) of student errors by (a) modeling response or modeling/leading students through strategy to obtain response, *and* (b) providing practice on the same or similar example. | | | |
| B. Classroom Environment | Observed | Not observed | No opportunity/ inappropriate given activity |
| 1. Classroom furniture was arranged so students could see teacher and visual presentations, teacher could easily monitor student behavior, and movement within room was possible without disrupting others. | | | |
| 2. The classroom environment was set up so the teachers and students could easily access materials, and clutter was minimized. | | | |
| 3. Expectations for student behavior were visible to everyone in the room, clearly defined using student-appropriate language, and stated positively. | | | |

*(continued)*

84

| | Observed | Not observed | No opportunity/ inappropriate given activity |
|---|---|---|---|
| 4. Routines appeared to have been established for common daily activities (e.g., transitions, gaining student attention, collecting homework, passing out materials, signaling for a choral response, asking for help, turning in work, selecting partners, using restroom). | | | |
| **Total Number of Features Observed** | | | |

## Part 2: Academic Engagement

*At the beginning of the observation, start the timer and after each 10-second interval, observe a student momentarily (e.g., <1 second) and decide if the student is on task or off task at that specific point in time. Mark a "+" in the box if a student appears to be on task or mark a "−" in the box if a student appears to be off task. Continue to observe and record until all boxes are marked.*

### A. On-Task/Off-Task Behaviors—10 minutes

| 1 | 2 | 3 | 4 | 5 | 6 | 7 | 8 | 9 | 10 |
|---|---|---|---|---|---|---|---|---|---|
| 11 | 12 | 13 | 14 | 15 | 16 | 17 | 18 | 19 | 20 |
| 21 | 22 | 23 | 24 | 25 | 26 | 27 | 28 | 29 | 30 |
| 31 | 32 | 33 | 34 | 35 | 36 | 37 | 38 | 39 | 40 |
| 41 | 42 | 43 | 44 | 45 | 46 | 47 | 48 | 49 | 50 |
| 51 | 52 | 53 | 54 | 55 | 56 | 57 | 58 | 59 | 60 |
| **Number of "+s" =** | | | | | | | | | |

### B. Opportunities to Respond—10 minutes

*Directions: Mark one (1) tally in the appropriate response box for every individual student or group academic response (i.e., oral or action) made during your observation of reading instruction.*

Start Time: \_\_\_\_:_____    End Time: \_\_\_\_:_____    Total Number of Minutes Observed: _____

| Group Responses | | Individual Student Responses | |
|---|---|---|---|
| Correct academic response | Incorrect response | Correct academic response | Incorrect response |
| | | | |
| Total = | Total = | Total = | Total = |
| **Total Group Responses =** | | **Total Individual Responses =** | |
| Was material covered mostly (≈80% or more) new or drill/practice?   **Y or N** (May need to ask teacher.) | | | |

*(continued)*

## C. Student–Teacher Interactions—10 minutes

*Mark one (1) tally in the "Responses to Appropriate Behaviors" box any time the teacher makes a response to an appropriate student behavior (e.g., meets the behavioral expectations for the task, is conducive to student's/classmates' learning). The teacher's response may be vocal, physical, or gestural and directed to the entire class, a small group of students, or individual students.*

*Mark one (1) tally in the "Responses to Inappropriate Behaviors" box any time the teacher makes a response to an inappropriate student behavior. The teacher's response may be a redirection or a showing of disapproval through words, physical prompts, or gestures. The teacher's response may be directed to the entire class, a small group of students, or individual students.*

*Specific vs. General Appropriate Responses: If the teacher's praise was specific (i.e., the teacher names the appropriate behavior when praising), then the tally is placed in the "Specific" column. If the teacher's praise was general (e.g., the teacher gives a "thumbs up" signal but does not name the behavior), then the tally is placed in the "General" column.*

| Responses to Appropriate Behaviors | | Responses to Inappropriate Behaviors |
|---|---|---|
| Specific | General | |
| | | |
| Total Specific Responses = <br> Total General Responses = <br> **Total Responses =** | | **Total Responses =** |

*(continued)*

## OBSERVATION SCORING GUIDELINES

**Part 1A: Explicit Teaching Strategies Checklist**

Number of Explicit Teaching Strategies Observed =

Criterion: 6 or more = 2 points     3 to 5 = 1 point     Less than 3 = 0 points

**Score for Explicit Teaching Strategies =** _____ **/ 2**

**Part 1B: Classroom Environment Checklist**

Number of Features Observed =

Criterion: 4 = 2 points     2 to 3 = 1 point     0 to 1 = 0 points

**Score for Classroom Environment =** _____ **/ 2**

**Part 2A: On-Task/Off-Task Behaviors**

Formula for Percentage of On-Task Behaviors:

Percentage of On-Task Behaviors = Number of "+"s ÷ 60 = _____ %

Criterion: 90% or more = 2 points     75–89% = 1 point     0–74% = 0 points

**Score for On-Task Behavior Percentage =** _____ **/ 2**

**Part 2B: Opportunities to Respond (OTRs**

(1) Formula for Total Student OTR Rate:

Student OTR Rate = Total Number of Responses ÷ Number of Minutes Observed = _____
Responses/Min.

Criterion for new material: 4 responses/minute = 2 points   2–3/min. = 1 point
        0–1/min. = 0 points

Criterion drill and practice: 9 responses/minute = 2 points     4–8/min. = 1 point
        0–3/min. = 0 points

**Score for OTR Rate =** _____ **/ 2**

(2) Formula for Percentage of Accurate Group Responses:

Percentage of Accurate Group Responses =

Total Number of Correct Group Responses ÷ Total Number of Group Responses = _____ %

Criterion for new material: 80% or more = 2 points     60–79% = 1 point     0–59% = 0 points

Criterion for drill and practice: 90% or more = 2 points     75–89% = 1 point
        0–74% = 0 points

**Score for Group Response Accuracy =** _____ **/ 2**

(3) Formula for Percentage of Accurate Individual Responses:

Percentage of Accurate Individual Responses =

Total Number of Correct Individual Responses ÷ Total Number of Individual Responses = _____ %

Criterion: 90% or more = 2 points     75–89% = 1 point     0% to 74% = 0 points

**Score for Individual Response Accuracy =** _____ **/ 2**

*(continued)*

**Part 2C: Student–Teacher Interactions**

(1) Formula for Total Interaction Rate:

Total Interaction Rate = Total Number of Positive Interactions ÷
Number of Negative Interactions = _____

Criterion: 3 or more = 2 points      1.5–2.9 = 1 point      Less than 1.5 = 0 points

**Score for Total Interaction Rate =** _____ **/ 2**

(2) Formula for Percentage of Specific Acknowledging Responses:

Percentage of Specific Acknowledging Responses =

Number of Specific Responses to Appropriate Behavior ÷ Total Number of Responses to Appropriate Behavior = _____ %

Criterion: 75% or more = 2 points      25–75% = 1 point      0–24% = 0 points

**Score for Specific Acknowledging Statements =** _____ **/ 2**

# Multi-Tiered Systems of Support Needs Assessment— Elementary Version

| Element of MTSS | 0<br>Not<br>Implementing | 1<br>Partially<br>Implementing | 2<br>Mostly<br>Implementing | 3<br>Fully and<br>Consistently<br>Implementing | Current Level<br>of Implemen-<br>tation in Our<br>School: |
|---|---|---|---|---|---|
| Element 1. Staff is knowledgeable about, organizes, and delivers school-based services using a **multi-tiered model** of service delivery. This service delivery incorporates both a systematic approach to the prevention of school difficulties for most students (a **public health model**) and a systematic approach to resolving identified system-level and student-level difficulties (a **problem-solving model**). | 1. In general, our staff understands and supports the rationale and components of a **multi-tiered model** of service delivery, and this model guides our practices. | | | | |
| | 2. In general, our staff understands and supports the rationale and components of a **public health model** of preventive service delivery, and this model guides our practices. | | | | |
| | 3. In general, our staff understand and support the rationale and components of a **problem-solving model** of service delivery, and this model guides our practices. | | | | |
| Element 2. Identify and conduct periodic schoolwide **screenings** of all students to examine the overall effectiveness of our school, both currently and over time. Screening data are examined from a prevention orientation and used to evaluate the overall "health" of all students in the school. The data are also disaggregated to assess the achievement of subgroups (e.g., freshmen, females/males, English language learners, students receiving special education services). Consider the reliability, validity, and usefulness of assessment tools. *Note:* Element 4 focuses on the use of screening data for purposes of identifying *individual* students at risk for or experiencing problems. | 1. In the area of academic skills/achievement in **reading/literacy** (e.g., STAR, DIBELS, AIMSweb) . . . | | | | |
| | a. A system for periodic **screening** of academic achievement is organized and utilized. | | | | |
| | b. We have reliable, valid, and useful tools for screening. | | | | |
| | c. We regularly evaluate the overall health of our school by examining the most current data for all students. | | | | |
| | d. We regularly evaluate trends in this area over time by examining current and previously collected schoolwide screening data (e.g., comparing schoolwide student performance and growth from fall, winter, and spring, across years). | | | | |
| | e. We regularly evaluate the achievement of various subgroups of students in our school using screening data. | | | | |
| | 2. In the area of academic skills/achievement in **math** (e.g., STAR, DIBELS, AIMSweb). | | | | |
| | a. A system for periodic screening of academic achievement is organized and utilized. | | | | |
| | b. We have reliable, valid, and useful tools for screening. | | | | |
| | c. We regularly evaluate the overall health of our school by examining the most current data for all students. | | | | |

*(continued)*

Reprinted with permission from Jenlyn Furey and Gary Stoner.

| Element of MTSS | 0<br>Not<br>Implementing | 1<br>Partially<br>Implementing | 2<br>Mostly<br>Implementing | 3<br>Fully and<br>Consistently<br>Implementing | Current Level<br>of Implemen-<br>tation in Our<br>School: |
|---|---|---|---|---|---|
| | d. We regularly evaluate trends in this area over time by examining current and previously collected schoolwide screening data (e.g., comparing schoolwide student performance and growth from fall, winter, and spring, across years). | | | | |
| | e. We regularly evaluate the achievement of various subgroups of students in our school using screening data. | | | | |
| | 3. In the area of **academic behavior and engagement** (e.g., attendance, homework completion, motivation, study and organizational skills, grades) . . . | | | | |
| | a. A system for periodic screening of academic behavior and engagement is organized and utilized. | | | | |
| | b. We have reliable, valid, and useful tools for screening. | | | | |
| | c. We regularly evaluate the overall health of our school by examining the most current data for all students. | | | | |
| | d. We regularly evaluate trends in this area over time by examining current and previously collected schoolwide screening data (e.g., comparing schoolwide student performance and growth from fall, winter, and spring, across years). | | | | |
| | e. We regularly evaluate the achievement of various subgroups of students in our school using screening data. | | | | |
| | 4. In the area of **mental health** and/or **personal or interpersonal adjustment** (e.g., anxiety, depression, attention problems, substance use, interpersonal relationships/connections) . . . | | | | |
| | a. A system for periodic screening of mental health/personal adjustment is organized and utilized. | | | | |
| | b. We have reliable, valid, and useful tools for screening. | | | | |
| | c. We regularly evaluate the overall health of our school by examining the most current data for all students. | | | | |
| | d. We regularly evaluate trends in this area over time by examining current and previously collected schoolwide screening data (e.g., comparing schoolwide student performance and growth from fall, winter, and spring, across years). | | | | |
| | e. We regularly evaluate the achievement of various subgroups of students in our school using screening data. | | | | |
| | 5. In the area of **problem behavior** (e.g., physical and verbal aggression, bullying, violation of school rules) . . . | | | | |
| | a. A system for periodic screening of problem behavior is organized and utilized. | | | | |
| | b. We have reliable, valid, and useful tools for screening. | | | | |
| | c. We regularly evaluate the overall health of our school by examining the most current data for all students. | | | | |

*(continued)*

| Element of MTSS | 0<br>Not<br>Implementing | 1<br>Partially<br>Implementing | 2<br>Mostly<br>Implementing | 3<br>Fully and<br>Consistently<br>Implementing | Current Level<br>of Implemen-<br>tation in Our<br>School: |
|---|---|---|---|---|---|
| | d. We regularly evaluate trends in this area over time by examining current and previously collected schoolwide screening data (e.g., comparing schoolwide student performance and growth from fall, winter, and spring, across years). | | | | |
| | e. We regularly evaluate the achievement of various subgroups of students in our school using screening data. | | | | |
| Element 3. Design and deliver **evidence-based practices** (differentiated instruction and systematic supports) for student academic achievement, academic behavior/ engagement, mental health and personal adjustment, and appropriate behavior. | 1. **Evidence-based practices** (instruction and supports) are used for *all students* (Tier 1) in the areas of . . . | | | | |
| | a. Promoting academic skills/achievement in **literacy**. | | | | |
| | b. Promoting academic skills/achievement in **math**. | | | | |
| | c. Promoting and supporting student **academic behavior and engagement** (e.g., attendance, homework completion, motivation, study and organizational skills, grades). | | | | |
| | d. Promoting positive **mental health/personal** and **interpersonal adjustment** (and preventing problems in areas such as anxiety, depression, attention, substance use, interpersonal relationships/ connections). | | | | |
| | e. Promoting and supporting appropriate, **expected behavior** (and preventing problem behavior such as physical and verbal aggression, bullying, violation of school rules). | | | | |
| | 2. Supplemental evidence-based practices (instruction and supports) are used for *some students* (Tier 2 supports are intended to provide additional support to students not fully benefiting from Tier 1 services alone, and are typically delivered in small groups) in the areas of . . . | | | | |
| | a. Promoting academic skills/achievement in **literacy**. | | | | |
| | b. Promoting academic skills/achievement in **math**. | | | | |
| | c. Promoting and supporting student **academic behavior and engagement** (e.g., attendance, homework completion, motivation, study and organizational skills, grades). | | | | |
| | d. Promoting positive **mental health/personal** and **interpersonal adjustment** (and preventing problems in areas such as anxiety, depression, attention, substance use, interpersonal relationships/ connections). | | | | |
| | e. Promoting and supporting appropriate, **expected behavior** (and preventing problem behavior such as physical and verbal aggression, bullying, violation of school rules). | | | | |
| | 3. Personalized, intensive, evidence-based practices (instruction and support) are used for *small numbers of students* (Tier 3 supports are intended to provide individualized support to students who are experiencing significant difficulties) in the areas of . . . | | | | |
| | a. Promoting academic skills/achievement in **literacy**. | | | | |
| | b. Promoting academic skills/achievement in **math**. | | | | |
| | c. Promoting and supporting student **academic behavior and engagement** (e.g., attendance, homework completion, motivation, study and organizational skills, grades). | | | | |

*(continued)*

| Element of MTSS | 0<br>Not<br>Implementing | 1<br>Partially<br>Implementing | 2<br>Mostly<br>Implementing | 3<br>Fully and<br>Consistently<br>Implementing | Current Level<br>of Implemen-<br>tation in Our<br>School: |
|---|---|---|---|---|---|
| | d. Promoting positive **mental health/personal** and **interpersonal adjustment** (and preventing problems in areas such as anxiety, depression, attention, substance use, interpersonal relationships/connections). | | | | |
| | e. Promoting and supporting appropriate, **expected behavior** (and preventing problem behavior such as physical and verbal aggression, bullying, violation of school rules). | | | | |
| Element 4. Use assessment linked to **data-based decision making**, with a focus on problem solving. Include assessment for (a) screening/benchmarking decisions, (b) **diagnostic and/or functional assessment** decisions, and (c) progress monitoring decisions. | 1. **Screening** assessments (from Element 2) are used to identify *individual students* potentially at risk in the areas of . . . | | | | |
| | a. Academic skills/achievement in **literacy**. | | | | |
| | b. Academic skills/achievement in **math**. | | | | |
| | c. **Academic behavior and engagemen**t (e.g., attendance, homework completion, motivation, study and organizational skills, grades). | | | | |
| | d. **Mental health/personal** and **interpersonal adjustment** (e.g., anxiety, depression, attention, substance use, interpersonal relationships/connections). | | | | |
| | e. **Problem behavior** (e.g., physical and verbal aggression, bullying, violation of school rules). | | | | |
| | 2. **Diagnostic** and/or **functional assessments** are conducted to identify specific problem areas/strengths for students at risk in the areas of . . . | | | | |
| | a. Academic skills/achievement in **literacy**. | | | | |
| | b. Academic skills/achievement in **math**. | | | | |
| | c. **Academic behavior and engagemen**t (e.g., attendance, homework completion, motivation, study and organizational skills, grades). | | | | |
| | d. **Mental health/personal** and **interpersonal adjustment** (e.g., anxiety, depression, attention, substance use, interpersonal relationships/connections). | | | | |
| | e. **Problem behavior** (e.g., physical and verbal aggression, bullying, violation of school rules). | | | | |
| | 3. **Progress monitoring** assessment is conducted regularly to aid in formative instructional decision making for students at risk in . . . | | | | |
| | a. Academic skills/achievement in **literacy**. | | | | |
| | b. Academic skills/achievement in **math**. | | | | |
| | c. **Academic behavior and engagemen**t (e.g., attendance, homework completion, motivation, study and organizational skills, grades). | | | | |
| | d. **Mental health/personal** and **interpersonal adjustment** (e.g., anxiety, depression, attention, substance use, interpersonal relationships/connections). | | | | |
| | e. **Problem behavior** (e.g., physical and verbal aggression, bullying, violation of school rules). | | | | |

*(continued)*

| Element of MTSS | 0<br>Not<br>Implementing | 1<br>Partially<br>Implementing | 2<br>Mostly<br>Implementing | 3<br>Fully and<br>Consistently<br>Implementing | Current Level<br>of Implemen-<br>tation in Our<br>School: |
|---|---|---|---|---|---|
| | 4. Screening data are analyzed in a timely manner (e.g., every 2–3 weeks) and used to identify at-risk students. | | | | |
| | 5. Diagnostic and/or functional assessment data are analyzed in a timely manner and used to inform instruction/interventions. | | | | |
| | 6. Progress monitoring data are analyzed in a timely manner to make decisions about a student's RTI. | | | | |
| | 7. Screening, progress monitoring, and diagnostic/functional assessment data are used to support team-based decision making. | | | | |
| | 8. Data reflecting student needs are used to form flexible intervention groups. These groups are flexible in that they are periodically adjusted based on student progress and reexamination of student need for intervention. | | | | |
| | 9. We systematically document and evaluate the extent to which our programs and supports are delivered with fidelity (i.e., programs are implemented as designed and with sufficient intensity). | | | | |
| | 10. Parents/families are systematically informed and included in decision making and problem solving relating to screening, progress monitoring, and diagnostic/functional assessment and decisions. | | | | |
| Element 5. Promote **shared responsibility** among all teaching and nonteaching staff, administrators, parents, and students for prevention and problem solving. Of particular importance is collaboration between general and special education and collaboration between specialized support professionals and teaching staff. | 1. General education teachers, special education teachers, and specialized support staff *share responsibility* for student progress/ outcomes in the areas of . . . | | | | |
| | a. Promoting and supporting academic skills/achievement in **literacy**. | | | | |
| | b. Promoting and supporting academic skills/achievement in **math**. | | | | |
| | c. Promoting and supporting **academic behavior and engagement** (e.g., attendance, homework completion, motivation, study and organizational skills, grades). | | | | |
| | d. Promoting and supporting positive **mental health/personal** and **interpersonal adjustment** (and preventing problems in areas such as anxiety, depression, attention problems, substance use, and relationships). | | | | |
| | e. Promoting and supporting appropriate, **expected behavior** (and preventing problem behavior such as physical and verbal aggression, bullying, violation of school rules). | | | | |
| | 2. Nonteaching staff members are involved in providing academic support for students within a multi-tiered framework. | | | | |
| | 3. Nonteaching staff members are involved in providing behavior support for students within a multi-tiered framework. | | | | |
| | 4. Staff regularly involves students as partners in prevention, problem solving, and decision making relating to the areas noted in Item 1 above. | | | | |
| | 5. Staff regularly involves parents/families as partners in prevention, problem solving, and decision making relating to the areas noted in Item 1 above. | | | | |
| | 6. There is parent/family representation on our MTSS leadership team. | | | | |

*(continued)*

| Element of MTSS | 0 Not Implementing | 1 Partially Implementing | 2 Mostly Implementing | 3 Fully and Consistently Implementing | Current Level of Implementation in Our School: |
|---|---|---|---|---|---|
| | 7. Parents/families are informed about how curricula programs and practices are used to support their children's achievement in the areas noted in Item 1. | | | | |
| Element 6. Organize and deliver effective **team-based problem solving** at each tier in a multi-tiered framework. | 1. We conduct effective problem-solving meetings at the building level. | | | | |
| | 2. We conduct effective problem-solving meetings at the grade or content area level. | | | | |
| | 3. Information about prior problem-solving efforts is effectively communicated at times of student transitions (e.g., from year to year). | | | | |
| | 4. Roles and responsibilities within teams are delegated clearly and understood by all team members. | | | | |
| | 5. Cross-team coordination occurs and is effective (e.g., cross-grade, cross-subject-area coordination). | | | | |
| | 6. Parents are engaged as team members regarding academic problem solving. | | | | |
| | 7. Parents are engaged as team members regarding problem solving for behavior concerns. | | | | |
| Element 7. Consider and incorporate **contextual factors** in prevention and problem solving. These include, but are not limited to, curricula, scheduling, cultural variables, students who are English language learners, resources, community factors, funding, contractual/union-related factors, and developmental considerations. | 1. Our school's prevention and problem solving efforts systematically attend to the following factors . . . | | | | |
| | a. curricula | | | | |
| | b. scheduling | | | | |
| | c. cultural variables | | | | |
| | d. students who are English language learners | | | | |
| | e. resources | | | | |
| | f. funding | | | | |
| | g. community factors | | | | |
| | h. contractual/union-related factors | | | | |
| | i. age, grade, and developmental appropriateness of supports. | | | | |
| | 2. Multiple school-based and community-based student support initiatives are coordinated and integrated within the school. | | | | |
| | 3. Parent/family goals and expectations are considered as part of our school's team-based problem-solving practices. | | | | |
| Element 8. Systematically use a multi-tiered approach to identify and support students with learning disabilities and behavioral disorders, and make special education eligibility decisions, including use of a **dual discrepancy** and/ or **functional assessment** approach to diagnosis | 1. A **dual discrepancy approach** is used to diagnose specific learning disabilities [SLD]. | | | | |
| | 2. Evidence-based instructional interventions are utilized prior to diagnosing specific learning disabilities. | | | | |
| | 3. The fidelity of instructional interventions is monitored and documented prior to concluding that a student is not responsive to an intervention. | | | | |
| | 4. A **functional assessment** approach is used to understand and intervene with behavior problems. | | | | |

*(continued)*

94

| Element of MTSS | 0<br>Not<br>Implementing | 1<br>Partially<br>Implementing | 2<br>Mostly<br>Implementing | 3<br>Fully and<br>Consistently<br>Implementing | Current Level of Implementation in Our School: |
|---|---|---|---|---|---|
| and documentation of intervention fidelity. *Note*: High-quality practices in this element are related to and dependent on the use of practices identified in Elements 3 and 4. | 5. Evidence-based behavior supports are utilized prior to diagnosing behavioral disorders. | | | | |
| | 6. The fidelity of behavior supports/interventions is monitored and documented prior to concluding that a student is not responsive to an intervention. | | | | |
| | 7. When data indicate that there may be a disability, families are informed of their due process rights. | | | | |
| Element 9. Provide strong, ongoing **leadership** for MTSS administration, staff development, and supervision of activities/personnel. | 1. The efforts of the MTSS leadership team are supported with adequate budgeting and other resources. | | | | |
| | 2. The MTSS leadership team conducts effective meetings. | | | | |
| | 3. The MTSS leadership team organizes and supports MTSS-related assessment activities, including provision of staff training. | | | | |
| | 4. The MTSS leadership team organizes and supports MTSS-related curricula and intervention program development, including provision of staff training. | | | | |
| | 5. The MTSS leadership team facilitates the integration of technology into MTSS initiatives. | | | | |
| | 6. The MTSS leadership team utilizes and coordinates MTSS-related activities with districtwide resources. | | | | |
| | 7. The MTSS leadership team aids in the development of a K–12 continuum of MTSS services and activities. | | | | |
| | 8. The MTSS leadership team organizes and supports staff development opportunities regarding parent/family engagement in MTSS-related activities. | | | | |

*(continued)*

**Multi-Tiered Systems of Support Needs Assessment—Elementary Version** *(page 8 of 9)*

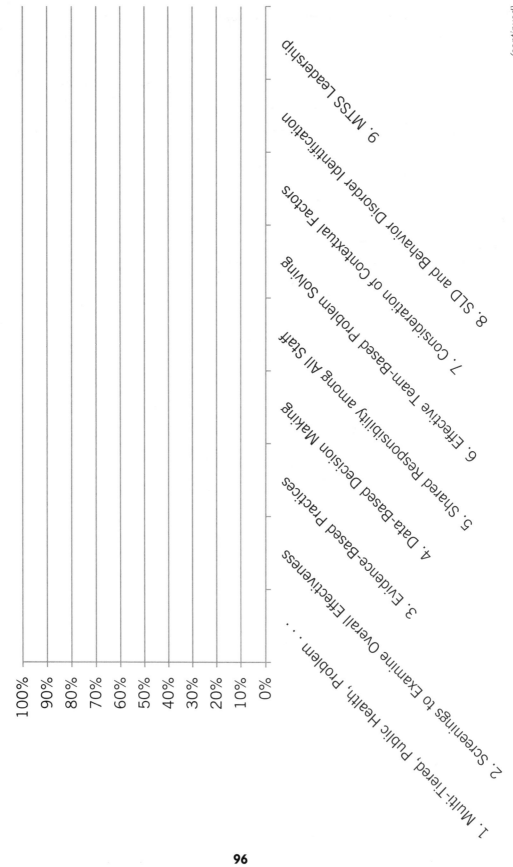

100%
90%
80%
70%
60%
50%
40%
30%
20%
10%
0%

1. Multi-Tiered, Public Health, Problem . . .
2. Screenings to Examine Overall Effectiveness
3. Evidence-Based Practices
4. Data-Based Decision Making
5. Shared Responsibility among All Staff
6. Effective Team-Based Problem Solving
7. Consideration of Contextual Factors
8. SLD and Behavior Disorder Identification
9. MTSS Leadership

*(continued)*

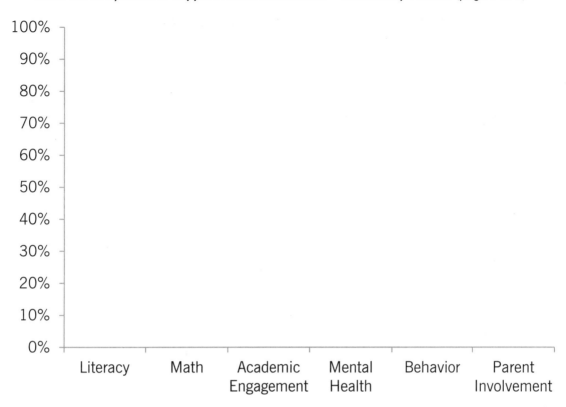

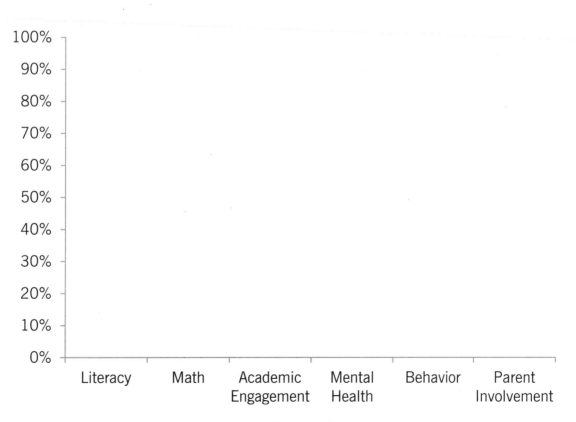

# Multi-Tiered Systems of Support Needs Assessment—
## Secondary Version

| Element of MTSS | 0<br>Not<br>Implementing | 1<br>Partially<br>Implementing | 2<br>Mostly<br>Implementing | 3<br>Fully and<br>Consistently<br>Implementing | Current Level of Implementation in Our School: |
|---|---|---|---|---|---|
| Element 1. Staff is knowledgeable about, organizes, and delivers school-based services using a **multi-tiered model** of service delivery. This service delivery incorporates both a systematic approach to the prevention of school difficulties for most students (a **public health model**) and a systematic approach to resolving identified system-level and student-level difficulties (a **problem-solving model**). | 1. In general, our staff understands and supports the rationale and components of a **multi-tiered model** of service delivery, and this model guides our practices. | | | | |
| | 2. In general, our staff understands and supports the rationale and components of a **public health model** of preventive service delivery, and this model guides our practices. | | | | |
| | 3. In general, our staff understands and supports the rationale and components of a **problem-solving model** of service delivery, and this model guides our practices. | | | | |
| Element 2. Identify and conduct periodic schoolwide **screenings** of all students to examine the overall effectiveness of our school, both currently and over time. Screening data are examined from a prevention orientation, and are used to evaluate the overall "health" of all students in the school. The data are also disaggregated to assess the achievement of subgroups (e.g., freshmen, females/males, English language learners, students receiving special education services). Consider the reliability, validity, and usefulness of assessment tools. *Note:* Element 4 focuses on the use of screening data for purposes of identifying *individual* students at risk for or experiencing problems. | 1. In the area of academic skills/achievement in **literacy** (e.g., STAR, portfolios, summative course grades) . . . | | | | |
| | a. A system for periodic **screening** of academic achievement is organized and utilized. | | | | |
| | b. We have reliable, valid, and useful tools for screening. | | | | |
| | c. We regularly evaluate the overall health of our school by examining the most current data for all students. | | | | |
| | d. We regularly evaluate trends in this area over time by examining current and previously collected schoolwide screening data (e.g., comparing schoolwide student performance and growth from fall, winter, and spring, across years). | | | | |
| | e. We regularly evaluate the achievement of various subgroups of students in our school using screening data. | | | | |
| | 2. In the area of academic skills/achievement in **math** (e.g., STAR, portfolios, summative course grades) . . . | | | | |
| | a. A system for periodic screening of academic achievement is organized and utilized. | | | | |
| | b. We have reliable, valid, and useful tools for screening. | | | | |
| | c. We regularly evaluate the overall health of our school by examining the most current data for all students. | | | | |

*(continued)*

Reprinted with permission from Jenlyn Furey and Gary Stoner.

| Element of MTSS | 0<br>Not<br>Implementing | 1<br>Partially<br>Implementing | 2<br>Mostly<br>Implementing | 3<br>Fully and<br>Consistently<br>Implementing | Current Level of Implementation in Our School: |
|---|---|---|---|---|---|
| | d. We regularly evaluate trends in this area over time by examining current and previously collected schoolwide screening data (e.g., comparing schoolwide student performance and growth from fall, winter, and spring, across years). | | | | |
| | e. We regularly evaluate the achievement of various subgroups of students in our school using screening data. | | | | |
| | 3. In the area of **academic behavior and engagement** (e.g., attendance, homework completion, motivation, study and organizational skills, grades) . . . | | | | |
| | a. A system for periodic screening of academic behavior and engagement is organized and utilized. | | | | |
| | b. We have reliable, valid, and useful tools for screening. | | | | |
| | c. We regularly evaluate the overall health of our school by examining the most current data for all students. | | | | |
| | d. We regularly evaluate trends in this area over time by examining current and previously collected schoolwide screening data (e.g., comparing schoolwide student performance and growth from fall, winter, and spring, across years). | | | | |
| | e. We regularly evaluate the achievement of various subgroups of students in our school using screening data. | | | | |
| | 4. In the area of **mental health** and/or **personal or interpersonal adjustment** (e.g., anxiety, depression, attention problems, substance use, interpersonal relationships/connections) . . . | | | | |
| | a. A system for periodic screening of mental health/personal adjustment is organized and utilized. | | | | |
| | b. We have reliable, valid, and useful tools for screening. | | | | |
| | c. We regularly evaluate the overall health of our school by examining the most current data for all students. | | | | |
| | d. We regularly evaluate trends in this area over time by examining current and previously collected schoolwide screening data (e.g., comparing schoolwide student performance and growth from fall, winter, and spring, across years). | | | | |
| | e. We regularly evaluate the achievement of various subgroups of students in our school using screening data. | | | | |
| | 5. In the area of **problem behavio**r (e.g., physical and verbal aggression, bullying, violation of school rules) . . . | | | | |
| | a. A system for periodic screening of problem behavior is organized and utilized. | | | | |
| | b. We have reliable, valid, and useful tools for screening. | | | | |
| | c. We regularly evaluate the overall health of our school by examining the most current data for all students. | | | | |
| | d. We regularly evaluate trends in this area over time by examining current and previously collected schoolwide screening data (e.g., comparing schoolwide student performance and growth from fall, winter, and spring, across years). | | | | |

*(continued)*

| Element of MTSS | 0<br>Not<br>Implementing | 1<br>Partially<br>Implementing | 2<br>Mostly<br>Implementing | 3<br>Fully and<br>Consistently<br>Implementing | Current Level of Implementation in Our School: |
|---|---|---|---|---|---|
| | e. We regularly evaluate the achievement of various subgroups of students in our school using screening data. | | | | |
| Element 3. Design and deliver **evidence-based practices** (differentiated instruction and systematic supports) for student academic achievement, academic behavior/ engagement, mental health and personal adjustment, and appropriate behavior. | 1. **Evidence-based practices** (instruction and supports) are used for *all students* (Tier 1) in the areas of . . . | | | | |
| | a. Promoting academic skills/achievement in **literacy**. | | | | |
| | b. Promoting academic skills/achievement in **math**. | | | | |
| | c. Promoting and supporting student **academic behavior and engagement** (e.g., attendance, homework completion, motivation, study and organizational skills, grades). | | | | |
| | d. Promoting positive **mental health/personal** and **interpersonal adjustment** (and preventing problems in areas such as anxiety, depression, attention, substance use, interpersonal relationships/ connections). | | | | |
| | e. Promoting and supporting appropriate, **expected behavior** (and preventing problem behavior such as physical and verbal aggression, bullying, violation of school rules). | | | | |
| | 2. Supplemental evidence-based practices (instruction and supports) are used for *some students* (Tier 2 supports are intended to provide additional support to students not fully benefiting from Tier 1 services alone, and are typically delivered in small groups) in the areas of . . . | | | | |
| | a. Promoting academic skills/achievement in **literacy**. | | | | |
| | b. Promoting academic skills/achievement in **math**. | | | | |
| | c. Promoting and supporting student **academic behavior and engagement** (e.g., attendance, homework completion, motivation, study and organizational skills, grades). | | | | |
| | d. Promoting positive **mental health/personal** and **interpersonal adjustment** (and preventing problems in areas such as anxiety, depression, attention, substance use, interpersonal relationships/ connections). | | | | |
| | e. Promoting and supporting appropriate, **expected behavior** (and preventing problem behavior such as physical and verbal aggression, bullying, violation of school rules). | | | | |
| | 3. Personalized, intensive, evidence-based practices (instruction and support) are used for *small numbers of students* (Tier 3 supports are intended to provide individualized support to students who are experiencing significant difficulties) in the areas of . . . | | | | |
| | a. Promoting academic skills/achievement in **literacy**. | | | | |
| | b. Promoting academic skills/achievement in **math**. | | | | |
| | c. Promoting and supporting student **academic behavior and engagement** (e.g., attendance, homework completion, motivation, study and organizational skills, grades). | | | | |
| | d. Promoting positive **mental health/personal** and **interpersonal adjustment** (and preventing problems in areas such as anxiety, depression, attention, substance use, interpersonal relationships/ connections) | | | | |

*(continued)*

| Element of MTSS | 0<br>Not<br>Implementing | 1<br>Partially<br>Implementing | 2<br>Mostly<br>Implementing | 3<br>Fully and<br>Consistently<br>Implementing | Current Level of Implementation in Our School: |
|---|---|---|---|---|---|
| | e. Promoting and supporting appropriate, **expected behavior** (and preventing problem behavior such as physical and verbal aggression, bullying, violation of school rules). | | | | |
| Element 4. Use assessment linked to **data-based decision making**, with a focus on problem solving. Include assessment for (a) screening/benchmarking decisions, (b) **diagnostic and/or functional assessment** decisions, and (c) progress monitoring decisions. | 1. **Screening** assessments (from Element 2) are used to identify *individual students* potentially at risk in the areas of . . . | | | | |
| | a. Academic skills/achievement in **literacy**. | | | | |
| | b. Academic skills/achievement in **math**. | | | | |
| | c. **Academic behavior and engagement** (e.g., attendance, homework completion, motivation, study and organizational skills, grades). | | | | |
| | d. **Mental health/personal** and **interpersonal adjustment** (e.g., anxiety, depression, attention, substance use, interpersonal relationships/connections). | | | | |
| | e. **Problem behavior** (e.g., physical and verbal aggression, bullying, violation of school rules). | | | | |
| | 2. **Diagnostic** and/or **functional assessments** are conducted to identify specific problem areas/strengths for students at risk in the areas of . . . | | | | |
| | a. Academic skills/achievement in **literacy**. | | | | |
| | b. Academic skills/achievement in **math**. | | | | |
| | c. **Academic behavior and engagement** (e.g., attendance, homework completion, motivation, study and organizational skills, grades). | | | | |
| | d. **Mental health/personal** and **interpersonal adjustment** (e.g., anxiety, depression, attention, substance use, interpersonal relationships/connections). | | | | |
| | e. **Problem behavior** (e.g., physical and verbal aggression, bullying, violation of school rules). | | | | |
| | 3. **Progress monitoring** assessment is conducted regularly to aid in formative instructional decision making for students at risk in . . . | | | | |
| | a. Academic skills/achievement in **literacy**. | | | | |
| | b. Academic skills/achievement in **math**. | | | | |
| | c. **Academic behavior and engagement** (e.g., attendance, homework completion, motivation, study and organizational skills, grades). | | | | |
| | d. **Mental health/personal** and **interpersonal adjustment** (e.g., anxiety, depression, attention, substance use, interpersonal relationships/connections). | | | | |
| | e. **Problem behavior** (e.g., physical and verbal aggression, bullying, violation of school rules). | | | | |
| | 4. Screening data are analyzed in a timely manner (e.g., every 2–3 weeks) and used to identify at-risk students. | | | | |
| | 5. Diagnostic and/or functional assessment data are analyzed in a timely manner and used to inform instruction/interventions. | | | | |
| | 6. Progress monitoring data are analyzed in a timely manner to make decisions about a student's response to an intervention. | | | | |

*(continued)*

| Element of MTSS | 0<br>Not<br>Implementing | 1<br>Partially<br>Implementing | 2<br>Mostly<br>Implementing | 3<br>Fully and<br>Consistently<br>Implementing | Current Level<br>of Implemen-<br>tation in Our<br>School: |
|---|---|---|---|---|---|
| | 7. Screening, progress monitoring, and diagnostic/functional assessment data are used to support team-based decision making. | | | | |
| | 8. Data reflecting student needs are used to form flexible intervention groups. These groups are flexible in that they are periodically adjusted based on student progress and reexamination of student need for intervention. | | | | |
| | 9. We systematically document and evaluate the extent to which our programs and supports are delivered with fidelity (i.e., programs are implemented as designed and with sufficient intensity). | | | | |
| | 10. Parents/families are systematically informed and included in decision making and problems solving relating to screening, progress monitoring, and diagnostic/functional assessment and decisions. | | | | |
| Element 5. Promote **shared responsibility** among all teaching and nonteaching staff, administrators, parents, and students for prevention and problem solving. Of particular importance is collaboration between general and special education and collaboration between specialized support professionals and teaching staff. | 1. General education teachers, special education teachers and specialized support staff *share responsibility* for student progress/outcomes in the areas of . . . | | | | |
| | a. Promoting and supporting academic skills/achievement in **literacy**. | | | | |
| | b. Promoting and supporting academic skills/achievement in **math**. | | | | |
| | c. Promoting and supporting **academic behavior and engagement** (e.g., attendance, homework completion, motivation, study and organizational skills, grades). | | | | |
| | d. Promoting and supporting positive **mental health/personal** and **interpersonal adjustment** (and preventing problems in areas such as anxiety, depression, attention problems, substance use, and relationships). | | | | |
| | e. Promoting and supporting appropriate, **expected behavior** (and preventing problem behavior such as physical and verbal aggression, bullying, violation of school rules). | | | | |
| | 2. Nonteaching staff members are involved in providing academic support for students within a multi-tiered framework. | | | | |
| | 3. Nonteaching staff members are involved in providing behavior support for students within a multi-tiered framework. | | | | |
| | 4. Staff regularly involves students as partners in prevention, problem solving, and decision making relating to the areas noted in Item 1 above. | | | | |
| | 5. Staff regularly involves parents/families as partners in prevention, problem solving, and decision making relating to the areas noted in Item 1 above. | | | | |
| | 6. There is parent/family representation on our MTSS leadership team. | | | | |
| | 7. Parents/families are informed about how curricula programs and practices are used to support their children's achievement in the areas noted in Item 1. | | | | |
| Element 6. Organize and deliver effective **team-based problem solving** at each tier in a multi-tiered framework. | 1. We conduct effective problem-solving meetings at the building level. | | | | |
| | 2. We conduct effective problem-solving meetings at the grade or content-area level. | | | | |

*(continued)*

| Element of MTSS | 0<br>Not<br>Implementing | 1<br>Partially<br>Implementing | 2<br>Mostly<br>Implementing | 3<br>Fully and<br>Consistently<br>Implementing | Current Level of Implementation in Our School: |
|---|---|---|---|---|---|
| | 3. Information about prior problem-solving efforts is effectively communicated at times of student transitions (e.g., from year to year). | | | | |
| | 4. Roles and responsibilities within teams are delegated clearly and understood by all team members. | | | | |
| | 5. Cross-team coordination occurs and is effective (e.g., cross-grade, cross-subject-area coordination). | | | | |
| | 6. Parents are engaged as team members regarding academic problem solving. | | | | |
| | 7. Parents are engaged as team members regarding problem solving for behavior concerns. | | | | |
| Element 7. Consider and incorporate **contextual factors** in prevention and problem solving. These include, but are not limited to, curricula, scheduling, cultural variables, students who are English language learners, resources, community factors, funding, contractual/union-related factors, and developmental considerations. | 1. Our school's prevention and problem solving efforts systematically attend to the following factors . . . | | | | |
| | a. curricula | | | | |
| | b. scheduling | | | | |
| | c. cultural variables | | | | |
| | d. students who are English language learners | | | | |
| | e. resources | | | | |
| | f. funding | | | | |
| | g. community factors | | | | |
| | h. contractual/union-related factors | | | | |
| | i. age, grade, and developmental appropriateness of supports. | | | | |
| | 2. Multiple school-based and community-based student support initiatives are coordinated and integrated within the school. | | | | |
| | 3. Parent/family goals and expectations are considered as part of our school's team-based problem solving practices. | | | | |
| Element 8. Systematically use a multi-tiered approach to identify and support students with learning disabilities and behavioral disorders, and make special education eligibility decisions, including use of a **dual discrepancy** and/or **functional assessment** approach to diagnosis, and documentation of intervention fidelity. *Note:* High-quality practices in this element are related to and dependent on the use of practices identified in Elements 3 and 4. | 1. A **dual discrepancy approach** is used to diagnose specific learning disabilities [SLD]. | | | | |
| | 2. Evidence-based instructional interventions are utilized prior to diagnosing specific learning disabilities. | | | | |
| | 3. The fidelity of instructional interventions is monitored and documented prior to concluding that a student is not responsive to an intervention. | | | | |
| | 4. A **functional assessment** approach is used to understand and intervene with behavior problems. | | | | |
| | 5. Evidence-based behavior supports are utilized prior to diagnosing behavioral disorders. | | | | |
| | 6. The fidelity of behavior supports/interventions is monitored and documented prior to concluding that a student is not responsive to an intervention. | | | | |
| | 7. When data indicate that there may be a disability, families are informed of their due process rights. | | | | |

*(continued)*

| Element of MTSS | 0 Not Implementing | 1 Partially Implementing | 2 Mostly Implementing | 3 Fully and Consistently Implementing | Current Level of Implementation in Our School: |
|---|---|---|---|---|---|
| Element 9. Provide strong, ongoing **leadership** for MTSS administration, staff development, and supervision of activities/personnel. | 1. The efforts of the MTSS leadership team are supported with adequate budgeting and other resources. | | | | |
| | 2. The MTSS leadership team conducts effective meetings. | | | | |
| | 3. The MTSS leadership team organizes and supports MTSS-related assessment activities, including provision of staff training. | | | | |
| | 4. The MTSS leadership team organizes and supports MTSS-related curricula and intervention program development, including provision of staff training. | | | | |
| | 5. The MTSS leadership team facilitates the integration of technology into MTSS initiatives. | | | | |
| | 6. The MTSS leadership team utilizes and coordinates MTSS-related activities with district-wide resources. | | | | |
| | 7. The MTSS leadership team aids in the development of a K–12 continuum of MTSS services and activities. | | | | |
| | 8. The MTSS leadership team organizes and supports staff development opportunities regarding parent/family engagement in MTSS related activities. | | | | |

*(continued)*

104

Multi-Tiered Systems of Support Needs Assessment—Secondary Version *(page 8 of 8)*

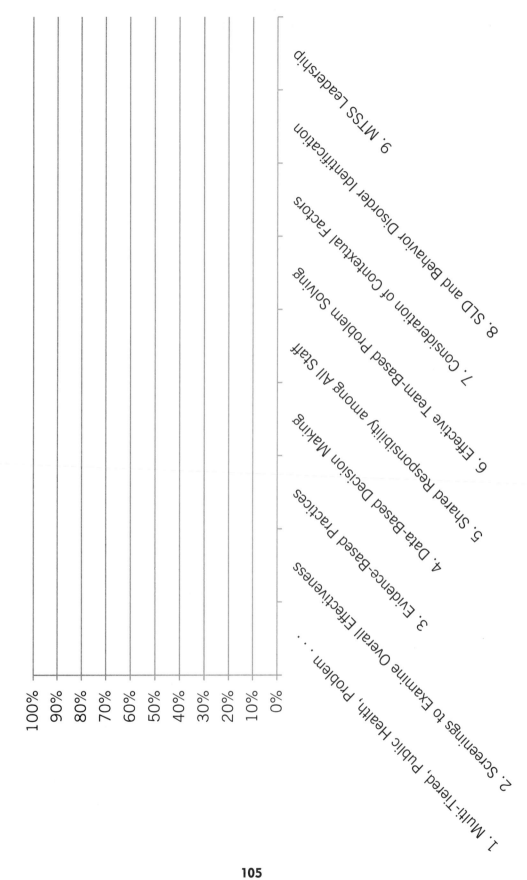

100%
90%
80%
70%
60%
50%
40%
30%
20%
10%
0%

1. Multi-Tiered, Public Health, Problem . . .

2. Screenings to Examine Overall Effectiveness

3. Evidence-Based Practices

4. Data-Based Decision Making

5. Shared Responsibility among All Staff

6. Effective Team-Based Problem Solving

7. Consideration of Contextual Factors

8. SLD and Behavior Disorder Identification

9. MTSS Leadership

# Integrated Academic and Behavior Request for Assistance Form

Date: _____  Teacher/Team: _____

Student Name: _____  Grade: _____  IEP (circle):  Yes  No

Concerns (circle):        ACADEMICS             SOCIAL BEHAVIOR             BOTH

Academic strengths (identify at least two): _____

_____

Social strengths (identify at least two): _____

_____

Interests (identify at least one): _____

**Routines Analysis:** For each period/activity, circle academic skill deficits (upper row of numbers), likelihood of problem behavior (lower row of numbers), and specific concerns.

| Schedule (Times) | Period/Activity | Academic Skill Deficits Likelihood of Problem Behavior Low                    High | Specific Academic Deficits and/or Problem Behaviors |
|---|---|---|---|
| | | 1  2  3  4  5  6<br>1  2  3  4  5  6 | |
| | | 1  2  3  4  5  6<br>1  2  3  4  5  6 | |
| | | 1  2  3  4  5  6<br>1  2  3  4  5  6 | |
| | | 1  2  3  4  5  6<br>1  2  3  4  5  6 | |
| | | 1  2  3  4  5  6<br>1  2  3  4  5  6 | |
| | | 1  2  3  4  5  6<br>1  2  3  4  5  6 | |

*(continued)*

Adapted with permission from Anne W. Todd from Todd, Horner, Sugai, and Colvin (1999) and March et al. (2000).

| Schedule (Times) | Period/Activity | Academic Skill Deficits Likelihood of Problem Behavior Low | | | | High | Specific Academic Deficits and/or Problem Behaviors |
|---|---|---|---|---|---|---|---|
| | | 1 2 3 4 5 6 | | | | | |
| | | 1 2 3 4 5 6 | | | | | |
| | | 1 2 3 4 5 6 | | | | | |
| | | 1 2 3 4 5 6 | | | | | |
| | | 1 2 3 4 5 6 | | | | | |
| | | 1 2 3 4 5 6 | | | | | |
| | | 1 2 3 4 5 6 | | | | | |
| | | 1 2 3 4 5 6 | | | | | |
| | | 1 2 3 4 5 6 | | | | | |
| | | 1 2 3 4 5 6 | | | | | |

**Identify Patterns:** Examine the periods of greatest concern. Do the periods with high academic ratings also have high behavior ratings?

**Specific Academic Concerns (if needed):**

| Content Area(s) | Specific Academic Needs |
|---|---|
| | |

Provide most recent screening/progress monitoring data in areas of concern:

Date: _____  Content Area: _____  Score(s): _____

Date: _____  Content Area: _____  Score(s): _____

Date: _____  Content Area: _____  Score(s): _____

What have you tried/used? How has it worked?

*(continued)*

**Specific Behavior Concerns (if needed):**

| Situations | Problem Behaviors | Most Common Result |
|---|---|---|
|  |  |  |
| What have you tried/used? How has it worked? | | |
|  |  |  |

**Integrated Concerns:** If academic task requests lead to problem behavior, describe the requests in detail below.

| **Academic tasks (e.g., reading, long division) that lead to problem behavior** |
|---|
| What tasks are MORE likely to lead to problem behavior? |
| What tasks are LESS likely to lead to problem behavior? |
| **Types of requests (e.g., read aloud, seatwork) that lead to problem behavior** |
| What types of requests are MORE likely to lead to problem behavior? |
| What types of requests are LESS likely to lead to problem behavior? |

How have you informed parents/caregivers? _____

_____

**Date of Meeting:** _____

# Inventory for Identifying MTSS Assessment Needs

| Content Area: _____ | Questions | | |
|---|---|---|---|
| Tool (e.g., assessment, measure, test) | Is it required? | Are data high quality? | What modifications are needed? |
| **Fidelity of Implementation** | | | |
| 1. | | | |
| 2. | | | |
| 3. | | | |
| 4. | | | |
| 5. | | | |
| Fidelity of Implementation Needs: | | | |
| **Screening** | | | |
| 1. | | | |
| 2. | | | |
| 3. | | | |
| 4. | | | |
| 5. | | | |
| Screening Needs: | | | |

*(continued)*

| Tool (e.g., assessment, measure, test) | Is it required? | Are data high quality? | What modifications are needed? |
|---|---|---|---|
| **Diagnostic Assessment** | | | |
| 1. | | | |
| 2. | | | |
| 3. | | | |
| 4. | | | |
| 5. | | | |
| Diagnostic Assessment Needs: | | | |
| **Progress Monitoring** | | | |
| 1. | | | |
| 2. | | | |
| 3. | | | |
| 4. | | | |
| 5. | | | |
| Progress Monitoring Needs: | | | |
| **General Outcomes Measurement** | | | |
| 1. | | | |
| 2. | | | |
| 3. | | | |
| 4. | | | |
| 5. | | | |
| General Outcome Measurement Needs: | | | |

# Tiers 2 and 3 Intervention Tracking Tool

**Directions:** Use this form to summarize information about how much each Tier 2 or 3 academic or behavioral intervention is used, how well students are responding to it, and how well it is being implemented. Information from benchmark or progress monitoring assessments is used to complete this form. If there are multiple sections or groups of the same intervention, record information separately for each section/group. Update monthly.

| Intervention (list each below) | Sept. | Oct. | Nov. | Dec. | Jan. | Feb. | Mar. | April | May |
|---|---|---|---|---|---|---|---|---|---|
| No. of students participating in the intervention | | | | | | | | | |
| No. of students responding/ making adequate progress | | | | | | | | | |
| Percent of students responding/ making adequate progress | | | | | | | | | |
| Average fidelity of implementation score | | | | | | | | | |
| No. of students participating in the intervention | | | | | | | | | |
| No. of students responding/ making adequate progress | | | | | | | | | |
| Percent of students responding/ making adequate progress | | | | | | | | | |
| Average fidelity of implementation score | | | | | | | | | |

*(continued)*

Reprinted with permission from the Michigan Department of Education.

Tiers 2 and 3 Intervention Tracking Tool *(page 2 of 2)*

| Intervention (list each below) | Sept. | Oct. | Nov. | Dec. | Jan. | Feb. | Mar. | April | May |
|---|---|---|---|---|---|---|---|---|---|
| No. of students participating in the intervention | | | | | | | | | |
| No. of students responding/ making adequate progress | | | | | | | | | |
| Percent of students responding/ making adequate progress | | | | | | | | | |
| Average fidelity of implementation score | | | | | | | | | |
| No. of students participating in the intervention | | | | | | | | | |
| No. of students responding/ making adequate progress | | | | | | | | | |
| Percent of students responding/ making adequate progress | | | | | | | | | |
| Average fidelity of implementation score | | | | | | | | | |

# CHAPTER 4

# Integrating Practices

In this chapter, we discuss how academic and behavior practices can be combined within an integrated MTSS model. By *practices*, we mean the curricula, instructional time, interventions, and strategies that are used with students across the school, in the classroom, and with individual students. Our intent is not to provide extensive details of specific academic and behavior interventions, as there are many excellent resources describing nonintegrated interventions for academics and behavior (e.g., Burns, Riley-Tillman, & VanDerHeyden, 2012; Crone et al., 2010; Rathvon, 2008; Stormont, Reinke, Herman, & Lembke, 2012). Instead, we describe how existing academic and behavior practices—ones that are commonly used in schools—can be integrated in a logical and efficient manner. Our goal with an integrated MTSS approach focuses on optimizing learning by providing a safe, welcoming learning environment with few distractions, keeping students in the classroom and engaged in classroom instruction, and making the most of instructional time through effective teaching strategies across academic and behavior domains. This integration leads to students' experience of success, which enhances outcomes across content areas.

## SMARTER INTEGRATION

With the research from Chapter 2 in hand, it seems logical to try to integrate every facet of academic and behavior systems. After all, if academic and behavior skills are intertwined and the systems are so similar, wouldn't providing an integrated set of interventions make the most sense? Not necessarily, and especially not if those integrated interventions become a third set of practices and student groups! Instead, integrated systems involve *integrated thinking*, considering the natural link between academics and behavior, doing good work on both the academic and behavior sides, and integrating where it makes the most sense. This step means resisting the temptation to implement additional, integrated interventions and instead thinking about which existing interventions provide both academic and behavior support and differentiating instruction to allow combined support to happen under existing structures and practices.

In the next section, we provide a useful way to integrate these practices without adding a third set of practices. Integration is described in terms of the three common tiers of support in MTSS, not simply because academic RTI and PBIS are organized into tiers, but because the approach used in integrating practices varies in relation to the specific tier. As will be seen, integrated Tier 1 practices often involve quality instruction in each content area, using the same set of core principles to guide intervention. Integrating practices at Tier 1 can be beneficial, but integrating at Tiers 2 and 3 is even more critical to improving outcomes for students requiring additional support. At Tier 2, practices can be integrated by identifying existing Tier 2 academic practices that also provide behavior support (and vice versa) or differentiating instruction to add efficient intervention across content areas. At Tier 3, support plans are fully integrated based on individual needs, which may indicate combined support or support only in a content area of need. The final section of this chapter describes strategies for selecting and managing integrated practices. We emphasize a practical, *doable* integration that uses synergy as an efficient means to improve outcomes.

## INTEGRATED PRACTICES WITHIN A TIERED MODEL

### Tier 1: Universal Supports

For both academic RTI and PBIS, the focus of Tier 1 is optimizing learning and preventing problems as early as possible. As we have discussed, unaddressed challenges in one area may lead to challenges in others. Conversely, success in one area may generalize to other areas, through use of universal skills or the experience that in general, attention and perseverance will lead to success. As such, Tier 1 practices are not selected specifically in response to individual challenges, but rather to maximize success for all students in all areas. From this logic, it is important to use practices that are most likely to help students rapidly develop academic and social–emotional skills.

### Six Principles of Effective Academic and Behavior Instruction

The most effective and durable interventions for both academic and behavior support involve teaching, and the higher the quality of instruction, the more powerful the intervention. In fact, when we encounter students who do not use skills we've just taught them or consistently use the wrong strategy for the situation, attending to the quality of teaching is the first step in solving the problem, whether it be academic or behavior in nature. As a result, it is worthwhile to review some key universal principles of instruction for Tier 1. These six principles, from Coyne, Kame'enui, and Carnine (2007), apply equally to academic and social–emotional instruction (see Table 4.1).

PRINCIPLE 1: FOCUS ON BIG IDEAS

Quality curricula focus on the big ideas of instruction. Big ideas are the core concepts or subdomains that are necessary for academic and social competence, and they serve to provide a focus to instruction that maximizes positive development and avoids providing students with an education that is "a mile wide and an inch deep." As Coyne, Kame'enui, and Carnine (2007) note, big ideas tell us what content is most important to teach. For example, in early literacy, research tells us that the big ideas are phonemic awareness, alphabetic principle, fluency with connected text, vocabulary, and reading comprehension (National Reading Panel, 2000). Regarding behavior, there is less collective agreement on what constitutes big ideas, but some possibilities can be found. For example, the Collaborative for Academic, Social, and Emotional Learning (CASEL) has described the big ideas of social and emotional competence as self-awareness, self-management, social awareness, relationship skills, and responsible decision making (Collaborative for Academic Social and Emotional Learning, 2003). If created well, a school's PBIS schoolwide expectations (e.g., be safe, be responsible, be respectful) encompass these ideas and serve as curriculum anchors for social behavior, much in the same way as the big ideas of early literacy guide academic instruction.

## PRINCIPLE 2: CONSPICUOUS STRATEGIES

In this principle of instruction, teaching actions are made explicit and unambiguous to the learner through clear explanations of not only the content, but also the learning process itself. Coyne, Kame'enui, and Carnine (2007) suggest that *conspicuous strategies* describe how we should teach. These strategies give students the skills needed to understand and analyze input from complex stimuli to produce their own knowledge, rather than simply memorizing facts. In beginning reading instruction, students are taught to produce sounds of individual letters and then blend the sounds together to say the printed word. This strategy is much more efficient than teaching only sight words because it gives students a skill to use when encountering unfamiliar words. In PBIS, students are taught social and emotional skills through explicit lesson plans, which provide a rationale (why to use the skill), the correct contextual cues (when to use the skill), clear examples and nonexamples (how to use the skill), and practice that includes performance feedback. This use of feedback for students strengthens the link of skills to rationale and natural reinforcement (e.g., "You showed respect by waiting until everyone had a turn. People will look up to you when you show them respect").

## PRINCIPLE 3: MEDIATED SCAFFOLDING

This principle focuses on providing additional supports to promote accurate and timely responding. These supports are eventually faded as student skills improve. Examples of mediated scaffolding may include adding verbal or visual prompts to ensure student success with new or difficult skills. In academic instruction, scaffolding may involve giving reminders to follow the strategies (e.g., "Remember to carry to the 10's place") that are gradually removed once the students can reliably use the skill (e.g., "Remember to carry"). PBIS scaffolding of behavior expectations in the classroom might include posters on the wall prompting behavior expectations. Early in the school year, the teacher may ask students to read the expectations off the posters and have them provide positive examples of expected behavior before transitions. As the year progresses, the teacher may simply point to the poster and later remove any prompts when students are transitioning efficiently.

**TABLE 4.1. Principles of Effective Academic and Behavior Instruction**

| Principle | Description | Reading example | Behavior example | Integrated support example |
|---|---|---|---|---|
| Big ideas | Focus on key and critical components | Big ideas of early literacy<br>• Phonemic awareness<br>• Alphabetic principle<br>• Fluency with connected text<br>• Vocabulary<br>• Comprehension strategies | Social and emotional learning<br>• Self-awareness<br>• Self-management<br>• Social awareness<br>• Relationship skills<br>• Responsible decision making<br><br>Schoolwide PBIS Expectations<br>• Be Safe<br>• Be Responsible<br>• Be Respectful | Directly connect behavior expectations to academic expectations (e.g., be responsible means engaging in class instruction). |
| Conspicuous strategies | Directly teaching strategies that are used by successful learners | Teach sounds of individual letters and then blend the sounds together to say the printed word. | Explicitly teach behavior expectations through examples and nonexamples connected to context; teach routines for responding to problems (e.g., bullying behavior). | Directly teach academic enabler skills (e.g., attending, engagement responses). |
| Mediated scaffolding | Providing guidance through prompting and fading of prompts | Point to letters for student to sound out and then slide finger across word to say it fast. | Post behavioral expectations as prompts; regular use of expectations as labels to describe behavior. | Prompt what the student should be doing (academic engagement) rather than not doing (problem behavior); schedule instruction to increase successful responding and reduce behavior problems. |

| | | | |
|---|---|---|---|
| Strategic integration | Previous learning applied to new, more complex content and contexts | Phonemic awareness is combined with alphabetic principle to promote fluency with connected text. | Behavior expectations are selected and taught to transfer to new settings and contexts (e.g., substitute teacher, field trip). | Teach students to use strategies learned in solving reading problems to apply to social problems (e.g., identifying context cues, understanding meaning). |
| Primed background knowledge | Linking current content to prior knowledge and experiences | Connect vocabulary instruction to student's existing vocabulary and understanding. | Use student's previous experiences to better understand rationale for using prosocial behavior. | Make connections from concepts previously learned in one area (e.g., content from story) as background knowledge for another area (e.g., importance of responsibility in social situations). |
| Judicious review | Planful and periodic review of skills and knowledge | Review vocabulary terms at end of initial lesson and also periodically based on student performance. | Review behavior expectations after each school vacation period or before common "spikes" in problem behavior; precorrect prior to challenging settings. | Monitor student performance within the instructional setting to assess need for review of both academic *and* behavior skills. |

*Note.* Based on Coyne, Kame'enui, and Carnine (2007).

PRINCIPLE 4: STRATEGIC INTEGRATION

The principle of strategic integration means to combine and sequence instructional components to increase student understanding in a broader and more meaningful way. It is accomplished by helping students understand critical features of previous learning that leads to the new learning. For example, after instruction is provided on various big ideas (as identified above), these big ideas are combined for deeper learning—phonemic awareness is combined with alphabetic principle and developing fluency with connected text. On the behavior side, once behavior expectations are identified and defined, students will then practice these expectations in the natural settings where the behaviors should occur.

PRINCIPLE 5: PRIMED BACKGROUND KNOWLEDGE

Learning is optimized when teachers connect the current lesson to previous knowledge. This connection provides a brief review, makes new content more familiar, and links the lesson to previous success. For example, understanding the vocabulary of *mean, median,* and *mode* as well as the concept of *standard distribution* will help the learner better understand measures of central tendency. When students' learning histories vary greatly from the teacher's, it is especially important to bridge the content to their background knowledge (Chaparro, Nese, & McIntosh, 2015). For behavior, a brief discussion of previous experiences and situations when social–emotional skills could have been beneficial allows the new skill to be taught in connection with the student's learning history. Such priming can enhance motivation to learn.

PRINCIPLE 6: JUDICIOUS REVIEW

We all know that frequent exposure helps students remember key concepts, but it is important to review not simply what has been taught, but to review it in a careful, purposeful manner. It is important to consider what content requires the most review and when the review should take place to maximize learning. A skillful instructor will consider student performance to evaluate and determine when review is beneficial. For example, after teaching the terms *transparent* and *opaque,* the instructor can monitor class discussions to assess any further need to review. In PBIS, students are taught behavior expectations at the beginning of the school year, but periodic review (in the form of booster lessons) is needed throughout the year. This review is most effective when it is based on data regarding periods when review is necessary (e.g., after vacation breaks), before changes in routines where difficulties may be anticipated (e.g., field trips, substitute teachers), or based on student needs. For example, teachers in kindergarten classes may review expectations every morning for the first few weeks of school to assist with school readiness.

## *Integrated Strategies*

An educator can use these common principles of instruction across academic and behavior instruction to increase effectiveness. Focusing on big ideas within an integrated MTSS model might involve directly connecting behavior expectations to desirable academic behaviors. For example, a behavior expectation to "be responsible" means not only following the school rules but also participating fully in academic instruction. The behavior expectation to "be prepared" is linked to having read assignments or completing homework prior to class discussion. In these two scenarios, effective behavior support makes academic instruction more efficient and effective. In addition, conspicuous strategies and mediated scaffolding can be used independently with either academic or behavior content. When we use these principles to help students to effectively and successfully learn academic content (particularly for activities that may have been difficult for them in the past), we can reduce interruptions and decrease the likelihood of escape-maintained problem behaviors. In an integrated approach, strategic integration becomes useful not only within a content area, but also across content areas. Developing prerequisite academic engagement behaviors (e.g., attending to teacher, requesting help, following directions) enhances academic success and becomes incompatible with unwanted behavior. Additionally, the principles help the teacher and student focus on what the student should be doing while providing preventive support to do it correctly, rather than spending time practicing errors in academic or behavior responding.

Consider the following example. In the classroom setting, we determine the universal supports (Tier 1 practices) associated with a content area (e.g., literacy, math, behavior). The universal reading program may focus on a 90-minute reading block using the district reading curriculum. This instruction would be connected with the universal behavior support program, which includes schoolwide behavior expectations. These expectations are then used within the classroom for mapping behavior expectations to classroom routines, such as turning in work or asking for help. Within Tier 1 interventions, the students are provided with quality instruction based on the principles and also explicitly taught how to interact during the instruction period using the strategies of mediated scaffolding and judicious review.

In addition to attending to principles of effective instruction in general, some specific Tier 1 strategies are particularly helpful in providing integrated academic and behavior support. Many of these strategies are based on the premise that maximizing both instructional time and student engagement will maximize student academic and behavior outcomes. It is important that educators use all available instructional time, and there is a critical difference between *time allocated for instruction* and *actual minutes spent in instruction*. Instructional time is reduced by behavior disruptions and transitions. Obviously, more instructional time equals more potential for academic engagement, which is a strong predictor of student achievement (Brophy, 1988; Fisher et al., 1981; Greenwood, Horton, & Utley, 2002; Wang, Haertel, & Walberg, 1997). The following strategies can help educators capitalize on time by understanding how Tier 1 behavior support can benefit academic outcomes, and vice versa.

## EFFECTIVE CLASSROOM MANAGEMENT PRACTICES

As described in Chapter 2, effective classroom behavior support can be considered a means to recover and utilize teacher time that might have been lost to addressing unwanted behavior. In addition, any strategies that can keep students in the classroom (as opposed to in time-out, in the principal's office, or serving a suspension) expose them to more instruction. To ensure that students receive quality instruction, teachers can use effective classroom PBIS strategies, such as defining, teaching, and acknowledging expected classroom behaviors to make the best use of instructional time. When behavior expectations are clear, teachers are free to provide quality instruction, and students can better attend to learning without interruption from unwanted behavior or fears of victimization (McIntosh, Chard, et al., 2006; McIntosh, Ty, & Miller, 2014). Moreover, schoolwide PBIS systems are more effective, more sustainable, and more equitable when classroom systems are implemented with fidelity (Childs, Kincaid, George, & Gage, in press; Mathews, McIntosh, Frank, & May, 2014; Tobin & Vincent, 2011).

## TEACHING CLASSROOM ROUTINES

Although most schools implementing PBIS include classrooms when they teach expectations across settings, there is an even greater benefit from teaching expectations not just for the classroom in general, but across separate settings and routines *within* classrooms. Expectations naturally vary based on the subject or mode of instruction, so "be respectful" often means *quiet talking* during group work but *no talking* during tests or teacher-led instruction. As a result, teaching expected behaviors for classroom activities (e.g., teacher-led instruction, group work, tests and quizzes), or routines (e.g., entering the classroom, getting materials, transitioning to new activities) is more effective than a blanket teaching of classroom expectations (Sprick, 2009). Figure 4.1 provides a typical classroom matrix that includes the schoolwide expectations (down the left side) and the activities or routines (listed across the top). The cells in the center include specific examples of how those broad expectations vary depending on each activity or routine. Explicit instruction in classroom routines is especially helpful in avoiding inadvertent misbehavior that would affect academic performance (e.g., failure to submit homework inde-

| Class Routines → / School Rules ↓ | Transitions | Independent Seat Work | Small-Group Activities | Teacher-Led Instruction |
|---|---|---|---|---|
| Be Respectful | • Use whisper voice<br>• Keep 8 inches between yourself and others in line | • Raise hand before talking<br>• Turn in work you are proud of | • Eyes on speaker<br>• Listen to each other<br>• Accept each other's answers | • Eyes on teacher<br>• Raise hand before talking |
| Be Responsible | • Start right on signal<br>• Put materials away | • Read and follow the directions<br>• Complete your own work | • Do your part<br>• Use time wisely | • Follow along<br>• Listen to teacher instructions<br>• Take notes |
| Be Safe | • Move quickly but safely<br>• Look out for others | • Sit with feet on the floor<br>• Stay in your space | • Keep objects out of hands<br>• Use materials carefully | • Sit with feet on the floor<br>• Keep objects out of hands |

**FIGURE 4.1.** Classwide behavior expectations matrix. From Fairbanks, Simonsen, and Sugai (2008). Adapted with permission from SAGE Publications.

| Getting Help |
|---|
| (How to ask for assistance with difficult tasks) |

| Teaching Examples |
|---|
| 1. When you're working on a math problem that you can't figure out, *raise your hand and wait until the teacher can help you.*<br>NONEXAMPLE: Raise hand and wave it around or call out.<br>2. You and a friend are working together on a science experiment but you are missing a piece of lab equipment. *Ask the teacher for the missing equipment.*<br>NONEXAMPLE: Skip steps that use this equipment.<br>3. You are reading a passage and don't know the meaning of a word. *Ask your neighbor.*<br>NONEXAMPLE: Ask your neighbor for the word and then keep talking. |

| Student Activity |
|---|
| 1. Ask two or three students to give an <u>example of a situation</u> in which they needed help to complete a task, activity, or direction.<br>2. Ask students to <u>indicate or show</u> how they could *get help.*<br>3. <u>Encourage</u> and support appropriate discussion/responses. Minimize attention for inappropriate responses. |

| After the Lesson |
|---|
| (during the day) |

| |
|---|
| 1. Just before giving students a difficult or new task, direction, or activity, ask them to tell you how they could *get help* if they have difficulty (<u>precorrection</u>).<br>2. When you see students having difficulty with a task (e.g., off task, complaining), ask them to indicate that they *need help* (<u>reminder</u>).<br>3. Whenever a student *gets help* the correct way, provide <u>specific praise</u> to him or her. |

**FIGURE 4.2.** Classroom routine lesson plan.

pendently) and in minimizing transition time (McIntosh, Herman, Sanford, McGraw, & Florence, 2004). A sample classroom routine lesson plan is provided in Figure 4.2.

## INCREASING OPPORTUNITIES TO RESPOND

Once effective behavior support practices are in place and the expectations for classroom activities and routines have been taught and practiced, it is important to consider academic instructional practices that maximize success. In other words, when we recover valuable instructional time lost through behavior disruptions, we need to use that time wisely. One strategy that enhances academic engagement, which increases achievement and reduces the likelihood of problem behavior, is increasing students' *opportunities to respond.* Providing students with frequent opportunities to respond to questions from the teacher, as well as feedback to encourage correct responding, makes students more active participants in the lesson, helps students build fluency, and allows teachers to check understanding or skills to see if it is time to move on. It is important for teachers to encourage students to respond so that additional practice is actually taking place. It is also important for teachers to monitor student responding carefully so that correct responding is acknowledged and errors are corrected.

Some examples of providing more practice might include choral (verbal) responses with the whole group, in which all students answer a question or practice a skill component in unison. A variation involves students writing responses on personal dry-erase boards, with all students displaying their responses at the same time following a teacher cue. Additionally, teachers may "randomly" call on individual students to respond by asking the question first and then identifying the student who is to answer. When we increase opportunities to respond by asking more questions but call on students in a predictable order (e.g., down each row), students easily learn when they can ignore instruction—which defeats the purpose of providing more opportunities to respond. Instead, when no student knows who is going to be asked next, each student needs to be ready to respond, which increases practice dramatically. This technique also provides the added advantage of enabling the teacher to call more frequently on students who may need additional practice or support in staying engaged, without overtly identifying that they are receiving more support. As students become more engaged in instruction, they are also less likely to engage in unwanted behavior.

## INCORPORATING PEER-MEDIATED INSTRUCTION

Another approach for increasing opportunities to respond is to teach students to instruct each other. This set of strategies involves pairing students or using small groups of students to provide more frequent opportunities to respond than a single teacher could ever manage (MacKay, Andreou, & Ervin, 2009). Students often take turns being the "teacher" and "student" so that each student has the chance to respond to questions. Peer-mediated instruction is generally better for providing additional practice and building fluency in skills that students have already acquired, as opposed to new or challenging content. Peer-mediated sessions can be fit into "free spaces" during the day to solidify teacher-led instruction in a range of content areas.

Peer-mediated instruction programs are most effective when they are highly structured and students are taught the peer-mediated instructional procedures. Preparing students for this approach involves teaching specific roles, the use of timers, and even the use of scripts for students to follow. By increasing structure, even complicated instructional procedures (e.g., error correction) can be delivered accurately by students. The structure also reduces misbehavior that can come from unclear directions and unsupervised academic time. In fact, in many effective programs, the first lesson focuses entirely on establishing the routines needed for effective peer-mediated instruction, without academic content.

Peer-mediated instruction is a beneficial integrated strategy because academic and social–emotional instruction can occur at the same time. Through one-on-one interactions with peers, students have enhanced academic engagement and learn skills of teamwork and coaching at the same time as practicing academic skills. They can also access peer attention for appropriate academic and behavior responses, which can motivate some students more than simply receiving teacher attention.

A number of resources are available for implementing peer-mediated instruction. In addition to free online materials (e.g., *http://interventioncentral.com/htmdocs/interventions/rdngfluency/prtutor.php*), specific programs have been developed and validated as well. One example is classwide peer tutoring (*www.specialconnections.ku.edu/~kucrl/cgibin/drupal/?q=instruction/classwide_peer_tutoring*). The classwide peer tutoring program is designed to double the amount of opportunities to respond than a student might receive in teacher-led instruction. Another is peer-assisted learning strategies (PALS; *http://kc.vanderbilt.edu/pals*). PALS has been shown to be effective for a range of academic and social outcomes, including improved academic engagement, academic skills, decreased problem behavior, and improved social standing (Barton-Arwood et al., 2005; L. S. Fuchs, Fuchs, Yazdian, & Powell, 2002; Locke & Fuchs, 1995; Sutherland & Snyder, 2007).

## UTILIZING UNIVERSAL DESIGN FOR LEARNING

It is challenging for educators to teach classrooms of diverse learners where there may be a difference of several grade levels of academic skills within the same class (Coyne et al., 2007). At the same time, presenting students with academic material that is too challenging for them increases the likelihood of problem behavior (Filter & Horner, 2009; McIntosh, Horner, et al., 2008). *Universal design for learning* (Hall et al., 2012) is a helpful concept to enhance success in diverse classrooms. One key principle is that practices that are critical for supporting students with additional needs may also benefit all students. For example, focused identification of the main ideas of a lesson helps everyone achieve the desired outcomes of the academic lesson.

An aspect of universal design for learning that is particularly helpful for integrated support is that of systematically varying task difficulty to increase success (Archer & Hughes, 2011; Carnine, Silbert, Kame'enui, Tarver, & Jungjohann, 2006). During teacher-led reading instruction, for example, teachers can guide students through more challenging content because they can carefully monitor student responding to minimize practicing errors. During independent work, it is more important that the task is structured for success (e.g., the content is at an easier level than teacher-led content) as a means of increasing success, decreasing frustration, and preventing the repeated practice of errors—which will all decrease the likelihood of problem behavior. It is also important to vary instructional techniques across academic content areas. For example, math instruction may require increased instructional support as compared to reading, due to the inherent motivational components of a storyline (Gersten, 2013).

## INCLUDING SOCIAL AND EMOTIONAL CONTENT IN LITERACY AND SOCIAL STUDIES OR HISTORY

In addition to changing the academic environment, it may be possible to infuse behavior lessons into the content of academic instruction. Although it is not inconceivable to embed behavior support content into science or math lessons, albeit awkwardly (e.g., "Dave has taken two deep breaths to calm down. How many more deep breaths does he need to get to five?"), it is more logical to consider how social lessons can be built into lessons in reading (e.g., narrative passages) or historical events. There are two promising strategies for doing so. The first is simply to select materials or content that includes social or emotional lessons (i.e., "morals"). Table 4.2 includes a list of children's literature that addresses a range of social and emotional themes. Teachers can use these resources preventively, as part of booster lessons on behavior expectations, or in response to classroom events or patterns of behavior. The second is to use comprehension or discussion questions that focus on social and emotional behavior when reading. For example, when reading a passage, the teacher might ask the following sample questions:

1. "How do you think that made her feel?" (to teach empathy)
2. "What do you think is going to happen next?" (to teach cause and effect)
3. "How could he have done things differently?" (to teach problem solving)

**TABLE 4.2. Teaching Social and Emotional Competencies through Children's Literature: A Brief Book List**

General social and emotional competencies

- Aesop. *The Ant and the Grasshopper*
- Aspinwall, Alicia. *Please*
- Cannon, Janell. *Stellaluna*
- Carle, Eric. *The Grouchy Ladybug*
- Demi. *The Empty Pot*
- Derolf, Shane. *The Crayon Box That Talked*
- Galdone, Paul. *The Little Red Hen*
- McDermott, Gerald. *Anasasi the Spider*
- Mora, Pat. *The Rainbow Tulip*
- Obligado, Lilian. *Three Little Kittens*
- Phister, Marcus. *The Rainbow Fish*
- Rathman, Peggy. *Officer Buckle and Gloria*
- Rey, Margret, and Rey, H. A. *Curious George Visits the Police Station*
- Scienscka, Jon. *The True Story of the Three Little Pigs*
- Stapleton, John T. *The Littlest Mermaid*

Self-awareness and self-management

- Aesop. *The Boy and the Nuts*
- Aesop. *The Fox and the Crow*
- Aesop. *The Frogs at the Well*
- Aesop. *The Goose That Laid the Golden Egg*
- Cook, Julia. *My Mouth Is a Volcano!*
- Dismondy, Maria, and Hiatt, Kathy. *Spaghetti in a Hot Dog Bun: Having the Courage to Be Who You Are*
- Gaeddert, LouAnn. *Noisy Nancy Norris*
- Gilbert, Nan. *Champions Don't Cry*
- MacLachlan, Patricia. *Sarah Plain and Tall*
- Reynolds, Peter. *The Dot*
- Sendak, Maurice. *Where the Wild Things Are*
- stone, elberta h. *I'm Glad I'm Me*
- Viorst, Judith. *Alexander and the Terrible, Horrible, No Good Very Bad Day*

Social awareness

- Blake, Olive. *Mystery of the Lost Letter*
- Butterworth, William. *Leroy and the Old Man*
- Byars, Betsy. *The House of Wings*
- Chinn, Karen. *Sam and the Lucky Money*
- Cohen, Miriam. *No Good in Art*
- De La Peña, Matt. *Last Stop on Market Street*
- Frank, Anne. *The Diary of Anne Frank*
- Krull, Kathleen, and Morales, Yuyi. *Harvesting Hope: The Story of Cesar Chavez*
- Levinson, Cynthia. *We've Got a Job: The 1963 Birmingham Children's March*
- Mahy, M. *The Seven Chinese Brothers*
- Mathis, Sharon Bell. *The Hundred Penny Box*
- Rathmann, Peggy. *Ruby the Copy Cat*
- Raven, Margot Theis, and Ellison, Chris. *Let Them Play*

*(continued)*

**TABLE 4.2.** *(continued)*

- Smith, Dennis. *The Little Fire Engine That Saved a City*
- Talley, Carol, and Paine, Penelope Colville. *Clarissa*

Relationship skills

- Allard, Harry. *Miss Nelson Is Missing*
- Berson, Harold. *Pop Goes the Turnip*
- Brenner, Barbara. *Mr. Tall and Mr. Small*
- Brett, Jan. *Berlioz the Bear*
- Brown, Laurene. *How to Be a Friend*
- Brown, Marcia Wise. *Stone Soup*
- Ernst, Lisa Campbell. *Zinna and Dot*
- Evans, Katherine. *A Bundle of Sticks*
- Galdone, Paul. *The Little Red Hen*
- Hoban, Lillian. *A Bargain for Frances*
- Lionni, Leo. *Swimmy*
- Lord, John Vernon. *The Giant Jam Sandwich*
- McCloud, Carol. *Have You Filled a Bucket Today? A Guide to Daily Happiness for Kids*
- Mitchell, Margarie King. *Uncle Jed's Barbershop*
- Silverman, Erica. *The Big Pumpkin*

Responsible decision making

- Abolafia, Yossi. *Harry in Trouble*
- Brown, Marc. *Arthur's Pet Business*
- Dahlstedt, Marden. *The Terrible Wave*
- Day, A. *Frank and Ernest*
- Deedy, Carmen. *The Library Dragon*
- Gardiner, John. *Stone Fox*
- Green, Norma. *The Hole in the Dike*
- Hoban, Lillian. *Awful Thursday*
- Javernick, Ellen. *What If Everybody Did That?*
- Levinson, Cynthia. *We've Got a Job: The 1963 Birmingham Children's March*
- Seuss, Dr. *Horton Hatches the Egg*
- Seuss, Dr. *The Lorax*
- Silverstein, Shel. *The Giving Tree*
- Wells, Rosemary. *Fritz and the Mess Fairy*

Bullying

- Lovell, Patty. *Stand Tall, Molly Lou Melon*
- O'Neill, Alexis. *The Recess Queen*
- Seuss, Dr. *The Sneetches*
- Sornson, Bob, and Dismondy, Maria. *The Juice Box Bully: Empowering Kids to Stand Up For Others*

Fairness

- Berenstain, Stan, and Berenstain, Jan. *The Berenstain Bears and the Slumber Party*
- Berenstain, Stan, and Berenstain, Jan. *The Berenstain Bears Go Out for the Team*
- Blume, Judy. *Pain and the Great One*
- Christian, Mary. *The Green Thumb Thief*

*(continued)*

**TABLE 4.2.** *(continued)*

- Clymer, Eleanor. *My Brother Stevie*
- Cohen, Marion. *Bee My Valentine*
- Cosgrove, Stephen. *Sniffles*
- Demi. *The Empty Pot*
- Foreman, Michael. *Moose*
- Fritz, Jean. *The Cabin Faced West*
- McGuire, Leslie. *This Farm Is a Mess*
- O'Brien, Robert. *Mrs. Frisby and the Rats of NIMH*
- Peck, Robert N. *Soup*
- Peck, Robert N. *Soup and Me*
- Pfeffer, Susan. *Kid Power*
- Pinkwater, Daniel. *The Big Orange Splot*
- Rockwell, Thomas. *How to Eat Fried Worms*
- Seuss, Dr. *The 500 Hats of Bartholomew Cubbins*
- Siiteri, Helen. *Adventures of Nicolas*
- Viorst, Judith. *Alexander, Who Used to Be Rich Last Sunday*
- Ward, Lynd. *The Biggest Bear*

Honesty

- Aesop. *The Boy Who Cried Wolf*
- Alexander, Lloyd. *The Truthful Harp*
- Avi. *Nothing but the Truth*
- Bauer, Marion Dane. *On My Honor*
- Berenstain, Stan, and Berenstain, Jan. *The Berenstain Bears and the Truth*
- Brown, Marc. *The True Francine*
- Bunting, Eve. *A Day of Work*
- Calmenson, Stephanie. *The Principal's New Clothes*
- Choroao, Kay. *Molly's Lies*
- Cole, Joanna. *The Secret Box*
- Coleman, H.C. *Tell Me No Lies*
- Collodi, Carlo. *Pinocchio*
- Demi. *The Empty Pot*
- Girion, Barbara. *Misty and Me*
- Havill, Juanita. *Jamaica's Find*
- Hoban, Russell. *A Bargain for Frances*
- Hughes, Dean. *Honestly, Myron*
- Ness, Evaline. *Sam, Bangs, and Moonshine*
- Turkle, Brinton. *The Adventures of Obadiah*
- Weinman, Marjorie. *A Big Fat Enormous Lie*
- White, E. B. *The Trumpet of the Swan*
- Wylie, David, and Wylie, Joanne. *A Big Fish Story*

Kindness

- Bang, Molly. *The Paper Crane*
- Brett, Jan. *The Wild Christmas Reindeer*
- Cazet, Denys. *A Fish in His Pocket*
- Cole, Brock. *The King at the Door*
- Fleischman, Sid. *The Scarebird*

*(continued)*

**TABLE 4.2.** *(continued)*

- Heyward, Du Bose. *The Country Bunny and the Little Gold Shoes*
- Rylant, Cynthia. *Silver Packages: An Appalachian Christmas Story*
- San Souci, Robert D. *The Talking Eggs*
- Seuss, Dr. *Horton Hears a Who!*
- Steptoe, John. *Murfaro's Beautiful Daughters*
- Whitcher, Susan. *Moonfall*
- Zolotow, Charlotte. *I Know a Lady*

Patience

- Erickson, Karen. *Waiting My Turn*
- Ets, Marie Hall. *Play with Me*
- Kibby, Marsha. *My Grammy*
- Kraus, Robert. *The Carrot Seed*
- de Larrea, Victoria. *Waiting for Mama*
- Rounds, Glen. *The Blind Colt*
- Steiner, Charlotte. *What's the Hurry, Harry?*
- Weiss, Nicki. *Waiting*
- Wells, Rosemary. *Max's Breakfast*

Punctuality

- Allen, Jeffrey. *Mary Alice, Operator Number 9*
- Boyd, Selma. *I Met a Polar Bear*
- Burningham, John. *John Patrick Norman McHennessy: The Boy Who Was Always Late*
- Friedrich, Priscilla. *The Easter Bunny That Overslept*
- Grossman, Bill. *The Guy Who Was Five Minutes Late*
- Hoban, Lillian. *Bedtime for Frances*
- Hoff, Sid. *Henrietta, the Early Bird*
- Sewell, Marcia, and Krasilovsky, Phyllis. *The Man Who Tried to Save Time*

*Note.* Adapted with permission from Florida's Positive Behavior Support Project (2004).

Historical events, such as interactions leading up to wars (e.g., World War I) and injustices (e.g., slavery, the Trail of Tears) or inspiring events (e.g., the civil rights movement, native language revitalization), are good examples of history class content that can be used to teach respect, responsibility, perspective taking, and problem solving. Students can describe how using the social and emotional competencies taught through PBIS may have aided understanding and prevented challenges.

## Tier 2: Secondary Supports

In contrast to Tier 1 supports, which are provided in the same way to all students, Tier 2 supports are added based on students' presenting needs. Because Tier 2 supports are meant to supplement and not replace Tier 1 supports (Baker et al., 2010), Tier 1 systems that provide high-quality supports in both content areas reduce the need for Tier 2 supports and provide more options for effective and efficient integrated Tier 2 interventions. In this sense, quality Tier 1 practices provide a base of support, meaning that students already receive at least some support in both academics and behavior. When considering Tier 2 interventions, it then becomes just a matter of identifying which practices might supplement Tier 1 supports.

Most schools already have a few Tier 2 academic and behavior practices in place, sometimes more informal than formal (i.e., systematized). Common Tier 2 practices range from brief individual or small-group instruction (academic or social) to accommodations that change the environment (e.g., point card, change in materials or level of work), and are categorized as either academic or behavior interventions (Yong & Cheney, 2013). As described at the start of this chapter, adding another layer of integrated interventions on top of these existing ones (particularly if existing interventions are systematized and effective) is more likely to overload the system than provide benefits. Instead, thinking again about *smarter integration* allows us to examine what already exists and identify how some practices may inherently provide both academic and behavior support simultaneously.

## Assessing Student Needs for Tier 2 Supports

A foundation of smarter integration includes analyzing student needs to select the best match for Tier 2 supports. There are four possibilities of student needs as illustrated in Figure 4.3, and each corresponds to a different approach for support:

1. *Academic problems only.* One category of concern is the student who is having solely academic challenges. An example would be the student who has challenges in understanding and applying math concepts. Difficulties may be seen only in terms of math content errors, but there may not be any related behavior difficulties. As such, only academic intervention is warranted.

2. *Behavior problems only.* A student may need support only for his behavior and not academics. An example might be a student who regularly harasses other students in the hall during passing periods to get attention from peers, but the behavior is not related to academic difficulties. In these situations, only a behavior intervention is needed.

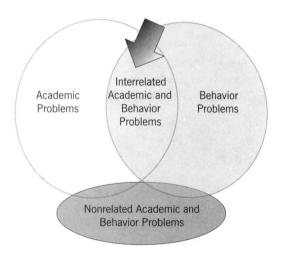

**FIGURE 4.3.** Four possible student needs based on type of problem.

**3.** *Nonrelated academic and behavior problems.* A third category of concern is the student who exhibits unwanted behavior and also has difficulties with academics, but problems in one area are not necessarily linked to problems in another. For example, a student may push other students at recess to obtain her preferred swing and also may have difficulty learning and using new vocabulary words. Although she is experiencing problems in both areas, they do not appear to be related to each other (and they occur in different routines as well). For this student, separate academic and behavior interventions may be needed, and the team may choose to implement them either simultaneously or in sequence, to build on successes and minimize task overload for the adults.

**4.** *Interrelated academic and behavior problems.* The final category involves a student whose problem behavior is directly related to academic problems. For example, a student who has difficulty reading grade-level material may engage in unwanted behavior that results in escape from the academic task. Yelling at the teacher during reading group may result in the teacher removing the student from the classroom. The unfortunate cycle that occurs in this scenario is that the student, who needs more instruction and academic practice, actually ends up with less because he is removed from the instructional setting, and as his peers build skills, the reading tasks become more and more difficult (McIntosh, Horner, et al., 2008). The student is facing challenges in both literacy and behavior, and although separate interventions could be effective, an integrated intervention that combines both academic and behavior support—or even the right academic intervention all by itself—may be more efficient, as well as more likely to work.

The first three possibilities described above are somewhat straightforward and fit nicely into siloed (i.e., independent) academic and behavior RTI systems. Students can be placed into the available Tier 2 academic or behavior practices as their needs suggest. As described in Chapter 2, identifying and addressing these students' needs as early as possible can help prevent their eventual movement into the fourth possibility, where the initial problem leads to interrelated challenges. It is for these interrelated problems, the fourth possibility, that integrated systems are most useful.

## Integrated Tier 2 Intervention

When considering the primary goal of efficient support at Tier 2, it is often best to utilize existing academic or behavior interventions that, by their nature, also provide a moderate level of support in other content areas. Such information is helpful in planning support that is effective yet minimizes disruption to Tier 1 support. For example, by selecting one practice that effectively supports multiple needs, a student may spend more time learning with her peers in the general education setting, rather than being pulled from class for two separate interventions. We also avoid the problem of adding more and more interventions to a fully loaded school. The process of instructional grouping is always complex, and adding instructional groups to target integrated challenges would add considerable energy to planning and management.

Instead, we suggest that integrated support may best be considered through differentiating instruction for students within existing instructional grouping structures. When supporting students with Tier 2 needs in both academics and behavior, we recommend placing students into small-group instruction for their primary area of *academic concern*. The teacher then adds behavior support strategies for the students in the small group based on the function of their behaviors, which is the most important data to drive integrated intervention selection (McIntosh, Campbell, Carter, & Dickey, 2009). In the examples below, we categorize some promising Tier 2 academic and behavior support practices that can provide integrated support based on function of behavior (see Table 4.3).

## INTERVENTIONS FOR STUDENTS WHO ENGAGE IN UNWANTED BEHAVIOR TO OBTAIN ADULT ATTENTION DURING INSTRUCTION

For students with attention-maintained behavior, it is important to provide access to adult attention for correct academic and social responding through three steps. First, provide students with brief additional lessons in behavior expectations to provide a better understanding of acceptable behavior and illustrate appropriate ways to obtain adult attention. For example, the student and teacher would review how to be respectful and responsible in interacting with the teacher during instruction as a short booster lesson of the classroom PBIS system. Second, use an instructional practice in the needed academic content area with many inherent opportunities for student responding and feedback from the teacher. For literacy, an example might be REWARDS (Reading Excellence, Word Attack, and Rate Development Strategies) by Archer, Gleason, and Vachon (2006). Increased teacher attention can be delivered to the student for following directions, with attention minimized for unwanted behavior. Third, arrange the instructional environment so that this additional adult attention is easy to provide and not disruptive to others. For example, the student could be placed closer to the instructor or taught to use a signal (e.g., hold a card or gesture) to request help quietly (Paine, Radicchi, Rosellini, Deutchman, & Darch, 1983). In addition, it may be helpful to add common Tier 2 behavior support practices to add structure and adult feedback, such as check-in/check-out (also known as the *behavior education program*; Crone et al., 2010). Check-in/check-out provides a systematic process for students to receive adult attention through increased feedback on their behavior through the use of daily progress reports.

## INTERVENTIONS FOR STUDENTS WHO ENGAGE IN UNWANTED BEHAVIOR TO OBTAIN PEER ATTENTION DURING INSTRUCTION

For students seeking peer attention, the previous interventions for adult attention could be used with modifications to provide more attention from peers in socially appropriate ways. Expectations, especially those for interacting with peers, can be taught and practiced with a respected peer. It is helpful for students in this support category to receive peer-mediated instruction (as described in the Tier 1 section) in the identified academic area of need. Peer-mediated instruction involves many opportunities for student responses and peer feedback, with structured peer attention for correct academic responding and prosocial behavior. These programs often also utilize group reinforcement strategies, which can provide further peer interactions for academic engagement. Environmentally, the whole class or small group can be taught to ignore any unwanted behavior of peers and continue with their work to help minimize attention for misbehavior and allow increased focus on the academic lesson. It is also helpful to seat

**TABLE 4.3. Integrated Tier 2 Practices Based on Function of Behavior**

In an integrated model, students are placed into small instructional groups based on their primary academic instructional needs. Then, accommodations and differentiation of instruction for social behavior are based on the following considerations.

| Scenario | Possible accommodations/differentiation |
|---|---|
| 1. Student engages in unwanted behavior to obtain adult attention during instruction. | • Teach, practice, and acknowledge behavior expectations, with specific focus on appropriate ways to obtain adult attention.<br>• Provide increased opportunities for student responding and feedback from instructor.<br>• Arrange the instructional environment so that appropriate adult-seeking attention is easy and not disruptive to others (e.g., seating near teacher, providing a "help signal" for independent work).<br>• Enroll in check-in/check-out (CICO). |
| 2. Student engages in unwanted behavior to obtain peer attention during instruction. | • Teach, practice, and acknowledge behavior expectations with peers, with specific focus on appropriate ways to obtain peer attention.<br>• Provide increased opportunities for peer-mediated instruction (e.g., peer tutoring, group work).<br>• Teach peers to ignore unwanted behavior and acknowledge appropriate, prosocial behavior.<br>• Arrange the instructional environment to minimize peer disruptions (e.g., seating changes). |
| 3. Student engages in unwanted behavior to avoid or escape interactions with adults or peers during instruction. | • Briefly teach and practice behavior expectations and acknowledge with responses that are reinforcing for the student.<br>• Provide opportunities for independent structured instruction (e.g., programmed instruction, computer-aided instruction).<br>• Teach needed social and emotional skills. |
| 4. Student engages in unwanted behavior to avoid or escape academic tasks. | • Develop skills in specific deficit areas.<br>• Provide instruction at student success level.<br>• Use evidence-based interventions to address deficit areas.<br>• Add reinforcement system to reward engagement.<br>• Enroll in Breaks are Better CICO modification. |
| 5. Student engages in unwanted behavior due to deficits in academic enabler skills. | • Teach, practice, and acknowledge behavior expectations, with specific focus on appropriate classroom behavior.<br>• Teach specific academic enabler skills (e.g., attending, organization, engagement).<br>• Enroll in CICO. |

the student near peers who can model appropriate behavior and away from those who are likely to respond to misbehavior, as well as monitor peer models to ensure high-quality interactions.

## INTERVENTIONS FOR STUDENTS WHO ENGAGE IN UNWANTED BEHAVIOR TO AVOID OR ESCAPE INTERACTIONS WITH ADULTS OR PEERS DURING INSTRUCTION

Conversely, students may engage in behavior to avoid or escape interactions with other students or adults. These patterns of behavior often arise from academic skill deficits and the resulting fear of making mistakes in front of others. The steps for intervention in these situations still include instruction in behavior expectations for when the student is in a group setting. However, supplemental academic instruction can be delivered through self-instruction or computer-aided instruction. Such instruction allows for skill development without the social interactions that may cause challenges. For example, following a period of small-group instruction, the student may have some time to work independently to further skill development. Some programmed instructional strategies include having students systematically work through problems on their own and then immediately check their work by comparing it to the answers provided. Another example, Read Naturally (*www.readnaturally.com*), has a computer-based component that focuses on building reading fluency and comprehension without social interaction. However, if the student lacks the social skills to interact effectively with others, social skills instruction will be necessary so the student is prepared for successful participation with others in a group. One example of a commercially available social skills program with strong supporting evidence is Second Step: A Violence Prevention Curriculum (Committee for Children, 1997). This program can be used as an intervention at Tier 1 for all students, Tier 2 for some students, or in combination, where all students receive Tier 1 instruction and some receive additional instruction or practice at Tier 2 (Merrell & Gueldner, 2010).

## INTERVENTIONS FOR STUDENTS WHO ENGAGE IN UNWANTED BEHAVIOR TO AVOID OR ESCAPE ACADEMIC TASKS

Although sometimes unwanted behavior arises from tasks that are too easy or boring, students who engage in behaviors to escape academic tasks typically lack the skills necessary to complete them. In this situation, we need to identify the specific skill deficit that is contributing to academic difficulties and provide instruction to remediate it. The goal is to strengthen academic skills (or fluency with these skills) until the task is no longer aversive. Once the task becomes easier, avoidance or escape becomes unnecessary. To do so, it is necessary to remediate the specific deficit area that occasions unwanted behavior. For example, a reading fluency intervention is unlikely to reduce the behavior for a student who is struggling with letter–sound identification.

The strategies for increasing opportunities to respond described as *Tier 1 integrated strategies* can be used as differentiated instruction at Tier 2 to improve academic skills. However, because the function of the behavior is to avoid or escape academic tasks, it is important to present tasks at the appropriate level or in such a way that the task is not aversive enough to evoke the behavior. It may also be necessary to add a structured reinforcement system to tip the scales in favor of academic task persistence. In addition, it may be worth considering implementing a task avoidance adaptation to check-in/check-out, called *Breaks are Better* (Boyd & Anderson,

2013). In this Tier 2 practice, students are taught a standardized break routine to use when academic demands become too aversive.

## INTERVENTIONS FOR STUDENTS WHO ENGAGE IN UNWANTED BEHAVIOR DUE TO DEFICITS IN ACADEMIC ENABLER BEHAVIORS

A final scenario for integrated academic and behavior needs involves the lack of the prerequisite skills needed to engage in instruction (e.g., organization, mindset, attending). These skills are variously called *academic enablers* or *academic facilitators* and have been defined as attitudes and behaviors that facilitate student participation in—and benefit from—academic instruction in the classroom (DiPerna, Volpe, & Elliott, 2002). When students are unprepared for the instructional setting, a chain of escalating problems may occur. For example, a student may not have materials ready or prerequisite work completed. Corrective feedback from the teacher may then evoke the student's unwanted behavior, which disrupts instruction and possibly results in his or her removal from the classroom, further reducing access to instruction. In these cases, it is important to teach these underlying skills. An example of such a curriculum is Skills for School Success (Archer & Gleason, 1990). This program provides students with strategies to improve their organization skills and includes intermediate (grades 3–6) and advanced (grade 7 and higher) versions. Once these skills are acquired, practices such as check-in/check-out can provide the additional feedback and incentives that may be needed to ensure their regular use.

## *Tier 3: Tertiary Supports*

Within a multi-tiered approach, less severe problems should be addressed through universal prevention (Tier 1) and strategic intervention at Tier 2 supports. Once we reach Tier 3, the student's needs are such that Tier 1 or 2 supports are insufficient to promote success. Those students who continue to have difficulties within comprehensive MTSS models will require our most powerful interventions—provided by our most skilled interventionists—to address the intensity and severity of their needs. Unfortunately, there are no ways to cut corners in providing effective Tier 3 support. In these situations, programs need to be intensive and tailored to the student's specific circumstances. Although there are common Tier 3 intervention strategies, each support plan incorporates interventions in a unique and specific manner to best address the individual student's needs. Table 4.4 provides some resources for developing Tier 3 support plans for either academic or behavior challenges.

In integrated MTSS models, it is even more critical than in Tiers 1 and 2 to consider the interactive relationship between academics and behavior. Schools are often arranged to provide independent systems of support for academics and behavior (e.g., separate referral procedures, separate teams, separate support plans). This separation can create problems in (1) alignment of supports, (2) responsibility for educating students as whole individuals, and (3) comprehensiveness of support plans. Separate interventions developed for academic and behavior problems may demand more time and attention than can be delivered, resulting in poor implementation of both. In situations in which a student has interrelated academic and behavior difficulties, it is important that the intervention plan focuses on academic problems that contribute to the behavior problems, and vice versa.

**TABLE 4.4. Resources for Developing Tier 3 Support Plans**

There are many excellent resources for selecting Tier 3 interventions for academic or social behavior challenges based on assessment data. Each of these resources focuses primarily on either academic or behavior support.

Tier 3 Academic Support

Archer, A. L., & Hughes, C. A. (2011). *Explicit instruction: Effective and efficient teaching.* New York: Guilford Press.

Although explicit instruction can help students be successful at each tier of support, it is particularly important for students receiving Tier 3 supports. This book provides information for designing lessons and organizing and delivering instruction. The strategies are useful for any grade level and content area.

O'Connor, R. E., & Vadasy, P. F. (Eds.). (2013). *Handbook of reading interventions.* New York: Guilford Press.

This handbook presents evidence-based approaches to address struggling readings. Chapters provide strategies for key areas of reading interventions, including phonemic awareness, phonic interventions, vocabulary, fluency, and comprehension. Interventions are presented for preschool literacy instruction, older students, English language learners, and students with learning disabilities.

Carnine, D. W., Silbert, J., Kame'enui, E. J., Tarver, S. G., & Jungjohann, K. (2006). *Teaching struggling and at-risk readers: A direct instruction approach.* Columbus, OH: Pearson.

This text provides a comprehensive description of explicit instruction principles and practices for beginning and intermediate readers. Although the domain is specific to reading and prereading, the content applies to all academic (and even social) domains.

Daly, E. J., Neugebauer, S., Chafouleas, S. M., & Skinner, C. H. (2015). *Interventions for reading problems: Designing and evaluating effective strategies* (2nd ed.). New York: Guilford Press.

Daly and colleagues lay out a systematic process for diagnosing reading problems to determine whether a student does not have adequate skills ("can't do" problem) or is not motivated ("won't do" problem). These results are then linked to interventions for the domain of reading.

Hall, S. L. (2012). *I've DIBEL'd, now what? Next edition: Designing interventions with DIBELS data.* Longmont, CO: Sopris West Educational Services.

If teams are using DIBELS to assess early literacy, this book provides helpful guidance in taking those results and designing small-group, individualized early literacy instruction. The author recommends specific intervention strategies to address common skill deficits that DIBELS results identify.

Shapiro, E. S. (2010). *Academic skills problems: Direct assessment and intervention* (4th ed.). New York: Guilford Press.

This book (and its associated workbook) provides a comprehensive guide to individual academic assessment across multiple domains and describes how to use these results to guide intervention selection and progress monitoring.

*(continued)*

**TABLE 4.4.** *(continued)*

Tier 3 Social Behavior Support

Crone, D. A., Hawken, L. S., & Horner, R. H. (2015). *Building positive behavior support systems in schools: Functional behavioral assessment* (2nd ed.). New York: Guilford Press.

Crone and Horner provide an approachable overview of school-based FBAs and behavior support planning. The book includes the *Functional Assessment Checklist: Teachers and Staff* (March et al., 2000), a research-validated brief interview tool for school personnel (McIntosh et al., 2008).

O'Neill, R. E., Albin, R. W., Storey, K., Horner, R. H., & Sprague, J. R. (2015). *Functional assessment and program development for problem behavior: A practical handbook* (3rd ed.). Independence, KY: Cengage Learning.

This newly updated text is an excellent resource for conducting FBAs and developing behavior support plans, particularly for individuals with more significant challenges and related health issues. The assessment process provided in the book includes a comprehensive interview tool and direct observation form.

Loman, S., Strickland-Cohen, M. K., Borgmeier, C., & Horner, R. H. (2013). *Basic FBA to BSP trainer's manual.* Eugene, OR: University of Oregon, Educational and Community Supports. Available at *www.pbis.org.*

This free resource is a manual with complete materials for training school personnel to complete "basic FBAs," which are relatively straightforward and can be completed by educators without extensive training. The second part of the training focuses on how to develop behavior support plans based on basic FBA results.

## The Importance of FBAs in Developing Effective Tier 3 Support Plans

The key driver in intervention selection for integrated Tier 3 plans is the function of behavior, as discussed in Chapter 3. Once the function is identified and confirmed through an FBA, a support team can brainstorm and select specific intervention strategies for a comprehensive support plan. Results of the FBA are used to create a competing pathways diagram (shown in Figure 4.4) and the specific predictors and consequences of unwanted behavior are used to select strategies that make the problem behavior irrelevant, inefficient, and ineffective (O'Neill et al., 2015). These goals are accomplished through environmental changes and teaching a student a functional skill that meets the same need as the unwanted behavior, but in a more socially acceptable manner (Loman et al., 2013).

## An Example of Integrated Tier 3 Support

The following case study (which follows from the case study in Chapter 3) describes different approaches to building Tier 3 support plans to address interrelated academic and behavior challenges.

Eddie is a third-grade student without any identified disabilities who can play guitar and enjoys playing team sports. He has been referred for behavior support by his teacher for chronic disruptive behavior in the classroom, despite repeated instruction and practice in prosocial behavior. Classroom observations indicate that he yells and threatens others when asked to read grade-level content. When he engages in this behavior, he is sent to a time-out desk in the corner of the room, where he immediately stops misbehaving. Recall that a review of his benchmark reading fluency data in Chapter 3 indicates that Eddie is actually reading far below his grade level, with significant skill deficits in decoding words. These results indicate that Eddie's unwanted behavior results from his academic skill deficits (see the preceding section, "Interventions for Students Who Engage in Unwanted Behavior to Avoid or Escape Academic Tasks"). We illustrate this process in the competing pathways diagram in Figure 4.4.

In any approach, the goal is for Eddie to complete his academic tasks successfully without engaging in unwanted behavior. To achieve this aim for him (and for all students), we work to implement adequate Tier 1 practices to promote academic and behavior success. We ensure that the core reading program is robust so that most students are successful. The core program should address the five big ideas of reading instruction as identified in the research. In addition, positive behavior is promoted through teaching, practicing, and acknowledging classroom behavior expectations, as well as providing instructional corrections for behavior errors. In Eddie's case, Tier 1 strategies are not enough to help him become successful in academic and behavior domains. Additionally, the frequency and intensity of his difficulties point to a need for support beyond Tier 2 interventions. As such, a Tier 3 function-based behavior intervention is developed for Eddie. This intervention can be developed in one of two ways: using the more common siloed approach, or using an integrated approach.

## SILOED APPROACH (FIGURE 4.4)

According to common, nonintegrated practice, the behavior support team may implement a function-based intervention with three components: prevention, teaching, and consequence

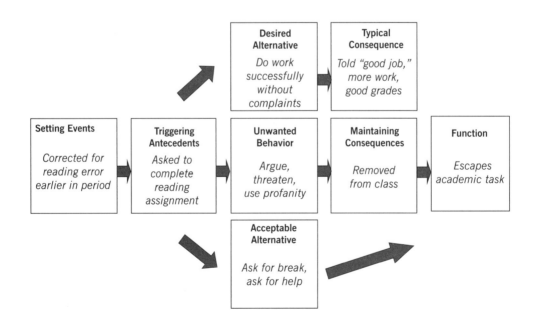

**FIGURE 4.4.** Competing pathways analysis of behavior.

strategies (see Crone et al., 2015, for a detailed guide to the process). The team could implement a strategy to prevent unwanted behavior by not providing him with grade-level reading material. That strategy may decrease the need for this behavior because it removes the aversive request that predicts unwanted behavior. Second, the team could teach an alternative response (asking for a break) that results in the same outcome as his unwanted behavior (escape). This plan is functional in that it is likely to reduce unwanted behavior because it provides Eddie with a more socially acceptable way to escape academic demands. The team could then use consequence strategies to ensure escape when breaks are taken correctly and prevent escape for unwanted behavior. The team is likely to be pleased because of the resulting reductions in such behavior. At the same time (but in isolation of behavior support considerations), the academic support team might implement a "double-dosing" approach where Eddie is provided with more of the same instruction with the hope that additional exposure and practice will result in improved reading proficiency. In this "integrated" plan, the behavior team has provided an intervention to reduce unwanted behavior, and the academic team has provided an intervention to increase academic skills. It seems that both areas are being supported.

So what's wrong with that approach? This plan is problematic because Eddie already engages in disruptive behavior to escape or avoid reading instruction. The addition of "more of the same" instruction and an encouraged use of breaks will most likely result in even further reduced access to academic instruction. A worrisome cycle develops in that Eddie needs additional instruction to be successful, but he engages in either unwanted or replacement behavior, either of which results in the removal of instruction. As a result, the teams have reduced unwanted behavior but not addressed the underlying issue of what make the academic task so aversive in the first place. A better intervention plan would address the same behavioral function while improving academic skills that make reading less aversive, thereby making avoidance of reading tasks unnecessary.

## INTEGRATED APPROACH (FIGURE 4.5)

An integrated intervention plan (see Figure 4.5) considers academic and behavior deficits at the same time, with a stronger focus on how they are related. Just as with typical support, it includes prevention, teaching, and consequence components. However, the components are more closely tied to Eddie's needs. Our immediate goal is to keep Eddie in the instructional environment so that further teaching can take place to improve his skills. As a result, he should not be given reading tasks in the same way as in the past, as is proposed in the siloed plan. Instead of simply avoiding grade-level reading tasks for Eddie, there would be a stronger emphasis on providing academic task demands at his level (e.g., easier content). Additionally, content can be presented in a way that is less threatening (e.g., the content is guided, prompted, and presented in smaller "chunks" by the instructor). Finally, there is a strong focus on firming up the prerequisite or requisite skills necessary for Eddie to be academically successful. As a result, Eddie is not simply being asked not to do hard work, but rather given tasks that are challenging, but less aversive, allowing for further academic development. In the plan's teaching components, we may still, if needed, teach the break procedure used in the previous plan. However, we add academic skill development as a stronger focus for the plan. This component involves academic instruction that is tailored to Eddie's specific skill deficits and is at his level (see Figure 4.6). Without this component, Eddie's skills will never develop, and reading will remain aversive, leading to further unwanted behavior or an excessive use of breaks whenever difficult tasks are provided to him.

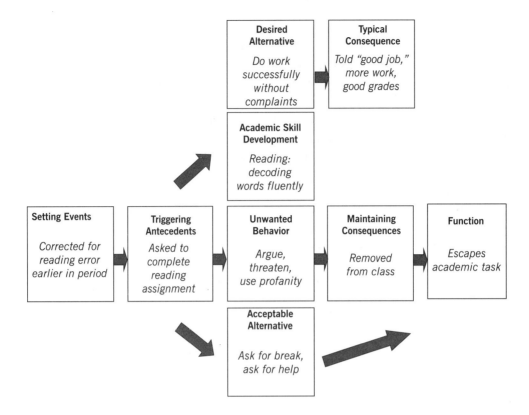

**FIGURE 4.5.** Integrated competing pathways analysis of academics and behavior.

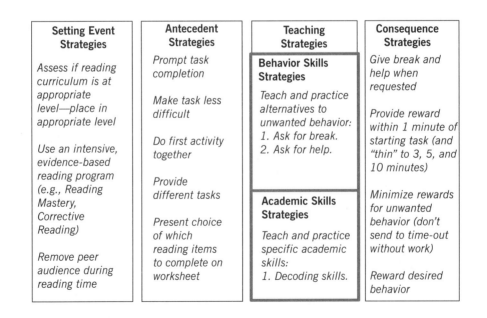

**FIGURE 4.6.** Possible intervention strategies based on integrated competing pathways analysis of academics and behavior.

Once the competing pathways diagram is developed and possible strategies are brainstormed, the strategies are then narrowed based on several decision rules (Albin, Lucyshyn, Horner, & Flannery, 1996). First, we need to consider the likelihood of each strategy's effectiveness in order to eliminate those that are not consistent with the FBA. Next, we also must consider whether we have adequate resources available (e.g., time, materials, intervention skills) so that the intervention can be implemented with fidelity. Given the complexities of the educational environment and the many demands placed on educators, it is also important to focus on the smallest change that we can make to promote educationally significant outcomes for the student. Finally, we must consider the context of the implementers to determine the likelihood of the intervention being implemented. The primary outcome of this process is to build a technically sound plan that can be implemented with fidelity. Sometimes we need to remember that a less-than-perfect plan, implemented well, is better than a very strong plan that won't be implemented at all.

## GUIDANCE IN SELECTING INTEGRATED PRACTICES

Because both academic RTI and PBIS are systems-level approaches and not interventions in and of themselves, adopting them (or an integrated MTSS) leads to the need to select and implement specific practices. As described in this chapter, practices may be curricula and other published programs, freely distributed interventions, or even simple strategies or tricks used to improve student performance. Both academic RTI and PBIS have three basic criteria for intervention selection. First, their quality (or fidelity) of implementation must be measureable (as well as measured!). Second, they must be evidence-based (alternatively called research-validated, or from IDEA, "scientific, research-based"; Individuals with Disabilities Education Improvement Act, 2004). Third, they must be adopted strategically to provide a continuum of tiered support with increasing intensity based on student need, and without so many interventions in place that they cannot be implemented well. Data used to assess the first criterion were covered in Chapter 3, and in this section, we discuss the second and third criteria.

### Selecting Evidence-Based Practices

There is no mistaking the importance of adopting evidence-based practices. Simply put, we can't waste the precious few resources we have available in education on practices that are not likely to work. If a particular practice is more likely to work (i.e., there is more research showing that it is effective across a range of schools and students), it is hard to justify choosing another one in its place. Yet how do we make decisions about which practices are and are not evidence-based?

### What Are Evidence-Based Practices?

The logical place to start in determining the evidence base for interventions is having clear criteria for just what is *evidence-based*. However, there are no common definitions across education or any regulations regarding those criteria (Kratochwill & Stoiber, 2002). As a result, it is easy for publishers to assert (often with a shiny sticker on the front of an expensive curriculum) that their programs are "evidence-based." In response, many associations (e.g., American Psychological Association, Association for Positive Behavior Support, Council for Exceptional Children, and Society for Prevention Research) have developed their own criteria for such a label. Although there are some differences among these various groups' definitions, there are far more similarities. Based partly on the work of these groups, we share here a fairly simple categorizing system that can be used to assess academic and behavior practices through three levels of increasing evidence: (1) *unsupported practices*, (2) *research-based practices*, and (3) *evidence-based practices*.

## UNSUPPORTED PRACTICES

Unfortunately, there are plenty of practices in use in schools that have no evidence supporting their effectiveness, or even have evidence that they may be harmful to students. It's hard to imagine practices with no evidence being used regularly in medicine, law, or even auto repair, and yet it is commonly the case in education. As expected, these practices should not only be avoided, but also actively discouraged. For example, a number of research studies to date have indicated that the standard format of the substance abuse prevention program D.A.R.E. (Drug Abuse Resistance Education) is either ineffective or potentially harmful (i.e., may increase substance use), and thus other practices should be adopted to prevent or reduce substance abuse (Cornell, 2006).

## RESEARCH-BASED PRACTICES

The next level of evidence, *research-based practices*, refers to practices that have not themselves been evaluated through rigorous research (as in the *unsupported practices* category), but are at least designed based on research indicating that they are likely to work. For example, an untested intervention designed to improve listening comprehension or emotional regulation (important foci as shown by research) using research-validated principles of instruction (like those described at the beginning of this chapter, pp. 114–118) may be considered research-based because it was created based on the best available information about what to target and how. Practices may also be considered research-based if there is some research demonstrating their promise, but through studies that are not rigorous. For example, a practice may have been shown to work in an evaluation or a study without random assignment to condition (i.e., students or schools were not selected at random either to receive the intervention or serve as controls). Although this level of evidence is still not high, research-based practices may be acceptable to adopt if there are no other interventions that have been shown to work in that area to date (Kratochwill & Shernoff, 2004).

## EVIDENCE-BASED PRACTICES

As opposed to the previous categories, *evidence-based practices* have been shown in multiple rigorous research studies to improve student outcomes. In our system, this label means more than just any research studies. The studies that earn an evidence-based label must adhere to standards that we derived from a few respected publications (Flay et al., 2005; Gersten et al., 2005; Horner, Carr, et al., 2005). From our perspective, to be called evidence-based, studies must meet the following four criteria: (1) There must be at least two, high-quality experimental studies (either group studies with random assignment to condition or experimental single-case designs); (2) these studies must be conducted by teams at different institutions (with at least one team that is not affiliated with the developers); (3) these studies must consistently document educationally meaningful, positive effects on valued outcomes without any negative side effects; and (4) there is evidence that the practice can be implemented fully by typical school personnel with typical resources. This last point is important because initial studies often evaluate a practice's efficacy (i.e., effects under ideal conditions, often with trained clinicians and extensive resources) as opposed to effectiveness (Bearman, Ugueto, Alleyne, & Weisz, 2010). As an example of this system of classification, the collection of common practices as part of PBIS meets the criteria for *evidence-based practice*, due to multiple, high-quality, randomized controlled trials with typical implementers showing positive, clinically meaningful effects on problem behavior, academic achievement, bullying behavior, school safety, and emotional regulation (Bradshaw et al., 2012; Horner, Sugai, & Anderson, 2010; Waasdorp et al., 2012).

## Data for Examining Evidence Bases

In making determinations about levels of evidence, it is important that the studies themselves are of high quality. Without tightly controlled designs, any positive effects are questionable, and practices with evidence only from less rigorous studies can be rated no higher than *research-based* until high-quality studies can be conducted. Readers interested in learning more about the criteria for high-quality research studies (which are then, in turn, used to evaluate a given practice's evidence base) can find clear guidelines in articles by Gersten and colleagues (2005) and Horner, Carr, and colleagues (2005).

However, these criteria are not, in and of themselves, all of the proof needed to feel confident in practices. Another level of evidence is also necessary: After its selection and implementation, the practice must be shown to work with the particular students who you are supporting, especially when supporting students who are culturally and linguistically diverse. In all cases, regardless of a practice's evidence base, it should be evaluated for effectiveness with the exact student or group of students for whom it is implemented (Kratochwill & Shernoff, 2004). We should not assume that because a practice has been shown to be effective in other schools, it will automatically be effective in *your* school. Only your own data for each of your students will tell you that answer.

## Selecting Practices by Assessing Practices Already in Place (Resource Mapping)

Before determining what practices to add, it is often helpful to identify what is already in place by cataloging the school's current academic and behavior support practices in a process called *resource mapping*. This practice allows a school or district team to take stock of existing practices to analyze strengths and areas with few options for support. This latter step, called *gap analysis*, helps teams prioritize needs for selecting and implementing new practices. In addition, when reviewing a resource map, it may become apparent that some practices are no longer utilized or needed and can be replaced by more relevant or effective practices. There are a number of different types of resource mapping activities, and each has its specific purpose.

## MTSS Quick Audit

In its simplest form, a resource map can be a one-page sheet with a depiction of a triangle and blank spaces for filling in the practices at each tier (see Figure 4.7 for a completed example and Appendix 4.1 for a blank version). This assessment of all tiers at once provides a simple and efficient means of identifying what is in place and what may be needed. Although this tool is often used to assess the entire school, it can be used with specific grade levels or classrooms as well. To complete the audit, team members list the practices for each tier of support next to the corresponding section of the triangle to indicate which practices are available within the school for both academic and behavior support (tools for integrated support are described later in this chapter). The next step is to write in any practices used, including commercially purchased programs, teacher-developed practices, and basic strategies. Additionally, some teams may want to distinguish between practices that are simply available and those that are actually in use. Once complete, the last step is to examine these practices to identify (1) gaps where practices are needed and (2) practices that could be eliminated or replaced with more systematic, evidence-based practices.

For example, consider the quick audit in Figure 4.7. Parks Elementary completed a quick audit for their grade 1 behavior and literacy support systems to assess gaps and areas for improvement. Although it is clear that the behavior practices may also serve as literacy practices, and vice versa, the quick audit allows teams and coaches to focus on quality implementation for one content area at a time. However, the literacy audit does include "instructional expectations lessons" because the team feels that it is important to emphasize this practice as a key Tier 1 practice for effective literacy instruction. The quick audit activity highlights some aspects of their systems that could be examined for improvement. For example, in Tier 2 for behavior, the presence of only one practice (which may itself vary widely in terms of services provided and effectiveness) indicates the need to add practices in this area. By selecting one cost-effective practice that can be adapted according to student need, such as check-in/check-out, the school may find that some students considered as needing Tier 3 support may actually be supported adequately at Tier 2. In Tier 2 for literacy, on the other hand, there appear to be so many practices that it may be difficult (or at least inefficient) to deliver them all with high fidelity. The team may consider removing one or more practices to allow time for implementing a new Tier 2 behavior practice. In Tier 3 for literacy, although there are some blank spaces, if the team feels that the students are adequately supported by the practices in place, there may not be the need to add more. The goal is to provide high-quality support, not to fill every line!

## Tier 2 Resource Maps

In addition to the broad view that the MTSS Quick Audit provides, resource mapping can be conducted in detail at each tier. This process is especially useful at Tier 2, where assessment results may indicate the need for different Tier 2 interventions based on specific skill deficits or needs. In PBIS, school teams sometimes map their Tier 2 interventions to identify specific matches in relation to the function of behavior (Horner & Todd, 2002; see Figure 4.8 for a completed sheet and Appendix 4.2 for a blank version). In the Tier 2 Function-Based Intervention and Resource Mapping Worksheet, school teams create a matrix of their available Tier 2 interventions and match them to functions of behavior and intervention features. As with the MTSS

## MTSS Quick Audit

School: *Parks Elementary*                    Date: *September 13, 2015*

Grade Level/Classroom: *Grade 1*              Domain: *Social Behavior*

### List practices (strategies, programs)

ALL (Tier 1):

*Expectations lessons (start of year)*

*Periodic expectations boosters*

*Bear PAWS tickets*

*Second Step lessons*

*Bullying Prevention PBIS lessons*

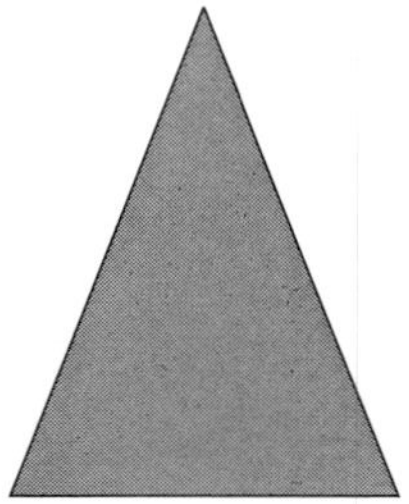

SOME (Tier 2):

*Referral to counselor*

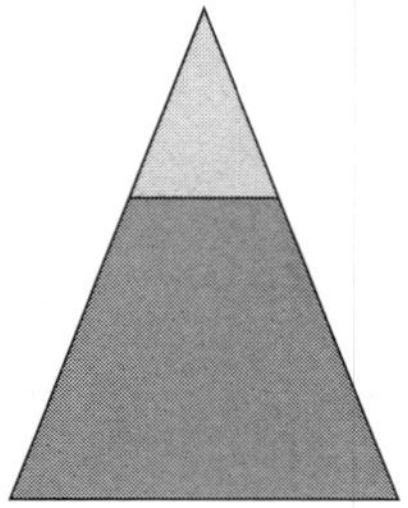

FEW (Tier 3):

*Function-based support plans*

*Referral to district behavior team*

*Wraparound support*

*Multisystemic therapy*

*Parent management training*

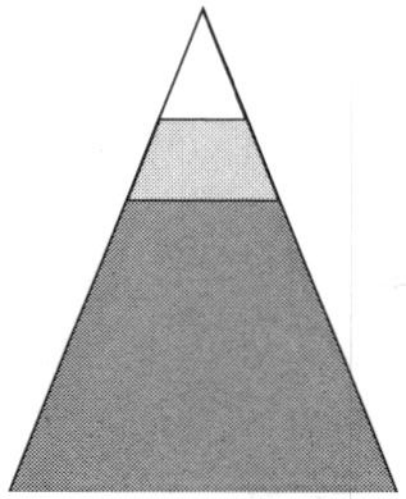

---

## MTSS Quick Audit

School: *Parks Elementary*                    Date: *September 13, 2015*

Grade Level/Classroom: *Grade 1*              Domain: *Literacy*

### List practices (strategies, programs)

ALL (Tier 1):

*90-minute core reading block*

*Flexible skill grouping*

*Instructional expectations lessons*

*Evidence-based core curriculum*

*Focus on alphabetic principle*

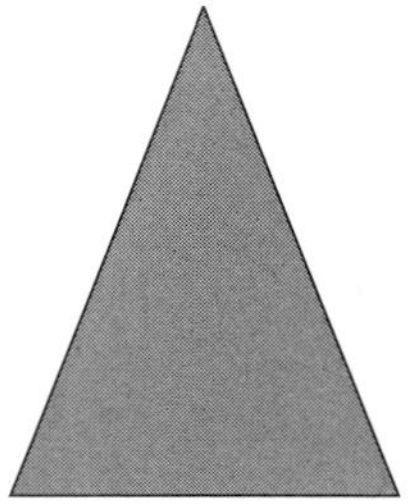

SOME (Tier 2):

*Double dosing with core curriculum*

*Peer-Assisted Learning Strategies*

*Read Naturally*

*Reading Recovery*

*Road to the Code*

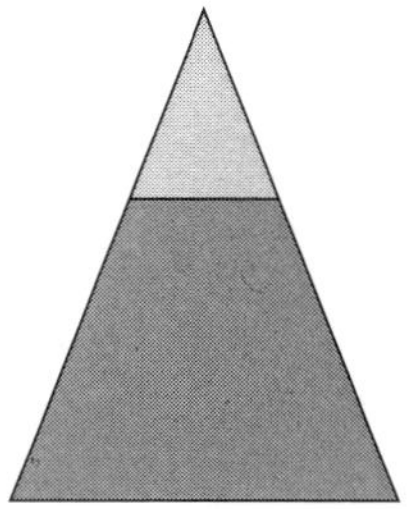

FEW (Tier 3):

*Small groups based on skill levels*

*Scott Foresman ERI*

*Reading Mastery*

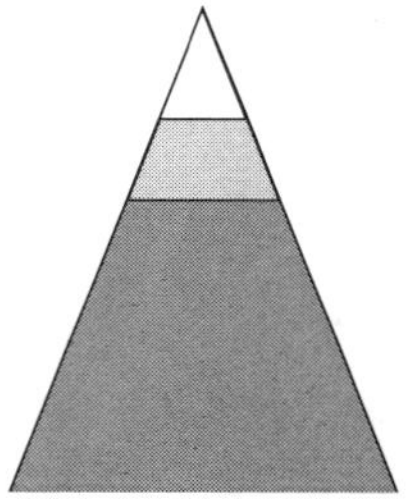

**FIGURE 4.7.** Example of completed MTSS Quick Audits of social behavior and literacy practices by MTSS tier.

**School:** _Riverview Elementary_ _____     **Date:** _October 30, 2015_ _____

| Tier 2 Interventions ➤<br>Features ↓ | Check-in<br>Check-out | Social Skills<br>Club | Grief/Loss<br>Group | Homework<br>Club | Lunch<br>Buddies |
|---|---|---|---|---|---|
| **Access to adult attention** | X | X | X | X | X |
| **Access to peer attention** | | X | X | | X |
| **Access to choice of alternative activities** | X | X | X | X | X |
| **Options for avoiding aversive activities** | X | X | X | X | X |
| **Options for avoiding aversive social attention** | | | X | | X |
| **Additional structural prompts for "what to do" throughout the day** | X | X | | | |
| **At least five structured times each day to receive feedback** | X | | | | |
| **School–home communication system** | X | | | X | |
| **Option to adapt into a self-management system** | X | X | | X | X |

**FIGURE 4.8.** Example of a completed Tier 2 Function-Based Intervention Resource Mapping Worksheet. Adapted with permission from Rob Horner and Anne W. Todd from Horner and Todd (2002).

Quick Audit, teams can also examine any gaps in practices to determine what interventions could be added to make their Tier 2 support more complete. The example school's interventions include check-in/check-out, a social skills club, a grief/loss group, a homework club, and a lunch buddy option. Each intervention is examined to determine the possible type of reinforcement available to participating students. The team then selects an appropriate Tier 2 intervention based on the probable function of the student's behavior. For example, a student whose unwanted behavior is maintained by adult attention may be placed in any intervention, but if the behavior is maintained by peer attention, the social skills club, grief/loss group (if appropriate), or lunch buddies option may be more appropriate. Each of these interventions provides regular, structured social interactions, allowing for peer attention in a controlled setting. Although some other interventions could be modified to provide peer attention (e.g., check-in/check-out), the others may be a more natural fit without the need for individualization, which limits the efficiency of Tier 2 interventions.

The previous examples of resource mapping do not necessarily indicate how academic and behavior practices can be integrated in the ways we describe in this book. However, resource mapping can be an important tool for integration. To illustrate an integrated academic and behavior Tier 2 resource map, Dawn Miller, from Shawnee Mission School District in Kansas, developed a more comprehensive matrix that matches function to components inherent in the delivery of Tier 2 academic interventions (see Figure 4.9). Although addressing the specific academic deficits that may evoke unwanted behavior is the most obvious way that academic interventions can provide behavior support, there are other considerations as well. For example, problem behavior that is maintained by peer attention may be addressed with peer-mediated academic intervention strategies such as PALS (*http://kc.vanderbilt.edu/pals*), which provides academic support through peer instruction. In this integrated approach, students are placed into existing Tier 2 academic interventions that inherently meet both academic and behavior needs for support by function. The function is then used to select interventions that not only support academic skill development but also inherently provide an opportunity to access similar functions that the unwanted behavior serves. This matching process makes engaging in unwanted behavior during the instructional time unnecessary because social needs are also met. Additionally, it assists with implementation because it helps school personnel identify the integrated practices they already have (i.e., academic interventions that inherently provide some behavior support), as opposed to selecting and implementing an entirely new array of integrated interventions.

## Integrated Instructional Plans

The final and most detailed form of resource mapping is an integrated instructional plan for each grade level or classroom (see Figure 4.10 for an example and Appendix 4.3 for a blank version). This instructional plan is adapted from another resource mapping tool called a *core, strategic, and intensive* (CSI) *map*, developed by Beth Harn as part of Project CIRCUITS (Chard & Harn, 2008). Typically, integrated instructional plans are completed twice per year (e.g., after the fall and winter benchmarking periods). In this process, a grade-level team or classroom teacher lists the students requiring support and available practices at each tier, as well as the educator responsible, time requirements, and progress monitoring measures and timing. The integrated considerations column describes how instruction can be enhanced by attending to integration. At Tier 1, the primary focus is on providing quality Tier 1 intervention for all students across all content areas, thereby preventing additional risk. At Tiers 2 and 3, the column describes the specific accommodations for students or groups of students that can provide integrated support within existing practices. The main benefit of this integrated instructional plan is that the instructor can readily identify the students receiving each prac-

| Tier 2 Interventions → Features ↓ | Open Court | K-PALS | PALS | REWARDS | Passport | Read Naturally |
|---|---|---|---|---|---|---|
| **Access to adult attention** | X | | X | X | X | |
| **Access to peer attention** | | X | X | X | | |
| **Options for avoiding aversive activities** | | | | | | X |
| **Options for avoiding aversive social attention** | | | | | | X |

**FIGURE 4.9.** Example of completed integrated academic and behavioral resource mapping. Adapted with permission from Dawn Miller from Miller and Goodman (2012).

tice of academic or behavior support at a glance and schedule groups accordingly. As a result, the level of specificity does not lend the tool to gap analysis, which is better achieved through the MTSS Quick Audit.

In the example in Figure 4.10, all students are provided with Tier 1 instruction that includes a core literacy program and supplemental activities intended to support academic growth, as well as schoolwide PBIS features to support positive social and emotional development. The integrated considerations column for Tier 1 describes strategies for all students that are intended to maximize success across content areas. At Tier 2, the same column shows how students can receive integrated supports without the need for additional interventions. For example, Daniel requires support in both areas, and accommodations are indicated to maximize his success in Tier 2 without the need for a completely individualized Tier 3 plan. In another case, Tran's performance in literacy is suffering, but the team believes that an emphasis on attending and task completion within check-in/check-out will provide enough support to allow for sufficient academic skill development. Conversely, the grade-level team believes that a Tier 2 literacy intervention will be sufficient to address Ian's mild escape-maintained disruptive behavior during core instruction. At Tier 3, Sam requires an integrated support plan, whereas Travis currently has Tier 3 behavior support needs but is served adequately by the strong Tier 1 literacy support. Thanks to careful resource mapping, all of this integrated support is provided within existing practices in the school, making the system more responsive yet still sustainable.

## Additional Approaches for Resource Mapping and Scheduling

In addition to or in place of audits, resource maps, and integrated instructional plans, some educators and teams use more visual approaches to identify practices and link them to student need, especially when gaps have already been addressed and the main task is to create schedules for each practice.

### POCKET CHARTS AND INDEX CARDS

At the classroom or grade level, teachers will sometimes use pocket charts that include a pocket for each student and index cards representing existing academic and behavior Tiers 2 and 3 practices (either with a different color for each practice or color-coded by tier). These cards are then placed into each student's pocket based on individual needs. Through this quick sorting process, it becomes easier to see which students need additional academic or behavior supports The patterns may also highlight where interventions can be integrated (e.g., teaching social skills and reading comprehension in the same intervention group) or where Tier 1 supports can be enhanced for more feasible scheduling (e.g., incorporating more math fluency intervention into Tier 1 supports if many students share this need).

### MASTER DISPLAY BOARDS

Many educators use display boards to visually display practices and their schedules, particularly when academic and behavior supports are arranged across classrooms and grade levels. Figure 4.11 shows an example of a display board in a staff meeting room with the school day's schedule down the side and grade levels across the top. Teams can then schedule interventions in the

## Integrated Instructional Plan: Literacy and Behavior

**School:** _Pleasant Valley Elementary_    **Grade:** _First Grade_    **Period:** _Fall to Winter_

**Team Members:** _J. Burns, M. Wilson, L. Thomas, R. Jones, K. Mallory_    **Date:** _9/24/15_

**Directions:** After reviewing your grade-level data, complete the cells below. The purpose of this tool is to direct support efforts within and across all classes for the grade level.

**Literacy Focus:** (Fall to Winter) _Phonemic Awareness. By fall of first grade, students should have established phonemic awareness skills as indicated by the DIBELS Phoneme Segmentation Fluency measure. If this is not true for more than 20% of your students, consider making your core reading block greater than 90 minutes and allocate 15–20 minutes 3–5 days per week for 6–8 weeks (make the adjustment to the kindergarten core program to prevent this remedial loop next year)._

_Alphabetic Principle. By January of first grade, students should be fluent with sound–symbol relationships and recoding as indicated by the Nonsense Word Fluency measure. Twenty to thirty minutes of small-group instruction in alphabetic principle is recommended as a daily part of the core instructional block. Students needing strategic or intensive instruction will need additional time and instruction. Students should also be able to read words at about a rate of one word each 2–3 seconds._

**Behavior Focus:** (Fall to Winter) _Modeling and Labeling of Prosocial Behavior. The purpose of behavior support is to teach prosocial behavior, teach expectations as vocabulary words with models for behavior appropriate for school, and structure the instructional environment to maximize time in instruction and minimize disruptions/removals._

_(continued)_

**FIGURE 4.10.** Example of a completed Integrated Instructional Plan: Literacy and Behavior.

| | Students | Program and Materials | Integrated Academic and Behavior Considerations (universal focus) | Instructor | Time/Days | Progress Monitoring | Weeks Until Next Benchmark |
|---|---|---|---|---|---|---|---|
| **Literacy** | All students | Core program: Harcourt Review, two to three small groups daily. | Ensure high rates of academic responding. | J. Burns K. Mallory R. Jones | 20 minutes daily | NWF once per month for all students | 9 Weeks |
| | | Alphabetic Principle: Practice three to five phoneme words each day—blending and segmenting before going into phonics instruction. | Goal of 90%+ correct responding to build momentum. | J. Burns K. Mallory R. Jones | 3–5 minutes | | |
| | | Use PALS for whole class to support the core. | Explicit instruction on PALS routines. | J. Burns | 3 times/ week for 35 minutes | | |
| **Behavior** | All students | Schoolwide behavioral expectations lesson plans to teach and review behavior expectations for classroom and nonclassroom settings | Link schoolwide behavior expectations to academics (e.g., "Be Responsible" means participating in instruction). | J. Burns | 10 minutes daily for first week, then review every Monday | Review SWIS office discipline referrals for first-grade classroom and playground monthly | 9 Weeks |
| | | Precorrection before instruction in new or challenging content | Explicit instruction in behavior expectations within classroom settings (e.g., teacher-led instruction, group work) and routines (e.g., asking for help, turning in assignments). | | | | |
| | | Gotcha tickets to reward academic engagement | | | | | |

**Benchmark/Universal Support**

For all students, provide a scientifically-based core program that focuses on the "Big Ideas" of each domain, and is effective for meeting the needs of most (≥ 80%) of students.

**FIGURE 4.10.** *(continued)*

(continued)

148

**Strategic/Targeted Intervention**

For students not making adequate progress with core. Students with similar needs are grouped and provided intervention in specific areas, based on student need and "Big Ideas."

| | Students | Program and Materials | Integrated Academic and Behavior Considerations (universal focus) | Instructor | Time/Days | Progress Monitoring | Weeks Until Next Benchmark |
|---|---|---|---|---|---|---|---|
| **Literacy** | Daniel<br>Ian<br>James<br>Juan<br>Kam<br>Neveah | Teacher-directed PALS | Pair Dan with peer who can model appropriate behavior and provide appropriate attention during instruction to address peer attention maintained problem behavior. | J. Burns | After reading block for 30 minutes each day, 3 days per week | PSF and NWF once per week | 9 weeks |
| **Behavior** | Daniel<br>James<br>Natashia<br>Kam<br>Terrence | Second Step Social Skills Program | Teach peers to ignore Dan's inappropriate behavior. | M. Wilson<br>T. Greene | 20 minutes per day, 3 days per week | Monthly SWIS Referrals | 9 weeks |
| **Behavior** | Tran<br>Shondel | Check-in/check-out (CICO) | Tran's CICO program should focus on improving his attending and completing assigned tasks. | M. Wilson<br>K. Malloy | Daily | CICO–SWIS Report<br>Monthly SWIS Referrals | |

**FIGURE 4.10.** (continued)

149

| Students | Program and Materials | Integrated Academic and Behavior Considerations (universal focus) | Instructor | Time/Days | Progress Monitoring | Weeks Until Next Benchmark |
|---|---|---|---|---|---|---|
| **Literacy** Ava Jerome John Sam Terrence | Reading Mastery | Provide Ava with increased opportunity for appropriate feedback and attention during instruction to address adult attention-seeking problem behavior. | M. Wilson | After Reading block for 30 minutes per day, 5 days per week | PSF and NWF twice per week | 9 weeks |
| **Behavior** Travis | Token economy system for appropriate language during transitions in classroom; purchase items with token before lunch and before going home | | L. Thomas | Daily | ISIS–SWIS report every 2 weeks; chart of tokens earned daily | 9 Weeks |
| Sam | See behavior intervention plan for aggression/property damage for escape–maintained behavior (provide break for appropriate request; modify instructional requirements). | Ensure that Sam's intervention plan focuses on skills development in phonemic awareness, with many opportunities for success. Additionally, monitor both academic and behavior responding. | J. Burns, L. Thomas | Daily | ISIS–SWIS report every 2 weeks; chart of appropriate requests for break | |

**Intensive/Individualized Support**

For students having significant challenges that are unlikely to be supported by core and strategic support. Students are provided highly specific and individualized interventions derived from assessment results.

**FIGURE 4.10.** (continued)

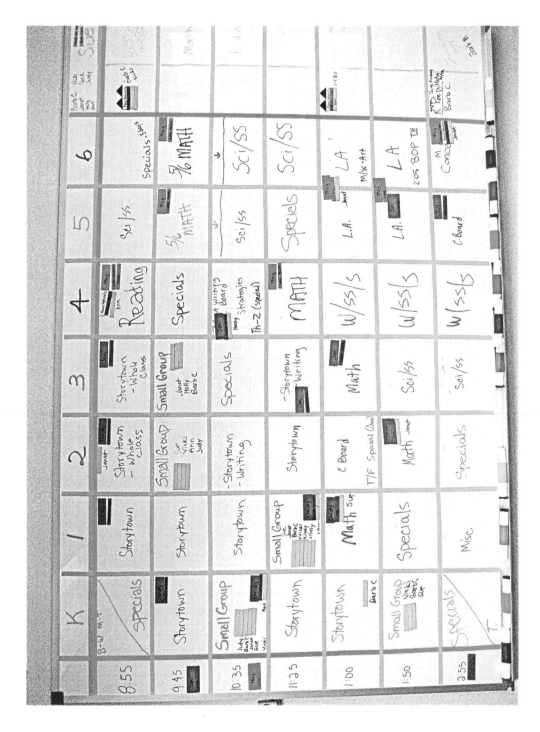

**FIGURE 4.11.** Visual display of schedule of practices across a school's grade levels. Reprinted with permission from Patrick Sorrelle.

151

boxes that can be accessed by any students at each time period in the school day based on their academic and behavior needs for support. Such a tool allows for more flexibility in intervention grouping and reduces duplication of intervention groups when planning and scheduling integrated practices.

## TEAM CHECKLISTS: INTEGRATING PRACTICES

The checklists in this chapter focus on activities for creating integrated practices at the building and district levels. They include common steps to focus on effective practice selection, implementation, and integration.

# SCHOOL-LEVEL TEAM CHECKLIST
# FOR INTEGRATING PRACTICES

| Implementation Step | Implementation Status | | |
|---|---|---|---|
| | Not in place | Partially in place | In place |
| 1. The team adopts schoolwide and classroom interventions based on their evidence base. | | | |
| 2. Interventions are selected and organized along a tiered continuum that increases in intensity (e.g., frequency, duration, individualization, expertise in support). | | | |
| 3. The team creates and maintains an MTSS Quick Audit to map the continuum of interventions provided in the school. | | | |
| 4. The team creates and maintains a Tier 2 Function-Based Intervention and Resource Mapping Worksheet to map their academic and behavior interventions onto the function of problem behavior. | | | |
| 5. Grade-level teams complete Integrated Instructional Plans at least twice per year. | | | |
| 6. Academic and behavior practices are implemented (a) with fidelity (Chapter 3) and (b) in line with the six principles of quality of instruction (see pp. 114–118). | | | |
| 7. Schoolwide behavior expectations are identified and taught to promote prosocial behavior, increase instructional time, and remove distractions from instruction. | | | |
| 8. Classroom management systems are consistent with the schoolwide PBIS systems (e.g., same as schoolwide expectations, access to schoolwide acknowledgment). | | | |
| 9. Classroom teachers provide explicit instruction in how the schoolwide behavior expectations apply to their classrooms. | | | |
| 10. Classroom teachers provide explicit instruction in classroom routines (e.g., turning in assignments, transitions to and from classroom, requesting assistance) that is consistent with schoolwide expectations. | | | |

| Priority for Action Planning (the three most important items from above) | Who is responsible? | By when? | How will we know when it is accomplished? |
|---|---|---|---|
| 1. | | | |
| 2. | | | |
| 3. | | | |

# DISTRICT-LEVEL TEAM CHECKLIST
# FOR INTEGRATING PRACTICES

| Implementation Step | Implementation Status | | |
|---|---|---|---|
| | Not in place | Partially in place | In place |
| 1. The district team creates and maintains a district-level MTSS Quick Audit to map the continuum of interventions supported within the district. | | | |
| 2. The district team develops and maintains a list of recommended evidence-based practices across the tiered continuum for both academic and behavior support. | | | |
| 3. The district team collects and shares sample MTSS Quick Audits, Tier 2 Function-Based Intervention and Resource Mapping Worksheets, and Integrated Instructional Plans. | | | |
| 4. The district team supports school-level teams in selecting evidence-based practices based on their existing practices, resources, and needs. | | | |
| 5. The district team provides schools with access to materials and training in implementing recommended interventions with fidelity. | | | |
| 6. The district team conducts needs assessments to identify additional practices that may be needed in schools. | | | |

| Priority for Action Planning (the three most important items from above) | Who is responsible? | By when? | How will we know when it is accomplished? |
|---|---|---|---|
| 1. | | | |
| 2. | | | |
| 3. | | | |

# MTSS Quick Audit

School: _____     Date: _____

Grade Level/Classroom: _____     Domain: _____

## List practices (strategies, programs)

ALL (Tier 1):

_____

_____

_____

_____

_____

_____

SOME (Tier 2):

_____

_____

_____

_____

_____

FEW (Tier 3):

_____

_____

_____

_____

_____

_____

# Tier 2 Function-Based Intervention Resource Mapping Worksheet

**School:** _____  **Date:** _____

**Purpose:** This worksheet is designed to be used as a map when discussing function-based behavior support needs. Use it as a reference when selecting intervention options for individual students or identifying school needs for additional practices.

**Tier 2 interventions defined:** *Common features include (1) additional skills instruction and practice, (2) increased structure and prompts, (3) increased feedback, (4) provided in the same way to most students, and (5) available to anyone within 72 hours.*

**Instructions:** List the targeted interventions that are available in your school across the top. Identify the possible functions (or features) that the intervention is designed to support by putting an *X* in each cell.

*Examples:*

- Check-in/check-out offers predictable adult attention, structure, feedback, and additional functions (e.g., peer attention, escape) with slight modifications.
- Social skills groups may offer adult and peer attention and instruction in skills to request choices or appropriate task avoidance.

| Tier 2 Interventions →<br>Features ↓ | | | | | |
|---|---|---|---|---|---|
| **Access to adult attention** | | | | | |
| **Access to peer attention** | | | | | |
| **Access to choice of alternative activities** | | | | | |
| **Options for avoiding aversive activities** | | | | | |
| **Options for avoiding aversive social attention** | | | | | |
| **Additional structural prompts for "what to do" throughout the day** | | | | | |
| **At least five structured times each day to receive feedback** | | | | | |
| **School–home communication system** | | | | | |
| **Option to adapt into a self-management system** | | | | | |

Adapted with permission from Rob Horner and Anne W. Todd from Horner and Todd (2002).

## Integrated Instructional Plan: Literacy and Behavior

School: _____ Grade: _____ Period: _____

**Team Members:** _____ Date: _____

**Directions:** After reviewing your grade-level data, complete the cells below. The purpose of this tool is to direct support efforts within and across all classes for the grade level.

**Literacy Focus:**

**Behavior Focus:**

157

(continued)

Integrated Instructional Plan: Literacy and Behavior *(page 2 of 4)*

**Benchmark/Universal Support**

For all students, provide a scientifically-based core program that focuses on the "Big Ideas" of each domain, and is effective for meeting the needs of most (≥ 80%) of students.

| Students | Program and Materials | Integrated Academic and Behavior Considerations (universal focus) | Instructor | Time/Days | Progress Monitoring | Weeks Until Next Benchmark |
|---|---|---|---|---|---|---|
| **Literacy** All students | | | | | | |
| **Behavior** All students | | | | | | |

*(continued)*

158

Integrated Instructional Plan: Literacy and Behavior *(page 3 of 4)*

| | Students | Program and Materials | Integrated Academic and Behavior Considerations (universal focus) | Instructor | Time/Days | Progress Monitoring | Weeks Until Next Benchmark |
|---|---|---|---|---|---|---|---|
| **Literacy** | | | | | | | |
| **Behavior** | | | | | | | |

**Strategic/Targeted Intervention**
For students not making adequate progress with core. Students with similar needs are grouped and provided intervention in specific areas, based on student need and "Big Ideas."

159

*(continued)*

Integrated Instructional Plan: Literacy and Behavior *(page 4 of 4)*

| Students | Program and Materials | Integrated Academic and Behavior Considerations (universal focus) | Instructor | Time/Days | Progress Monitoring | Weeks Until Next Benchmark |
|---|---|---|---|---|---|---|
| **Literacy** | | | | | | |
| **Behavior** | | | | | | |

**Intensive/Individualized Support**

For students having significant challenges that are unlikely to be supported by core and strategic support. Students are provided highly specific and individualized interventions derived from assessment results.

**CHAPTER 5**

# Integrating Teaming

It takes a tremendous amount of time and resources from both the school and the district level to establish an integrated MTSS model. When planning these efforts, there is likely a nagging thought in the back of everyone's head regarding how we invest this time in a way that maximizes both implementation and sustainability. Many of us have experienced major initiatives that either failed to take root (i.e., inadequate implementation) or did take root initially but then withered away (i.e., adequate implementation but inadequate sustainability; McIntosh et al., 2013; Sindelar, Shearer, Yendol-Hoppey, & Liebert, 2006). After all of this investment, how do we implement systems change in a way that is both deep and durable, especially as we deal with the inevitable changes in staff and settings? In our experiences, the best way to achieve both of these outcomes is through a *team approach*.

## THE TEAM APPROACH

A team is more than a group of individuals who come together periodically and call themselves a team. A team is a group that forms for a common purpose to achieve an outcome by working together. The purpose of teaming in education is to support staff members in their work to support students. This definition makes it clear that teams are systems that allow us all to work more effectively in achieving our aims.

However, at times, it can seem as if teams are stopping us from meeting these goals. Having an endless parade of meetings across our calendars may make us feel that the time could be better spent *doing* the work instead of talking about it. In our experience, this feeling comes not from too much teaming, but rather, from too much dysfunctional teaming. For example, when the team primarily serves a social function, or a venting function, or simply to enact one person's vision without collaboration, it may be less effective in supporting students than having no team at all. Such team experiences (which we all have from time to time) can ruin morale and leave individuals feeling jaded about the entire teaming process, leading to disengagement and further dysfunction. In this chapter, we describe teams, teaming structures, and specific strategies to move teams from dysfunctional to functional, with specific attention to the challenges and opportunities of implementing and sustaining integrated MTSS models.

## Why Is a Team Approach So Important?

Despite our common experiences with dysfunction and the temptation to move fast and light without so many meetings, there are a few key reasons why we stress the importance of teaming. First, the fundamental function of teams is to distribute the workload among multiple individuals. This aspect, in and of itself, has many advantages. It can reduce the stress (or reliance) on any single person in the initiative. By distributing the load, we make the work efficient and reduce burnout. A by-product of spreading tasks across a number of people is reducing the chance of relying on one individual too heavily to run a system. Any systems that rely too much on the knowledge and efforts of one person are more susceptible to abandonment when that person (often a champion for the initiative) moves on to another position (Strickland-Cohen, McIntosh, & Horner, 2014). In contrast, when a well-functioning team runs the system, the initiative has continuity and resists diminishment through staff turnover. A strategy used by schools and districts that sustains PBIS is to refresh the school leadership team membership each year (Andreou et al., 2015). New staff members are encouraged to join the team, while veteran staff members rotate off. This process builds capacity of new staff (who often lack training in classroom management), brings new ideas to the team, decreases burnout of key members, and populates the general school staff with those who know and support the approach.

Another key benefit of teaming is the opportunity for enhanced collaboration. In today's world, we educators are assumed to be experts in so many areas. Closing our doors and working in isolation is an unrealistic and unhealthy expectation that sets us up for failure and cuts us off from the collective expertise of a group of experienced teachers. Instead, collaborating as part of a team gives us this access in a systematic manner. We can improve our problem solving due to the variety of skill sets, experience, and expertise of the team members. Our decisions are likely to be better because they are informed by multiple staff perspectives. As a result, staff buy-in is often increased because the group as a whole feels more represented than if one individual or a small group makes the key decisions.

## TEAMS IN MTSS

When discussing teams, it is useful to have a sense of what teams exist in most schools, their purposes, typical members, and common activities. Schools that have been dabbling in integrated MTSS often have multiple types of each of these teams (e.g., a schoolwide academic RTI team and a schoolwide PBIS team). There is no ideal team makeup or number of teams that will work perfectly in each school, but knowing the makeup and functions of each team can assist in selecting which teams to add or combine. In Figure 5.1, we propose different levels of teams at the school and district levels and how they fit with each other. It is worth considering how the functions of these teams might be accomplished in specific schools given the teams that already exist. Within each possibility, it is useful to consider the most efficient and effective methods for integration.

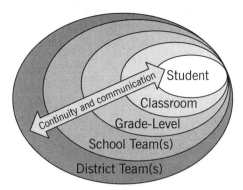

**FIGURE 5.1.** Nesting of teaming structures within schools and districts.

## Common MTSS Teams at the School Level

### Individual Student Team

At the heart of all teams is a team that is sometimes overlooked: each individual student's team. Although this team is rarely viewed as a formal team unless a student is receiving special education services, it is useful to consider in the school's overall teaming structure. The team should be responsible for the student's academic and social growth, career development, and quality of life. The default members include the student, teacher(s), and family or caregivers. Family members and caregivers should always be viewed as partners in ensuring student outcomes, and they can provide critical information needed to support the student to meet broader life goals. When additional supports are needed to be successful, the team may include more members, such as case managers, administrators, and community agency liaisons. When the student is receiving special education services, this team becomes the IEP team. This team meets at least once per year during student conference times (or also at IEP meetings). In these meetings, the team often reviews report cards, academic and behavior screening data, and IEP goals and progress, if applicable. Because this team is responsible for all aspects of the student's education, the student team is already integrated by necessity.

### Classroom Team

Although the classroom may not be considered to be a team in the traditional sense, there are often a number of individuals who work together to improve outcomes within the classroom. Led by the classroom teacher(s), this team has primary responsibility for implementing the educational programming directly with students, primarily at Tier 1 but also at Tiers 2 and 3. As such, the teacher is key in intervention planning and implementation in an integrated MTSS model. In addition to teachers, classroom aides or volunteers may be part of the classroom team. Additionally, support staff (e.g., specialists, therapists) may join the class to work with students. Individuals who contribute to the classroom "team" may never meet altogether as one team, especially when the membership is small. However, as the team size increases, the team may meet more often. For example, co-taught classroom teams often meet (or communicate systematically) at least weekly to ensure consistency and address issues preventively. The classroom team's core activities include implementing whole-class, small-group, and sometimes individual student interventions. The data that are most useful for the teacher focuses on individual student performance, particularly to assess which students need specific additional support. As with the individual student team, classroom teams are already integrated because of the need to deliver both academic and behavior support to all students in the classroom.

## Grade-Level Team

Many schools incorporate a grade-level teaming structure to increase consistency across classrooms and facilitate collaboration in problem solving for continuous improvement. The traditional focus of the grade-level team is on improving academic outcomes for students and not necessarily on PBIS implementation. In an integrated MTSS model, the grade-level teams may focus on both academic and behavior support. In high schools, grade-level teams may be replaced with academic departments (e.g., math, science) that serve a similar general purpose but cut across grade levels.

Membership of the grade-level team usually consists of all of the teachers at each grade level within the school. Given the size of the school or the topics discussed, it may be more beneficial for several grade levels to form one team (e.g., a primary and intermediate team in a smaller elementary school). Participating members include classroom teachers, paraprofessionals, support staff, and a school administrator. When multiple grade-level teams meet at the same time (e.g., an early-release day), the principal or assistant principal will need to rotate across the various meetings. In addition, an external or district coach may attend these meetings to help build team capacity. These teams often meet weekly or every other week during common planning times.

Core activities of grade-level teams include evaluating the effects of practices supporting all students within their specific grade and classrooms, as well as taking steps to strengthen them. These teams review student screening data after each academic benchmark period for grouping and intervention considerations. By sharing students across classrooms through flexible grouping, teams can more efficiently differentiate instruction based on similar need. Integrated grade-level teams also consider ODRs as data to adjust behavior support. In addition, grade-level teams review overall student progress and compare results against grade-level targets to assess whether to modify instruction and practices. Tier 2 supports are created as "packages" around a specific need identified for groups of students. As described in Chapter 4, these packaged programs may be developed by staff or purchased commercially.

As just described, grade-level teams are commonly formed for academic purposes but not necessarily for PBIS. Teams may want to address this issue through full integration (i.e., grade-level teams focus on both academics and behavior). However, school personnel may perceive a need to work primarily at the grade level for academics but at the school level for behavior. Another option is for grade-level teams to continue to focus more on academic support, leaving Tier 1 behavior support to a schoolwide PBIS team (which may also be the school leadership team, described next). In these situations, it is beneficial for a member of each grade-level team to serve as a member of the school team.

## School Leadership Team

School leadership teams provide the guiding oversight for initial and sustained implementation in integrated MTSS models. Each school leadership team primarily coordinates implementation of Tier 1 systems, although it may also oversee systems for Tiers 2 and 3. Whereas individual, class, and grade-level teams are most concerned with implementing practices, the school leadership teams takes a broader view, with emphasis on developing local implementation capacity to implement practices and long-term action planning for sustainability.

Because of this significant role, it is important that the school leadership team's work is embedded within the school improvement process. Some schools have a school improvement team that is responsible for developing and implementing the school improvement plan. The work of school improvement clearly overlaps with the academic and behavior MTSS process. For this reason, we suggest that the functions of the school improvement team and the school leadership team be combined into the same team. Fusing these teams is especially useful when managing initiatives that overlap but could be implemented under an MTSS umbrella (e.g., equity, family–school partnerships; McIntosh, Girvan, et al., 2014). Minimally, there should be alignment, communication, and collaboration across school improvement and MTSS teams.

Membership on the school leadership team consists, as one would expect, of leaders across the school. The team should be representative of the school (e.g., across grade levels and content areas). The principal is a critical member of the team because he or she has the responsibility to create and enhance systems through securing resources, acknowledging success, and demonstrating priority of programs to staff, families, and the district. Because the school leadership team monitors and supports the development of systems that address all students and classrooms, it is important that its members include representatives from the other teams in the school. These team members provide leadership in implementation and ensure regular communication across the school. An external or internal coach often facilitates the team's processes to ensure effective and efficient meetings, allow for problem solving, and celebrate successes. We do not recommend that the principal serve as facilitator for two reasons. First, he or she may be called away for other responsibilities, leaving the team without a facilitator. Second, having a staff member serve as coordinator cements the school's integrated MTSS model as a bottom-up—as opposed to top-down—initiative.

In many schools, family members and students participate as full or limited members of the school leadership team. Including family perspectives on the school leadership team can enhance family–school partnerships (Garbacz, McIntosh, Eagle, Dowd-Eagle, Hirano, & Ruppert, in press). As such, it is important that the family member(s) on the team can represent the concerns and priorities of all families and not just a subset. As with any team process, it is important to maintain confidentiality regarding students and families. This is particularly true when students, families, or members of the community participate on the team. In some situations, including them on subcommittees (e.g., students on a student PBIS subcommittee, families on a school improvement team) may feel like an appropriate balance, but in others, it may feel even more exclusionary.

Core activities of the school leadership team include assessing Tier 1 fidelity of implementation and creating and monitoring a detailed action plan to further enhance the fidelity of implementation, aligned with school improvement goals. The action plan often involves steps to build local capacity by creating access to the training and coaching needed to develop core competencies. This team also gathers information from teams working more directly with individual students (e.g., individual student teams, student support team).

To complete these activities, the team uses a range of data for decision making, including fidelity of implementation data, intervention success data, and student outcome data (all described in detail in Chapter 3). The team utilizes individual student data not to monitor the progress of individual students but rather to ensure that the existing tiered supports are improving student outcomes in both academics and behavior. When the school leadership team reviews data, we recommend a "no student names" rule. This policy helps to keep the focus on prevention—developing effective schoolwide educational environments as opposed to responding to individual needs (the purpose of the student support team, described next). Furthermore, the "no names" policy maintains confidentiality when students or family members are on the team.

In addition to collecting and analyzing data, the school leadership team plays an important role of communicating current status and outcomes of the integrated MTSS model to stakeholders. The team often provides regular updates to staff, students, the community (e.g., parent–teacher association) and the district (e.g., district administration, school board) through presentations, newsletters, and reports. In addition to providing useful information about integrated MTSS progress and successes, this communication helps to leverage broader supports needed to accomplish the school improvement plan.

When considering integrated MTSS models, it can be beneficial to have one school leadership team that coordinates all academic and behavior systems. However, schools in initial or staggered implementation often establish separate Tier 1 academic and behavior teams. Unless these separate teams work efficiently, some schools may find it difficult to integrate schoolwide teams. The agenda of one integrated school leadership team may be too packed for efficient operation, especially when the team is early in the implementation process for either academic or behavior systems. Alternatively, school leadership teams could meet every other week and alternate between an academic RTI or PBIS focus, especially if separate teams would have the same members anyway! In considering these decisions, the research in Chapter 2 tells us that integrating teams that coordinate Tiers 2 and 3 systems (described next) is a more important priority.

## Student Support Team

The student support team (alternatively, the student assistance team, school-based team, or student study team) addresses the needs of students requiring more than Tier 1 support to be successful. An MTSS conceptualization of this team has a broader focus than some existing teams by this name, as well as each individual student team. The student support team's primary aims are to establish, monitor, and adapt the *systems* at Tiers 2 and 3. The team maintains ongoing interventions for students requiring some additional support (Tier 2) and develops and monitors intensive, individualized programs of support for students with significant difficulties (Tier 3). Larger schools may even have separate Tier 2 and Tier 3 teams. The student support team may also be involved in the eligibility determination process for special education services. However, this team is most effective when it focuses primarily on providing and monitoring the effectiveness of supports for all students, regardless of their designation. As a result, it may take some deliberate changes to existing student study teams to adjust to the expanded scope of student support teams.

Members of the student support team may include special education teachers, content specialists (e.g., behavior consultants, reading coaches), counselors, social workers, psychologists, and liaisons to community agencies. Due to the challenges students face at this level, it is important that the team include individuals with knowledge and skills in specific areas of intervention, such as literacy, numeracy, applied behavior analysis, and person-centered or wraparound support planning. The student support team may regularly or occasionally include expertise from the district level. District personnel can serve three important functions. First, they help to develop intervention plans for students with complex and severe difficulties that exceed the school team's capacity. Second, they can support teams in building fluency with Tiers 2/3 systems teaming process. Third, they provide an important communication link with district administrators. A designated student support team member plays the important role of coordinator. In addition to facilitating meetings, the coordinator examines individual student progress data before meetings to prioritize students for discussion by the team (e.g., those not making adequate progress). Student support teams typically meet every other week.

Core activities for the student support team include identifying students needing additional support, designing student support (i.e., intervention) plans, monitoring the ongoing effectiveness of those plans, and supporting staff in implementation. As such, the team uses individual student screening, diagnostic, and progress monitoring data extensively. Academic and behavior screening data indicate which students are discussed at the next meeting. The team may use these data for diagnostic purposes or complete additional diagnostic assessments, particularly FBAs (Crone et al., 2015). Teams may invite classroom teachers or other staff to complete FBA interviews at team meetings. These data are used to assign students to Tier 2 interventions or to design Tier 3 intervention plans for students. Once plans are developed and implemented, the team uses progress monitoring data to assess whether students are experiencing more success or if adjustments are needed. This role may be new for teams that simply take special education referrals and create intervention plans without following up. As such, having clear decision rules for intervention changes (e.g., 3 data points below the goal or an aimline toward the next benchmark goal) makes these decisions more efficient (Riley-Tillman & Burns, 2010). Finally, the team collects information on how many students are accessing Tier 2 and Tier 3 interventions and the percent of students who are successful with each intervention (see Appendix 3.8). This information is then summarized and sent to the school leadership team for planning and evaluation.

Some schools have separate student support teams to address academic or behavior concerns. We strongly suggest combining these teams into one integrated team that coordinates both academic and behavior support. The focus on systems, as opposed to specific interventions, means that the teams should already have similar agendas, making integration easier than for the other types of teams described previously. In addition, for the reasons explained in Chapter 2, although academic support teams may not always need to consider behavior support, behavior support teams are more effective when they also consider students' academic needs. As such, an alternative integration option would be to have one academic support team and add behavioral expertise when the meeting agenda includes behavior support systems or behavior support for individual students.

## Common MTSS Teams at the District Level

### District Leadership Team(s)

District leadership teams support their school leadership teams by promoting funding, visibility, and political support for the integrated MTSS model. As is described in more detail in

Chapter 6, leadership teams at the district level may be separated into cabinet and implementation teams. Regardless of the configuration, district leadership team members work to ensure a strong, unified vision, provide long-term planning and evaluation, and coordinate training and coaching for schools (Sugai, Horner, Algozzine et al., 2010).

Membership on district leadership teams includes district personnel with the authority to make funding and policy decisions. It is important to have members who can make these decisions during the meetings without the need to first check with others for approval. Members may include the superintendent, curriculum director, special education director, local community agency representatives, juvenile court representatives, teacher association representatives, family members, some school administrators, district coaches, and a district MTSS coordinator. District leadership teams often meet on a monthly or quarterly basis.

Core activities for district leadership teams include evaluating fidelity of implementation and effects of MTSS systems, building local capacity to implement, and long-term (e.g., 3- to 5-year) action planning for sustainability. For effective evaluation and planning, these teams need school-level fidelity of implementation and outcomes data. Key analyses include combining these data to document both improvement over time and the association between fidelity of implementation of the integrated MTSS model and student outcomes. For example, the team may build reports that compare outcomes for schools implementing with and without adequate fidelity (e.g., Figure 3.5). The team uses this information to increase political support and identify how best to support individual school leadership teams in their implementation efforts, including removing barriers to implementation. One barrier that the team may address is the misalignment of academic and behavior MTSS initiatives. Considering this barrier, integrating all district teams helps to bring separate initiatives together into one unified system of supports.

## District Student Support Team

District student support teams exist to help each school's student support team in its functioning. These teams provide oversight for Tiers 2 and 3 systems through two primary functions. First, they provide general guidance regarding district-supported Tiers 2 and 3 interventions and the systems needed to implement them well. Second, they may also develop intensive, individualized programs of support for students with significant difficulties that involve specialized skills beyond the capacity of the individual school to provide.

Due to the complex challenges inherent in supports that are elevated to the district level, the team has to be able to support students with whom school teams have tried to intervene and are still struggling. As a result, the team needs to include individuals with expertise in specific areas of assessment, intervention, and service delivery. These specialists may be district employees or from outside agencies that provide supports to students in the district.

Core activities for the district student support team include building capacity within each school's student support team to enhance its practices and systems, as well as responding to individual student needs or emergencies. Although school personnel (and even district administrators) may view the team's primary function as responding to emergencies, attention to helping schools with their systems is the only way to make this team's workload manageable (Lewis-Palmer, Bounds, & Sugai, 2004). Assessing system implementation and identifying needs for training and coaching will help school teams support more students more effectively. Given that the district team provides support for both systems and individual students at Tiers 2 and 3, the team uses the same data as the school student support teams. To build capacity, district teams may assist school teams in analyzing their own data.

As with the school level, we strongly recommend integrating district student support teams. Because the systems at Tiers 2 and 3 are similar across academics and behavior (e.g., tiered organization, data-based decision making, use of meeting agendas), the same knowledge and skills are used to support school teams in their tiered systems of support. However, depending on the direct support needs of individual students, the schools' individual student teams may not need integrated individual student consultation. Table 5.1 summarizes the common teaming structures used in schools and districts.

## STRATEGIC INTEGRATION OF TEAMS

Throughout this book we have stressed some key reasons for integrating academic RTI and PBIS. Teaming is one place where the true advantages of an integrated MTSS model shine. First, because of the interactive nature of academics and behavior, teams that consider both academics and behavior can be more effective in addressing student needs. Second, consolidating teams with the same or similar functions—as opposed to simply adding more of them—is a unique opportunity to build efficiency in complex systems. In theory, we suggest that schools integrate teams whenever possible, so that all teams consider both academic and behavior data in problem-solving efforts, using the same problem-solving process to tackle the range of student needs. However, this type of full integration may not meet the needs of all schools, which is why we recommend strategic integration—a careful consideration of which teams make the most sense to integrate and in what order to integrate.

### *Finding the Right Balance*

It's not uncommon for schools implementing both academic RTI and PBIS to have completely separate teaming structures. During initial implementation this plan makes sense, but once the ad hoc academic RTI or PBIS exploration committees become standing teams (see Chapter 7), the number of teams in the school may become unsustainable. In larger schools (with more available faculty), it may be beneficial to have different teams to address specific components of student support (either by tiers or by domain). For example, a schoolwide academic RTI team may focus on academic instructional practices, independent of the schoolwide PBIS team and a school improvement planning team. A concern, particularly with smaller schools, is assigning staff to too many teams. The key point is to find the balance between effectiveness and efficiency, landing at the right number and configuration for each school's needs, so that teams can find the time to meet *and* get through their agendas. The basic premise focuses on identifying the functions that are important for an integrated model to be successful and then to make sure that these functions are addressed. The form (i.e., number and types of teams) used to address the function will vary based on resource availability, administrator priority, and staff experience. Just as there is no ideal team makeup or number of teams in each school, there is no magic, ideal solution for how to integrate them. Because starting with the most logical teams to integrate in each school makes sense, we present three methods to go about this task: (1) adapting existing teams, (2) integrating across domains, and (3) integrating across tiers.

**TABLE 5.1. Common Teaming Structures Used in Schools and Districts**

| Team | Makeup | Typical meeting frequency | Student focus | Key purposes |
|---|---|---|---|---|
| Individual student team | • Student<br>• Family members<br>• Classroom teacher<br>• Specialists (as needed) | • Yearly or more frequently as needed | • The individual student | • Set goals for academic, social, and career success.<br>• Review individual student progress. |
| Grade-level team | • Teachers at the grade level (e.g., sixth grade, intermediate)<br>• Classroom aides | • Every other week | • *Most* students within the grade level, with a primary emphasis on prevention at Tier 1<br>• Secondary emphasis on intervention at Tiers 2 and 3 | • Collect and review student data at grade level.<br>• Coordinate and schedule integrated grade-level interventions.<br>• Collaborate to implement integrated academic and behavior practices. |
| School leadership team | • Principal<br>• Grade-level team representatives<br>• Specialists<br>• Family representative(s)<br>• Student(s) | • Monthly | • *All* students in school, with a primary emphasis on prevention at Tier 1<br>• Secondary emphasis on systems at Tiers 2 and 3 | • Coordinate and manage schoolwide interventions in an integrated academic and behavior MTSS model.<br>• Review fidelity, academic, and behavior data at schoolwide level and adjust schoolwide action plan. |
| Student support team | • Tiers 2/3 coordinator<br>• Special education teachers<br>• Content specialists<br>• Support personnel<br>• District personnel (as needed) | • Every other week | • Systems for specific students requiring additional support, with a primary emphasis on intervention at Tiers 2 and 3 | • Coordinate and manage Tiers 2 and 3 interventions in an integrated academic and behavior MTSS model.<br>• Design and monitor effectiveness of Tiers 2 and 3 interventions. |
| District leadership team(s) | • District administrators<br>• School administrators<br>• Community representatives<br>• Family representatives<br>• District MTSS coaches<br>• District MTSS coordinator | • Quarterly | • Systems capacity for each school in the district, with a primary emphasis on prevention at Tier 1 | • Evaluate implementation and effectiveness of model.<br>• Build capacity (training, coaching) in schools.<br>• Develop and implement long-term action plan. |
| District student support team | • District behavior specialists<br>• District and/or external interventionists<br>• Family liaisons<br>• District MTSS coaches<br>• District MTSS coordinator | • Monthly | • Systems capacity for each school in the district, with a primary emphasis on intervention at Tiers 2 and 3<br>• Secondary emphasis on intervention at Tier 3 (students with the most needs) | • Evaluate implementation and effectiveness of Tiers 2 and 3 interventions.<br>• Build capacity (training, coaching) in schools.<br>• Provide direct support to school student support teams. |

## Adapting Existing Teams

Considering that schools already have a number of teams (some of them mandated), it is always wise to explore whether one of these teams can take on the responsibilities of an MTSS team. As described earlier, an existing school leadership team or school improvement team may be able to take on Tier 1 MTSS coordination. In addition, a school-based team or teacher assistance team could become the student support team. However, when repurposing teams for integrated MTSS, it is important to be clear about changes in team responsibilities and common activities. For example, a student support team that previously handled only special education eligibility referrals (and perhaps only academic ones) may need additional training and ongoing coaching to become comfortable with the new role of monitoring the ongoing progress of students receiving Tier 2 or 3 support.

## Integrating across Domains

Another obvious opportunity for integration is to merge teams that address academic and behavior domains. An existing schoolwide academic RTI or PBIS team could have an expanded mandate as the schoolwide MTSS team. Although this configuration is advantageous for many schools, others may find it too difficult to get the important work done. In these situations, we've found a few alternatives that may work as well or better for some schools. Given that it is so powerful to integrate academic and behavior support at Tiers 2 and 3, we recommend integrating these teams first. If these teams would like to merge academic and behavior support but find it difficult to cover all of the students (both the initial referrals and progress monitoring), alternating an academic or behavior focus every other meeting could be a manageable solution. As teams are integrated, it is helpful to keep in mind that although an integrated MTSS team needs to be knowledgeable about academic and behavior supports, not everyone on the team needs to be an expert in both areas. Integrated teams allow for the sharing of skill sets and the building of collective capacity to solve problems.

## Integrating across Tiers

Team overload doesn't come solely from integrating support—it also comes from teaming for the multiple tiers in an MTSS model. Another approach for integration is to integrate teams vertically (i.e., merging teams by tier). The easiest way to merge teams across tiers is to consolidate the coordination of Tiers 2 and 3 systems into one team. A contemporary view of MTSS conceptualizes support as more of a gradient than as distinct levels. As an example, a team may implement a standard protocol check-in/check-out with a student and later tweak that intervention to prevent escape-maintained behavior more effectively. This change would likely fall somewhere between Tiers 2 and 3 support, and therefore it is advantageous to have this continuum of support managed by a single team. However, trying to coordinate services for all students needing additional support may be too much for one team, especially in high schools. As with integrating across domains, an alternative is to have a single team alternate a Tier 2 or 3 focus every other meeting. Finally, some schools may attempt to consolidate all three tiers into one team. Although this approach may seem like a good solution (or the only solution for small schools), there are disadvantages, particularly when discussing individual student support. Talking about individual students may violate confidentiality (if parents or students are team members), or the discussions regarding individual student support may crowd out the prevention practices at Tier 1, which will eventually lead to more students requiring support at Tiers 2 and 3.

### Alignment of Teams

Regardless of the number and configuration of MTSS teams within the school, it is important to ensure that each team is aligned with other teams and with the mission of improving student outcomes. Alignment across the various teams ensures that progress is made while reducing competition for staff time and energy, as multiple teams may compete with each other for resources and cognitive focus. Staff should view the implementation of MTSS as a way to enhance their current activities in school improvement. Administrators can help by describing MTSS activities as ways to implement existing and future school, district, and state initiatives (e.g., achievement, school safety, equity).

## STRATEGIES FOR EFFECTIVE TEAMING

Earlier in this chapter, we mentioned one of the challenges of integrated teams: the additional agenda items resulting from more data to consider and the complexity of examining integrated data and interventions in the same meeting. Teams that currently do fine addressing one content area without clear structures and processes are likely to find themselves overwhelmed when adding a new content area and team members. As a result, it is absolutely critical to assess and improve team functioning. The research is clear that having effective teams is a key factor in effective implementation and sustainability (Coffey & Horner, 2012; McIntosh et al., 2013; McIntosh, Mercer, Nese, Strickland-Cohen, & Hoselton, in press).

To address team functioning, it is worthwhile to consider one's experiences with teaming. Individuals may join a team for a range of reasons. They may be interested in the work to be accomplished, feel obligated to contribute to the school, enjoying working with colleagues, or were selected to join. No matter the reason, the likelihood that each member of the team will stay motivated to continue teaming increases when he or she sees the team as productive and successful. As a result, a focus on effective teaming will enhance team morale and functioning in the long run. It may take sustained efforts for the team to adjust to this change (i.e., from a group of individuals spending time together to a group functioning collaboratively and effectively with an outcome-oriented focus). However, team members can be assured that these skills easily transfer to teaming in other domains.

### Effective Teaming Structures

Regardless of the structure of teams in a school or district and how they are integrated, *all teams* can benefit from a small set of strategies for organization, effective interaction during meetings, and useful problem solving (Sugai & Todd, 2004). Many of these strategies are included in a structured teaming process developed for PBIS teams, called *team-initiated problem solving* (TIPS; Newton et al., 2014). TIPS provides a comprehensive model for forming teams and running effective meetings that focus on using school data for problem solving and linking this information to action planning. Experimental research has shown that adoption of TIPS results in significantly improved team functioning and decision making (Newton, Horner, Algozzine, Todd, & Algozzine, 2012; Todd et al., 2011). The following teaming structures, many of which are defined in TIPS, can enhance teaming in integrated MTSS models.

## Clear Mission and Purpose

Before even considering how well teams work, it is important for each team to have a clear mission, as well as clear outcomes for each meeting. A clear and brief statement of purpose makes it easy for the team and each of its members to assess whether they are addressing the team's overarching mission or taking on the purposes of other teams in the school. For example, a well-intentioned school leadership team may spend time in their meeting discussing the needs of individual students, which is a task better suited for the student support team's mission. A mission statement for a school leadership team might be:

"We coordinate the MTSS universal prevention systems by (1) collecting, analyzing, and sharing schoolwide data regarding implementation and outcomes with school staff and community; (2) identifying schoolwide needs (in literacy, math, and behavior); (3) developing schoolwide goals/priorities/strategies to meet identified needs; and (4) ensuring completion of overall goals/priorities/strategies."

This mission statement establishes a distinct emphasis of this team's role as one of coordinating schoolwide systems. As such, both the team and general school staff understand this team's responsibilities as they relate to their integrated MTSS model.

In addition, although staff members may enjoy each other's company, generally educators connect in work settings to see outcomes and accomplishments. Meetings will become burdensome and stressful without meaningful work that nets observable accomplishments. Team members should enter each meeting knowing what decisions need to be made and how these decisions fit in with the team's mission.

## Agreements and Norms

Working effectively as a team involves a team culture of shared values and understandings. Effective teams also use skills specific to productive meeting processes and collaboration. In Chapter 4, we discussed the importance of identifying clear behavior expectations for our students so that they know exactly what they are being asked to do and, as a result, can be more successful in school. Similarly, it is helpful for team members to agree on behavior expectations for their team. Table 5.2 illustrates one example of behavior expectations for teams.

## Specified Meeting Roles

In addition to team expectations, it is beneficial to identify roles and responsibilities for each member of the team, so that each knows what to do and what others will do. The TIPS protocol includes four roles: facilitator, minute taker, data analyst, and team member (Newton et

**TABLE 5.2. Sample Team Behavior Expectations**

| Expectation | Specific examples |
|---|---|
| Be Responsible. | • Start and end on time.<br>• Arrive prepared for the meeting (i.e., complete action items).<br>• Follow agenda.<br>• Take responsibility for ensuring the meeting outcomes and keeping the meeting moving forward. |
| Be Respectful. | • Consider all of the voices we represent.<br>• Be considerate of team members connecting through conference call.<br>• Assume good intentions.<br>• Support and honor expertise and experience of all staff. |
| Be Productive. | • Work efficiently.<br>• Be present with the conversation.<br>• Focus on team mission.<br>• Define action items for achieving team outcomes. |

al., 2014). As another example, Table 5.3 provides a set of roles and responsibilities of team members. One key aspect of specifying roles is not that these specific titles (e.g., timekeeper/note taker/recorder) and even divisions of responsibilities are used (e.g., the facilitator may also have the responsibilities of timekeeper), but rather that there is agreement on who will perform them. As such, specific titles and responsibilities may vary from school to school, and the number of roles will vary based on the members on the team. With regard to integrated MTSS models, teams may need to have separate data coordinators for different data sources (e.g., literacy, math, behavior). Another key aspect of this sample set is that each member has a role. The final role in the table is active team member, as all members of effective teams have responsibilities. Finally, it is useful to have specified backups (in case core members cannot attend) and have the attending school administrator serve as an active team member, because of the chance of missing some or all of meetings to address emergencies.

Team member responsibilities include not only actions during the meeting, but also tasks to be completed before and after them as well. Preparation and follow-up helps to make sure that the work of the team is carried out between meetings. One important example involves the role of the data coordinator. As seen in the table, one key responsibility of each data coordinator is to make sense of the data *before* the team examines it. Because team meeting time is extremely valuable and individuals bring skill sets that vary across domains in an integrated MTSS model, it is inefficient and often overwhelming for the entire team to look at raw data during the meeting. Instead, having someone (or a small group) examine the raw data, identify trends, and give a summary to the team with updates and identified areas for discussion is immensely helpful. For example, when examining fidelity data, it is helpful to start the meeting with an overall snapshot (e.g., Are we implementing to criterion?) and then provide some suggestions for action planning, or alternatively, guide the team through this process quickly to build capacity. When examining schoolwide or grade-level data, the data coordinator can utilize academic benchmark data to determine in which areas the Tier 1 systems are working and which areas the core curriculum needs supplementation. When examining Tier 2 or 3 progress monitoring data, the data coordinator can check the rosters, calculate what percent of students is (1) performing successfully, (2) could move down a tier of support, and (3) needs additional problem solving. When these decisions are straightforward, the data coordinator can simply update the team and note any changes to action plans. This efficiency creates more time for problem solving any challenging circumstances. As such, the other team members can focus more on making important decisions than identifying which decisions need to be made.

**TABLE 5.3. Sample Team Member Roles and Responsibilities**

| Team Member Role | Team Member Responsibilities |
|---|---|
| Facilitator | • Sends meeting agenda and reminder before meeting.<br>• Ensures that agenda is followed.<br>• Guides discussions.<br>• Ensures that all team members are engaged in team mission and outcomes. |
| Note taker | • Documents key items.<br>• Clarifies outcomes of discussions during the meeting.<br>• Circulates meeting minutes promptly after meetings. |
| Action item recorder (may be combined with meeting note taker) | • Documents actionable item next steps assigned to team members, including:<br>  o Clear description of task.<br>  o Who will complete the task.<br>  o When the task completion is due.<br>  o Possible resources needed to complete the task. |
| Timekeeper | • Keeps track of time and related agenda items during the team meeting.<br>• Provides prompts when nearing end of allocated time for item and when allocated time is over. |
| Data coordinator | • Analyzes fidelity and outcome data (i.e., turns data into information) before meeting.<br>• Prioritizes items for discussion (e.g., Tier 1: specific areas of challenge, Tiers 2/3: specific student needs for problem solving).<br>• Brings data summaries to meeting for discussion. |
| Active team member | • Engages in conversations and contributes to problem solving and feedback regarding the team's work.<br>• Completes assigned tasks as documented by the action item recorder. |

## Structured Agenda

One of the most critical tools for improving meetings is the meeting agenda. Teams with unfocused agendas or tendencies to deviate from them are unlikely to meet their objectives. In light of this challenge, developing a structured agenda form that helps guide the team can vastly improve meeting quality and accountability. A structured agenda can be viewed as a series of prompts to engage in effective collaboration and decision making. For example, the TIPS process includes a structured meeting agenda form that focuses on utilizing data to enhance problem solving. A TIPS-inspired agenda helps to prompt teams to analyze their data, move from general problem statements (e.g., "Behavior in the hallways is out of control") to precise ones (e.g., "There has been a steady increase over the fall in ODRs for inappropriate language for grade 6 students in the hallways in the afternoons"), which are more actionable and lead to more effective and efficient solutions (Todd et al., 2012). This type of agenda is appropriate for any teams in the integrated MTSS model, including the school leadership team, grade-level team, student support team, and the various district teams. Additionally, this process works well for addressing academic, behavior, or integrated academic and behavior challenges.

Effective structured agendas have a number of key features that help the team to function in a maximally effective manner (Sugai & Todd, 2004). First, such agendas focus the team on using data to make key decisions; they provide time to discuss and make plans regarding not only student outcomes, but also fidelity of implementation of practices. In addition, they also prompt a common element that is forgotten among teams: conducting follow-up on effectiveness of plans to address previous challenges. Second, structured agendas include suggested times (i.e., number of minutes) for each agenda item so that the team can get through the entire set during the allotted time. Third, as indicated by the specific role of the action item recorder in Table 5.3, good agendas provide space (which serves as a prompt) to define specific tasks to be completed, including the person responsible and the due date for completion of the task. It is common to discuss challenges and solutions effectively but neglect to note the details needed to carry out the plan. Fourth, these agendas include a brief self-assessment at the end of the meeting for team members to evaluate whether they are following agreements and working effectively. This feature allows teams to validate their efforts and self-correct error patterns before sliding into inefficient or ineffective meeting habits. Optionally, agenda forms may also include space that allows them to serve as the meeting minutes as well. This type of form makes it easier for teams to follow and ensures that the agenda items and minutes are aligned, without any items falling through the cracks.

Once structured agendas are developed, teams can take a number of steps to maximize their utility. It is helpful to distribute the agenda prior to the meeting with identified outcomes so that members can come to the meeting as more active participants. Additionally, it is wise to make the agenda and meeting minutes electronic by projecting them so that everyone can see the notes as they are typed. This small step allows for everyone to follow along with the agenda, minutes, and decisions in real time, as well as access the minutes immediately, without the note taker having to type them up after the meeting. Instead, the note taker can e-mail them directly to the group as soon as the meeting is over.

Two sample team meeting agendas are provided in Figures 5.2 and 5.3, with blank forms in Appendices 5.1 and 5.2. The first agenda is used by an integrated MTSS school leadership team in their regular meeting to coordinate Tier 1 academic and behavior systems. This agenda

# School Leadership Team Meeting Agenda

School: *Lakeview Elementary*                   Date: *October 8*

Facilitator: *Rhonda*

Note Taker/Recorder: *Charleen*

Timekeeper: *DeSean*

Data Coordinator: *Karyn*

Active Team Members Present: *Kenneth, Howard*

**Team Purpose:** *We work to improve schoolwide academic and behavior outcomes for all students through coordinating integrated systems. We also ensure alignment with school, district, and state initiatives.*

1. **Celebrate Successes** (5 minutes):

   *Plan to reduce classroom ODRs is working—all teachers completed lessons on time.*

2. **Review Tier 1 Implementation Data** (10 minutes):

   a. Review most recent fidelity data.

      - *Literacy: R-TFI Total Score : 91%*
      - *Behavior: SWPBIS TFI Tier I Scale : 83%*
        *Student/Family/Community Involvement item score : 0 (not implemented)*

   b. What barriers are interfering with implementation?

      - *Intermediate teachers seem unclear on differentiation of whole-group reading instruction for low performing students.*

   c. What can we do to improve implementation? Update action plan below.

      - *Review general principles for differentiation of instruction at next intermediate grade-level team meeting.*
      - *Administer PBIS Family Input and Satisfaction Survey.*

3. **Review Tier 1 Student Outcomes Data** (15 minutes):

   a. Review most recent student outcomes data.

      A. *Literacy: Students at or above fall AIMSweb benchmarks :*
         i. *Grade K: 41%*
         ii. *Grade 1: 78%*
         iii. *Grade 2: 87%*
         iv. *Grade 3: 79%*
         v. *Grade 4: 77%*
         vi. *Grade 5: 77%*
      B. *Behavior:*
         i. *Percent of students with 0–1 ODRs (last full year): 83% (81% in previous years)*
            a. *White students : 92%*
            b. *Black students : 73%*
            c. *Latino/a students : 94%*
         ii. *Classroom ODRs last month : 26 (33 in month before last)*

*(continued)*

**FIGURE 5.2.** Example of a completed School Leadership Team Meeting Agenda.

b. What can we do to improve outcomes? Update action plan below.

- *Monitor outcomes after instruction review in intermediate grades (consider as topic for next inservice day).*
- *Complete review of ODRs to identify precise problem statement of vulnerable decision points (specific situations with more disproportionality for black students).*
- *Get risk ratios from SWIS Ethnicity Report to monitor disproportionality.*

**4. Ongoing Business** (15 minutes):

a. Review issues and action items from previous meeting.

*Reducing classroom ODRs; teach/reteach classroom routines.*

i. What is status (completed, in process, not started)?

*Completed—all teachers completed by last Friday.*

ii. What do we need to continue/stop/add?

- *Continue to monitor classroom ODRs each month.*
- *Assess need for booster lessons in classrooms.*

**5. New Business** (10 minutes):

a. What new issues need to be addressed to ensure improved implementation and/or outcomes?

- *Discussion about implicit racial bias in ODR decisions and providing equitable opportunities to respond in classroom instruction.*
- *Continue to identify nature of the problem with precise problem statements; topic for next meeting.*

b. What are continuing barriers or risks to implementation?

*Staff overload—try to focus on a few small things each month.*

**6. Meeting Self-Assessment** (5 minutes):

| Evaluation of Team Meeting | Yes | So-So | No |
|---|:---:|:---:|:---:|
| 1.  Did we follow our expectations in the meeting today? | X | | |
| 2.  Did we focus on our team's purpose in the meeting today? | X | | |
| 3.  Did we do a good job of completing the tasks we agreed on at previous meetings? | X | | |
| 4.  In general, are the completed tasks having the desired effects on student outcomes? | | X | |
| **If some of the ratings are "So-So" or "No," what can we do to improve things?** | | | |
| *Continue to complete tasks, especially for equity—good outcomes will come from this team's hard work!* | | | |

*(continued)*

**FIGURE 5.2.** *(continued)*

**Ongoing Action Planning Items**

| Activity | Who is responsible? | Target start date | Target completion date | How will we know if it's working? |
|---|---|---|---|---|
| Complete R-TFI | Coach and team | January 8 | January 8 | Discussed at Feb. meeting |
| Complete SWPBIS TFI again | Team with PBIS coach | December 2 | December 2 | Entered on PBIS Assessment site |
| Teach classroom routines | Classroom teachers | October 1 | October 15 | Staff room checklist—Done |
| Monitor classroom ODRs | Data coordinator | October 1 | Monthly | Data summary sent before each meeting |
| Send Family Input and Satisfaction Survey link to families in school newsletter | Administrative assistant | November 5 | December 5 | At least 75% return rate |

**FIGURE 5.2.** *(continued)*

includes the team's purpose as a reminder for members to stick to their most important tasks. The facilitator may read it to the team as a precorrection, especially if the team has drifted from this aim in past meetings. The first official item is to celebrate successes with the Tier 1 systems, such as strong implementation of a new curriculum or improved schoolwide student outcomes in a particular area. Next, the team reviews systems-level fidelity of implementation data and discusses progress. After reviewing fidelity, the team examines schoolwide data (e.g., percent of students successful), with care taken not to discuss individual students. At this point, the team reviews ongoing business, including progress in follow up actions from previous meetings. This team followed up on their previous plan to reduce ODRs in the classroom, which had increased compared to previous years. Next, the team identifies new business, including a discussion regarding their ODR data indicating racial disproportionality. Finally, the team self-assesses their functioning. At the bottom of the agenda is the action plan for ongoing entry and updating throughout the meeting.

The second team meeting agenda is intended for use by the school's integrated MTSS student support team. As can be seen, the agenda closely resembles the school leadership team's agenda, with some key differences. Agenda item 4 ("Systems Decisions Updates from Data Coordinator") is an important component of the meeting. This item is intentionally brief, as it is a simple update of student progress that highlights decisions regarding graduation or modification (students not in these categories continue with current support). The time saved by keeping this agenda item brief in this section can be used to discuss modifications for students who are not being successful. Of course, individual team members may ask to discuss any student's progress in detail.

# Student Support Team Meeting Agenda

School: _Lakeview Elementary_      Date: _October 15_

Facilitator: _Cesar_

Note Taker/Recorder: _Sandee_

Timekeeper: _Michael_

Data Coordinator: _Karyn_

Active Team Members Present: _Chanti, Howard_

**Team Purpose:** _We primarily work to build effective academic and behavior systems of support for our students requiring more than Tier 1 support to be successful. We also handle new referrals for support and monitor and problem-solve progress for individual students._

1. **Celebrate Successes** (5 minutes):

   _Great implementation check for REWARDS!_
   _Aria spent 100% of last week in her regular classroom!_
   _Eddie's decoding is improving rapidly!_

2. **Review Tiers 2/3 Implementation Data** (10 minutes):

   a. Review most recent fidelity data.

      - _Literacy: REWARDS fidelity observations: 88% (average)_
      - _Behavior: SWPBIS TFI Tiers 2 and 3 scales : 76% and 51%_
        _Tier 3 support plans subscale score : 33%_
        _FBAs on file are good, but support plans are missing key components (e.g., comprehensive support, family preferences)._

   b. What barriers are interfering with implementation?

      - _Less capacity for building support plans after Carol left._

   c. What can we do to improve implementation? Update action plan below.

      - _Request FBA to BSP training for team and district coaching support._

3. **Review Tiers 2/3 Student Outcomes Data** (15 minutes):

   a. Review most recent student outcomes data.

      A. _Literacy: Students being successful (at or above aimlines in progress monitoring):_
         i. _Early Reading Intervention : 91%_
         ii. _Read Naturally: 83%_
         iii. _REWARDS: 88%_

      B. _Behavior: Students being successful (meeting daily point goals on 4 of 5 days per week):_
         i. _FRIENDS for Life : 89%_
         ii. _CICO (check-in/check-out): 89%_
         iii. _CICO + Second Step: 82%_
         iv. _CICO + Tier 3 plan : 42%_

_(continued)_

**FIGURE 5.3.** Example of a completed Student Support Team Meeting Agenda.

b. What can we do to improve outcomes? Update action plan below.

*Review all Tier 3 behavior support plans for adequacy and improve plans.*

4. **Systems Decisions Updates from Data Coordinator** (5 minutes):
   a. Literacy:
      i. Students ready to graduate from support.

      *Kaylee (Read Naturally)—drop to Tier 1*

      ii. Students not being successful (discuss in #5).

      *None at this time (nice work, team!)*

   b. Behavior:
      i. Students ready to graduate from support.

      *Aria (CICO)—fade to self-monitoring*

      ii. Students not being successful (discuss in #5).

      *Ned (Tier 3)—discuss next*

5. **Problem Solving for Individual Students** (15 minutes):
   a. Student(s) of concern: *Ned (grade 4)*
      i. Current plan
         - *CICO + Tier 3 (individualized plan) teaching appropriate skills to obtain peer attention*
         - *No additional academic support.*
      ii. Issues
         - *Four ODRs in past week for work refusal during math and defiance after teacher check-outs.*
         - *Below benchmark in math problem-solving fluency.*
      iii. What do we need to continue/stop/add?
         - *Reteach Ned how to accept constructive CICO feedback and teacher how to provide it supportively.*
         - *Additional diagnostic assessment in math (start by checking benchmark probes).*

6. **New Referrals for Support** (5 minutes):
   a. What new referrals need to be handled?

   *Aiden R. (grade 2) classroom disruption. Student is reading at benchmark, and teacher has reviewed expectations.*

   b. What steps are needed for implementation? Update action plan below.

   *Start Aiden on check-in/check-out. Cesar to do initial teaching tomorrow. Karyn to be mentor.*

*(continued)*

**FIGURE 5.3.** *(continued)*

**7. Meeting Self-Assessment** (5 minutes):

| Evaluation of Team Meeting | Yes | So-So | No |
|---|---|---|---|
| 1. Did we follow our expectations in the meeting today? | X | | |
| 2. Did we focus on our team's purpose in the meeting today? | | X | |
| 3. Did we do a good job of completing the tasks we agreed on at previous meetings? | X | | |
| 4. In general, are the completed tasks having the desired effects on student outcomes? | X | | |
| **If some of the ratings are "So-So" or "No," what can we do to improve things?** | | | |
| Remind each other to share only relevant student information during problem solving to keep meeting efficient. | | | |

**Ongoing Action Planning Items**

| Activity | Who is responsible? | Target start date | Target completion date | How will we know if it's working? |
|---|---|---|---|---|
| Continue fidelity observations for literacy interventions | Literacy coach | November 15 | Monthly | Discussed at next meeting |
| Complete SWPBIS TFI again | Team with PBIS coach | December 15 | December 15 | Entered on PBIS Assessment site |
| Request district FBA to BSP training | Facilitator | October 22 | November 1 | Response from district coordinator |
| Request district behaviorconsultant to attend meetings | Facilitator | October 22 | November 1 | Response from district coordinator |
| Review Tier 3 behavior support plans | Data coordinator | October 22 | Monthly (three per month) | Summary sent to team |
| Reteach CICO rating process with Ned and his teacher | Facilitator | October 16 | October 22 | Report at meeting |
| Review Ned's math benchmarks | Facilitator | October 22 | November 1 | Discuss at next meeting |
| Enroll Aiden in CICO | Facilitator | October 16 | October 22 | Data summary at meeting |

**FIGURE 5.3.** *(continued)*

## *Annual Timetable for Agenda Items*

Obviously, integrated MTSS teams have a huge set of tasks to undertake. To avoid overwhelming teams and maintaining effective functioning, it is useful to spread these tasks across meetings throughout the year in a thoughtful way. Such a timetable is often developed by district administrators and built into a calendar of trainings and deadlines for activities. Table 5.4 provides a sample annual timetable with monthly focus points for an integrated MTSS school leadership team. The activities identified in the table correspond with key events (e.g., academic benchmark assessments) that take place at predictable times during the year and link information into action planning. Additional activities represent progress monitoring and adjusting the team's actions to ensure that students have access to effective interventions and experience improved outcomes as a result. This timetable corresponds closely to the data collection and use schedule provided in Figure 3.3 (p. 65). As an example of a time-specific agenda, Appendix 5.3 provides a sample grade-level team meeting agenda for meetings that follow academic benchmark data collection, which culminate in a revised integrated instructional plan (see Figure 4.10 [p. 147] and Appendix 4.3 [p. 157]).

## *Integrated Problem-Solving and Decision-Making Processes*

During meetings, integrated teams can be more effective and efficient by using the same standard process for addressing challenges at various levels (e.g., schoolwide, classroom, individual student) and domains (e.g., academics, behavior, integrated support). Once a standard problem-solving process is defined and adopted, team members can devote more of their energy to solving problems rather than spending meetings trying to figure out what to do next. Using a standard process for problem solving is certainly no guarantee of success on the first try, but going through iterative problem-solving cycles will help the team become more accurate and fluent in the problem-solving process, which will also increase the likelihood of solving the problem.

### *Integrated Problem-Solving Processes*

Although there are many different problem-solving models that educators use to improve the quality of instructional programs and associated student outcomes, the models share many features and can be considered variations of a general problem-solving process (Newton et al., 2014). Different models may include a few simple steps (e.g., plan, do, study, act) or a more complex process. For the purpose of this book, we suggest a general six-step problem-solving process that any teams across tiers or content areas can use. This process is derived from the school psychology literature (Deno, 1995), TIPS (Newton et al., 2012), and the outcomes-driven model (Good, Gruba, & Kaminski, 2002).

STEP 1: PROBLEM IDENTIFICATION

This first step involves bringing a problem to the attention of the team. Typically the problem identification step begins with a broad and general statement (e.g., third-grade reading scores are too low, students are too loud in the main hallway). The main purpose of this step is to determine whether a problem exists, define it as precisely as possible, and decide whether it is

**TABLE 5.4. Annual Timetable for Integrated MTSS School Leadership Team Meetings**

| Month | Focus of team meeting | Team activities | Key questions to answer |
|---|---|---|---|
| September | Integrated implementation plan revision | • Coordinate fall academic benchmarking/screening assessments and fidelity assessments for year.<br>• Use schoolwide student outcomes data to track progress.<br>• Adjust school improvement plan based on schoolwide student data. | • Are school personnel adequately supported to conduct data collection?<br>• Do we need to change our academic interventions and supports based on screening data? |
| October November December | Fidelity and behavior progress monitoring | • Use Tier 1 fidelity data to track progress and identify successes and barriers.<br>• Identify and correct implementation issues proactively.<br>• Build implementation capacity of team and school staff.<br>• Use monthly behavior screening data to identify successes and challenges. | • Are school personnel implementing interventions correctly?<br>• What additional professional development opportunities are needed for improved implementation? |
| January | Integrated implementation plan revision | • Coordinate winter academic benchmarking/screening assessments.<br>• Use schoolwide student outcomes data to track progress.<br>• Adjust school improvement plan as needed. | • Do we need to change our interventions and supports based on screening data? |
| February March April | Fidelity and behavior progress monitoring | • Use Tier 1 fidelity data to track progress and identify successes and barriers.<br>• Identify and correct implementation issues proactively.<br>• Build implementation capacity of team and school staff.<br>• Use monthly behavior screening data to identify successes and challenges. | • Are school personnel implementing interventions correctly?<br>• What additional professional development opportunities are needed? |
| May | Evaluation and revision of integrated implementation plan for next school year | • Conduct yearly evaluation of implementation and student outcomes.<br>• Share evaluation report with staff, families, district, and community.<br>• Develop next year's school improvement plan based on both implementation and outcomes data. | • How well did we implement an integrated MTSS model?<br>• How successful were students with the integrated MTSS model?<br>• What should we do next year to enhance our integrated MTSS model? |

a problem worth addressing. To assist in this decision, it is helpful to compare current data to specific criteria (e.g., academic benchmarks, local or national norms for behavior, performance in previous years).

## STEP 2: PROBLEM CLARIFICATION

Once identified, it is important to understand the problem in greater detail. During the problem clarification process, the team seeks to identify why the problem is occurring, similar to diagnostic assessment for students (described in Chapter 3). The contextual variables that may trigger or maintain the problem are identified. Careful data collection and analysis during this step will help to develop solutions that are more directly linked to the problem.

## STEP 3: SOLUTION PLANNING

The team takes the information from Step 2 to begin identifying possible interventions. This process can include three actions: (a) brainstorming possible strategies, (b) selecting strategies that are both feasible to implement *and* likely to be effective, and (c) developing a clear action plan for implementing and assessing outcomes (Scott, Anderson, & Alter, 2012).

## STEP 4: GOAL SETTING

A frequently overlooked step in problem solving is to set a clear goal that will indicate whether the plan is successful. This goal can often be derived from the criteria used in Step 1 to identify the problem. This goal should be accompanied by a date for reaching it and a plan for assessing progress.

## STEP 5: INTERVENTION IMPLEMENTATION

Once a solution is identified and a goal is set, the intervention is implemented. It is critical to ensure that implementers have the necessary resources to implement well, including a plan to monitor the fidelity of implementation. Sometimes the individuals implementing the plan will require additional training to implement the solution(s) well.

## STEP 6: EVALUATION

During this last stage, the success of the plan is evaluated (in a process mirroring Step 1) to determine whether the problem still exists. If so, the problem-solving steps will begin again while applying the new information learned during the previous problem-solving cycle. If the process is successful, it is useful to celebrate and use the learning from this cycle for future problem solving.

## EXAMPLES

As described, this process can drive decision making for any team in the school or district. To provide a few brief examples of the model in action, Figure 5.4 briefly shows the problem-

## PROBLEM-SOLVING STEPS IN ACTION
### School Leadership Team (see agenda in Figure 5.2)

| |
|---|
| **Problem:** Racial/ethnic disproportionality in ODRs |
| **Step 1: Problem Identification** |
| The data coordinator identifies that black students are overrepresented in ODRs. A total of 73% of black students had 0 to 1 ODRs last year, compared to 92% of white students and 83% overall. |
| **Step 2: Problem Clarification** |
| Before the next meeting (November), the data coordinator assesses ODRs by problem behavior, location, and time of day and finds that black students are more likely to receive ODRs for disrespect and more likely to receive these ODRs in the bus area in the afternoon. |
| **Step 3: Solution Planning** |
| After brainstorming solutions at the next meeting, the team decides to (a) revisit ODR definitions for disrespect; (b) review instructional approaches to problem behavior; (c) reteach expectations for the bus area; (d) increase use of acknowledgment tickets, ensuring equity across groups, at the bus area; and (e) monitor ODRs for improvement by assessing risk ratios for black students (% of black students with an ODR / % of white students with an ODR). |
| **Step 4: Goal Setting** |
| The team notes a current risk ratio of 2.85 and sets a goal to reduce it to below 1.25 by the end of the school year. |
| **Step 5: Intervention Implementation** |
| The team plans to review ODRs, instructional responses to behavior, and bus area expectations at the next staff meeting; reteach expectations to students in the next week; and observe implementation of responses to prosocial and problem behavior at the bus area. The team creates a quick checklist to assess completion. |
| **Step 6: Evaluation** |
| The team plans to revisit its plan and observe outcomes each month until the goal (described in Step 4) is met, revising plans if no decrease is seen in the risk ratio each month. |

### Student Support Team (see agenda in Figure 5.3)

| |
|---|
| **Problem:** Progress for Ned (grade 4) |
| **Step 1: Problem Identification** |
| Ned received four ODRs in the past week. He received seven last year but none this year until last week. |
| **Step 2: Problem Clarification** |
| Classroom teacher reports that problems are related to work refusal in math and defiance after teacher check-outs (CICO). Additional clarification through file review (fall academic screening assessment) shows that he is below benchmark in math problem solving. The data coordinator examines error patterns and notes correct problem comprehension but multiple operations errors. |
| **Step 3: Solution Planning** |
| The team decides to (a) teach Ned how to accept constructive CICO feedback; (b) review effective strategies for the teacher to provide CICO feedback; (c) reteach math operations; and (d) monitor CICO points, ODRs, and CBM math progress monitoring data for improvement. |
| **Step 4: Goal Setting** |
| The team sets a goal of 80% of CICO daily points earned and progress on an aimline toward meeting the winter math benchmark by January 15. |

*(continued)*

**FIGURE 5.4.** Example of school leadership team and student support team problem-solving steps.

| |
|---|
| **Step 5: Intervention Implementation** |
| The team creates an action plan to ensure that each of the components is completed. The facilitator will observe CICO feedback sessions at least once per week to ensure effective use of feedback by the teacher and accepting feedback by Ned. |
| **Step 6: Evaluation** |
| The team will monitor Ned's data at each student support team meeting as usual through January, revising the plan if there are 3 consecutive days missing CICO points goals or below the math aimline. |

**FIGURE 5.4.** *(continued)*

solving steps in action for two problems identified by teams in their meetings (minutes shown in Figures 5.2 and 5.3). Other examples can be found in the literature for Tier 1 team problem solving (Todd et al., 2012) and Tier 2 team problem solving (Albin & Todd, 2015).

## Integrated Student Request for Assistance Processes

At the point when the problem-solving model indicates that students require more support than Tier 1 to be successful, having a single, systematic referral process that is flexible enough to address the range of student challenges will immensely benefit integrated student support teams. This process allows teams to capitalize on their shared expertise across content areas and build capacity by examining complex problems in a clear, straightforward manner. Effective student support teams teach staff how to request support by, for example, completing an integrated request for assistance form (see Chapter 3 and Appendix 3.4). Having received a referral, the team begins the process shown in Figure 5.5. Whether the primary concern is academics or behavior, the first step (one part of problem clarification) is to verify that Tier 1 supports have been implemented with fidelity. It is important to rule out that the student is having difficulty simply from lack of access to quality Tier 1 support. If the student did not receive quality Tier 1 instruction, then the team works with the classroom teacher or school leadership team to improve fidelity at Tier 1 (e.g., explicit instruction in academic skills or expectations, practice, and feedback), then continue to monitor student progress. If it is determined that quality Tier 1 instruction was in place, the next step is to gather information on previous strategies to address the problem. This information is then summarized by the data coordinator and documented by the note taker so that it can be utilized for the next step in developing an intervention plan, as well as to start a record of intervention attempts. At this point, the team may either select an existing Tier 2 intervention to implement (not shown in the figure) or gather additional diagnostic information to guide the selection of interventions (further problem clarification).

To gather more information, the team then conducts either a brief or extensive functional assessment in either behavior (FBA; Crone et al., 2015) or academics (functional academic assessment; Witt et al., 2000). These processes are described in Chapter 3 and illustrated in Figure 3.1 (p. 49). The results of this step indicate whether an integrated academic and behavior support plan is needed. For behavior challenges, the team's FBA indicates whether avoiding or escaping academic tasks maintains the student's behavior. If neither of these is a factor, the team can develop a solely academic support plan. If either avoidance or escape is a factor, the team can then complete a functional academic assessment to identify which academic task demands

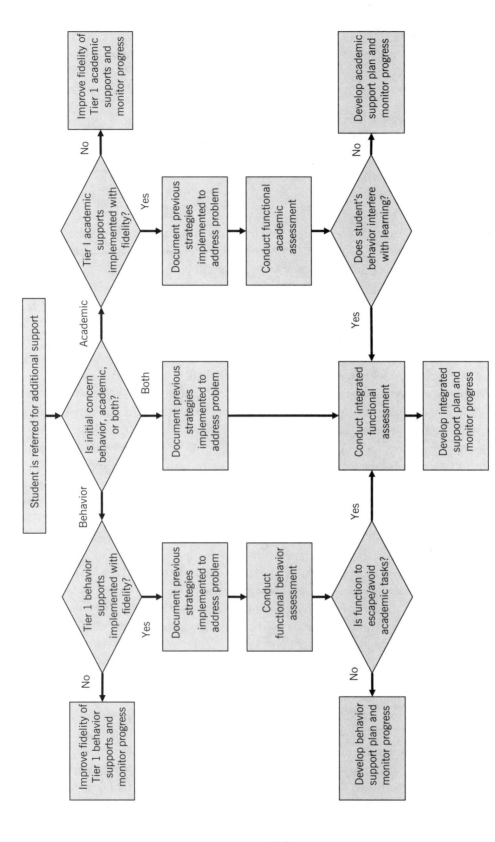

**FIGURE 5.5.** Suggested integrated MTSS request for assistance process. *Note:* Figure 3.1 describes the functional assessment process for behavior, academics, and integrated concerns.

trigger problem behavior and require intervention. These results are used to build an integrated support plan, which the team will monitor for effectiveness and any needed changes. For academic challenges, the core determination is whether the student's behavior interferes with academic learning opportunities. For example, disruptive student behavior may result in regular removal from instruction. If not, the team can develop a solely academic support plan. If so, the team conducts an FBA to determine the contextual variables that contribute to the problem behavior. These contextual variables are considered along with the functional academic assessment results to develop an integrated academic and behavior support plan.

## Data-Based Decision Rules

Both of the processes just described, as well as all aspects of the meetings where the processes take place, benefit greatly from having some clear decision rules for common points in the problem-solving process. For example, the efficient decisions made by the data coordinator in the system's decision updates can happen only if the coordinator and the team have agreed upon specific criteria for determining whether to continue, modify, or fade support. In decision making at Tier 1, it is common to apply an "80% rule" to evaluate the adequacy of this first tier. This rule states that if fewer than 80% of students are successful (either in academics or behavior) with Tier 1 support, then the team should make efforts to implement fully or intensify Tier 1 supports until at least 80% of students are successful. In some situations, schools serving high-risk communities may have Tier 1 systems that look like Tier 2 systems in other schools. Without this intensity of support, too many students will need support at Tiers 2 and 3, and the reactive systems will consume more resources than are needed. In decision making at Tiers 2 and 3, common criteria for the need to modify support include three consecutive data points below an aimline that closes the gap with peers (academic support) or 3 consecutive days not meeting daily progress report goals (behavior support). Of course, team members may choose to override such decision rules for various reasons (e.g., provide sufficient time to evaluate a change in support), but without such rules, decisions will be inefficient, and as a result, teams will be inefficient.

## TEAM CHECKLISTS: INTEGRATING TEAMS

The checklists in this chapter focus on common steps for integrating teams in schools and districts. Although the form of teaming structures (e.g., number of teams, configurations) may vary, the same functions (e.g., purposes, core activities) are necessary for optimal functioning. For some teams, integration provides an efficient method of streamlining activities, and for others, integration may be more cumbersome than existing structures. These checklists focus specifically on function over form.

# SCHOOL-LEVEL TEAM CHECKLIST FOR INTEGRATING TEAMS

| Implementation Step | Implementation Status | | |
|---|---|---|---|
| | Not in place | Partially in place | In place |
| 1. The school leadership completes an audit (i.e., identifies teams, purposes, and membership) to identify teams that could be dissolved, integrated, or take on integrated roles. | | | |
| 2. All teams in the school have clear missions and purposes that do not overlap with each other. | | | |
| 3. All teams in the school have regular meeting times and spaces. | | | |
| 4. All teams in the school establish norms and expectations for team members. | | | |
| 5. All teams in the school define meeting roles and procedures for assigning backup roles as needed. | | | |
| 6. All teams in the school use a structured agenda and common problem-solving process. | | | |
| 7. All teams in the school use agreed-upon decision rules for assessing student progress and making instructional and intervention adjustments. | | | |

| Priority for Action Planning (the three most important items from above) | Who is responsible? | By when? | How will we know when it is accomplished? |
|---|---|---|---|
| 1. | | | |
| 2. | | | |
| 3. | | | |

---

# DISTRICT-LEVEL TEAM CHECKLIST FOR INTEGRATING TEAMS

| Implementation Step | Implementation Status | | |
|---|---|---|---|
| | Not in place | Partially in place | In place |
| 1. The district leadership completes an audit (i.e., identifies teams, purposes, and membership) to identify district teams that could be dissolved, integrated, or take on integrated roles. | | | |
| 2. All teams in the district have clear missions and purposes that do not overlap with each other (or overlap purposefully). | | | |
| 3. All teams in the district have regular meeting times and spaces. | | | |
| 4. All teams in the district establish norms and expectations for team members. | | | |
| 5. All teams in the district define meeting roles and procedures for assigning backup roles as needed. | | | |
| 6. All teams in the district use a structured agenda and common problem-solving process. | | | |
| 7. The district leadership provides schools with recommended decision rules for assessing student progress and making instructional and intervention adjustments. | | | |
| 8. The district leadership develops an annual timetable/calendar of common activities and decisions for school teams to use in defining meeting agendas. | | | |

| Priority for Action Planning (the three most important items from above) | Who is responsible? | By when? | How will we know when it is accomplished? |
|---|---|---|---|
| 1. | | | |
| 2. | | | |
| 3. | | | |

# School Leadership Team Meeting Agenda

School: _____ Date: _____

Facilitator: _____

Note Taker/Recorder: _____

Timekeeper: _____

Data Coordinator: _____

Active Team Members Present: _____

**Team Purpose:**


**1. Celebrate Successes** (5 minutes):


**2. Review Tier 1 Implementation Data** (10 minutes):
   a. Review most recent fidelity data.



   b. What barriers are interfering with implementation?



   c. What can we do to improve implementation? Update action plan below.



**3. Review Tier 1 Student Outcomes Data** (15 minutes):
   a. Review most recent student outcomes data.



*(continued)*

_____

b. What can we do to improve outcomes? Update action plan below.

4. **Ongoing Business** (15 minutes):

   a. Review issues and action items from previous meeting.

       i. What is status (completed, in process, not started)?

       ii. What do we need to continue/stop/add?

5. **New Business** (10 minutes):

   a. What new issues need to be addressed to ensure improved implementation and/or outcomes?

   b. What are continuing barriers or risks to implementation?

6. **Meeting Self-Assessment** (5 minutes):

| Evaluation of Team Meeting | Yes | So-So | No |
|---|---|---|---|
| 1. Did we follow our expectations in the meeting today? | | | |
| 2. Did we focus on our team's purpose in the meeting today? | | | |
| 3. Did we do a good job of completing the tasks we agreed on at previous meetings? | | | |
| 4. In general, are the completed tasks having the desired effects on student outcomes? | | | |
| **If some of the ratings are "So-So" or "No," what can we do to improve things?** | | | |
| | | | |

*(continued)*

## Ongoing Action Planning Items

| Activity | Who is responsible? | Target start date | Target completion date | How will we know if it's working? |
|---|---|---|---|---|
|  |  |  |  |  |
|  |  |  |  |  |
|  |  |  |  |  |
|  |  |  |  |  |
|  |  |  |  |  |
|  |  |  |  |  |
|  |  |  |  |  |
|  |  |  |  |  |
|  |  |  |  |  |

# Student Support Team Meeting Agenda

School: _____ Date: _____

Facilitator: _____

Note Taker/Recorder: _____

Timekeeper: _____

Data Coordinator: _____

Active Team Members Present: _____

**Team Purpose:**

1. **Celebrate Successes** (5 minutes):

2. **Review Tiers 2/3 Implementation Data** (10 minutes):
   a. Review most recent fidelity data.

   b. What barriers are interfering with implementation?

   c. What can we do to improve implementation? Update action plan below.

3. **Review Tiers 2/3 Student Outcomes Data** (15 minutes):
   a. Review most recent student outcomes data.

*(continued)*

b. What can we do to improve outcomes? Update action plan below.

**4. Systems Decisions Updates from Data Coordinator** (5 minutes):
   a. Literacy:
      i. Students ready to graduate from support.

      ii. Students not being successful (discuss in #5).

   b. Behavior:
      i. Students ready to graduate from support.

      ii. Students not being successful (discuss in #5).

**5. Problem Solving for Individual Students** (15 minutes):
   a. Student(s) of concern:
      i. Current plan

      ii. Issues

      iii. What do we need to continue/stop/add?

**6. New Referrals for Support** (5 minutes):
   a. What new referrals need to be handled?

   b. What steps are needed for implementation? Update action plan below.

*(continued)*

**7. Meeting Self-Assessment** (5 minutes):

| Evaluation of Team Meeting | Yes | So-So | No |
|---|---|---|---|
| 1. Did we follow our expectations in the meeting today? | | | |
| 2. Did we focus on our team's purpose in the meeting today? | | | |
| 3. Did we do a good job of completing the tasks we agreed on at previous meetings? | | | |
| 4. In general, are the completed tasks having the desired effects on student outcomes? | | | |
| **If some of the ratings are "So-So" or "No," what can we do to improve things?** | | | |
| | | | |

## Ongoing Action Planning Items

| Activity | Who is responsible? | Target start date | Target completion date | How will we know if it's working? |
|---|---|---|---|---|
| | | | | |
| | | | | |
| | | | | |
| | | | | |
| | | | | |
| | | | | |
| | | | | |
| | | | | |

*(continued)*

197

Student Support Team Meeting Agenda (page 4 of 4)

## Tiers 2/3 Student Update Sheet

| Student Name | Referral Date | Initial Meeting Date | 1st Review Date | 1st Review Consideration | 1st Review Period Data | 2nd Review Date (2 weeks after initial meeting) | 2nd Review Consideration | 2nd Review Period Data | 3rd Review Date (6 weeks after initial meeting) | 3rd Review Period Data |
|---|---|---|---|---|---|---|---|---|---|---|
| | | | | ☐ Continue ☐ Modify ☐ Graduate | | | ☐ Continue ☐ Modify ☐ Graduate | | | |
| | | | | ☐ Continue ☐ Modify ☐ Graduate | | | ☐ Continue ☐ Modify ☐ Graduate | | | |
| | | | | ☐ Continue ☐ Modify ☐ Graduate | | | ☐ Continue ☐ Modify ☐ Graduate | | | |
| | | | | ☐ Continue ☐ Modify ☐ Graduate | | | ☐ Continue ☐ Modify ☐ Graduate | | | |
| | | | | ☐ Continue ☐ Modify ☐ Graduate | | | ☐ Continue ☐ Modify ☐ Graduate | | | |
| | | | | ☐ Continue ☐ Modify ☐ Graduate | | | ☐ Continue ☐ Modify ☐ Graduate | | | |
| | | | | ☐ Continue ☐ Modify ☐ Graduate | | | ☐ Continue ☐ Modify ☐ Graduate | | | |

# Grade-Level Team Postbenchmarking Meeting Agenda

School: _____     Date: _____

Facilitator: _____

Note Taker/Recorder: _____

Timekeeper: _____

Data Coordinator: _____

Active Team Members Present: _____

**Team Purpose:**

**Meeting Purpose:** *Develop an instructional plan for ALL students that reflects student need and optimizes student outcomes.*

1. **Recap Benchmarking Data Collection Process (10 minutes):**
   a. Successes

   b. Suggestions for next benchmarking period

2. **Review Academic Benchmarking Data (30 minutes):**
   a. Review grade-level benchmark goals for:
      i. Fall

      ii. Winter

      iii. Spring

*(continued)*

b. Assess current academic status for both grade level and classroom:

    i. Percent of students at low risk (at or above benchmark):

    ii. Percent of students with some risk:

    iii. Percent of students at risk:

c. Compare to behavior data (ODRs or systematic screening):

    i. Percent of students at low risk:

    ii. Percent of students with some risk:

    iii. Percent of students at risk:

d. Compare academic and behavior data to Tier 1 goals (e.g., 80% of students successful with Tier 1 systems).

**3. Write/Revise Grade-Level Instructional Plan until Next Benchmark (45 minutes):**

a. Review previous plan in light of Tier 1 goals. Discuss any needed changes.

b. Design instructional plan specifics.

    i. Identify interventions, instructors, and schedule for students to access the interventions.

    ii. Identify students who will receive progress monitoring, and by whom.

c. Finalize action plan.

    i. Identify action plan steps for implementation.

    ii. Identify additional support that may be needed to implement plan.

    iii. Assign tasks.

    iv. Set follow-up dates.

*(continued)*

## 6. Meeting Self-Assessment (5 minutes):

| Evaluation of Team Meeting | Yes | So-So | No |
|---|---|---|---|
| 1. Did we follow our expectations in the meeting today? | | | |
| 2. Did we focus on our team's purpose in the meeting today? | | | |
| 3. Did we do a good job of completing the tasks we agreed on at previous meetings? | | | |
| 4. In general, are the completed tasks having the desired effects on student outcomes? | | | |
| **If some of the ratings are "So-So" or "No," what can we do to improve things?** | | | |
| | | | |

### Ongoing Action Planning Items

| Activity | Who is responsible? | Target start date | Target completion date | How will we know if it's working? |
|---|---|---|---|---|
| | | | | |
| | | | | |
| | | | | |
| | | | | |
| | | | | |
| | | | | |
| | | | | |
| | | | | |

# CHAPTER 6

# Integrating District Support Systems

Up to this point, the primary focus of this book has been on what schools can do to integrate their systems. In this chapter, we go into much greater detail regarding what kinds of district support are needed to assist schools in their integration efforts. When working in a school, it is easy to overlook the district's influence when it appears that more immediate, school-level enablers and barriers are more influential. The district leadership seems so far away from the actions of the grade-level team or individual educator. For example, leadership from the school administrator seems much more important for building momentum than from a district administrator. However, the district's leadership can affect the school in many ways, including the leadership of school administrators. As an example, when district leaders promote specific approaches as a high priority, direct funds to implementation, and embed the practice into job descriptions and hiring decisions, school administrator support can be enhanced (McIntosh, Kelm, & Canizal Delabra, in press; Strickland-Cohen et al., 2014). Through this lens, districts are seen as pivotal in the implementation and sustainability process, particularly as they help their schools troubleshoot through obstacles that might sink an individual school's implementation capacity (Andreou, McIntosh, Ross, & Kahn, 2015; George & Kincaid, 2008).

There are some useful metaphors that help describe the district's complex role in supporting schools. District support is somewhat like the offensive line in football or using the latest technology (e.g., connecting to wireless Internet or an LCD projector). One never realizes it when things are going well behind the scenes—it just seems that everything is going exceptionally smoothly. But when things go wrong, it feels like everything is going wrong. That difference is the effect of district support. Strong district support is like the keel on a boat—it allows schools to move forward in one direction through the changes in current and wind. With the keel down, you may not notice the breezes that could have been blowing you off course.

This chapter is primarily intended to provide information about what kinds of district supports are needed to ensure that schools can implement an integrated MTSS model for academics and behavior with fidelity and sustainability. We could write an entire book solely on district support, so this chapter should be considered only an overview of district support and, in particular, the role of districts in supporting integrated MTSS models in individual schools. Our basic message is that an integrated schoolwide approach is strengthened through a specific set of supports provided by the district. For those who are working at the district level, this chapter addresses the key functions involved in supporting schools that are implementing an integrated MTSS model. This chapter describes strategies with which district teams can increase the use and longevity of practices and systems in their schools. For those working in a school, this chapter describes the external supports that are needed and why. Schools need external support to sustain their efforts in the long run, and we hope that members of the school leadership team can use this information to advocate for these supports from the district. Understanding what is needed from the district will help the school leadership function as better consumers, make better investments into schoolwide programs, and increase the likelihood of obtaining the district supports that will result in improved student outcomes.

## HOW DISTRICTS CAN SUPPORT INDIVIDUAL SCHOOLS IN IMPLEMENTING MTSS

Throughout this book, we promote an integrated MTSS model as a means to produce socially significant student outcomes. We all know that developing a schoolwide system to implement academic and behavior practices requires more than simply telling educators which practices to implement. Educators need to know *how* to implement these practices through effective processes. Educators also need adequate supports for their work in these implementation processes. Figure 6.1 shows how effective interventions are braided with effective implementation and enabling contexts to promote socially significant outcomes (Fixsen, Blase, Horner, & Sugai, 2009a). It also highlights that these strands are combined for one singular purpose: to produce valued student outcomes, in both academics and behavior.

### Effective Practices

Effective practices are the most tangible components of Figure 6.1 because they are what we do when we work directly with the whole student body, classrooms, groups, and individual

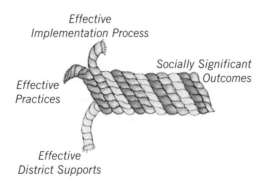

**FIGURE 6.1.** How district supports work to improve outcomes. Adapted with permission from Bohanon, Goodman, and McIntosh (2009).

students. In Chapter 4, we presented details regarding integrated practices and how to select them. By selecting practices based on evidence of their effectiveness, we know that we are investing in practices that are the most likely to improve student outcomes. The use of evidence-based practices becomes even more important when considering that we also need to invest in the implementation processes (i.e., systems) to implement them well. This investment multiplies the resource commitment for practices and further highlights the need to select them wisely.

### Effective Implementation Process

As just described, an effective implementation process helps us to put practices in place well enough to see changes in student outcomes. Although we emphasize the implementation process throughout this book, Chapters 5 (Integrating Teaming) and 7 (Integrating Entire Systems) provide the most detail regarding processes for implementing practices effectively. By focusing on what is needed for quality implementation as much—or more than—on the practices themselves, we can maximize the likelihood that the interventions will produce the highest impact on student outcomes. After all, students cannot benefit from interventions that they do not receive (Fixsen et al., 2005)!

### Effective District Supports

District supports can be considered as the systemwide organizational environment that enhances or inhibits practice implementation over time. These district supports are adapted in response to the specific needs of educators and the unique contextual variables of the district and its schools. A district can support effective implementation through enacting district policies that promote an integrated model and problem-solving barriers to effective implementation (e.g., principal or staff turnover, changes in community, budget issues, RTI-PBIS turf battles). By troubleshooting these obstacles, providing training, and building capacity, the district can create a context in which it is easier for school personnel to implement practices well, just like the environmental modifications we make when supporting student behavior (McIntosh, Lucyshyn, Strickland-Cohen, & Horner, 2014). These aspects of district support make up what are sometimes known as effective "host environments" in which effective practices can take place (Kame'enui, Simmons, & Coyne, 2000).

Figure 6.2 shows another representation of how the emphasis across the braided components of the MTSS model changes at different levels. For teachers, the primary focus is on delivering the practices to students, although aspects of implementation (e.g., fidelity self-assessment, progress monitoring) are still part of the job. As the unit of implementation expands, the focus shifts more from the practices themselves to the implementation process and external supports. At the district level, there is often still a role in selecting particular practices, but there is much more of an emphasis on how to get those practices into place through methods that are durable.

## THE DRIVERS OF DISTRICT SUPPORT

From their review of research on effective implementation, Fixsen and colleagues (2005) identified a number of key avenues for providing effective external support, called *implementation*

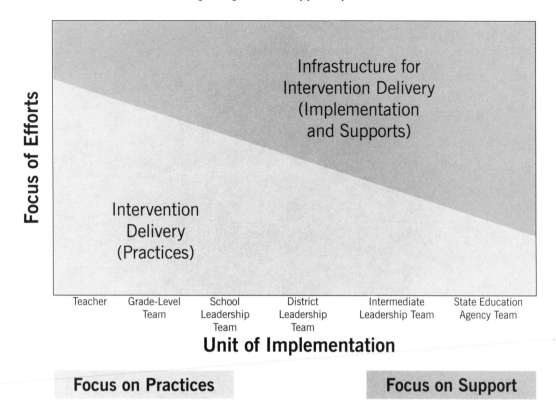

**FIGURE 6.2.** Focus of efforts for implementing effective practices.

*drivers.* These are fundamental elements that promote the implementation of practices with fidelity and durability and can be brought to scale. School districts can support their schools through ensuring that these drivers are in place so that the practices of academic RTI and PBIS can be implemented with fidelity over time. The drivers we present in this chapter are specific to school systems and come from (1) the drivers promoted by the National Implementation Research Network (Blase, Van Dyke, & Fixsen, 2013), (2) functions of the leadership team from the schoolwide PBIS implemention blueprint (Sugai, Horner, Algozzine, et al., 2010), and (3) the seminal leadership work of Thomas Gilbert (1978). Nine individual drivers are organized within three categories that are essential to effective organizations: leadership, contexture, and competency (see Figure 6.3). Each driver is instrumental in guiding the implementation process through designing and enhancing school environments so that practices are implemented fully and outcomes are measurably improved.

It is important to note that these drivers are both integrated and compensatory (Blase, Van Dyke, et al., 2013). Each driver is connected to the others to improve the district's efficiency and effectiveness in facilitating desired outcomes. For example, training will be more efficient when there is a specific process to identify appropriate individuals who will implement the practice. In addition, weakness in a specific driver may be compensated by other drivers. For example, effective training and coaching may compensate for less optimal selection procedures.

Additionally, using these drivers as a map of district support assists in understanding and improving the implementation process. The absence of any particular driver may be due to

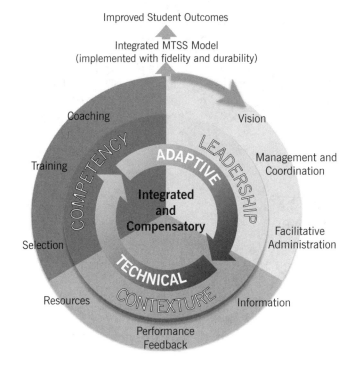

**FIGURE 6.3.** MTSS implementation drivers. Adapted with permission from Karen A. Blase from Blase, Van Dyke, and Fixsen (2013).

either *technical* or *adaptive* problems (Heifetz, Grashow, & Linksy, 2009). Technical problems pertain to the "what" and "how" of implementation, meaning the mechanics of selecting practices and tools and learning how to use them in keeping with key principles of MTSS. These problems are rather straightforward and can be addressed by sharing exactly what current research tells us to do regarding the specific steps of implementing MTSS data, systems, and practices. In contrast, adaptive problems pertain to the "why" of implementation, as well as to the alignment or reconciliation of the model with philosophical or pedagogical beliefs, values, and attitudes. Adaptive supports are provided to connect with the contextual political, philosophical, and cultural needs associated with adopting the practices. Adaptive problems often require an assessment of the context and an adaptation of practices to improve fit, considering social barriers to implementation and removing disincentives for engaging in implementation. Using this lens of technical and adaptive problem solving, it is likely that as the district evolves throughout the MTSS implementation process, district teams will need to adapt how the drivers are put into place to meet new needs and challenges.

Although each driver can be developed independently, it may be helpful to prioritize a place to start. We suggest beginning with the leadership drivers and then address each driver moving clockwise around Figure 6.3. By moving in this direction, each subsequent driver builds on the previous drivers, which improves both the effectiveness and efficiency of the entire implementation support process. However, the process of installing implementation drivers is not expected to be linear, and individual districts may have easier points of entry for change. Table 6.1 includes the drivers and common installation activities.

**TABLE 6.1. Implementation Drivers and Common Activities for Installation**

| Category | Driver | Common activities |
|---|---|---|
| Leadership: *Providing the direction and coordination to guide the implementation process* | *Vision:* Defining the desired future state of the district in terms of its fundamental goals and objectives | • Build and document a shared philosophy and values.<br>• Embed support and guidance toward this vision in written policy.<br>• Identify goals and standards for the initiative.<br>• Secure political and social support from administration and stakeholders. |
| | *Management and Coordination:* Directing and monitoring finite resources efficiently and effectively | • Use existing teaming structures to manage and monitor ongoing implementation activities.<br>• Develop and use a coordinated district plan with goals, objectives, activities, and timelines to transform the vision into action and strategies.<br>• Allocate adequate funding and time to complete implementation activities.<br>• Assess and expand implementation of drivers (e.g., administer the District Capacity Assessment). |
| | *Facilitative Administration:* Assisting implementation by making it easier and removing barriers | • Use schoolwide data (fidelity, outcomes, process) to improve educational environments.<br>• Identify barriers to effective implementation and address via policy, regulation, funding, and support.<br>• Ensure that the drivers within the contexture and competency categories are integrated, aligned, and compensatory.<br>• Use the stages of implementation logic to enhance implementation. |
| Contexture: *Engineering the host environment to enhance individual performance* | *Information:* Basing decisions on a clear, objective understanding of current status and next steps | • Build an electronic data system (online or using a spreadsheet or database software program) to store and access student outcome data, fidelity of implementation data, and process data.<br>• Integrate data systems across content areas to allow for integrated decision making.<br>• Set clear, understandable standards for performance regarding the integrated MTSS model.<br>• Use data systems to provide timely evaluation data for assessing progress and setting action plan goals. |
| | *Performance Feedback:* Sharing meaningful information to promote continuous improvement | • Provide regular, understandable feedback to staff regarding student outcomes and fidelity of implementation.<br>• Build and use regular schedules for two-way feedback loops to share data and discuss progress. |

*(continued)*

**TABLE 6.1.** *(continued)*

| Category | Driver | Common activities |
|---|---|---|
| Contexture *(continued)* | *Resources:* Providing the necessary means to implement practices and systems well | • Ensure that educators have adequate time to plan and accomplish activities.<br>• Develop common processes and procedures for effective implementation of integrated MTSS models.<br>• Build and maintain a library with manuals, materials, and tools (sample forms, quick reference guides). |
| Competency: *Developing individuals' knowledge and skills to implement the systems and practices* | *Selection:* Hiring the right people with the right skills and attitudes | • Build MTSS responsibilities directly into job descriptions and postings.<br>• Include demonstrations of MTSS competencies in interview processes.<br>• Select staff based on (1) specific skills and experience and (2) "intangibles" (e.g., philosophy, collaborative spirit) related to implementing an integrated MTSS model. |
| | *Training:* Providing formal structures for knowledge and skill acquisition | • Provide training to build awareness, knowledge, or initial skills.<br>• Focus on building necessary skills for the contexts in which those skills will be used.<br>• Develop a regular calendar of trainings with clear purposes and intended outcomes.<br>• Differentiate training based on audience and needs. |
| | *Coaching:* Facilitating competency development through prompting, modeling, acknowledging, and giving feedback | • Provide coaching to help school personnel develop and perform critical skills following training sessions.<br>• Differentiate coaching based on school and individual needs.<br>• Provide on-site coaching (with modeling) as needed.<br>• Provide school team networking sessions.<br>• Develop and maintain capacity among a group of individuals who can serve coaching functions.<br>• Provide professional development for coaches as well. |

## Leadership Drivers

The first set of drivers, leadership drivers, includes activities to enhance priority and provide the visibility and resource allocation needed for an integrated model (McIntosh, Filter, et al., 2010; Sugai, Horner, Algozzine, et al., 2010). These leadership drivers—vision, management and coordination, and facilitative administration—primarily set the stage to enable the other drivers to be put in place. When considering these drivers, it is important to note that an effective conceptualization of leadership is broad, by necessity. The term *leadership* refers to the function of leadership rather than to an individual's position within the organization. Many individuals can provide leadership, although it is certainly easier to do so when one can direct financial resources.

## Vision

Because school teams are often consumed with the regular tasks of implementation, it is important for a larger organizational group to provide the overarching foresight and long-term planning needed to move toward the goal of implementing and sustaining effective school practices across the district. By promoting fundamental objectives based on effective practices, prioritizing important initiatives, and seeking alignment of high-priority practices, the district can provide a general vision for the direction of its schools. With a clear direction based on the research and principles behind quality instruction and its implementation, the district can greatly enhance the durability and scalability of its schools' implementation efforts. A common vision can also increase visibility. When the district promotes a model and shares local evidence of its effectiveness, more stakeholders may be brought in to support the vision.

An effective district vision reflects the values of school personnel, students, families, and the broader community. This consensus can be built by identifying common, shared values and the outcomes that reflect these values (McIntosh, Horner, & Sugai, 2009). Any district initiative can be improved by including these values, outcomes, and a description of ongoing staff, family, and community involvement and communication in its implementation plans.

Vision is important because it allows for a coordinated application of resources. When this vision is shared widely, the district can allocate more resources to implementation across schools in the district, often in a way that is more efficient than funding an array of short-term, uncoordinated projects. This shared vision is particularly important for integrated MTSS models, where separate visions and priorities for district academic RTI and PBIS initiatives can sometimes pit each model at odds with the other. By promoting an inclusive vision that highlights the research showing the benefits of an integrated model (as seen in Chapter 2), as well as efficient ways to integrate key features (Chapters 3, 4, and 5), fragmentation of vision and competition for existing district resources can be avoided.

## Management and Coordination

This next leadership driver can be seen as the avenue through which the district's vision becomes action. Districts can install this driver by ensuring that there is an entity responsible for managing and monitoring the initiative's ongoing activities. This group coordinates the actions of the district and its schools in implementation of the integrated MTSS model. Its work includes developing and following a detailed plan with goals, objectives, activities, and timelines for implementation. As will be described, it is not necessary for this entity to be a new group. Instead, it is generally preferable to use existing structures than to create new ones, although sometimes it may be easier to create a new group than try to retool an existing group that already has a heavy agenda or is not well suited for the tasks. In some cases, it is a good idea to consider expanding an existing district RTI or PBIS leadership team to take on coordination of an integrated MTSS model. These individuals are often skilled in the management and coordination of their respective models, which generalizes well to support across content areas.

## Facilitative Administration

The work of the management and coordination entity is enhanced when its actions are informed by research in effective implementation. For example, schools require different types and levels of support depending on their stage of implementation (Mercer, McIntosh, Strickland-Cohen, & Horner, 2014; Turri, Mercer, McIntosh, Nese, & Hoselton, in press), as is described in Chapter 7. When district leaders operate based on this understanding, they can create plans that more effectively move schools through the process of exploring, installing, and sustaining practices. Facilitative administration creates a "hospitable" environment by identifying and addressing potential barriers and facilitators, while ensuring effective use of the contexture and competency drivers.

## Contexture Drivers

The second set of drivers includes the three contexture drivers. *Contexture* (which is indeed a real word) is the process of integrating different aspects of the environment for a common purpose. The contexture drivers help educators create and sustain more effective and efficient organizational systems. In other words, these drivers are elements of "effective host environments" that make it easier to implement practices well (Kame'enui et al., 2000). In essence, building a system that supports effective practices is more beneficial than hiring effective individuals to work in an unsupportive environment. The goal is a self-modifying system of continuous improvement in which data, practices, and systems are regularly modified as part of the typical implementation process. The drivers that cultivate this type of system include both data systems and methods for using the data for improvement.

### Information

In Chapter 3, we discussed the kinds of data needed for integrated MTSS models in great detail. This driver, information, encompasses not only the tools but also the processes and procedures for collecting data, as well as the processes and procedures for summarizing, analyzing, and reporting results (i.e., turning data into information). An effective district information system provides results that are timely and understandable both to those who need to act on this information and those who need to be informed on implementation efforts. The comprehensive information systems needed for successful integrated MTSS models include student outcome data, fidelity of implementation data, and data regarding the systems themselves (e.g., capacity, processes). Integrated MTSS models multiply this complexity by adding content areas. One-time or isolated efforts by one or two people in the district may work for one area (e.g., early literacy, PBIS), but coordinated systems are needed to manage this added complexity, especially when school initiatives become district initiatives.

The process of evaluation is a key component of the information driver. One goal of evaluating an integrated MTSS system is to determine whether it is being fully implemented. Another goal is to determine the worth of the model in meeting the needs of the district's students, families, communities, and staff. Just as important, evaluation allows for a formative process to improve efficiency and effectiveness. Within this driver, staff needs to understand which types of data to collect and how to compare results to a standard (e.g., benchmark goals for student reading performance or established scores for adequate fidelity of PBIS implementation).

### Performance Feedback

It is also important to make sure that evaluation information is used within a continuous process of quality improvement. The performance feedback driver completes the process that is started with the information driver. Because performance feedback is a powerful facilitator of both student and adult learning (Gilbert, 1978; Hattie, 2009), it is wise to build systems to deliver it in a regular, timely, and understandable manner. The regular use of positive feedback creates a culture wherein competence and success are valued; in contrast, feedback that is delivered haphazardly or only when problems arise is less likely to be received in ways that improve performance (Gottman, Coan, Carrere, & Swanson, 1998).

When important data are collected *and* provided to individuals in feedback loops (current status and comparison to goals), the individuals in the system have an increased capability to improve outcomes. These feedback loops are reinforcing and help to highlight the importance of the practice and what can be done to improve it. For example, regular collection, viewing, and sharing of both implementation and outcome data are strongly related to sustained fidelity of PBIS implementation (Andreou et al., 2015; McIntosh et al., 2013). These feedback loops can be built for teams and individuals at district, school, grade, classroom, and student levels.

## Resources

For continuous improvement, school personnel need to have both time to complete activities and clear guidance regarding effective selection, use, and modification of practices and data. Without adequate planning time or knowledge of what effective practices look like or how they are best implemented, it is difficult to find the next steps for positive change. Content and implementation expertise helps to guide teams in their action planning efforts and when addressing uneven implementation. To implement integrated MTSS models, school personnel need to be able to access specialized knowledge in academic and behavior support. This knowledge includes information regarding populations of interest (e.g., high school students, elementary students with autism) and how best to serve them. It is important to have theoretical and practical knowledge in the research bases of academic RTI, PBIS, and an integrated MTSS model.

However, this expertise should not come from one individual—if this were the case, the system would be vulnerable to breakdowns when that person changes positions or leaves the district. One way to protect against the loss of proficiency and knowledge is through a clear plan to institutionalize school and district expertise. Creating and providing a library of materials and tools for successful implementation of integrated MTSS models helps to avoid dependence on any one person. When materials are readily available for school teams in a form that makes them easy to use (e.g., brief informative handouts, summaries and checklists of key points), the expertise from the district expands dramatically. Resources can involve more than guidance in practices; the district team can build a set of local examples of the various processes and procedures needed for effective implementation (e.g., agendas, forms, reports, schedules).

## Competency Drivers

The final set of drivers includes mechanisms to develop, improve, and sustain the skills of individual school personnel in implementing the various aspects of integrated MTSS models. These drivers are used to ensure that each individual has the competencies needed to implement the practices with fidelity and in an efficient manner. The vast number of skills needed for the implementation of integrated MTSS models necessitates the creation of systems for supporting school personnel, who are likely to have a wide range of skill levels in all of these competencies. Attending to the competency drivers can help ensure that school personnel are equipped to successfully implement an integrated MTSS model. These drivers include selection, training, and coaching.

## Selection

Often, when we consider developing competency to implement integrated models, we think first about providing inservice trainings. Yet the application of the drivers suggests that even before training, the first step is to select individuals who have the knowledge, skills, and experience to implement MTSS well. Bringing the right people onboard is more efficient than building capacity solely through training and coaching. In addition, it helps to minimize opposition to core features, such as using evidence-based practices and data for decision making. Attending to selection also increases the likelihood of sustainability because properly selected school personnel have a common view of MTSS as "typical practice" in the schools (McIntosh, Predy, et al., 2014). The selection driver includes building integrated MTSS models explicitly into district policy, job descriptions and postings, and hiring practices (Blase, Fixsen, Naoom, & Wallace, 2005). Interviews may include common scenarios of MTSS implementation, such as examining fictitious student or school academic and behavior data to design an intervention plan.

## Training

This familiar driver is used to strengthen the skills or knowledge development of educators who were not necessarily selected for their skill sets in and integrated MTSS models. Training is particularly useful in building capacity when selection is not an option (e.g., staff is already in place). Unfortunately, many professional development calendars in education include trainings in a wide range of unrelated topics—including approaches without solid evidence—instead of coordinated plans that are sequenced to build deep knowledge and skills regarding a single approach.

Training is most effective when viewed as one limited component of an overall plan to build capacity, and it is particularly useful in building awareness of big ideas or key concepts, knowledge acquisition, and initial skill development for a set of defined set of activities. As a result, it is most effective when there is a skill or knowledge deficit among staff ("can't do"), rather than a motivational deficit ("won't do"). In the trainings themselves, quality trainers communicate training expectations, use active engagement strategies, promote positive learning environments, and use appropriate pacing to address participant needs. Most important, trainers and participants alike should be clear on the purpose and specific outcomes of each training session (Lewis, Barrett, Sugai, & Horner, 2010). Without a defined purpose and outcome, improvement in knowledge or skill level is much less likely.

Although school teams may conduct informal or incidental training for new team members or general school personnel, it is much more efficient and effective to have districts take on the role of training. Districts can provide a more coordinated approach based on a long-term vision of MTSS implementation and differentiated training needs. For example, nearly all schools in any given district will have new staff members who need a general orientation to MTSS principles, practices, and procedures. Holding a centralized introduction to MTSS training for new staff and new administrators is a key district action that can enhance sustainability and reduce costs (McIntosh, Kelm, et al., 2014).

## Coaching

Although training is a key driver, it is important not to assume that providing quality training will lead to improved implementation. Joyce and Showers (2002) demonstrated that even the best inservice training is unlikely to change educational practices without ongoing coaching. Unfortunately, the same is true for reading this book! Adding regular technical assistance to training efforts further enhances competency in a district's schools.

Coaching primarily takes the form of assisting individuals and teams to implement the selected MTSS practices with fidelity. Without coaching, these practices are unlikely to be implemented with fidelity. In turn, without fidelity, outcomes are unlikely to improve. As a result, coaching is a key mechanism for making integrated MTSS models work. This vision of coaching is shared across academic RTI and PBIS.

Coaching works by deepening a conceptual understanding of the core elements of the practices and processes introduced in training, and it is most important in assisting individuals to use the skills following training sessions, gain experience, and to see how implementing the practices improves outcomes (i.e., reinforcement of implementation; Andreou et al., 2015). Coaching not only helps develop skills to fluency, but it also facilitates transferring the knowledge and skills from training to the specific context of the school setting. After training, skills may be considered to be fragile, with low likelihood of correct use or generalization to unique uses (e.g., from teaching behavior expectations to reteaching them effectively with individuals). The assistance and guidance of coaching allows individuals to take chances and try out new skills with less effort and fear of failure. The coaching process includes rapport building, communication, precorrection (i.e., reminders to use the skills), performance feedback, and reinforcement for use of practices (Sprick, Knight, Reinke, & McKale, 2006). However, it should not be a part of formal evaluation, or rapport between the coach and consultee may be harmed.

It is important to note that coaching should be considered a function rather than a specific person (Sugai & Todd, 2006). Although an individual may be hired in a formal position as "coach," a range of individuals (with varying job titles) may serve the function of a coach. This point is especially important in integrated MTSS models, wherein one person may not have deep skills in all of the key areas, such as systems change knowledge, consultation skills, academic RTI, and PBIS. Instead, coaching is more likely to happen as a shared function for a number of individuals. School teams need access to the expertise in all of these areas, not necessarily a person whose job title is *coach*. Regarding these areas, Appendix 6.1 provides an MTSS coach competency self-assessment from Kathleen Ryan Jackson and Erin Chaparro at the University of Oregon. As can be seen, coaching in MTSS models is not an easy task! Correspondingly, coaches themselves need support in building their competencies as well. Regular coaches meetings and training opportunities are necessary for coaches to feel comfortable in their roles assisting schools.

The extent of support provided in coaching varies based on the skills of the educators, their experience with an integrated academic and behavior model, and the availability of resources. Karen Blase suggests that less coaching (or less skilled coaching) is needed when implementers have established skill sets and are implementing within familiar contexts. When implementation takes place within new contexts and requires new skills, there is a greater need for skillful coaching. Figure 6.4 shows how much coaching may be needed depending on the situation.

|  | | Skills | |
|---|---|---|---|
|  | | New | Established |
| Context | New | High-Level Intensity | Mid-Level Intensity |
|  | Familiar | Mid-Level Intensity | Low-Level Intensity |

Intensity of Supports
Based on Need and Experience

**FIGURE 6.4.** Varying intensity of district MTSS coaching. Adapted with permission from Karen A. Blase from Blase, Van Dyke, and Fixsen (2013).

The intensity of coaching entails more than simply providing more hours or access to more expertise. There is a systems component as well. Fixsen, Blase, Horner, and Sugai (2009b) emphasize this point:

> A key distinction between Basic TA and Intensive TA is the degree to which the TA providers take responsibility for outcomes. Basic TA relies upon recipients to make good and effective use of the information and training provided to them. Intensive TA takes responsibility for providing information and necessary supports and for doing whatever it takes to assure intended outcomes occur in a timely and effective manner. (p. 1)

### Assessing Implementation Drivers

In addition to assessing student progress and fidelity of implementation, it is also helpful to assess district status in implementing these drivers. The District Capacity Assessment (DCA; Duda et al., 2012) is an instrument designed to evaluate how well district teams are implementing the supports needed for effective school implementation of evidence-based practices, including an integrated MTSS model. The DCA considers each of the implementation drivers to evaluate the extent to which the district has adequate support mechanisms in place. It allows district teams to complete a few important activities, including (1) assessing the need for capacity building at the district level, (2) assessing the effects of capacity development efforts, and (3) identifying next steps for the district.

## A MODEL FOR ORGANIZING DISTRICT SUPPORT

As described above, districts provide the organizational structure to ensure that schools can implement an integrated MTSS model with fidelity and durability. Because function is more important than form, there is a range of ways to structure how to install these drivers in districts. However, it is often helpful to see an example of how these drivers can work in district structures. Figure 6.5 illustrates a district coordination model that has been used to organize support in many districts. The structure includes three groups: (1) a cabinet team (executive administration), (2) an implementation support team, and (3) training and coaching providers. The boxes in the figure identify which MTSS implementation drivers are the primary responsibilities of each group.

To varying degrees, each group addresses two components: (1) the structure for providing support and (2) the delivery of that support. The structure component sets up the conditions for more effective delivery of support to schools and provides for the development of materials, processes, and procedures that schools can implement. The delivery component provides a mechanism to transfer information and resources to school personnel. The cabinet and implementation planning teams are placed in the structure section because these teams primarily work on structural components. However, there is also a function of delivery with these groups as well. For example, the district superintendent may share information or problem solving regarding MTSS implementation in meetings with principals. The schools then participate in the model by implementing practices with students and providing feedback to the district teams on their needs for support.

## District Teams and Their Functions

We recommend using existing teams for district support whenever possible, as opposed to creating new teams. Existing organizational structures are far more durable and avoid the temporary

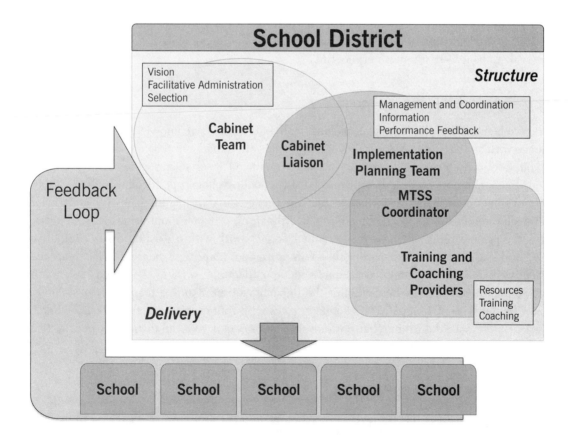

**FIGURE 6.5.** A model for organizing district MTSS support.

"project mentality" that comes from adding new positions and teams with initial project funding that has a clear end date (Adelman & Taylor, 2003). Because all districts have an executive-level administrative team, it is logical to use this existing team and allocate a small portion of regularly scheduled meetings to address MTSS implementation considerations. Additionally, districts may not have a team that specifically addresses MTSS implementation, but there may be a district RTI, PBIS, or school improvement team that can serve this function.

## Cabinet Team

The cabinet team is typically an existing group made up of the district executive management personnel, including the district superintendent, assistant superintendents (e.g., curriculum and instruction), and directors (e.g., special education). This cabinet team typically meets on a regular basis (e.g., weekly) and addresses the function of leadership by promoting top-priority initiatives, political support, visibility, funding, allocation of resources, and "barrier busting" (e.g., removing barriers that impede successful implementation). A key member of the cabinet team is the cabinet liaison. This individual is often in a position of leadership, such as assistant superintendent or director. The cabinet liaison sits on both the cabinet team and the implementation planning team and has a primary function of providing direct communication between the teams. When on the cabinet team, the liaison is responsible for providing implementation status updates to the cabinet. Common updates include the number of schools implementing an integrated MTSS model, results of fidelity of implementation assessment, student outcomes related to implementation efforts, and possible barriers to implementation. Generally, this process takes about 5–10 minutes per meeting.

## Implementation Planning Team

The implementation planning team includes individuals who have knowledge, skills, and experience with an integrated MTSS model. This team is often made up of five to seven individuals whom administrators would approach to learn about MTSS or set priorities for implementation. Team members may be reading specialists, school psychologists, social workers, or school improvement consultants. It is critical that the implementation planning team has sufficient time allocated to do the work of planning, coordination, progress monitoring, and evaluation. It is the responsibility of this team to embed project work within existing district initiatives (i.e., braiding efforts into a coherent school improvement plan; see Chapter 7). The team also attends regional and/or state-focused implementation planning sessions. The team leader is the MTSS coordinator; he or she facilitates the implementation planning team meetings, coordinates the implementation plan, and communicates with trainers and coaches. The coordinator works closely with the cabinet liaison to ensure alignment across the district support systems and consistency in messaging.

## Training and Coaching Providers

The third group at the district level is the training and coaching providers. These individuals are district-level trainers, coaches, and content experts in academics, behavior, and evaluation. The function of the training and coaching providers is to develop staff competencies within the schools through training and coaching. They may facilitate school leadership teams in their work within their individual schools, coordinate sharing among schools, or coach individual teachers to develop skills in implementing MTSS practices. This group may not meet regularly as a team, so it is important that communication, coordination, and support are provided by the MTSS coordinator to ensure that schools receive effective assistance.

## Coordination across Teams

There are strong advantages to spreading district leadership and implementation functions across two teams. We have found that it is important for initiatives to have strong political support, especially from those with direct budget authority to allocate district resources. It is also important to have a group of individuals who understand the content and can devote time to the details of ongoing implementation support. In small districts, one team may serve the function of both teams. However, in typical districts, these functions come from individuals with more specialized roles. District administrators may have the power to change policy and allocate resources but may not have expertise in the practices and processes in integrated MTSS models. Implementation planning team members may have time for the work and a strong understanding of the process but do not have the power to make districtwide decisions. By separating the two teams, each gains a clear purpose.

There are several steps needed for effective coordination across the cabinet and implementation planning teams, as shown in Figure 6.6. The cabinet team works to communicate and support the development of a vision for implementation of a districtwide integrated MTSS model (1). Once this vision gains political support and priority, it is passed onto the implementation planning team to operationalize. With this district administrator support, the implementation planning team collects data to develop a district plan, creates and utilizes materials, and identifies any barriers to implementation. This information is then passed back to the cabinet team (2). In response, the cabinet team commits the resources needed for successful implementation and removes barriers to implementation (3). The process continues in an ongoing cycle as data indicate the need to change plans.

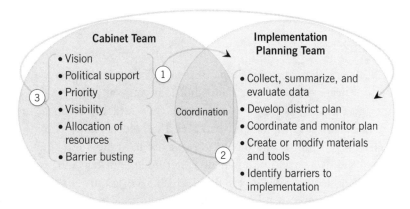

**FIGURE 6.6.** Coordination processes across district teams.

As shown in the previous two figures, a fundamental component of district support is gathering data on the quality of implementation and feedback on what activities might improve implementation. Information is gathered from school teams on fidelity of implementation, student outcomes, and implementation barriers. This information is shared with the cabinet team, implementation planning team, and training and coaching providers to adjust each group's actions. These information channels allow for enhanced alignment across district and school teams. The problems and needs identified at one level can then be addressed by the other levels. Alignment helps to ensure a common focus across the system and efficient allocation of resources by minimizing redundant or inefficient activities across the various levels, particularly in schools.

## VARIATIONS IN DISTRICT SUPPORT

So far in this chapter, we have described both districts and the support provided to schools somewhat generically. However, not all districts will have similar organizational structures, and not all schools in each district will need similar support. As we have described throughout this book, function is far more important than form. Rather than trying to fit an ideal district support structure onto all districts, it is better to consider these systems based on each district's context and the contexts of its schools. Within the common variations in district structures and supports, two general variations are useful to consider: variations in district MTSS structures based on size and differentiation of district support for school needs.

### Variations in District Support Based on District Size

It is an understatement to note that districts vary significantly in their available resources and ability to support the schools within their purview. Depending on the size of the district, there are relative advantages and disadvantages of various aspects of district support. Exactly how that support is organized is far less important than providing the functions needed to support schoolwide implementation of an integrated MTSS model. We provide guidance based on three general sizes of school districts: (1) large urban districts, (2) stand-alone districts, and (3) small school districts.

### Large Urban Districts

Large urban districts are characterized by more resources, more personnel, and more underserved populations. Larger districts have more staff that can contribute to supporting MTSS. As a result, these larger districts may have an easier time establishing local implementation support capacity because district personnel can afford to hold specialized roles—that is, skill sets to provide coaching, training, and technical expertise in academic RTI and PBIS without relying on outside trainers. As a result, it may be easier in large districts to provide more hours of support to schools and more people to join district teams. Larger districts may also have more experience in implementing and sustaining multiple initiatives. However, large urban districts must also face the challenges of poverty; frequent mobility of students; and high rates of staff, administrator, and particularly superintendent turnover. In addition, there are often multiple and competing initiatives, and supports are more likely to be siloed in separate departments that share overlapping functions (Nese et al., 2016). Although it may seem nice to have whole departments that provide support for academic RTI or PBIS, it is easy for turf battles to erupt when integrating, especially when budgets are integrated. These districts need to connect funding to cohesive and sustainable programs, with clear direction from the district and adequate support for implementation efforts. These challenges highlight the need to install the leadership drivers well. Additionally, changes in district and school administration present challenges for maintaining priority, continuity, and durability of integrated models. As a result, competency drivers, especially training, may need to be built up to ensure local school capacity through training new school and district personnel.

## Stand-Alone Districts

Stand-alone districts often have a moderate level of resources available for training, coaching, and evaluation, with relatively fewer contextual challenges than urban districts. Many of these stand-alone districts have fewer political challenges and much more stability in district administration. This continuity is helpful in promoting visibility and priority for district initiatives, including integrated MTSS models. As a result, it is relatively easier to develop systems that are more durable, with less of a need for extensive retraining.

## Small School Districts

In contrast, districts with only a few schools (or just one school) and enrollments under 3,000 students have their own unique challenges. Fewer personnel bring both advantages and disadvantages. For example, the reduced number of district personnel makes siloing less possible and allows for building a consistent vision more easily. On the other hand, small school districts often lack the resources for installing contexture and competency drivers. District administrators may need to think more creatively about teaming, and in particular, combining school and district teams to compensate for the vastly smaller number of staff. The cabinet team, implementation planning team, and training and coaching providers may all be the same group. The gains in communication efficiency are countered by the fact that that number of tasks does not diminish when teams are combined. These smaller districts may need to leverage other structures to address the implementation support needs of their schools.

## Additional Structures for Support

If districts cannot mobilize the resources to support their schools' implementation efforts, it is important to explore other avenues for supports rather than leaving schools to implement on their own. Smaller districts may be able to overcome their limited resources by obtaining support for implementation functions from larger agencies. In many states, the department of education may provide training and coaching supports. Some state educational agencies fund intermediate units to bridge the organizational support between states and districts. Examples of intermediate units include Area Education Agencies (Iowa), Boards of Cooperative Educational Services (New York, Colorado), Education Service Centers (Texas), Education Service Districts (Oregon), and Intermediate School Districts (Michigan). Intermediate units enable school districts to operate more efficiently and comply with state and federal mandates. Finally, if an intermediate unit is unavailable or unable to support small district implementation efforts, it may be possible to leverage supports across several small districts by pooling resources.

## Differentiating Support for Schools Based on Need

Another variation in district support is the type or level of support provided to each school in the district. Just as we differentiate support for individual students in the classroom, support for school teams is more effective when it is tailored to local expertise, needs, and available resources. And just like in the classroom, individualizing supports for each school is often impractical and inefficient. Although it may be possible for districts supporting only a few schools (e.g., for an initial pilot), individualized supports are difficult to coordinate for larger initiatives. As such, it is worth considering how schools may be grouped for differentiated support based on their stage of MTSS implementation (see Chapter 7) and level of need for additional implementation support.

### Differentiated Training

Districts with extensive and durable integrated MTSS models have a coordinated and planful professional development calendar, which allows for trainings for multiple schools in each event and efficient use of external trainers as needed. This approach is far more sensible than leaving schools to coordinate their trainings on their own, but it also has its disadvantages. Although larger training sessions may be efficient, they may also be less effective because school teams are often at different stages of implementation, with different needs for knowledge and skill development. Differentiating training allows districts to provide content to match schools' stages and needs with a balance of effectiveness and efficiency.

There are two common strategies for differentiating integrated MTSS training. The first method involves using general case instruction (Becker & Engelmann, 1978; Horner, McDonnell, & Bellamy, 1985). *General case instruction* is the delivery of key content with attention to the critical features and core principles of MTSS and with sufficient examples that a range of both new and experienced school teams can benefit. With multiple examples, school teams can see the variation in practices that allow for initial and advanced implementation and adaptation of practices to a range of school contexts. Although some individuals will see this training approach as repetitive, repetition builds fluency, and consistent training leads to more consistent practice across staff. General case programming is an efficient use of training resources, but some schools will need more coaching to apply this type of training to their specific settings.

Another format for differentiating training involves delivering some specialized training to smaller groups during a shared professional development day. First, all participants are presented with the same initial content in a plenary session. This session would be delivered with attention to general case programming—the content should be key concepts important for introduction or review. After the plenary session, participants would attend different breakout sessions based on their current implementation levels or need for knowledge or skills. These sessions would cover a range of content topics based on identified needs. To allow for efficient differentiation, content may be delivered by a combination of external trainers, the MTSS coordinator, district coaches, and advanced school team implementers in the district. Districts may also be able to access professional development through regional or state conferences.

## Differentiated Coaching

Although it is important to differentiate training for schools based on their stage of implementation, it is even more critical to differentiate coaching based on the intensity of their needs. It may be helpful to consider supporting schools in a multi-tiered approach similar to the multitiered framework used to support students. Although all schools can benefit from coaching, some schools can implement effectively with less support, particularly as they gain experience in integrated MTSS. Teams from these schools may need additional support at key points (e.g., when implementing RTI in a new content area, after significant staff turnover), but otherwise, periodic training and coaching contacts can be sufficient. In other schools, the team may need frequent scaffolded support, even for foundational activities.

The primary focus of differentiated coaching is to vary the support provided to groups of schools within the district so that all schools are able to implement integrated MTSS practices. By varying the intensity of support to match school need, the district teams can free up resources to apply them where they are needed most. Although it may be tempting to discuss schools as "green zones," "yellow zones," or "red zones," schools may need support for a variety of reasons, which makes these kinds of labels inappropriate and counterproductive. As with students, there are many aspects of the school context that can lead to inconsistent implementation, not simply willful resistance to an MTSS model (McIntosh, Lucyshyn, et al., 2014). We have found that it is more helpful instead to describe the different levels of district support provided to these groups of schools: standard support, supplemental support, and focused support.

### STANDARD SUPPORT

Schools receiving standard support can drive their own implementation efforts as well as troubleshoot past basic implementation barriers with minimal outside assistance. Through standard support, school leadership teams work as independently as possible to develop local implementation capacity within their schools. Standard support commonly includes providing basic integrated MTSS training through a typical training calendar. Schools may also access additional trainings that are provided by the district based on self-assessment of their implementation and needs. Additionally, the district provides some coaching, generally as part of monthly or quarterly school team networking sessions, where school teams or their facilitators meet on a regular (e.g., monthly, quarterly) basis to discuss implementation and share ideas. In addition, the district provides access to some on-demand coaching to ensure that training concepts are applied and adapted based on each school's context.

Just as with students, the proportion of schools successful with standard support can be increased through a number of strategies at the district level. First, before schools even receive initial training, the district can implement selection processes to ensure readiness for MTSS implementation. These processes include a review of applications from schools to participate in the initiative. Appendix 6.2 includes a sample school application for a district integrated MTSS model. Using a selection process is important because it serves as an efficient self-study guide for teams to take on initial steps and secure support before beginning and requiring much coaching. Schools can be required to collect and submit data, which helps clarify that use of data is a necessary core feature of implementation. The process also avoids implementation before school staff (or administrators) are aware of the resources required and are fully committed to it. Such adoption without investment or commitment can easily derail efforts and require much more district coaching than if the district works with teams that have already demonstrated commitment (Fixsen et al., 2005). A formal selection process also generates enthusiasm among school staff for being selected to participate. School teams that are not selected can be provided with brief tips on how to improve their readiness (and thereby their applications) in the future. Second, a focus on high-quality training for schools may decrease (but not eliminate) the need for coaching in schools with strong local capacity. Third, the use of common, group-delivered coaching opportunities (e.g., the school team networking sessions described in the preceding paragraph) can provide a foundation of support that is more efficient than coaching visits to individual schools. Receiving support from fellow school teams engaged in implementation, sometimes called a community of practice or professional learning community, can serve the same function, more efficiently and perhaps as effectively, as individual coaching (Stoll, Bolam, McMahon, Wallace, & Thomas, 2006).

## SUPPLEMENTAL SUPPORT

Supplemental support is added to typical support for school teams needing additional district help to implement data, practices, and systems with strong fidelity. School teams may need this level of support for a variety of reasons, such as challenging contexts or less local capacity for implementation at the staff, team, or administrator level. This support may be needed temporarily when school teams are starting a new phase of implementation or when they are experiencing brief setbacks (e.g., administrator or team facilitator turnover).

Supplemental support commonly includes increasing the frequency or intensity of coaching communication and visits (Lorhmann & Davis, 2014). It is beneficial to provide a point person who is available for questions and is proactive in communication. Schools receiving supplemental support are not always in regular contact with the district teams, and there are a number of common reasons. First, they may not be aware that they need support at key times. Teams just learning about the key principles and practices may not fully understand them and believe that they are implementing well when they may not be doing so (Rasplica, McIntosh, & Hoselton, 2016). In these situations, on-site coaching can help ensure quality implementation and assist teams in accurate self-assessment and action planning. The goal of these coaching contacts is to build the expertise of the school team to implement more independently. In addition, school teams may lose contact because of competing work priorities. Coaching in these cases involves providing gentle prompts and precorrections (the role Susan Barrett calls the "positive nag") that tip the scales from inactivity to taking the steps that the team knows will lead to improved implementation and student outcomes. Supplemental support may also include additional training opportunities, such as encouraging staff or team leaders to attend regular district orientations or to utilize existing district resources, such as online modules or practical reference books.

As with student support, there is no clear line between standard and supplemental support, and no clear way to differentiate which schools are receiving which type of support at any given time. School teams may request supplemental support themselves, or district staff may identify the need for additional support based on their interactions with teams (e.g., lack of communication, pushback on common tasks). District teams should also review their schools' fidelity of implementation data at least annually to identify schools that might benefit from more help.

## FOCUSED SUPPORT

Whereas supplemental support involves "light touch" prompts and contacts that generally refer school teams to their previous training and existing resources, focused support includes intensive, guided coaching to overcome persistent barriers to implementation that school teams are facing. These barriers may come from significant contextual challenges, such as community poverty, frequent turnover and mobility, severe student need, or staff or administrator commitment issues, such as resistance to MTSS practices or "implementation fatigue" (Lohrmann, Forman, Martin, & Palmieri, 2008; Tyack & Cuban, 1995). The good news is that contextual challenges may not be as much as a barrier as initially perceived and may even provide the motivation to improve practices (Bradshaw & Pas, 2011; McIntosh et al., 2013), and once schools reach adequate implementation, the effects of these barriers on sustainability become diminished (Turri et al., in press).

Coaching in focused support includes regular communication and more extensive visits. It is not assumed that school teams requiring this level of support will be proactive in contacting the district teams, so districts will take on this role, with regular contacts and follow-ups as needed, especially before and after team meetings or key data collection times (e.g., academic benchmarking). It is extremely helpful for these schools to have a district coach or MTSS coordinator attend meetings to ensure that they run smoothly. A coach can model how to run meetings efficiently and effectively, so that teams can see that it can be done well, even with the issues that they face. A key feature of effective focused support is that the coaching itself is explicit in both content and delivery. Coaches can provide support through a "think-aloud" approach to help build the capacity of the team for independent problem solving. Coaches can use the problem-solving approach described in Chapter 5 to help the team troubleshoot specific concerns in implementation efforts that interfere with successful implementation (e.g., allocation of funds/resources when there are minimal resources currently available). Focused support often also includes providing these school teams with regular training each year, such as new team trainings that are typically provided during initial implementation only. This training helps to build local capacity and counteract frequent turnover and misunderstandings about MTSS.

When providing focused support, it is helpful to revisit the distinction (from the implementation drivers section) between technical and adaptive problems. For technical problems (the "what" and "how" issues), focused coaching provides school personnel with competence in the components of integrated MTSS practices as identified in Chapters 3, 4, and 5. Coaching includes providing clear next steps and modeling these skills for the team to see firsthand. For adaptive problems (the "why" issues), focused coaching directly addresses concerns with practices. It often involves directly addressing individual concerns about implementation and using a clear approach to dispel misperceptions and adjust practices to meet needs (Feuerborn, Wallace, & Tyre, 2013). Coaching expertise is needed for this process because it is important to keep the critical features of the practice intact when adapting practices to enhance contextual fit (McIntosh, Horner, & Sugai, 2009). Any strategy or intervention has critical features that make the practice work, as well as "window dressing" that is not relevant. For example, acknowledgment tickets used in PBIS include an active ingredient (i.e., recognition for prosocial behavior) and irrelevant ingredients (e.g., color or shape of the ticket, raffle process). Without local or external coaching expertise, school teams may inadvertently remove the active ingredients when adapting strategies, resulting in "lethal mutations" (McLaughlin & Mitra, 2001). In most cases, the problems associated with focused support are a combination of technical and adaptive problems, which require coaches to attend to both.

## TEAM CHECKLISTS: INTEGRATING DISTRICT SUPPORT

Although each chapter in this section has included both school- and district-level checklists, this chapter's checklists are somewhat different from those in other chapters. As described at the start of this chapter, the focus is on strategies at the district level, but school teams should still advocate for needed district supports. As a result, the school-level checklist closely parallels the district-level checklist.

# SCHOOL-LEVEL TEAM CHECKLIST
# FOR INTEGRATING DISTRICT SUPPORT

| Implementation Step | Implementation Status | | |
|---|---|---|---|
| | Not in place | Partially in place | In place |
| 1. The school leadership team regularly (e.g., yearly) asks various stakeholders (e.g., students, families, staff) to identify shared values and how MTSS is meeting their needs (e.g., through surveys, community nights, focus groups). | | | |
| 2. The school leadership team presents data on implementation and outcomes to district administrators and the school board to advocate for district support of MTSS. | | | |
| 3. To the greatest extent possible, the school leadership team embeds MTSS implementation into (a) job descriptions, (b) postings, and (c) hiring preferences. | | | |
| 4. The school leadership team regularly (e.g., yearly) identifies barriers to implementation and implements plans or requests district support to overcome them. | | | |
| 5. The school leadership team acts (e.g., through hiring and training) to build in-school expertise in MTSS implementation. | | | |
| 6. The school leadership team helps build MTSS capacity among staff by bringing new members onto the team each year and sending members to relevant trainings. | | | |
| 7. The school leadership team maintains regular communications (including sharing successes) with district teams. | | | |
| 8. The school leadership team requests coaching support when needed. | | | |
| 9. The school leadership team networks with other school teams to share their successes and barriers to overcome. | | | |

| Priority for Action Planning (the three most important items from above) | Who is responsible? | By when? | How will we know when it is accomplished? |
|---|---|---|---|
| 1. | | | |
| 2. | | | |
| 3. | | | |

# DISTRICT-LEVEL TEAM CHECKLIST
# FOR INTEGRATING DISTRICT SUPPORT

| Implementation Step | Implementation Status | | |
|---|---|---|---|
| | Not in place | Partially in place | In place |
| 1. The district administration establishes teams (or a team) to serve the following functions: (a) cabinet (i.e., executive leadership), (b) implementation support, and (c) training and coaching. | | | |
| 2. Teams establish a cabinet liaison and an MTSS coordinator to facilitate team efforts. | | | |
| 3. Teams use a process to identify the shared values of various stakeholders (e.g., students, families, staff). | | | |
| 4. The cabinet team builds an integrated MTSS model into various district policies (e.g., prioritizing resources, professional development). | | | |
| 5. The cabinet team embeds MTSS implementation into (a) job descriptions, (b) postings, and (c) hiring preferences. | | | |
| 6. Teams regularly identify barriers to school implementation and implement plans to overcome them. | | | |
| 7. The implementation support team ensures that data systems are designed to generate meaningful information for decision making. | | | |
| 8. Teams use evaluation from information systems to provide performance feedback to improve implementation at all levels. | | | |
| 9. The district has access to training and coaching capacity and acts to build local training and coaching capacity. | | | |
| 10. The training and coaching providers conduct professional development through a common training calendar that includes (a) MTSS orientations, (b) administrator academies, (c) trainings for coaches, (d) peer networking, and (e) special topics. | | | |
| 11. The district makes coaching available to schools and differentiates access by need for support (e.g., standard, supplemental, focused). | | | |
| 12. The training and coaching providers hold training and regular meetings (e.g., quarterly) for those who provide coaching in the district. | | | |
| 13. The training and coaching providers hold regular school team networking sessions (e.g., quarterly) for school teams to share their successes and barriers to overcome. | | | |
| 14. The implementation support team regularly (e.g., quarterly) self-assesses the district's capacity for providing support (e.g., District Capacity Assessment) and develops action plan goals based on results. | | | |

*(continued)*

| Priority for Action Planning (the three most important items from above) | Who is responsible? | By when? | How will we know when it is accomplished? |
|---|---|---|---|
| 1. | | | |
| 2. | | | |
| 3. | | | |

# EBISS Systems Coach Self-Assessment

### Kathleen Ryan Jackson and Erin A. Chaparro
### *Center on Teaching and Learning, University of Oregon, 2014*

EBISS Coach Name: _____     Years of Coaching Experience: _____

District or Agency: _____

Please rate yourself on the specific coaching and content skills required of Systems Coaches supporting districts in the implementation of Effective Behavioral and Instructional Support Systems (EBISS) or Multi-Tiered Systems of Support (MTSS). You can use this self-assessment as a tool to set goals for your own professional development. You can also share these results with your district so that the district office can support you with the appropriate professional development.

**Please identify if you:**

Strongly Disagree (1),   Disagree (2),   Agree (3),   Strongly Agree (4)

### A. EBISS Evidence-Based Practices (EBPs):

I have the knowledge and skills to implement:

1. Scientifically validated or evidence-based tiered programs for reading.

   I am fluent with this knowledge          I am skilled to coach others in this area
   ①     ②     ③     ④                  ①     ②     ③     ④

2. Scientifically-validated or evidence-based tiered programs for behavior.

   I am fluent with this knowledge          I am skilled to coach others in this area
   ①     ②     ③     ④                  ①     ②     ③     ④

3. Screening of all students to identify students at risk of poor outcomes (reading and behavior).

   I am fluent with this knowledge          I am skilled to coach others in this area
   ①     ②     ③     ④                  ①     ②     ③     ④

4. Progress monitoring to assess student's reading and behavioral performance, student's rate of improvement, and responsiveness to instruction.

   I am fluent with this knowledge          I am skilled to coach others in this area
   ①     ②     ③     ④                  ①     ②     ③     ④

*(continued)*

Elements of this assessment were informed by the work of the National Implementation Research Network (*nirn.fpg.unc.edu*) and the Technical Assistance Center on Positive Behavioral Interventions and Supports (*pbis.org*). Specific references and resources can be found at the end.

The development of this assessment was supported by the Oregon Department of Education, through ED Grant No. H323A060007 to the University of Oregon. Reprinted with permission from Kathleen Ryan Jackson and Erin A. Chaparro.

5. Decision-making guidelines and timelines that guide tiered-program implementation.

I am fluent with this knowledge
① ② ③ ④

I am skilled to coach others in this area
① ② ③ ④

6. Data-based decision making that occurs at all levels (i.e., board, district, school, classroom).

I am fluent with this knowledge
① ② ③ ④

I am skilled to coach others in this area
① ② ③ ④

## B. Leadership and Team Facilitation:

I have the knowledge and skills to:

1. Develop a teaming framework (i.e., EBISS Teaming Framework) to establish communication loops and *Improvement Cycles* between all stakeholders.

I am fluent with this knowledge
① ② ③ ④

I am skilled to coach others in this area
① ② ③ ④

2. Guide teams in the use of *Implementation Stages* (Fixsen et al., 2013).

I am fluent with this knowledge
① ② ③ ④

I am skilled to coach others in this area
① ② ③ ④

3. Lead completion of a validated district-tiered program fidelity tool annually.

I am fluent with this knowledge
① ② ③ ④

I am skilled to coach others in this area
① ② ③ ④

4. Analyze outcome and fidelity data from district and school(s).

I am fluent with this knowledge
① ② ③ ④

I am skilled to coach others in this area
① ② ③ ④

5. Develop, align, and monitor district and school(s) action plan(s) using a problem-solving model (e.g., PDSA, TIPS).

I am fluent with this knowledge
① ② ③ ④

I am skilled to coach others in this area
① ② ③ ④

6. Guide development of Continuous Improvement Plan that links multiple initiatives, district policy, and school(s) practices

I am fluent with this knowledge
① ② ③ ④

I am skilled to coach others in this area
① ② ③ ④

7. Support design of a district budget that reflects equitable resource allocation and shared responsibility for student outcomes across all district- and school-level departments.

I am fluent with this knowledge
① ② ③ ④

I am skilled to coach others in this area
① ② ③ ④

*(continued)*

8. Identify important stakeholders, solicit input, and analyze feedback.

I am fluent with this knowledge
① ② ③ ④

I am skilled to coach others in this area
① ② ③ ④

## C. Systems Coordination:

I have the knowledge and skills to:

1. Assess district and school's level of implementation and *readiness* for change.

I am fluent with this knowledge
① ② ③ ④

I am skilled to coach others in this area
① ② ③ ④

2. Assess implementation barriers and make practical recommendations.

I am fluent with this knowledge
① ② ③ ④

I am skilled to coach others in this area
① ② ③ ④

3. Support selection and implementation of EBPs that are a contextual fit for district and school(s).

I am fluent with this knowledge
① ② ③ ④

I am skilled to coach others in this area
① ② ③ ④

4. Develop action plans that integrate training, coaching, hiring, satisfaction, and evaluations.

I am fluent with this knowledge
① ② ③ ④

I am skilled to coach others in this area
① ② ③ ④

5. Collect, analyze, and report multiple sources of outcome and fidelity data for behavior at Tier 1, 2, and 3 (e.g., *SET, BoQ, ODRs, TFI, MATT, ISSET*).

I am fluent with this knowledge
① ② ③ ④

I am skilled to coach others in this area
① ② ③ ④

6. Collect, analyze, and report multiple sources of outcome and fidelity data for literacy at Tier 1, 2, and 3 (e.g., *R-TFI, OTISS*, program specific fidelity measures).

I am fluent with this knowledge
① ② ③ ④

I am skilled to coach others in this area
① ② ③ ④

7. Lead development and presentation of easy-to-read reports on EBP fidelity and student outcomes to multiple stakeholders.

I am fluent with this knowledge
① ② ③ ④

I am skilled to coach others in this area
① ② ③ ④

*(continued)*

### D. Professional Development and Coaching:

I have the knowledge and skills to:

1. Administer a needs assessment to identify the knowledge and skills district and school teams require prior to MTSS implementation.

   I am fluent with this knowledge     I am skilled to coach others in this area
   ① ② ③ ④          ① ② ③ ④

2. Develop and implement a skill-based professional development (PD) service delivery plan in your area of expertise and secure additional supports when needed.

   I am fluent with this knowledge     I am skilled to coach others in this area
   ① ② ③ ④          ① ② ③ ④

3. Establish a clearly defined fidelity of implementation system that is conducted regularly to measure staff competence and to develop PD and coaching plans.

   I am fluent with this knowledge     I am skilled to coach others in this area
   ① ② ③ ④          ① ② ③ ④

4. Use multiple sources of data to evaluate effectiveness of PD and to inform coaching.

   I am fluent with this knowledge     I am skilled to coach others in this area
   ① ② ③ ④          ① ② ③ ④

5. Use multiple sources of data to evaluate effectiveness of coaching and to inform hiring and selection of new staff.

   I am fluent with this knowledge     I am skilled to coach others in this area
   ① ② ③ ④          ① ② ③ ④

6. Develop and implement a districtwide coaching service-delivery plan that responds to the unique needs of individual school(s).

   I am fluent with this knowledge     I am skilled to coach others in this area
   ① ② ③ ④          ① ② ③ ④

7. Coach district leadership teams (e.g., development of decision rules, application of data analysis skills for action planning and resource allocation).

   I am fluent with this knowledge     I am skilled to coach others in this area
   ① ② ③ ④          ① ② ③ ④

8. Coach school leadership teams (e.g., use of decision rules, application of data analysis skills for action planning and resource allocation).

   I am fluent with this knowledge     I am skilled to coach others in this area
   ① ② ③ ④          ① ② ③ ④

*(continued)*

## SCORING DIRECTIONS:

The knowledge category and the coaching category each have three different types of scores.

1. Raw item scores are 1, 2, 3, or 4 for each item.
2. Subscale total score is the number of raw points you add up from all items in each section. There are 4 points possible per item.
3. Subscale percentage is the number of points received divided by the number of points possible for that section.

Last you can average the subscale percentages together for your total average percentage.

Please use the table below to calculate subscale scores and percentages.

| SYSTEM COACH'S SELF ASSESSMENT: TOTAL SUMMARY SCORE | | | | |
|---|---|---|---|---|
| *I am fluent with this knowledge* | | | *I am skilled to coach others* | |
| **EBISS EVIDENCE-BASED PRACTICES** | | | | |
| # of items | Points Received/ Points Possible | Percentage of Points Possible | Points Received/ Points Possible | Percentage of Points Possible |
| 6 | /24 | % | /24 | % |
| | | | | |
| **LEADERSHIP AND TEAM FACILITATION** | | | | |
| # of items | Points Received/ Points Possible | Percentage of Points Possible | Points Received/ Points Possible | Percentage of Points Possible |
| 8 | /32 | % | /32 | % |
| | | | | |
| **SYSTEMS COORDINATION** | | | | |
| # of items | Points Received/ Points Possible | Percentage of Points Possible | Points Received/ Points Possible | Percentage of Points Possible |
| 7 | /28 | % | /28 | % |
| | | | | |
| **PROFESSIONAL DEVELOPMENT AND COACHING** | | | | |
| # of items | Points Received/ Points Possible | Percentage of Points Possible | Points Received/ Points Possible | Percentage of Points Possible |
| 8 | /32 | % | /32 | % |
| | | | | |
| | **Average Percentage** | % | **Average Percentage** | % |

*(continued)*

## REFERENCES AND RESOURCES

### Implementation Science

Fixsen, D., Blase, K., Metz, A., & van Dyke, M. (2013). Statewide implementation of evidence-based programs. *Exceptional Children, 79*, 213–230.

Frank Porter Graham Child Development Institute. (n.d.) *State Implementation and Scaling Up of Evidence Based Practices (SISEP)*. Retrieved from *http://sisep.fpg.unc.edu/*.

National Implementation Network (NIRN). (n.d.). *National Implementation Network*. Retrieved from *http://nirn.fpg.unc.edu*.

State Implementation and Scaling Up of Evidence Based Practices (SISEP) & National Implementation Network (NIRN). (2013-2014). AI Hub: The active implementation hub. Retrieved from *http://implementation.fpg.unc.edu/*.

*Key terms:* Improvement Cycles, Implementation Stages, OTISS (Measure), DCA (Measure).

### PBIS

Educational and Community Supports. (2014). *PBISApps*. Retrieved from *https://www.pbisapps.org/Pages/Default.aspx*.

Positive Behavioral Interventions & Supports (PBIS). (2014). *OSEP Technical Assistance Center*. Retrieved from *https://www.pbis.org/*.

Sugai, G., & Horner, R. (2002). The evolution of discipline practices: School-wide positive behavior supports. *Child and Family Behavior Therapy, 24*(1), 23–51.

*Key terms:* Team Initiated Problem Solving (TIPS), BoQ (Measure), TFI (Measure).

### Schoolwide Reading Model

Kame'enui, E. J., & Simmons, D. C. (1998). Beyond effective practice to schools as host environments: Building and sustaining a school-wide intervention model in reading. *OSSC Bulletin, 41*(3), 3–24.

Oregon Department of Education. (2011). *Oregon K-12 literacy framework: Reading*. Salem, OR: Co-author. Retrieved from *http://www.ode.state.or.us/search/page/?id=3519*.

OrRTI Oregon Response to Intervention. (2013). *Oregon RTI: Reading service delivery plan*. Tigard, OR: Author. Retrieved from *http://www.oregonrti.org/wpcontent/uploads/2013/09/OrRtI-Service-Delivery-Model_9-9-13-copy.docx*.

### EBISS

Chaparro, E.A., Ryan-Jackson, K., Baker, S. K., Smolkowski, K. (2012). Effective Behavioral and Instructional Support Systems: An integrated approach to behavior and academic support at the district level. *Advances in School Mental Health Promotion, 5*, 161–176.

Chaparro, E. A., Smolkowski, K., Baker, S. K., Hanson, N., & Ryan-Jackson, K. (2012). A model for system-wide collaboration to support integrated social behavior and literacy evidence-based practices. *Psychology in the Schools, 49*, 465–483.

# Integrated MTSS Implementation Readiness Application

The purpose of this application process is to help determine school readiness and commitment to the implementation of an integrated academic and behavior multi-tiered systems of support (MTSS) and to participate in the district initiative.

Listed below are requirements for participation in the district's integrated MTSS initiative.

☐ A schoolwide MTSS leadership team is identified to attend all required trainings and lead MTSS efforts in the building.

☐ Commitment from the school principal to attend all required trainings and allocate the needed time for the initiative's activities (e.g., professional development, trainings, and meetings).

☐ Literacy and social behavior are each indicated as one of the top three school improvement goals for this year.

☐ Commitment of at least 80% of staff to participate in the MTSS initiative for the next 3 years (please include a statement explaining how this commitment was obtained and documented).

☐ Commitment to build resources for implementing the integrated MTSS activities into the annual school budget.

☐ Completion of the *Multi-Tiered Systems of Support Needs Assessment* (please include in application).

Please answer the following questions.

1. What are the needs of your students that would be best addressed by an integrated MTSS model?

2. How does the MTSS framework fit into your school culture, philosophy, and values?

*(continued)*

3. Do you have the adequate staff capacity to implement the MTSS model well? (Please elaborate.)

4. Do you have adequate additional resources to implement the MTSS model well? (Please elaborate.)

5. Describe how this initiative will contribute to the achievement of your school improvement plan.

6. Describe other initiatives that you are currently implementing in the areas of social behavior and literacy. How long have these initiatives been under way? How do these initiatives support or compete with MTSS? How do you plan to integrate MTSS into your current initiatives?

# CHAPTER 7

# Integrating Entire Systems

Throughout this book, we have discussed the reasons for integrating RTI systems for academics and behavior. We described a rationale and strategies for integrating data in Chapter 3, practices in Chapter 4, teaming in Chapter 5, and district systems in Chapter 6. In this chapter, we take a broader view to examine more of the "how" for putting all of these elements together into one integrated system. As you might guess, this is no easy task. To do it well, we need to consider current systems and the foundational research behind implementation so that we can be most successful.

As we have previously emphasized, integration is best viewed not as a goal in of itself. The true goal is improved student outcomes, and any efforts at integration should be viewed in terms of whether or not they help us meet that goal. Figure 7.1 shows how we conceptualize this process. On the right of the figure, we see our goal of improved student outcomes. Then, at the middle, we implement systems to improve outcomes, and to the extent that they are effective, efficient, equitable, and sustainable, we will see durable improvements in student outcomes.

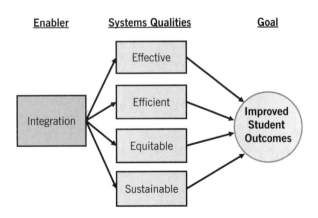

**FIGURE 7.1.** How integration might indirectly improve student outcomes.

236

Integration, then, is a vehicle for helping us make our educational systems better by addressing these four qualities of systems. If we reach the point at which more integration does not make our systems better, we may want to focus on other enablers until it does.

Considering integration as an enabler of better systems helps us understand how and why school and district efforts at integration will always vary along a continuum. One end of this continuum is represented by parallel (or siloed) systems. In parallel systems, the school is implementing academic RTI and PBIS as separate initiatives within the building. Each initiative might have separate teams doing the work, with separate data systems and separate practices. Some may view this approach as an integrated MTSS model (because both academic RTI and PBIS are in place in the school), but true integration is something different than simply trying to implement two separate initiatives at the same time. At the other end of this continuum, true integration involves the same people (i.e., the same team) implementing both academic RTI and PBIS as interrelated pieces of the larger educational system. Many schools will find themselves at, or initially aiming for, a reality somewhere between these extremes.

A good approach to integration is purposeful. Our actions are more effective if we understand when integration is best started and how this integration can take place. Through a strategic integration approach, we recognize that it is neither possible nor advantageous to force an integration of every academic and behavior practice with every student. Instead, it is helpful to look for and consider opportunities where integration is logical and makes teaching easier.

In this chapter, we describe various strategies for integrating entire systems of academic RTI and PBIS and explain how to plan a logical order for the integration process. Next, we discuss stages of implementation, informed by the field of implementation science, with an aim of maximizing the implementation and sustainability of any practice, but with a particular focus on integrated MTSS models. Finally, we address common barriers to implementation and offer suggestions for overcoming them.

## MOVING TO INTEGRATED MTSS MODELS: HOW DO WE GET THERE?

There are a few general paths that schools may take for integrating their systems. In some schools, one initiative (i.e., academic RTI or PBIS) may already be in place. The plan in this case is more straightforward. The integrated MTSS model can be developed by using the existing system as a framework and expanding the scope, especially if the system is both implemented well and seen as effective on student outcomes. In others, neither academic RTI nor PBIS systems are in place (or they are in place, but without high fidelity). The question then becomes whether to implement one fully and then the other or, alternatively, to implement an integrated system from the start. In both approaches, the desired outcome is an integrated MTSS model. The choice of how to get there depends on each school's circumstances and needs, as well as the systems-level factors we describe in this chapter.

### Simultaneous Adoption and Implementation

When schools have neither academic RTI nor PBIS strongly in place, implementing a fully integrated model from the start is one option. The main benefit of starting "fresh" by adopting a fully integrated MTSS model involves the expectation that academic and behavior will be integrated right from the beginning. In this path, administrators provide a clear message that the goal is an integrated MTSS model, and therefore all training is described as part of the same initiative. This initiative may have stronger support because of its acknowledgment of the importance of teaching the "whole child." In addition, rolling out MTSS as one initiative is often more efficient because of combined training and systems development. Systems that would require development and then integration can simply be built with the final goal in mind. It also avoids fragmentation and the misconception that we need to stop current work in academic support to focus on behavior support, or vice versa. In the same way, it preempts the development of silos of RTI and PBIS. Key staff members often champion academic RTI and PBIS initiatives (Andreou et al., 2015). These individuals typically invest a great deal of time and energy in these initiatives. The longer academic or behavior RTI systems have been in place in isolation, the greater the risk of conflict when integration eventually happens. The champions may feel a sense of loss or reduced competence or expertise with an integrated MTSS model. Adopting an integrated model from the beginning may minimize or preclude these potential issues.

However, there are also possible challenges associated with the simultaneous adoption and implementation path. Today more than ever, educators are often given more work to do than is reasonable. With increased calls for higher student proficiency, demands for teacher accountability, and introduction of new state standards, educators may feel overwhelmed with a true overhaul of the educational system all at once. This perception can be aggravated if the benefits of an integrated approach are not shared with staff in a manner that communicates how this approach will be better for both students and educators in achieving successful outcomes. It may also seem like too much too soon to tackle an integrated MTSS model due to cognitive overload and limited resources to support the work. If this feeling is common, it may be better to start small (i.e., one domain), experience success there, and then build on that success.

## A Staggered Approach to Integration

An alternative to the simultaneous adoption and implementation path is a staggered process, in which one domain is implemented to criterion and then another is added to it. This path can be taken whether or not an existing system is already in place (e.g., PBIS). If neither is in place, the school or district implementation team selects one domain to implement and adds the other in the future. A key advantage of this path is that educators will have already developed skill sets and hopefully experienced success in one domain of MTSS before adding complexity. In this "build-on" procedure, the key concepts, resources, and structures have been developed, refined, and can be relied upon to implement any other MTSS model. Another benefit with the staggered approach is that staff may be more motivated and open to integrate a second component in an integrated model when benefits and similarities of an integrated model are presented.

As described above, the possible challenges with the staggered path are the ones that make a simultaneous approach advantageous. For example, the staggered approach may lead to "turf wars" for priority of systems. In addition, without clear articulation of the objective of a fully integrated model, educators may feel that they are supposed to abandon one domain to make room to focus on the other. One possible way to take advantage of both the simultaneous and staggered approaches is by starting with a clear, consistent, and continual message from school and district administrators of the vision of a fully integrated model that will be implemented within a 5- to 7-year time frame, starting with one domain and adding others. If this message is consistent, school personnel may be able to keep the ultimate goal in mind when doing the work to put one domain in place, then the other. Throughout training and professional development events, trainers and coaches can share the vision and provide explicit training and examples of how the separate components can be integrated.

## Which Comes First: Academics or Behavior?

A common question for schools or districts that choose the staggered implementation path is which domain to implement first. This decision primarily depends on the strengths and needs of the school. For example, if a school has some items in one domain already in place (e.g., schoolwide behavior expectations and a matrix), moving from partial implementation to full implementation in that domain may be easier, leading to a strong sense of accomplishment and momentum to address the other domain. Showing quick progress in a large initiative can motivate staff and reduce resistance to change. In other circumstances, preferences of the staff may help determine the order of implementation. For example, the school staff may be more committed to improving academic outcomes than reducing problem behavior. Just as it is helpful with student behavior, providing choice (in terms of a vote) is a powerful tool to increase ownership in the implementation process.

### Reasons to Start with Academics

In the absence of a clear majority of support for one direction or the other, there may be some advantages to starting with academic RTI before adding in behavior systems. A primary reason for choosing academic RTI first is student need. Many schools are in situations where there is a sense of urgency to improve student academic outcomes. Starting with an academic approach can reduce political pressure and meet the needs of staff members who are concerned about student achievement. Starting with academic RTI may also align more easily with state and district mandates for improving student outcomes on high-stakes assessments.

### Reasons to Start with Behavior

However, there may be even more advantages to starting with an emphasis on behavior support. First, implementing PBIS often involves immediate changes in the physical school environment, such as posting behavior expectations throughout the school. Although these initial changes are superficial, it can be helpful for staff to see visible differences to prompt and motivate further implementation efforts. Further, it is more common to see rapid, noticeable improvement in student behavior than in academic skills, further reinforcing staff for implementation efforts. In addition, it is often difficult to implement academic RTI if considerable instructional time is lost to dealing with problem behavior. Implementing PBIS first in the sequence can thus set the stage for more efficient and effective implementation of academic RTI. Finally, sometimes changing one's approach to academic instruction can be more challenging. Although there are also philosophical differences to overcome in explicit teaching of social behavior, adding brief instruction in social expectations and routines, especially when lesson plans are provided, may be easier than changing one's personal academic teaching style for the entire period. It's best to avoid wars (e.g., reading wars, math wars) until there is enough belief in the system to be willing to bridge the gaps between philosophical differences in academic instruction.

## STAGES OF IMPLEMENTATION

Regardless of the path or order of implementation selected, there is some foundational theory and research that can guide the integration process. Too often in schools, new initiatives are selected without considering the science that supports quality implementation and integration. For example, a new practice may be chosen because someone from the district read a book or saw an engaging speaker present on a topic. All of a sudden, this initial enthusiasm results in contracts, one-shot trainings, manuals, and expectations that teachers will then implement this practice districtwide, with sanctions for those who do not implement it correctly. Attention to research (or simply common sense in many cases) would highlight a number of potential pitfalls to this approach. Any of these pitfalls may sink the entire initiative, even if it is a sound, evidence-based practice that meets school needs.

The study of how systems and practices are adopted, implemented, and sustained is known as *implementation science* (Cook & Odom, 2013). Knowing about implementation science can be as important as knowing the content of instruction, as it permeates every part of integrated MTSS models. One aspect that is particularly helpful in integration is the concept of stages of implementation (Fixsen et al., 2005; Horner & Sugai, 2006). These stages do more than simply track the progress of implementation of MTSS within a school or district; they also provide a framework with which to identify specific activities and accomplishments at each stage that can expedite implementation and integration (Goodman, 2013a). Each stage requires a different

| Focus | Stage | Activities |
|---|---|---|
| **Should we do it?** | Exploration/ Adoption | • Understand implementation requirements.<br>• Evaluate "goodness of fit."<br>• Develop implementation commitment. |
| **Work to do it right!** | Installation | • Create leadership teams and data systems.<br>• Audit current resources and capacity.<br>• Plan and prepare for implementation. |
| | Initial Implementation | • Test the practices on a small scale to learn best methods for broad implementation.<br>• Provide intensive support to implementers. |
| **Work to do it better!** | Elaboration | • Expand to new areas, individuals, and times.<br>• Adjust practices and systems based on initial implementation. |
| | Continuous Regeneration | • Make it more effective and efficient.<br>• Embed within current practices.<br>• Adjust to changing contexts. |

**FIGURE 7.2.** Stages of implementation.

emphasis, so strategies that are critical in one stage may be less so in others (Mercer, McIntosh, Strickland-Cohen, & Horner, 2014; Turri et al., in press). By attending to these stages, we can prevent seemingly insurmountable barriers (e.g., lack of buy-in, competing initiatives) to integrating systems in education.

A visual depiction of the five stages is provided in Figure 7.2. There are five distinct stages, but they can be chunked into three larger categories: (1) *Should we do it?*, (2) *Work to do it right*, and (3) *Work to do it better!* Although the stages and their order are common across systems, it is important to note that the speed at which schools and districts move through them will vary based on the experience of staff and the allocation of resources (Schaper, McIntosh, & Hoselton, in press; Nese et al., 2016). In addition, it is not uncommon to cycle back to earlier stages, particularly if personnel or resources shift. For each stage, we provide an overview, the intended outcomes, and how the stage can help us identify and avoid common pitfalls. Schools working to adopt a fully integrated model or starting to implement a first MTSS would consider these systems as the practice or model to use throughout each stage. For schools working toward integrating existing component systems (either integrating two parallel systems or adding on a new system to an existing academic RTI or PBIS model), we also provide considerations for integration within each stage of implementation.

## Stage 1: Exploration/Adoption

The exploration/adoption stage includes the process by which a team decides whether to select a given practice or initiative. So many of us educators are solution-focused, and when we see a problem, we immediately start thinking about fixes to try the very next day. Although this focus on changing outcomes immediately is admirable, the large systems-level decisions involved in implementing or integrating an MTSS require slowing down the selection process and ensuring that the options are sound. This stage can be used to determine whether an integrated MTSS model is the "right thing" for the school or district to do. This determination involves consideration of student need, fit with the school, and evidence that this approach will be successful for the students in that setting. The key point of this stage is not to rush ahead with implementation before considering whether there is a problem, what its presumed causes are, what options are available, and how to plan for success. This series of questions fits well within the integrated problem-solving process described in Chapter 5 (see p. 183).

The steps in this stage are led by an exploration team charged with investigating the possible adoption of practices or models, such as an integrated MTSS model. If the school already has an existing school leadership team (or the district has a district leadership team), that team will take on this role. This scenario is common for schools using the staggered implementation approach, in which one team (e.g., school PBIS team) considers whether to expand their model. For schools or districts without existing leadership teams, an ad hoc exploration team may be created for the sole purpose of this stage of implementation. As with any leadership team, it is important for the team to include those with administrative and budgetary authority, as well as representative leaders from the school or district. Even for school teams, it is crucial that the district administration plays a role in the exploration/adoption stage. Central administration can articulate the vision for the district (e.g., an integrated MTSS model), provide political support to school teams, allocate needed resources, and ensure alignment between the integrated model and other district initiatives. It is also helpful to engage with the local parent–teacher organization and gather input from the school community through family and student surveys. This information can be used to galvanize support for integrating systems.

Before considering any specific practice or model, a good first step for the exploration team is to collect data on current student outcomes. As described in Chapter 3, common methods include reporting the percent of students performing at or above academic expectations on high-stakes achievement tests or CBM benchmarks, as well as rates of exclusionary discipline (e.g., ODRs, suspensions). When sharing this information, it is important to show how these outcomes compare to district, state, or national averages. It is also important to consider the rate of growth (i.e., are student outcomes improving over time?). If student outcomes are lower (or growing more slowly) than expected, there may be stronger motivation to change current practices, particularly if team members ask themselves, "Do we think that our student outcomes will improve if we continue with our current educational program?" Starting with student outcomes, as opposed to evaluating a particular program, allows the team to assess both the level of student need as well as what types of supports will best address the need.

Once student outcomes have been identified and a need for change is established, the team can then evaluate possible approaches for improving outcomes, including integrating current systems. Figure 7.3 (adapted from the National Implementation Research Network's hexagon tool; Blase, Kiser, & Van Dyke, 2013) illustrates the key areas that should be addressed when evaluating a new practice or model for adoption. There are six components of the new approach to consider. Three of the components (the shaded triangles) address the question, "Is it the right thing to do?" This question generally explores the goodness of fit between the practice and the needs of the school or district. The other three components address a related question, "Can we do it in the right way?" This question assesses what would be needed to implement the practice or model both fully and durably. Table 7.1 guides implementation teams through using this tool to evaluate whether particular practices or models are worth adopting.

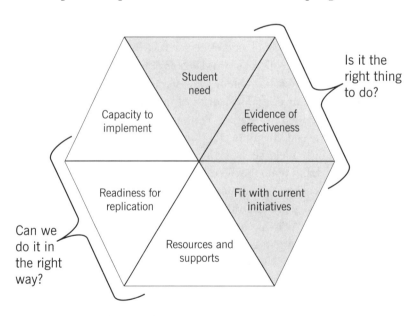

**FIGURE 7.3.** Hexagon tool for evaluating adoption of practices. Adapted with permission from Karen A. Blase from Blase, Kiser, and Van Dyke (2013).

**TABLE 7.1. Using the Hexagon Tool for Exploration and Adoption Decisions**

The following steps can be used to guide exploration teams through the evaluation process shown in the hexagon tool in Figure 7.1. If multiple options are being evaluated, the process is repeated for each practice (or model).

*"Is it the right thing to do?"*

- *Student need.* Consider the previously collected student outcomes data and assess whether the proposed practice meets these needs. Practices may generally be good ideas and worth implementing, but that doesn't necessarily mean that they will address the specific needs of students that have been identified.

- *Evidence of effectiveness.* Use the criteria described in Chapter 4 to evaluate the practice's potential to improve student outcomes. Given the investment in resources that is necessary to implement new initiatives well, it is absolutely critical to select the options that are most likely to be effective.

- *Fit with current initiatives.* Assess how the practice aligns with current initiatives by completing the MTSS Initiative Alignment Worksheet in Appendix 7.1 (see p. 264). First, list all existing school or district initiatives in the rows. For each current initiative, note its intended recipients, outcome measure(s) used to gauge success, and whether it is a mandated (i.e., required) initiative. Next, describe how the potential practice aligns with each existing initiative (e.g., does it conflict with or duplicate efforts?), and what value it adds for each existing initiative. Once complete, consider whether the proposed practice (1) meets a need, (2) could be integrated with or replace an existing initiative, and (3) could make other initiatives (especially mandated ones) better. This value added can be shared with administrators, staff, and the school community to mobilize support for a new practice. In addition, identify any initiatives that can be removed or modified to make room for a new initiative.

*"Can we do it in the right way?"*

- *Capacity to implement.* Assess existing skill levels of school personnel in practice implementation, which existing systems could support implementation, and what components of the practice may already be in place. In many cases, schools already have some effective practices or structures in place that can be used or adapted for the new initiative. Complete a self-assessment of fidelity of implementation to understand more about the practices and which critical features are already being implemented (see Chapter 3 for tools). These tools can also be used for needs assessment. For example, the PBIS Self Assessment Survey (Sugai, Horner, & Todd, 2000) includes ratings for each critical feature of PBIS that assess both whether the feature is already in place and the perceived priority for implementation. This information can be shared again with the team to document support for implementation, as well as build the habits of collecting and using data for decision making. Having low capacity to implement does not mean that the practice shouldn't be implemented, but it does mean that additional resources and supports may be needed to compensate.

- *Readiness for replication.* Consider how easily the practice can be put into place in the school or multiple schools in the district. Identify the extent to which the practice is clear and understandable. Is there access to high-quality materials and experts who can guide the implementation process? Has the practice been implemented in a range of schools, with documentation of the resources needed for implementation and sustainability? Identify if there are demonstration sites nearby that can be visited to see the practice in action. If a district is considering it, create a plan for supporting pilot schools to create local demonstration sites.

*(continued)*

**TABLE 7.1.** *(continued)*

---

- *Resources and supports.* Determine what types of support school personnel may need to implement the practice with fidelity. For any systems-level initiative to be implemented well, schools need specific support from the district, including the implementation drivers described in Chapter 6. A true evaluation of any practice will need to include evaluation of the proposed action plan for obtaining the resources needed to put the practice in place in a manner that is strong and durable.

---

## Outcomes of the Stage

The exploration/adoption stage of implementation is complete when a particular practice or model has been selected for implementation. However, there are two key underlying components of this selection process that are both important and often overlooked. First, there must be broad support to implement the practice or model before this stage is considered complete. A common criterion for academic and behavior systems is commitment to implement from 80% of staff and all administrators at the school (Horner, Sugai, et al., 2005). Second, for the commitment to be genuine, teachers and administrators must have a basic understanding of the practice or model that is being adopted. Individuals need to be able to identify the practice or model's critical features (e.g., explicit instruction in academic and behavior, progress monitoring), how these critical features are implemented, and how they relate to their classroom or administrative responsibilities. All should also understand the requirements, activities, and multiyear time commitment involved with implementing the program. This point is particularly true for the school administrator, as he or she will be leading the effort (McIntosh, Kelm, et al., in press; Strickland-Cohen et al., 2014). Table 7.2 provides a set of critical features for administrative leadership in cultivating and maintaining staff support for MTSS. As an outcome of these leadership efforts, all staff should know both the benefits and drawbacks of the approach before signing on. Without this understanding, a true commitment to implement the practice or model is not possible.

## Pitfalls to Avoid

As we've noted, the key pitfall of the exploration/adoption stage is pushing forward too quickly to adopt the new initiative without a clear, measured decision that is supported by a vast majority of staff. The point of spending time in this stage is to avoid the tendency to adopt practices that are either (1) a poor match for the school or district's needs or resources or (2) not understood or supported by school personnel. In addition, it is key that before an adoption decision is made, the exploration team identifies whether the school has the capacity to support implementation (e.g., funding, resources, time, skills) and has a plan for building adequate capacity before moving forward. Moving deliberately through the exploration/adoption stage can help address each of these pitfalls.

## Considerations for Integrating Separate Systems

Although this stage is easier to understand when considering adoption of specific programs, the same steps and strategies pertain to the decision to integrate existing systems as well. The hexagon tool and the MTSS Initiative Alignment Worksheet are completed in the same way, but with

**TABLE 7.2. Critical Features of School and District Administrator Support for Integrated MTSS Models**

| Critical feature | Rationale | Examples |
|---|---|---|
| 1. Make public statements of support. | Visible support by the building administrator signals priority and helps to mobilize staff support. | • Discuss support of MTSS model at staff meetings.<br>• Provide statements of support in staff communications. |
| 2. Build staff consensus. | Developing a "critical mass" of staff support helps to get the initiative started. Obtaining broad support provides defense against small numbers of detractors. Consensus helps to keep the initiative moving forward during the fragile initial implementation phase. | • Review school improvement goals (integrated MTSS should be considered within the top three school goals).<br>• Share current status of student academic and behavior outcomes with staff.<br>• Ask staff if things are likely to improve if the school continues in the same way.<br>• Help staff see how the chosen practices address needs and have documented effectiveness and "goodness of fit." |
| 3. Establish and support school leadership team(s). | By promoting a team approach, administrators can build local capacity for leadership without having to be there to "run the show." Building the skills of teams enhances effectiveness and sustainability beyond the time frame of an administrator's position at the school or district. | • Communicate a common vision for schoolwide supports.<br>• Work to establish the team's capacity to support all students.<br>• Commit resources to integrated MTSS model.<br>• Ensure that the team has regular meeting schedule and effective meeting structures. Develop methods for evaluating progress toward measureable outcomes.<br>• Build action plans based on data. |
| 4. Set and maintain standards for implementation. | Teams and staff need a clear framework and criterion for what successful implementation of integrated MTSS looks like. Once the vision is created, it is important to use this information to guide implementation plans. | • Collect fidelity of implementation data and update action plans.<br>• Review implementation efforts on a monthly basis.<br>• Compare implementation to fidelity criteria and provide performance feedback to staff. |
| 5. Guide decision-making/ problem-solving process. | The building administrator can help to establish ongoing cycles for collecting data and use information for decision making. It is important for administrators to monitor implementation activities and provide feedback to staff. | • Examine multiple data sources, including fidelity and student academic and behavior outcomes.<br>• Revise implementation plans based on data. |

*(continued)*

**TABLE 7.2.** *(continued)*

| Critical feature | Rationale | Examples |
|---|---|---|
| 6. Reinforce leadership team and school faculty. | Administrators play critical roles in providing staff recognition for accomplishment. Acknowledgment is especially important any time an activity is new or difficult for staff. | • Acknowledge faculty and staff for moving in the "right direction" toward goal.<br>• Focus on acknowledging activities related to the critical implementation features (i.e., fidelity data).<br>• Consider ratios of feedback provided (e.g., five acknowledgments to every one suggestion for change or correction). |

integration as the practice. For example, the exploration team assesses how integration would fit with, or add value to, existing initiatives, as well as current capacity and resources. Two issues should be addressed when considering whether to integrate systems. First, because the process of integration is often tailored to each school's strengths and needs, integration has a lower readiness for replication than a packaged, manualized program. As such, teams may need more resources and supports (e.g., coaching) to compensate and to make integration work. However, integration may add more value to existing initiatives than other options. The second issue, as we described above, is addressing the sense of loss that champions may feel when they are asked to work with each other. Including those who have strong program ownership as members of the exploration team will help the team make decisions that are more reflective of staff needs and build support instead of resistance.

### Stage 2: Installation

Once the school has decided to move forward with the new practice (e.g., an integrated MTSS model), there is important work to be done to install the necessary structures to ensure adequate implementation. The installation stage does not include actual implementation with students. Instead, the stage helps teams focus on what needs to be in place to support the initiative. Because this distinction is somewhat subtle, well-intentioned teams often skip this stage entirely; in their efforts to accelerate systems change, they move directly from adoption to implementation. This mistake is one of the biggest problems in education today (Fixsen et al., 2005), and it can be addressed with careful attention to the components of the installation stage.

As with exploration/adoption, the installation stage is facilitated by a team. The team may be an existing school leadership team, district leadership team, school improvement team, or a repurposed team (e.g., school discipline team, professional learning community, even the exploration team). This team will then take on the job of moving the practice or model through the rest of the stages of implementation. In light of this point, it is important for the membership of this team to be representative and to have administrative authority to make key decisions (see Chapter 5 for more details).

During this stage, the school leadership team creates and follows a comprehensive installation plan that addresses practices, data, and district support. Team members can complete the MTSS Quick Audit described in Chapter 4 (provided in Appendix 4.1) to take stock of current practices and assess the need to remove or add practices before initial implementation.

They can complete a similar audit of assessment tools in use (e.g., fidelity, screening, diagnostic assessment, progress monitoring; described in Chapter 3). Once these assessments have been identified (with removal of redundant tools and additions of new tools to address gaps), this information is combined into an integrated evaluation component of the plan to assess and report progress as part of the school's continuous improvement process. Finally, during this stage, a plan is created to provide training and coaching (see Chapter 6) in both the practices and assessment procedures. This plan may include support provided by the school leadership team, but more often than not, it will include district, regional, or state training, with coaching and coordination provided locally. As part of this support, it is important to clarify the roles and responsibilities for all involved in the implementation process, including school administrators, the school leadership teams, the staff, district administrators, and the school community. Although all of these individuals should have acquired a basic understanding of the practice by the end of the exploration/adoption stage, the specific tasks of involvement need to be articulated clearly during installation. Of course, the team also needs to acquire or develop the materials for implementation (e.g., posters of expectations for the classroom, integrated teaching lesson plans) and train staff in their use. The plan for support may also include formal structures for staff or school teams to collaborate by sharing strategies, as well as by modeling and viewing the teaching of lessons in a peer-to-peer community of practice.

A related part of the installation plan is considering how to integrate the practices into existing work. The MTSS Initiative Alignment Worksheet (described in the previous stage and in Appendix 7.1) is a useful tool to guide the integration of initiatives. The alignment column may identify both opportunities for integration (e.g., integrating teams that do similar work) and potential barriers that need addressing (e.g., a potential turf war, such as an initiative with a different philosophy). In addition, the value-added column indicates where there is common ground and shared objectives. This visioning work, either for integration or busting barriers, is more easily accomplished before the initial implementation stage, when the focus shifts more to the fine details of intervention. District teams may want to complete a separate MTSS Initiative Alignment Worksheet for aligning their work with state initiatives. This process can be extremely helpful in showing everyone how an initiative such as an integrated MTSS model can be used to meet multiple state requirements. Of course, astute school teams can do the same for district initiatives, providing a mechanism to avoid initiative overload (McIntosh, Horner, & Sugai, 2009).

Another useful method to enhance integration is the school improvement plan process. Because it is required in most schools, aligning the practice (e.g., integration) with school improvement goals gives it both instant priority and an existing framework for implementation. Implementing the practice with fidelity should be one of the top three goals of the school improvement plan, and the activities for implementation can be embedded within its steps. This approach may be easier for installing academic RTI systems than for PBIS. Although there is consensus among educators and stakeholders that improving academic outcomes is a top priority for schools, some educators do not include behavior supports within their school improvement plans because they believe (or are told) that the plan should address only academic concerns. In these circumstances, we suggest framing behavior initiatives in a way that stresses the positive academic outcomes of PBIS, such as developing an educational environment that is conducive to learning (e.g., safe and free from disruption). Those who are integrating their systems will find this task even easier.

Installation is also the time to consider the terminology used in the new practice. The words that are used in this stage may seem insignificant, but they are surprisingly important in facilitating systems change. For example, Adelman and Taylor (2003) recommend avoiding the use of terms such as *project* because they are associated with time-limited work and not with an enduring change to typical job responsibilities. Regarding *integration*, if the ultimate goal is an integrated MTSS model, it is useful to start using this term early and explain that academic RTI and PBIS systems *are* MTSS models. Otherwise, staff may oppose it simply because they think that it is a whole new way of doing things that disregards the strategies that are currently working for them.

## Outcomes of This Stage

The main outcome of the installation stage is that the practice or model is ready to be rolled out with students. By the end of installation, teams should have built the practices, data, and teaming structures to ensure strong implementation, and educators should have been trained in what they are expected to do and how to do it. Without this level of preparation, the likelihood of an easy initial implementation is low.

## Pitfalls to Avoid

The primary pitfall during the installation stage involves underestimating the need for careful work *before* the actual implementation begins. Too often, once a practice is selected, administrators expect staff to "just do it." As noted by many researchers and practitioners, expecting school staff to implement simply because they have been provided an initial training is both ineffective and unfair (Fixsen et al., 2005; Joyce & Showers, 2002). It is important to assess and adjust existing job requirements to make room for the new work, as well as to identify what district supports are needed to do it well. For quality implementation, these supports need to be in place prior to implementation. Often, there are pressures (from administrators, families, or community partners) to move quickly to the implementation stage, but rushing installation is unlikely to lead to the results that these stakeholders really want to see—a durable, fully implemented initiative.

## Considerations for Integrating Separate Systems

When integrating separate systems, alignment is an absolutely critical part of the installation stage. If schools have separate teams for academics and behavior, it is important to integrate these teams when feasible. One team can better manage, coordinate, and communicate implementation efforts than two teams doing the same work—or worse, working at cross efforts. It is also important that work is done at this stage to help educators see the similarities across academic and behavior systems (e.g., similar features, processes) so that integration will be as easy as possible. Integration is tricky business, and so it is important not to assume that everyone can draw connections across systems (e.g., using data for decision making, focusing on quality core instruction). Much professional development in education focuses on facilitating practical understanding (i.e., the steps and procedures of assessment or intervention). Such specific skill sets rarely generalize to new domains, however. For generalization (e.g., applying academic RTI components to PBIS), educators need to have a conceptual understanding (i.e., the theory of why practices work) as well. Therefore, training for the integrated MTSS model is most effective when it builds both practical and conceptual understanding (Gersten, Chard, & Baker, 2000).

Whenever possible, we suggest starting to combine actions from each separate initiative into one overall school improvement plan, even if these tasks are still completed in isolation. The framework for the school improvement plan provides a logical process for combining the work of parallel systems into a central plan. Essentially, it is easier to see opportunities to integrate when you're actively looking for them. The simple act of putting all of the tasks from both initiatives on one page can highlight areas where integration makes the most sense.

## Stage 3: Initial Implementation

During the initial implementation stage, the practice or model is finally implemented with students. Too often, this stage is viewed as a full roll-out of the practice, either with staff implementing all elements in the school at once or every school in the district implementing. Although this view is a good ultimate goal, the true intent of initial implementation is to pilot-test the new practice on a small scale so that there is (1) documentation of successful local implementation and (2) a model of the implementation process (i.e., what is needed for successful implementation) that can be improved upon when expanding the practice. Starting small in a school may involve implementing at one grade level initially, or beginning with foundational Tier 1 supports in one area before adding tiers or another content area. Starting small in a district may involve working with one or two schools in the same way. Purposefully limiting the number of initial implementation sites allows the team to provide adequate resources. At this stage, there is a heavy investment in initial implementation through intensive training and coaching. Failure at this stage means certain doom for the initiative. With more resources to bear, the implementation can start on a slightly larger scale, but it is important to resist the temptation to go too big too soon.

The first step in initial implementation is to select sites that are enthusiastic about trying out the practice and willing to work through the various bumps in the first steps of implementing something new. Initial attempts are often clumsy and inefficient. Selecting "early adopters" (Rogers, 2003) for piloting is helpful because they will be aiding in troubleshooting the systems and their implementation, which can take time and drain enthusiasm. It is far better to learn from mistakes that take place in a small-scale pilot, with staff who understand the challenges of going first, so that risks can be minimized without frustrating the rest of the staff, who may be understandably less willing to endure these problems. At the district and state levels, we have found that using a selection process, whereby schools apply to be the pilots (using readiness criteria such as those in Appendix 6.2), can generate excitement about implementation and help identify the strongest candidates for this initial undertaking.

Once the initial implementation sites are identified, it is useful to use a structured process for providing support and eliciting feedback from these sites. For the team to identify the most effective and efficient methods for implementing on a larger scale (e.g., schoolwide, district-wide), it is key to document what types of support were provided and how useful they were perceived to be. It is important to adjust the support provided to make implementation stronger for these schools, but also to learn from this experience. There should be ongoing two-way communication with administrators to share data on fidelity of implementation and feedback regarding what support is most useful to increase it.

## Outcomes of This Stage

The key desired outcomes of initial implementation are a demonstration that the practice can be done locally, a practice that has some of the bugs worked out, and a catalog of the lessons learned as school personnel actively engage in implementation and create the systems to support implementation. Although it is helpful to learn from experts and other implementers, having local implementation sites is incredibly valuable in understanding what is needed to support local staff in their work.

## Pitfalls to Avoid

The main pitfall to avoid in initial implementation is the temptation to implement in too many schools too soon. Limiting the number of initial implementation sites is an absolutely critical strategy for success. Implementing in too many places at the outset runs the risk of spreading resources too thin and trying to implement in infertile ground (e.g., with implementers who are only partially committed; Rogers, 2003). Initial implementation is truly a fragile stage. Schools are more likely to abandon new practices in the first year or two of implementation, before they are firmly in place (Nese, McIntosh, et al., 2016). As such, it is necessary to provide intensive support to staff members in their efforts. There is often an expectation that implementation will be perfect. In reality, initial implementation is more typically an experience of repeatedly running into unforeseen obstacles. There is a simple need to get started—even imperfectly—with a group that is willing to be pilot testers, and then to use this stage to learn how to be more perfect. If staff is not enthusiastic about the practice, it may be abandoned as soon as that inevitable first barrier is encountered.

On a related note, it is also important to be patient in this initial implementation stage. In many situations, staff will expect to see immediate changes in student outcomes. Although these results are possible (and usually more likely with PBIS than academic RTI), it is important to provide the message that change in outcomes comes from *high fidelity of implementation*. Complex, systems-level models such as academic RTI and PBIS can take 3–5 years to implement all of the critical features (Horner, Sugai, et al., 2005). Therefore, change in student outcomes could take that long (or longer) to see as well. Selecting sites (e.g., schools, classrooms) with this long-term commitment in mind is helpful in avoiding abandonment of the entire undertaking (Nese, McIntosh, et al., 2016).

## Considerations for Integrating Separate Systems

Initial implementation for integration can be a distinctive challenge, because there is much variation in how integration can happen and there are no true local examples in this stage. It is much easier to understand piloting a new program that comes with a manual and clear steps for implementation. However, the advice to implement in fertile ground pertains equally well to integration. When school personnel face conflict or uncertainty regarding integration, they may be tempted to revert back to the "old days" of using parallel academic and behavior systems. As a result, it is useful to look for the easiest opportunities to integrate, where initial successes can build confidence and trust. As described in previous chapters, integrating the practices, teaming, and decision making at Tiers 2 and 3 may be a logical place to start.

One key point in this stage of initial integration is not to underestimate the level of coaching that may be needed, even for experienced MTSS teams. Implementing one domain of MTSS well does not always generalize to the other, so more obstacles should be expected. On-site coaching can help teams identify the easier first steps for integration, as well as keep in mind the ideas of improved efficiency and effectiveness, which can bolster support for integration.

## Stage 4: Elaboration

After successful initial implementation, the next stage is expanding the practice to new settings, areas, and students, or alternatively, simply more complete implementation. It is tempting to call this stage "full implementation," because it is the extension of the practice beyond its pilot to a broader audience. Full implementation (e.g., implementation of more of the practice's critical features) is certainly a core aspect of the elaboration stage, as more staff and schools become engaged, but a deeper understanding of this stage includes continued testing and learning through the implementation process. More complete implementation often leads to more lessons learned, which enhances efficiency and effectiveness. As the model is further improved through several implementation iterations (e.g., multiple grade levels, multiple cohorts of implementing schools), it becomes more stable and more articulated, with increasingly clear identification of what works and what does not—in terms of both practice and support. We learn not only what components of the practices are effective but also how to effectively support those practices with fidelity. The structures that were created for initial implementation become more developed through continued use. In addition, daily implementation of the practice becomes, more and more, a part of typical job responsibilities—or, in other words, "what we do here." This shift toward institutionalization is a key part of both elaboration and sustainability (Adelman & Taylor, 2003; Gersten, Chard, & Baker, 2000; McIntosh, Predy, et al., 2014).

In the context of MTSS, this stage often involves both horizontal and vertical elaboration. The Tier 1 systems can be spread across multiple grade levels or schools, as described above, and schools that have implemented Tier 1 systems to criterion can begin building up the tiers and enhancing their systems at Tiers 2 and 3 for complete MTSS models. Elaboration may also mean moving further along the path toward full integration, with teams finding more opportunities to integrate as they move forward.

One aspect of the elaboration stage is particularly worth noting. Elaboration is intended to include (1) implementation of systems that have been tested and proven through initial implementation or (2) changes that carry few political or social risks. It may be more effective to consider bigger changes as comprising a new practice and start again at the exploration stage, with another adoption decision, installation, and pilot process. For example, expanding PBIS to include systematic supports for Tiers 2 and 3 may be more effective if tried again in one or two schools as opposed to implementing such a change districtwide. The existing system strengths and the availability of district resources will also help determine how cautiously to move forward with these changes.

## Outcomes of This Stage

Elaboration is considered complete when the practice or model becomes a mature, accepted schoolwide or districtwide initiative. This level of use doesn't necessarily mean that all parts are fully implemented or that all schools are implementing, but rather that it is recognized and promoted by administrators as a worthwhile initiative for all teams. One mark of this outcome is the embedding of the practice into school and district policy (Fixsen et al., 2005). The practice can be included as a recommended model for meeting district goals, incorporated into the budget, evaluations (both for school improvement and individual performance), job descriptions, hiring criteria (e.g., experience in implementation), and ongoing professional development plans. For example, the district may include new staff trainings for the practice as a regular and required offering instead of relying on each school to train their new staff.

Another important district-level outcome of the elaboration stage is the additional demonstration of the effects of the initiative on (1) the number of schools participating, (2) the number of schools implementing with adequate fidelity, and (3) valued student outcomes, for schools implementing adequately (Algozzine et al., 2010). Although the pilot effects that can be seen from initial implementation are useful in garnering more interest, the effects from broader, more complete implementation will be more compelling for more stakeholders, including the superintendent, school board, and community agencies.

### Pitfalls to Avoid

Pitfalls within the elaboration stage involve the temptation to scale up too much and too quickly. Unless there is a strong district commitment, there are often not enough resources to support elaboration with all implementation sites at once. In such cases, it is helpful to use a cohort model of implementation, in which waves of schools receive the level of attention and resources that the initial implementation sites received. Another problem during the elaboration stage is neglecting Tier 1 systems when moving to implement practices at Tiers 2 and 3. When too much effort is placed on expansion up the tiers, there can be a loss of focus on fidelity of implementation at Tier 1, which has damaging effects on installation of the upper tiers. It is helpful for administrators and coaches to continue to prompt implementation of Tier 1 strategies while assessing fidelity and providing feedback to educators on their efforts in this area.

### Considerations for Integrating Separate Systems

In the context of integrating systems, *elaboration* often means moving beyond the easy steps and taking on areas to integrate that are more challenging but also yield rewards in terms of increased effectiveness and efficiency. As with individual practices, integration itself can be embedded into policy, with a stronger expectation that systems will be more interactive and collaborative. Once teams have been successful with their initial integration efforts and have fostered the trust and commitment to move forward, some of the harder work becomes more feasible. This work is often done by combining or removing some of the structures that were developed when these separate systems were initially implemented. Merging district teams, professional development calendars, and budgets in particular will help to hasten elaboration. Obviously, however, this integration process may need more time to be successful than was needed to establish the parallel systems in the first place.

## Stage 5: Continuous Regeneration

The final stage of implementation is one that we call *continuous regeneration*. Alternatively, this stage is sometimes called *sustainability* or *continuous improvement*. We prefer the term *continuous regeneration* because this stage is characterized by making ongoing, iterative changes to the practice or model to enhance efficiency, effectiveness, and durability in response to changes in the environment (McIntosh, Filter, et al., 2010). These changes in the environment could include shifting district or state priorities, extensive turnover, or changing community demographics. In essence, if a practice or its support structure can't be modified to better fit current needs, it is far less likely to be sustained.

By this point, the practice or model should be running smoothly. There has been sufficient time both to test and refine the content and systems for each tier. The main purpose of this stage is to make it more effective on student outcomes, easier to implement, and more durable. Efficiency becomes a key mantra, because the initiative can no longer rely on the enthusiasm evoked by a new way of doing things. Instead, it must become so easy to do that it is not compelling to stop doing it. The incorporation of the practice into typical job responsibilities continues, with more standardization of activities, highlighting the key mechanisms for why specific strategies work (Embry & Biglan, 2008). In addition, there is an important need for administrators to communicate the purpose, priority, and vision for the approach at the start of each new school year. If there is a new school, district, or state initiative, it is key for administrators to explain how it connects to the existing initiatives, or how the practice is the preferred way to meet that initiative's goals (McIntosh, Horner, & Sugai, 2009). For example, it is much easier to address a state anti-bullying initiative through adding lessons within PBIS than it is to adopt a whole new program that may compete with PBIS for time and resources (Good, McIntosh, & Gietz, 2011).

## Outcomes at This Stage

This stage does not have the clear outcomes that the others do because it is the ultimate stage, and therefore there is no need to identify when to move on. However, deep continuous regeneration is reflected in a few important aspects. First, there is an institutionalized memory of the practice through manualization, documentation, and a system for storing and sharing information. Second, there is an ongoing cycle for reviewing and acting upon MTSS data (e.g., fidelity, student outcome, progress monitoring) at all tiers. Third, the practice is fully embedded within existing school structures and official policy. Fourth, there is ongoing professional development to increase the skills of existing staff and to orient new staff. Fifth, there is an ongoing process for administrators to integrate the practice with new initiatives and assess and remove barriers to implementation.

## Pitfalls to Avoid

There are two major pitfalls to anticipate and prevent during the continuous regeneration stage. The first pitfall is to slowly neglect implementation over time, either deliberately or unknowingly. In many circumstances, the primary motivation to adopt and implement a practice comes from alarming student outcomes, in either academics or behavior. When a practice is first implemented, the effects are often apparent and clearly linked to fidelity of implementation (e.g., students did better as soon as staff was implementing with fidelity). However, over time, as fewer staff members were at the school before implementation, this link may become less apparent, and some may question the need to continue (e.g., "Our students are fine—maybe they don't need to be taught the expectations"). In these situations, it is vital for administrators to stress measurement of fidelity of implementation, to provide a strong rationale for continuing, and even to describe what outcomes might look like if current practices were abandoned.

The second pitfall is to continue implementation just as it has always been done without addressing changes in context. Over time, the practice may become stale, even when implemented well, or slowly become less of a fit with the current needs of students and staff. The practice then becomes more endangered because it becomes dull and too routinized. Although standardization brings efficiency, new ideas can bring life back to a practice and help it meet needs better, enhancing its effectiveness. One helpful strategy is to regularly refresh membership on the various teams (Andreou et al., 2015). Bringing new staff onto the teams can bring fresh ideas and enthusiasm, enhance staff capacity, and allow veterans to cycle off to avoid burnout.

## Considerations for Integrating Separate Systems

Continuous regeneration for integration generally means getting iteratively better at the integration process. It is important to attend to fidelity of implementation, as there are many working parts, and thus many aspects that can slip without attention. The recommendations regarding effective meetings in Chapter 5 are helpful to consider, as it is easy for some systems to crowd out others if no one is paying attention. Issues such as turnover of key staff or emerging student challenges may require additional coaching as teams work through how best to adapt their systems to become more effective, efficient, and durable. For teams that are highly skilled in integration, continuous regeneration may mean integrating systems beyond academic RTI and PBIS, such as by implementing school-based mental health, technology, or physical activity initiatives.

## ADDRESSING CONCERNS REGARDING INTEGRATION

Even with close attention to implementation science and the stages of implementation, it is still common to encounter resistance in efforts to integrate academic and behavior systems. When faced with these challenges, we always reflect back on our strong belief that educators are doing the best they can, given their skills and support systems. From our experiences, there are a number of common and understandable barriers that are frequently voiced when teams specifically work to integrate academic RTI and PBIS models. The following sections explore common statements of concern we hear when educators work to implement an integrated MTSS model, along with strategies we have used to address them.

### "I Teach Science, Not Behavior."

### The Concern

There is a general tendency to view educational skills and the practices used to teach them as unique and discrete from one another. For example, math concepts differ from key components of reading, which in turn, focus on different skills than those to develop social and emotional competence. This separation and specificity in teaching the content areas tends to increase dramatically during high school, as content becomes more specialized and educators feel the accountability to get through the academic content. As a result, it may seem natural to teach them independently. Such a statement may reflect one's personal values, but it may also reflect how difficult it can be to change the status quo of silos within the field of education.

## Possible Solutions

Although each content area has distinct skill sets and strategies to develop those skill sets, there are still commonalities and benefits to integration. To increase motivation to integrate systems, it is helpful to begin with communicating why integration is good for students and staff. As described in Chapter 2, the time saved for instruction and increased academic engagement from implementing PBIS means that teachers will be better able to get through their academic content over the course of the year. Sharing this information is useful in showing how the systems are complementary. In addition, if the team has completed the MTSS Initiative Alignment Worksheet (Appendix 7.1, described earlier in this chapter), then they can describe the value that is added through integrating systems.

## "I Just Don't Want to Integrate Practices."

### The Concern

Even when the advantages of integration are shared, there may be more resistance to the idea, reflecting a range of possible deeper issues. One is general resistance to change. Change is difficult for anyone to go through, even when that change will likely make our jobs easier and outcomes better. There may be general inertia, or possibly the notion of sunk costs—that we've already invested too much in the current system to change it. Making a change may mean admitting that we didn't get it right initially. In addition, combining two established, siloed systems may be even more challenging when individuals associated with these systems have difficulty in sharing ownership.

### Possible Solutions

Generic resistance is tough to address because we may not have discovered the underlying cause for opposition. One method for finding a more specific cause is to look back on previous attempts at systems change by completing an "initiative autopsy." In an initiative autopsy, a team considers promising initiatives that were introduced and subsequently abandoned, noting perceived reasons for the failure. In many cases, patterns across initiatives may emerge, and these patterns can be used to prevent some of these concerns. Sticking with the status quo is more comfortable when there are few exemplars for integrating practices, little technical assistance provided in how to do it, and little priority at the policy level. Preventing these barriers to integration are more likely to be successful than challenging beliefs and attitudes after implementation has begun. The exploration/adoption stage is the best time to listen to the concerns of educators and address them before moving forward (Feuerborn et al., 2013; Walker & Cheney, 2012).

Another approach is to use the same lens we might use when assessing student behavior. When a student refuses to complete a task, we consider whether it is a "can't do" or "won't do" problem (VanDerHeyden & Witt, 2008). Although it is tempting to blame the educator's personal philosophy for such a statement, it may be more accurate—as well as more helpful—to consider the context in which the educator works. Educators need to hear a convincing argument that adopting the initiative will lead to improved outcomes for their students and themselves. If the answer is "won't do," perhaps for ideological reasons, it can be helpful to keep the focus on valued outcomes (e.g., student success) rather than feelings regarding a specific set of practices. That general aim provides a shared common ground for moving forward, even if there are conflicts regarding specific pedagogical practices (Dixon & Carnine, 1994).

## "I Don't Know How to Do Integration."

### The Concern

This concern describes the "can't do" issue from above. We all want to feel competent in our jobs. It is uncomfortable to have to use skills that we are just learning, ones that we are not sure we will do well. There is a common sentiment among educators that we now all have to be experts in all areas. By engaging in this complex task of integrating systems, some may feel that they are setting themselves up for embarrassment or criticism. It's no wonder why this feeling would lead to resistance.

### Possible Solutions

There are obviously specific sets of knowledge and skills required for implementing academic RTI and PBIS, not to mention an integrated MTSS model. It is crucial for staff to have regular opportunities for high-quality professional development, based on their needs (identified through both fidelity data and staff requests). This professional development can be provided as a continuum of opportunities, such as inservice training, peer and external coaching, access to materials or webinars, and professional learning communities. Additionally, it is helpful to share that the team approach we emphasize in integrated MTSS models allows us to capitalize on shared expertise so that no one individual needs to be expert in everything. In reality, for each skill set, the team simply needs one member with expertise or access to external (e.g., district) expertise.

## "I Will Not Be Adequately Supported to Integrate."

### The Concern

Educators are exposed to many initiatives throughout their careers, most of which will not be sustained (Nese, et al., 2016). New initiatives are often introduced with little planning for how the staff will be supported to implement the initiative, or if supports are promised, they may not be fully made available or for the time needed to allow deep implementation. Individual educators may have personal experiences of "unfunded mandates," where teachers are directed to implement a practice and then left on their own to figure out how to do it. As a result, new school or district initiatives may be perceived as an exercise in futility because of a history of initiative abandonment (Tyack & Cuban, 1995).

### Possible Solutions

This concern is most easily addressed with careful attention to the stages of implementation and the outcomes of each stage. As described above, the tendency to move too quickly through the stages comes from a sincere interest in helping students, but it tends to backfire. With regard to adequate support for staff, installation is a particularly key stage. It is helpful to consider here what structures are needed to maximize support for implementation. Asking school personnel is useful here—experienced staff members often have useful suggestions for what types of support they feel would be best in improving implementation. In addition, to counter personal learning histories of unfunded mandates, it is critical to ensure and communicate explicitly how this initiative's implementation will be different (and better) than what has been done in the past.

### *"Our Policies and Procedures Don't Allow for Integration."*

#### The Concern

This statement is based on the perception that some aspects of integration may not be permitted given the current rules of the school or district. Educational systems are indeed governed by policies that dictate what educators can do and how funds can be utilized. However, this barrier is sometimes based more on how policies and practices are interpreted by administrators or educators than actual prohibition of integration.

#### Possible Solutions

It is important to remove this concern entirely as an excuse not to integrate. Prior to beginning an integrated approach, it can be helpful to collect all relevant policies and procedures to determine which ones may facilitate or inhibit integration. Noting policies that support integration and changing policies that do not will be helpful in disputing disagreements. Sometimes the concern of policy is raised by individuals in parallel positions of power (i.e., different administrators at the same rank within the system). In these situations, one solution is to request support from a higher-level administrator to clarify policy and help settle the conflict.

### *"If We Add This New Focus, We May Stop Doing What We Do Well."*

#### The Concern

This statement is based on a fear of being spread too thin by expanding on successful academic or behavior systems and then losing those gains by trying to do too much. Although building on strengths is a wise choice, overloading a strong team with too many responsibilities may result in initiative fragmentation. Educators may have experienced systems that worked exceptionally well with a focused outcome before getting too big and then slowly deteriorating as those systems were overstressed.

#### Possible Solutions

It is obvious to everyone that adding another initiative and then losing the gains that were previously made helps no one. In reality, this is a legitimate concern whether or not systems are being integrated. The best solution is to be continuously vigilant in monitoring fidelity of implementation for the original systems. When integrating systems, initial implementation is a useful stage to assess overload. Generally, the weak point where integration may result in deterioration is in the teaming process. It is important to integrate teams slowly so that agendas do not become so full that activities are consistently missed. A common MTSS mistake is to take preventive systems for granted and neglect Tier 1 systems when moving onto implementing supports in Tiers 2 and 3. Delaying (or even stopping) integration before this breaking point occurs may help preserve the strength of existing systems. For these meetings, efficiency must be the mantra. Chapter 5 provides strategies for both increasing meeting efficiency and finding creative solutions through partial integration of teams.

## *"There Is Not Enough Time to Work on Integration."*

### The Concern

This concern is probably the most valid of all, as educators are always extremely busy, and there never seems to be enough time to do what needs to be done, let alone work on something that is new and unfamiliar. There will always be competing initiatives that demand our attention, such as implementation of new state standards or evaluation processes, not to mention instruction. Just getting through the curriculum on schedule may leave little time and energy to devote to the heady process of integrating existing parallel systems that may be perceived as working fine as siloed systems.

### Possible Solutions

There is no getting around the fact that the process of integration will start with investing more time than is currently spent. Ultimately, the way we see it, the time spent in integrating systems will pay off in even more time recovered for instruction. Integration can make us more efficient in our work, but these savings come only after an initial, often serious, investment. Our main suggestion is to work with school and district administrators to create the room needed for integration to take place. Administrators can support integration by being clear that it is a top priority and removing tasks and meetings or discouraging activities that compete with this priority. At times, this idea may include pushing back against higher-level administrators on other, less important initiatives to provide a buffer to allow school teams the time to integrate without adding another initiative.

   One tool that is particularly useful for this process is the MTSS Initiative Alignment Worksheet. Although we described this worksheet primarily as a way to assess whether a proposed practice fits with existing initiatives, it can also be used to identify opportunities to reduce competing initiatives and save time for high-priority work. Teams can look for initiatives with similar intended recipients and outcome measures to find opportunities to be more efficient. Options include braiding new practices into an existing initiative, integrating two existing initiatives, or removing low-priority (and nonmandated) initiatives that are a poor use of valuable staff time. Using this process, teams may be able to reduce redundancies, eliminate siloed systems that work at cross-purposes, and strengthen the alignment of the work across initiatives.

   The MTSS Initiative Alignment Worksheet can also be used to show how current efforts align with state initiatives. To complete it for state-level alignment, state initiatives are listed in each row instead of district or school initiatives. Then, the Alignment column is used to indicate how the integrated MTSS model may already meet the requirements of these initiatives.

If the worksheet shows that MTSS fulfills a state initiative's requirements without the need for a separate initiative, the district can document its steps in MTSS implementation as evidence of compliance and avoid more fragmented work. As a result, staff can see that implementing an integrated MTSS model is not an add-on initiative. Instead, it is central to the mission of the district and state.

## TEAM CHECKLISTS: INTEGRATING ENTIRE SYSTEMS

This final set of checklists serves to provide a concise list of the strategies for integrating systems, whether the process is simultaneous, staggered, or simply involves integrating existing parallel systems. Across each of these paths, there are common steps and strategies for building support and maximizing success throughout the stages of implementation.

# SCHOOL-LEVEL TEAM CHECKLIST
# FOR INTEGRATING ENTIRE SYSTEMS

| Implementation Step | Implementation Status | | |
|---|---|---|---|
| | Not in place | Partially in place | In place |
| 1. The school forms an exploration team to decide whether to adopt an integrated MTSS model. | | | |
| 2. The exploration team completes the hexagon tool (Figure 7.3 and Table 7.1) and MTSS Initiative Alignment Worksheet (Appendix 7.1). | | | |
| 3. The exploration team informs staff about basic concepts and responsibilities for integration. | | | |
| 4. The exploration team obtains 100% commitment from administrators and at least 80% commitment from staff to integrate before adopting an integrated MTSS model. | | | |
| 5. School administrators provide a clear, consistent message of a vision of an integrated MTSS model for staff. | | | |
| 6. The school leadership team develops and maintains an ongoing action plan for integrating (a) practices, (b) data, and (c) teams, as well as evaluating implementation and outcomes. | | | |
| 7. The school leadership team builds integration goals and steps into the school improvement plan. | | | |
| 8. The school leadership team aligns integration with existing initiatives. | | | |
| 9. School administrators buffer staff against new initiatives during the initial implementation period. | | | |
| 10. The school leadership team uses an application or selection process to determine the best areas for initial integration. | | | |
| 11. School administrators provide high rates of reinforcement during the initial implementation period. | | | |
| 12. The school leadership team establishes a structured process for gathering feedback and improving implementation. | | | |
| 13. The school leadership team continues to monitor fidelity of implementation and identify ways to make implementation more efficient. | | | |
| 14. The school leadership team refreshes team membership, bringing new staff on and easing roles of veterans. | | | |

*(continued)*

| Priority for Action Planning (the three most important items from above) | Who is responsible? | By when? | How will we know when it is accomplished? |
|---|---|---|---|
| 1. | | | |
| 2. | | | |
| 3. | | | |

# DISTRICT-LEVEL TEAM CHECKLIST
# FOR INTEGRATING ENTIRE SYSTEMS

| Implementation Step | Implementation Status | | |
|---|---|---|---|
| | Not in place | Partially in place | In place |
| 1. The district team identifies whether the district will support a simultaneous or staggered approach to integration. If staggered, the team selects academics, behavior, or school choice for order of implementation. | | | |
| 2. The district forms an exploration team to decide whether to adopt an integrated MTSS model. | | | |
| 3. The district exploration team completes the hexagon tool (Figure 7.3 and Table 7.1) and the MTSS Initiative Alignment Worksheet (Appendix 7.1) for both district and state initiatives. | | | |
| 4. The district exploration team informs staff about basic concepts and responsibilities for integration. | | | |
| 5. The district exploration team obtains at least 80% commitment from administrators, staff, and families to integrate before adopting an integrated MTSS model. | | | |
| 6. District administrators provide a clear, consistent message of a vision of an integrated MTSS model for the district. | | | |
| 7. The district installation team identifies terminology to align integration with existing initiatives. | | | |
| 8. District administrators delay implementation of other initiatives to allow time for integration. | | | |
| 9. District administrators articulate how integration helps schools meet requirements of state initiatives. | | | |
| 10. The district installation team builds integration goals and steps into the district improvement plan and assists schools in building integration into their school improvement plans. | | | |
| 11. The district installation team establishes training and coaching systems to support integration. | | | |
| 12. The district installation team uses an application or selection process to determine enthusiastic pilot schools. | | | |
| 13. District administrators provide high rates of reinforcement during the initial implementation period. | | | |

*(continued)*

| Implementation Step | Implementation Status | | |
|---|---|---|---|
| | Not in place | Partially in place | In place |
| 14. The district installation team establishes a structured process for gathering feedback and improving implementation. | | | |
| 15. The district installation team continues to monitor fidelity of implementation and identify ways to make implementation more efficient. | | | |

| Priority for Action Planning (the three most important items from above) | Who is responsible? | By when? | How will we know when it is accomplished? |
|---|---|---|---|
| 1. | | | |
| 2. | | | |
| 3. | | | |

# MTSS Initiative Alignment Worksheet

**Directions:** List all existing initiatives (school and/or district), their intended recipients, outcomes measures used to gauge success, and whether they are mandated. Then, for each practice (or model) being evaluated for adoption, complete the worksheet by describing how the practice aligns with each existing initiative (e.g., does it conflict with or duplicate efforts?), and what value it adds for each existing initiative. If multiple options are being evaluated, complete a separate worksheet for each practice. Once complete, consider whether the proposed practice (1) meets a need, (2) could be integrated with or replace an existing initiative, and (3) could make other initiatives (especially mandated ones) better. This value added can be shared with administrators, staff, and the school community to mobilize support for a new practice. In addition, identify any initiatives that can be removed or modified to make room for a new initiative.

**Practice (or model) being evaluated for adoption:**

| Existing Initiative | Intended Recipients | Outcome Measure(s) | Mandated Initiative? | Alignment with Practice Being Evaluated | Value Added by Adopting Practice |
|---|---|---|---|---|---|
| | | | ☐ Yes ☐ No | | |
| | | | ☐ Yes ☐ No | | |
| | | | ☐ Yes ☐ No | | |
| | | | ☐ Yes ☐ No | | |
| | | | ☐ Yes ☐ No | | |
| | | | ☐ Yes ☐ No | | |

Adapted with permission from George Sugai (2010).

# PART III

# CASE STUDIES
# OF SUCCESSFUL SYSTEMS

This last major part of the book is devoted to case studies describing the implementation of integrated MTSS models. In the next three chapters, authors share their systems and histories of implementation and integration for three separate initiatives that have endured over time. We have asked these accomplished implementers and researchers to write these chapters to illustrate the ideas we've presented in the first two parts, and more important, to give a sense of possibilities for the different approaches that can be used when integrating systems.

We ask you to read these chapters with a few specific aims in mind. As you go through them, we encourage you to consider the stories not only as examples to follow, but also as proof of the success of varied approaches to integration. In much of the content in this book, we've tried to stress the importance of function over form, and these case studies provide further evidence that there is no single roadmap or set of procedures that will work across schools, districts, and states. Context shapes implementation, and without attention to each site's unique context, initiatives will lack fit, scalability, and sustainability.

In addition, we asked the authors to provide not only a report of their current status (which is impressive), but also the stories of how these initiatives came to be. When considering their current scale and successes, reading their work may be intimidating, especially if you are just starting to plan for integration, but it is important to recognize that these groups started out in very much the same way. In each case, a few committed individuals came together to test out an idea of doing things differently in schools. That often started out at the classroom or school level, even if it was a pilot for a larger initiative. Whether you are a classroom teacher, school administrator, or state official, there can be lessons for your integration efforts. We think you'll find that each of these initiatives has humble (and repeatable) roots.

# CHAPTER 8

# Oregon's Effective Behavioral and Instructional Support Systems Initiative

*Implementation from District- and State-Level Perspectives*

Erin A. Chaparro, Sally Helton, and Carol Sadler

## OVERVIEW

In this chapter we describe the journey of many Oregon school districts. The work of one district, Tigard–Tualatin School District, inspired the scaling up of MTSS at the state level. Each of the following sections begins with the story of Tigard–Tualatin as the district leading the vanguard in Oregon, and the second part describes the efforts to scale up MTSS to districts in the rest of the state.

### District Level

The Tigard–Tualatin School District (TTSD) is a suburban district just south of Portland, Oregon. It began implementing PBIS in 1996 and RTI in 2002, in a system that became known as *effective behavior and instructional support* (EBIS). From 1996 to 2013, the student population has grown from 11,300 to over 13,000 in 16 schools: 10 elementary, 3 middle schools, 2 comprehensive high schools, and 1 alternative school. During that same time, the district's nonwhite population grew from 13 to 39%. Implementation began as a grassroots effort with groups of teachers and administrators eager to implement a schoolwide behavior model. The initial suc-

**Erin A. Chaparro, MS, PhD,** College of Education, University of Oregon, Eugene, Oregon.

**Sally Helton, MS,** Tigard–Tualatin School District, Tigard, Oregon.

**Carol Sadler, PhD,** Tigard–Tualatin School District (retired), Tigard, Oregon.

cess and growth of the model into a successful integrated academic and behavior MTSS was due to the guidance and inspiration of two champions: Carol Sadler and Petrea Hagen Gilden. As teachers and administrators saw the successful outcomes from EBIS, which integrated PBIS and RTI into one coherent system, there was more and more buy-in by staff, administrators, and the school board, so that now in TTSD, it is "the way we do business."

### State Level

As with all states, Oregon has a unique set of contextual variables. Our geography, economy, and changing student demographics set the stage for implementation strengths and challenges. Oregon has a population density of approximately 40 persons per square mile (U.S. Census Bureau, 2013), with mountain ranges splitting the state in half, separating the coastal areas from the primary population corridor. The majority of the 197 school districts in Oregon serve rural communities. These geographic characteristics can make outreach and professional development challenging. Economically, Oregon has consistently experienced higher rates of unemployment than the national average. As a result, many Oregon families struggle with much more than helping their students with homework. In the 2010–2011 school year, 51% of students enrolled in K–12 schools were eligible for free or reduced-price lunch as compared to the national average of 48% (Oregon State Archives, 2011). The economy also affects the public school system in that fiscal support for K–12 education comes from state income taxes, lottery funds, property taxes, and federal funds (Oregon State Archives). The state of Oregon does not have a state sales tax, which would typically supply additional funds to schools. During times of high unemployment, state education funds are greatly reduced, resulting in furlough days and higher student–teacher ratios.

Last, across the country many states have experienced a change in their student demographics and especially an increase in the number of students categorized as English language learners. Oregon is no different. Between the 1997–98 and 2009–10 school years, students identified as non-native English speakers increased by 387%. During the same period, other demographic changes in Oregon included a decrease in the percent of white students by 16%, an increase in students identified as Hispanic by 151%, and an increase in students identified as Asian/Pacific Islander by 35%. Through the Effective Behavioral and Instruction Support Systems (EBISS) initiative at the state level, we built on previous research and the work of TTSD to blend evidence-based academic and social behavior practices for greater efficiency of resources and improved student outcomes. The EBISS initiative uses ongoing high-quality professional development and coaching delivered to school and district personnel on the essential features of the practices to improve implementation and outcomes.

## HISTORY OF IMPLEMENTATION

### District Level

TTSD's foray into multi-tiered systems of support began in 1995 (Sadler, 2000), when a group of teachers and administrators, sponsored by the Oregon Department of Education and Behavioral Research and Teaching (a research unit at the University of Oregon), participated in a behavior support cadre to explore effective behavioral support (EBS), later known as schoolwide positive behavioral interventions and supports (PBIS). The following year, eight of the district's then 14 schools began implementing EBS. They received training from Dr. George Sugai, formed EBS teams at each of those schools, agreed on school rules, taught and rein- forced those rules with students, and began collecting data on ODRs. By the spring of that year (1996–97), the school board had adopted EBS as a districtwide program and created a half-time position for a district coordinator. Dr. Carol Sadler, a school psychologist in the district, was hired for that position and became the first district coach. In the following year, the remaining six schools began implementing EBS. From the onset, there was strong support for this program from all parties involved, from district-level administrator and principals to teachers and students. There was a marked decrease in the number of ODRs, suspensions, and expulsions each year.

As PBIS became well established in the district, it became increasingly clear that the vast majority of the students with multiple ODRs also struggled academically. Dr. Sadler and TTSD's Director of Student Services, Petrea Hagen Gilden, led a group in studying the possibility of using universal screenings to identify students with reading difficulties early and provide them with additional support. In January of 2001, the U.S. Department of Education, Office of Spe- cial Education Programs, funded a proposal written by the district to integrate early reading and special education evaluation using RTI into the district's EBS model. This became known as *effective behavior and instructional supports*, or EBIS (Sadler & Sugai, 2009). At the district level, a full-time EBIS literacy coordinator was hired to complement the EBS coach. EBIS was first implemented in all of the district's elementary schools. Initially, each building created one EBIS leadership team to help with the implementation. These teams were tasked with the responsibility of focusing on both reading instruction and behavior. The teams included English language learner (ELL) and Title I specialists, special education teachers, administrators, coun- selors, and teacher representatives. A district task force was also created to develop decision rules for grouping, monitoring, and adjusting instruction and curriculum based on a student's RTI. The work of this group became the foundation of the district's shift from a discrepancy model for learning disability eligibility to a problem-solving model featuring RTI.

At the school level, teachers were encouraged to use the core reading curriculum with fidelity and teach reading for 90 minutes per day. DIBELS was chosen as the universal screen- ing and progress monitoring tool. All students were screened three times per year for reading. The schoolwide data were reviewed after each screening period to determine the effectiveness of the core program, as well as to identify those students in need of more than core instruction. Evidence-based interventions were selected, and decision rules for when to start, intensify, and/or discontinue interventions were created. These decision rules also included a list of the evidence-based interventions from which teams could choose and the amount of time (in addi- tion to core instruction) that the students were to receive interventions. A half-time literacy specialist was hired at each school to oversee the reading interventions, which were delivered by trained instructional assistants. These literacy specialists became the school-level reading coaches, and the counselors and school psychologists became the school-level behavior coaches.

Grade-level EBIS teams began meeting monthly to review student progress in interven- tions, in both social behavior and reading. These meetings included all teachers of that grade level, as well as a core group that attended each grade-level meeting. The core group included the principal, counselor or school psychologist, English language teacher, special education teacher, and literacy specialist. These teams used the district decision rules and protocols when reviewing the progress of students who were receiving reading and/or behavior interventions. Students who did not make adequate progress after two group interventions and one individualized intervention were referred for a special education evaluation, with evidence of a dual discrepancy used as the criteria for special education learning disability eligibility. Because of their success with this model, in 2005 the Oregon Department of Education asked TTSD to write Oregon's RTI Technical Assistance Paper (Oregon Department of Education, 2007). This paper provides guidelines for implementing MTSS for specific learning disability (SLD) eligibility decisions. Since that time, TTSD has held a contract for a state-level initiative, Oregon Response to Intervention (OrRTI), which has supported the development of MTSS in school districts throughout the state of Oregon.

## State Level

Inspired by and attempting to build on the momentum of the success in TTSD, the Oregon Department of Education, under the guidance of Drs. Nancy Latini and Jennifer Coffey, wrote and submitted a grant application to train district-level administrators in the foundations of a blended model of PBIS and the school-wide reading model (SWRM). In 2007, the Oregon Department of Education was awarded a State Personnel Development Grant (SPDG) from the Office of Special Education Programs (OSEP). This funding assists state education agencies and their partners to improve systems of professional development, technical assistance, and dissemination of knowledge regarding best practices.

In the fall of the 2007–2008 school year, the Oregon Department of Education (ODE) announced a request for applications from school districts that were interested in receiving the grant and participating in the EBISS initiative. School districts completed an application that included questions covering five areas: (1) districtwide goals; (2) district leadership and commitment; (3) use of data-based teaming; (4) professional development and coaching; and (5) districtwide assessment, curriculum, and instructional practices. For the districtwide goals section, districts were asked to provide a list of their current goals from the state-required Continuous Improvement Plan. They also listed their goals for their district's participation in the EBISS initiative if their district was selected to participate. If a district had a district-level leadership team in charge of implementation of practices, they were asked to supply the names and roles of the members of this team. Districts were also asked to share information about the team, such as the different levels of expertise of the members, how often the team meets and for how long, and its general responsibilities and accomplishments. Although a small amount of money was awarded to participating districts, districts were asked to identify internal resources that they could use to support the initiative.

With regard to professional development and coaching, districts were asked if they already had coaching resources in place for literacy and PBIS. They were also asked to describe what professional development they had received previously on the topics of PBIS and the SWRM. Districts described their current within-district professional development plan, as well as ongoing technical assistance or coaching. Districts were also asked to provide information about districtwide screening and progress monitoring for early literacy and for social, emotional, and behavior issues. The last set of questions asked the district if it had adopted the same reading curriculum and a comprehensive set of social–behavior interventions and supports at a districtwide level. Over the course of the 4 years of the initial grant, 30 school districts applied for the grant, and 26 districts participated for all 4 years.

## Funding

Each participating district received a modest amount of money that was intended to support their participation in the EBISS initiative. For the first 2 years of the grant, districts were asked to use the funds to support the role of one person at the district level who worked toward implementing the EBISS model. This person was called the *systems coach*. The goal was that each district would have a leader available (for approximately 25 days throughout the school year) to facilitate district and building data meetings, professional development calendars, and attend EBISS-sponsored professional development activities. In the second 2 years of the grant, the same funds were allowed for uses beyond the systems coach. Some districts were able to support travel of new team members to professional development opportunities.

## Technical Assistance

The Oregon Department of Education contracted with three private consultants and granted the Center on Teaching and Learning at the University of Oregon funds to employ other educators to provide professional development and technical assistance to all participating districts. These state technical assistance providers met with each district's systems coach and provided tailored support based in part on their literacy and behavior data. Through this process, districts and schools received a range of support, including (but not limited to) assistance with analyzing data reports, training on the administration and scoring of literacy assessments, and modeling of effective instructional practices in both literacy and classroom behavior management. Each systems coach received technical assistance at a minimum of one district leadership team meeting per year, and most received consultative communication on a monthly basis (e.g., phone call, e-mail).

## Professional Development Conferences

Professional development provided to districts included sessions on implementation of SWPBIS and the SWRM, as well as general features of the EBISS teaming framework to integrate both systems. The Oregon Department of Education and the EBISS state technical assistance providers collaborated with other experts in the state, including the NorthWest PBIS Network and OrRTI, to provide strands and sessions over the course of the school year. The systems coaches attended 2 days of professional development, once in the fall and once in the winter, targeted toward systems-level implementation of both SWPBIS and SWRM. Each spring, a team of representatives from across each district was brought together for a 1-day workshop focused on collaborative teaming and data-based action planning. These district representatives included teachers from various grade levels, principals from all levels, and district-level administrators from both special and general education. Representatives occasionally included instructional assistants, parent volunteers, board members, and superintendents or assistant superintendents. Systems coaches were required to attend these trainings with their teams and were given the primary responsibility of facilitating the transfer of information from professional development to their schools.

# CURRENT STATUS

## District Level

Currently in TTSD, EBIS is in place in all schools, K–12, and is used for reading, math, writing, and behavior, including mental health issues. From its inception, EBIS has truly been a partnership between general education and special education. Members of both groups are part of the EBIS team, and the system is designed to flow smoothly from one to the other. All students are considered "our students." With the exception of one self-contained class at each level (elementary, middle, and high) for students with the most challenging behavior and emotional problems, there are no other self-contained programs in the district; all students receive instruction in the general education setting, and all students' progress is monitored and discussed at EBIS meetings. An RTI dual discrepancy model is used to determine special education eligibility for reading and math. The multi-tiered levels of support are also used as part of the evaluation for attention-deficit disorder, communication disorder, and emotional disturbance. Social workers from an outside agency and representatives from the county's juvenile justice department are regular members of Tier 2 teams.

All teachers use the same research-based core curriculum with a commitment to implementing it with fidelity. In the elementary schools, students "walk to read," meaning that they receive instruction in flexible skill groups, which allows them to be taught at their instructional level and have more opportunities to respond. Coaching, training, open communication, and continuous data-based decision making are important components of the EBIS system in TTSD. Each year, policies and procedures are reviewed and the district's EBIS handbooks (elementary and secondary) are revised and improved upon. In 2013–14 school year, protocols for English language development as well as dual language reading were added. The EBIS process is strongly in place in all schools, and EBIS is now considered the way we do business in TTSD.

EBIS was really begun by two local "champions" who had a vision for how to improve student outcomes. To sustain and improve on the process they began, the district has embraced the teachings of implementation science as outlined by Blase and colleagues (2005). The district focuses especially on their implementation drivers: selection, training, coaching, performance assessment, systems intervention, facilitative administration, decision support data systems, and leadership. TTSD has revamped its hiring process to ensure that instructional leaders are chosen as principals. Fidelity measures are used regularly to help reduce drift.

Since its inception in 2005, OrRTI, the initiative for which TTSD holds the contract, has trained more than 60 of the 197 districts in the state on MTSS. As part of this effort a progress monitoring data system was created. The Intervention Planning and Assessment System (IPAS; Tigard–Tualatin School District, 2008) allows for all screening and progress monitoring scores to be entered and creates aimlines and trendlines. It also provides a space to document and share all intervention data, such as curriculum, group size, and duration. Teams use these data to determine placement into interventions, evaluate the effectiveness of interventions, and make changes as necessary.

## State Level

In the fall of 2011, the Oregon Department of Education was awarded a second SPDG. This new SPDG has two major professional development branches, described as *depth* and *breadth*. Depth professional development targets the 26 districts served by the former SPDG. These districts are receiving continuing professional development and are provided with a small stipend for travels and a modest incentive to support the district in their implementation of EBISS. Each district team was also asked to choose one depth strand area. There are five strands to choose from, including secondary literacy, PBIS, RTI, RTI for SLD eligibility, and implementation science. Each professional development package includes 3 days of in-person trainings and a series of five webinars, plus phone and e-mail consultation. The online learning component of this recent effort was developed to address the challenge and expense of traveling across our large state for multiple in-person trainings and consultation meetings.

Breadth professional development targets both new and continuing EBISS school districts. After districts receive either breadth or depth professional development, they are offered ongoing coaching and technical assistance. This combination of professional development and technical assistance is being rolled out over the course of 4 years with the intention of reaching all of the 197 Oregon school districts. There are five regional implementation zones across the state currently being developed. Support for the continuing districts is intended to train new staff in the foundations of EBISS and implementation science. Over the course of the 3 days of in-person professional development and 20 brief webinars, the goal is to build and disseminate knowledge about (1) the foundations of RTI, PBIS, and the SWRM; (2) the EBISS teaming framework; and (3) implementation science.

## UNIQUE FEATURES

As schools and districts across the country are working to install MTSS, what is it that makes Oregon and Tigard–Tualatin worth highlighting? The implementation features that come together to create the EBISS model are (1) leadership and commitment, (2) action planning with schools, (3) coordination and coaching, (4) professional development and training, (5) ongoing assessment and evaluation systems, (6) visibility and political support, and (7) funding. Most of these features are typical in most MTSS, but several parts of this model may be unique to TTSD and to Oregon.

## District Level

EBIS is the system that TTSD uses to ensure that its mission, "Every student thrives in school and graduates prepared to succeed," is achieved. The structures of EBIS and the professional development to ensure that those structures are in place are developed at the district level with input from the schools. It is important that all students in the district receive the same opportunities for academic and social development no matter whose classroom or which school they happen to attend. With that in mind, there are several structures in place to ensure fidelity to the process as well as feedback communication loops between schools and the district.

## Leadership Teams

At the district level, there is a leadership team that makes final decisions about the EBIS process and any changes needed. There are two district-level coaches who meet with school teams on a regular basis and provide training and feedback on the process at the schools. Within each school, there is a literacy specialist who is the school-based coach for reading and a counselor or school psychologist who is the school-based coach for behavior. The principal is the instructional leader at the school and checks fidelity of instruction by conducting frequent classroom walk-throughs. There are monthly meetings at the district for these school-based coaches: one for literacy specialists, another for counselors and psychologists, and a third for principals. The coordinators of these teams are district-level coaches and administrators who are on the district leadership team. These monthly meetings are used for training, reviewing data, sharing information, and obtaining feedback from the practitioners.

## New Initiative Alignment

Because EBIS is the system used in TTSD, before the district takes on any new initiatives or activities, it considers how the proposed new initiative fits into the EBIS system. For the past several years, the district has been involved in the process described in *Courageous Conversations about Race* (Singleton & Linton, 2005). More recently we have initiated professional learning communities (PLCs; Eaker, Dufour, & Dufour, 2002) and a digital learning collaborative, a district-developed system that supports teachers in learning new ways to use technology as a means of increasing engagement and access to content through differentiation in order to raise the level of success for all students. Each of these has become part of the EBIS process. In that way, rather than feeling overloaded by competing initiatives, personnel understand there is one process, with multiple components that help ensure a strong core and effective interventions.

## Special Education Eligibility within MTSS

One last unique feature of EBIS in TTSD is that it is the system used to determine special education eligibility. Our teams ask three questions when determining eligibility:

1. Are the student's skills significantly lower than his or her peers?
2. Does the student make less than adequate progress despite interventions?
3. Does the student need specially designed instruction?

Very rarely are intelligence assessments needed. This aspect frees up our counselors and school psychologists to focus on behavior. These specialists have become the PBIS leaders in the schools and, together with other team members, they help ensure a positive climate as well as provide behavior interventions for those students in need of more than the universal supports.

## State Level

Following in the footsteps of TTSD, it was clear that district-level support systems for building-level implementation were warranted. Because EBISS is funded as a SPDG, the emphasis is on dissemination of knowledge and building capacity within districts. The EBISS initiative is unique in that most of the professional development is targeted at district-level administrators with the goal of providing the information necessary to install evidence-based practices across a district. At the state level, the key features include (1) a systems coaching role, (2) an EBISS teaming framework, (3) an EBISS district systems support plan, and (4) collaborative professional development.

## A Systems Coaching Role

With the EBISS teaming framework, the role of the systems coach is highlighted as a pivotal team member who facilitates communication between district-level and school-level stakeholders. The systems coach was not always a part of the EBISS teaming framework. Within the first year of the EBISS initiative, it became clear that there was a need for at least one person in the district who saw it as his or her job and responsibility to move the district forward in the installation of EBISS. We call this person the *systems coach* (*blogs.uoregon.edu/systemscoaching/*). This coach, as the name indicates, works at the district level to instruct and support the district leadership team in the principles of implementation. The scope and sequence of the systems coaches' professional development begins with the foundations of PBIS and the SWRM and integrates the vocabulary of implementation science and the stages of implementation (Fixsen et al., 2005). The goal is for the systems coach to be knowledgeable enough about PBIS, the SWRM, and implementation science to facilitate and coach the district leadership team effectively throughout the implementation process.

Although the role of the systems coach is a critical and uniform component of the EBISS framework, districts can make adjustments in the role to improve contextual fit. For instance, in larger districts it is not uncommon to have two or three team members share the role of the systems coach in addition to their primary role at the district office. For smaller districts, the systems coach is sometimes an educational specialist hired as a consultant from the regional education service agency or a teacher on special assignment. In our experience, as long as the systems coach is in frequent communication with the district's executive leadership, the work of the district leadership is supported.

## EBISS Teaming Framework

The Oregon Department of Education enacted the Oregon Coach Task Force, which included experts in both PBIS and SWRM from schools, districts, regional service districts, and universities. This group was charged with synthesizing the known research base and real-life examples from high-implementation schools and districts to design a teaming structure. In addition to the Oregon Coach Task Force, TTSD had previously determined that each school building should have a leadership team working on the implementation of PBIS and eventually EBIS (Sadler, 2000). With this information, coupled with lessons learned from other initiatives, in which each building also had its own leadership team (e.g., Reading First), we took the leadership team up a level and asked each district to create a district leadership implementation team (D-LIT). The resulting EBISS teaming framework is a central professional development theme.

The EBISS teaming framework is displayed in Figure 8.1. This framework ensures the functioning of effective and efficient communication loops and improvement cycles between

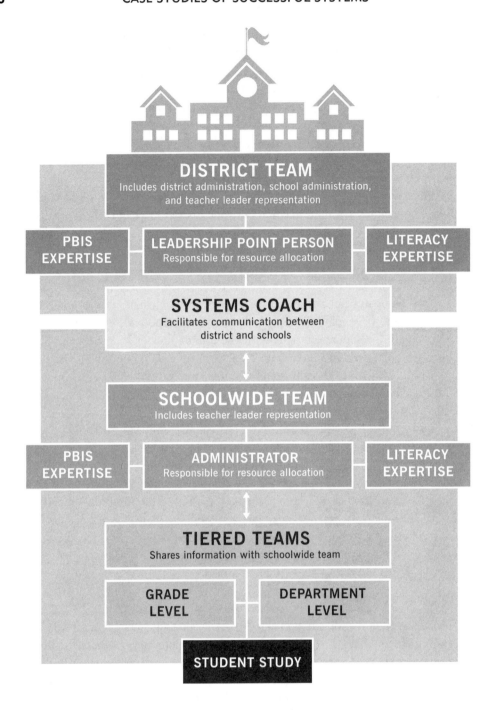

**FIGURE 8.1.** EBISS teaming framework.

the district and school teams, and among team members within a school building. The district team includes representatives from the district as well as school-level leaders. The school-level leaders can be teachers, specialists, and/or principals. Eventually all members of the district team should have the skills to interpret systemwide behavior and reading data (Todd et al., 2011). At first, however, there may be only one or two people who are confident in data analysis skills. Often this data analyst role is played by district PBIS or instructional coaches. As seen in the figure, the systems coach acts as a liaison between the D-LIT and the building leadership implementation team (B-LIT). This role can be filled by one person or shared by several people within the district leadership team.

The B-LIT focuses on blending the behavior and literacy data to allow school personnel and other stakeholders to respond to both sets of data for a more comprehensive view of building implementation. Systems coaches, along with building level representatives, facilitate the communication of the district level implementation plan to the school buildings. Similarly, the school level representatives hold the responsibility of sharing practical implementation concerns and feedback with the district team.

## District Systems Support Plan

With the strong EBISS emphasis on district-level implementation, it was soon realized that a fidelity measure would be needed at the district level. D-LITs needed a method to evaluate their strengths and the extent to which they were achieving their implementation goals. The Oregon Department of Education, in collaboration with the EBISS technical assistance providers, developed a measure of fidelity that helps districts determine how well they are, or are not, progressing toward specific implementation features. We call this fidelity survey the EBISS District Systems Support Plan (DSSP; University of Oregon, Center on Teaching and Learning, 2007). Initial validation efforts have indicated that the tool has strong reliability and moderate construct validity (Chaparro, Park, Baker, & Ryan-Jackson, 2011). The survey tool focuses teams on the seven EBISS features: (1) leadership and commitment, (2) action planning with schools, (3) coordination and coaching, (4) professional development and training, (5) ongoing assessment and evaluation systems, (6) visibility and political support, and (7) funding. D-LITs rate their district's systems and then select no more than three priority areas for which they develop an action plan. Initially, EBISS technical assistance providers facilitate administration with D-LITs. As district teams and systems coaches gain experience with the tool, they can complete the survey with the systems coach as the facilitator. A DSSP scoring rubric (Oregon Coach Task Force, 2011) is available to guide systems coaches in the facilitation of the DSSP administration process.

## Collaborative Professional Development

EBISS personnel worked with a range of technical assistance providers across the state to deliver the scope and sequence of EBISS professional development. Through ODE, EBISS technical assistance providers partnered with the NWPBIS Network (*www.pbisnetwork.org*). Each year the NWPBIS Network provides a series of conferences throughout the school year in Oregon and in Washington. These conferences, along with the Confederation of Oregon School Administrators (COSA; *www.cosa.k12.or.us*), provide the conference infrastructure to provide a diverse and rich mix of high-quality professional development. Similarly, since 2007, 13 districts in the EBISS initiative have also received varying levels of technical assistance from OrRTI as well. These collaborations among professional development providers give districts a consistent and repeated message about the importance of effectively implementing MTSS.

## EVALUATION OF OUTCOMES

### District Level

The results on student achievement of the EBIS system have been outstanding. Regular universal screening helps us identify and provide interventions quickly for those students who are in need of extra instruction. Protocols and decision rules ensure that a standardized process is followed and students receive the support they need regardless of whether they are in general or special education. In the fall of 2012, TTSD was recognized as one of a select few of outstanding districts in the country by Moving Your Numbers, a website maintained by the National Center on Educational Outcomes (NCEO; *www.movingyournumbers.org*). Our district was selected based on our districtwide system (EBIS) that all schools follow, along with the resulting improvements in student outcomes.

### Behavior Outcomes

Although EBIS is used for multiple subject areas, the focus in TTSD has been and remains threefold: reading, behavior, and decreasing the racial achievement gap. This focus has helped us to achieve the following results. In Figure 8.2, the number of ODRs per hundred students per month is shown to decline steadily since the implementation of PBIS. This decrease in ODRs reduces the amount of time that students miss instruction due to these incidents and also frees up administrators' time to be more effective instructional leaders rather than disciplinarians. Figure 8.3 shows the results from the School-wide Evaluation Tool (SET; Sugai, Lewis-Palmer, et al., 2001), which is designed to assess and evaluate the critical features of schoolwide PBIS. Schools scoring 80% and above are implementing universal schoolwide behavior support at an adequate level. Our fidelity has not always been consistent, but the trend has steadily increased and been maintained. Whenever our SET scores dropped, we answered that drop with renewed professional development efforts.

### Academic Outcomes

As our fidelity to PBIS increased and behavior outcomes improved, we also saw an increase in state assessment scores (Sadler & Sugai, 2009). OAKS (Oregon Assessment of Knowledge and Skills) is a statewide assessment of content mastery. Figure 8.4 shows the percent of all TTSD students, 3rd through 11th grades, that met or exceeded standards on OAKS during the given year. As we mentioned, the third focus area for TTSD has been to close the achievement gap between white non-Hispanic students and Hispanic students, our largest group of minority students. Figure 8.5 shows the percentage of white non-Hispanic students compared with Hispanic students meeting or exceeding on OAKS each year, and the achievement gap (or difference) between the two. With the use of EBIS, the gap has decreased from 43% in 2007–08 to 11% in 2012–13.

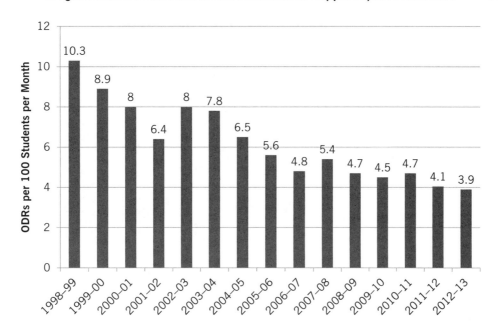

**FIGURE 8.2.** ODRs per 100 students per month, Tigard–Tualatin School District, 1998–2013.

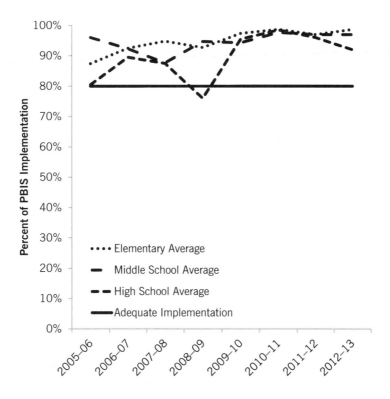

**FIGURE 8.3.** Schoolwide Evaluation Tool (SET) results.

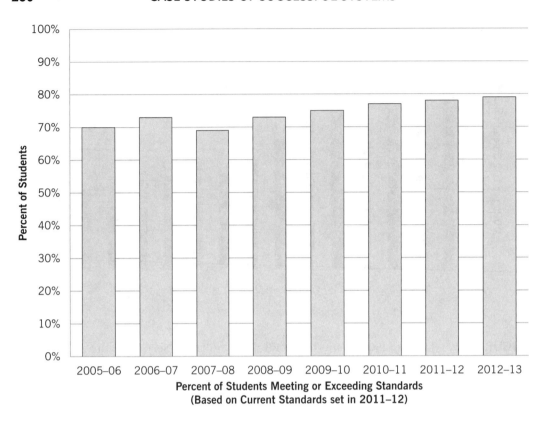

**FIGURE 8.4.** Percent of TTSD students meeting or exceeding on OAKS Reading.

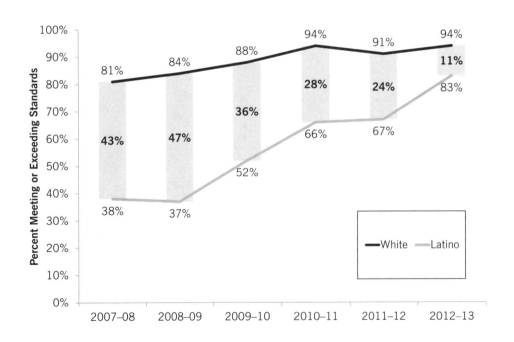

**FIGURE 8.5.** High School OAKS Reading achievement gap.

## State Level

An external evaluator conducts the evaluation of state-level EBISS outcomes. Because these data were collected as part of a professional development grant, the primary goal of the data was to show changes in adult behavior. Districts were asked to submit school-level and district-level data annually. The systems coach from each district was in charge of submitting the district and school data to the state team. Schools were asked to report data in three major categories: (1) EBISS systems, (2) student outcome data collection and use, and (3) fidelity data collection and use. EBISS systems questions asked if schools had literacy and behavior leadership teams in place and if they offered a continuum of support services for students. Schools provided information about the collection of literacy and behavior screening and progress monitoring data as well as the type of data systems they used to enter and analyze the data. Schools also reported the extent to which there was a set continuum of services in both literacy and behavior. Districts also completed the DSSP at the beginning and end of each year. This self-assessment allowed the technical assistance providers to adjust the scope and sequence of professional development to address areas of need.

We have been able to demonstrate that school districts participating in the state-level EBISS initiative have experienced improvements in both adult behavior change and student literacy outcomes, as measured by the questions asked in the school-level data summary. Chaparro, Smolkowski, Baker, Hanson, and Ryan-Jackson (2012) published the first 2 years of implementation data, which also included statistically significant improvement in oral reading fluency in the first and fifth grades as an indirect descriptor of district outcomes during their participation in the EBISS initiative.

### School-Level EBISS Systems

Through the collection of school-level data summaries, we were able to learn that from the first year through the fourth year, elementary schools in EBISS districts increased the use of several key EBISS features pertaining to both behavior and literacy systems. As shown in Figure 8.6, many of the schools already had the basic features of PBIS in place, including a leadership team, a continuum of behavior supports, a data system, and a building action plan, and schools were already using the SET or the Benchmarks of Quality (BoQ; Kincaid, Childs, & George, 2005) to monitor their building's PBIS fidelity. Figure 8.7 displays similar information but in regard to literacy systems. As can be seen, fewer schools started with literacy EBISS features in place. Early in the EBISS initiative, just over half of the elementary schools reported that they had MTSS in place for literacy, but by the third year, the vast majority of elementary schools had implemented a tiered system. We were also initially surprised to learn that only a few schools had a building action plan for literacy implementation in place (31%), and by the end of the fourth year, the vast majority of schools (95%) reported that they did, indeed, have an action plan in place.

### District-Level EBISS Systems

The average percentages on the DSSP from all EBISS districts are displayed in Figure 8.8. Over the four years of implementation, all of the seven EBISS features as measured by the DSSP

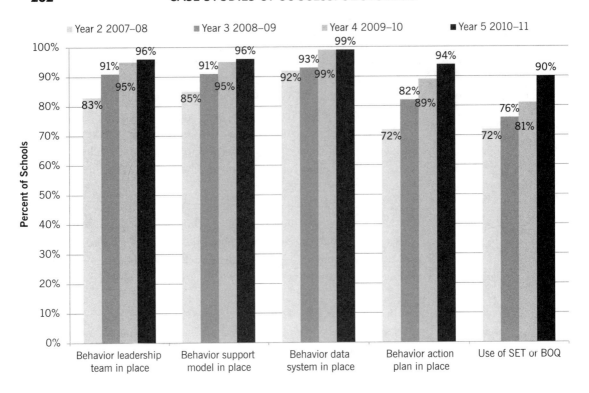

**FIGURE 8.6.** Percent of schools implementing MTSS for behavior.

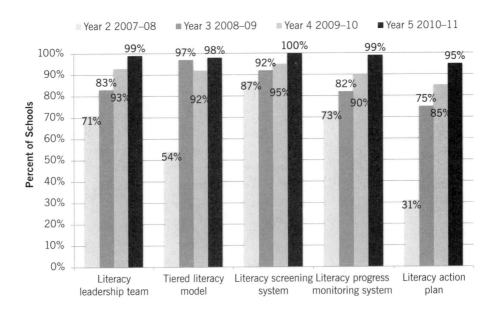

**FIGURE 8.7.** Percent of schools implementing MTSS for literacy.

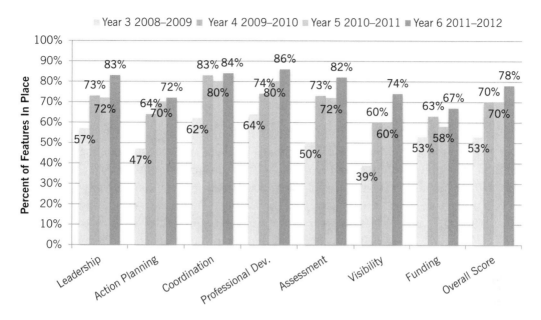

**FIGURE 8.8.** Average DSSP scores across all districts.

increased. The overall scores at the far right show that, on average, districts increased from having 53 to 78% of the features in place. In the final year, there were overall increases in all areas of the DSSP.

## LESSONS LEARNED

### District Level

TTSD has been implementing EBIS for over 10 years, and several points have become clear. A few of the lessons that we've learned are described here.

### It's OK to Start Small

Our first piece of advice is to begin with a narrow focus. In TTSD, the focus has been and remains reading and behavior. Before moving on to other areas, it is critical to have these two in place. Having a positive climate helps increase instructional time so that the evidence-based core program and interventions can be delivered with fidelity in order to improve student outcomes and help ensure that all students have the opportunity for a good life.

### Leadership Is Key

In order for EBIS to function well, administrators must understand and believe in its components, ensure fidelity to the system, and continually review outcomes with staff to ensure increased student growth. As a result, TTSD has revised its administrator application process. For example, we ask applying principals how they would teach reading to a first grader and to a fifth grader. We also ask them to analyze aimlines and trendlines and use TTSD decision rules to determine actions. Finally, we ask applicants how they will work with staff to ensure fidelity to the EBIS process. Hiring the proper leaders—those who can support EBIS—ensures our continued success and growth.

## Success Builds Success

When EBIS was first implemented in TTSD, many teachers were teaching reading using materials they had developed and collected instead of the core program. A few principals did not hold them accountable to the features of EBIS. Soon the district put pressure on principals to ensure that the core program was delivered with fidelity. Some teachers came and talked with the superintendent, saying that they were good teachers but would leave if they couldn't teach their own program. He agreed with them that they were good teachers and he would hate to lose them, but that the evidence-based program was going to be used in all classrooms and all schools. A few teachers did leave. Within a year of delivering the core program with fidelity, it was clear that students were reading better. As outcomes increased, so did the acceptance of the new way of doing things. Whereas at first teachers complained about having their students screened three times per year with DIBELS, now they insist that they get the results the day that screening occurs. As staff members retire or move to other positions, the selection of new staff willing to work in this system occurs and does not change the district focus on EBIS. In fact, TTSD has become a sought-after district for employment due to the successful outcomes for students.

Implementing a multi-tiered system of support is like a voyage of discovery. It takes preparation, leadership, training, and patience. It's hard work, but it's the right work. Increasingly, standards are becoming more rigorous for students, as demonstrated by the Common Core State Standards. MTSS helps to ensure that all students get the instruction they need when they need it.

When Columbus sailed West, he had his sights set on India, where he could gain access to the spices and other valuables of that country. He ended up somewhere completely different, but actually much more worthwhile. So it is with MTSS—the journey is long and sometimes takes us to unexpected but important places. The MTSS journey of discovery never really ends; there are always improvements and changes to be made in response to the data. However, by having a structure for teams of skilled educators to evaluate student outcomes, valuable information is gained and decisions are made to help ensure that "every student thrives in school and graduates prepared to succeed."

## State Level

Despite our many years working at implementation, we are still learning. As we bring new districts into the fold, we are learning how to make changes within the context of a lean fiscal landscape. With the districts that have been implementing for years, we are learning how to navigate changes in leadership and how to add on new, but complementary initiatives. Although our lessons have been many, from the state-level perspective, we've narrowed our lessons learned to three critical implementation factors. When districts had these implementation factors in place, they were able to navigate other challenges with the personnel and fiscal resources needed.

When districts did not have them in place, they sometimes reached their goal, but it usually was a bumpier and more time-consuming path. For this reason, we suggest that when installing MTSS, be sure (1) to have the correct people on the district leadership implementation team; (2) that all stakeholders are involved in the MTSS; and (3) to plan, plan, and plan some more before installing MTSS.

### Build a Leadership Implementation Team with All the Right People

In the early years of EBISS, there was a misconception that it was only a special education initiative. Therefore, the leadership teams were made up of mostly district-level special education staff and specialists. We quickly learned that we needed to work with the systems coaches to determine the proper stakeholders in their district. The other key person that was also often missing was a point person or that person on the team who holds authority to make budgetary decisions. We also learned that teams with a superintendent or assistant superintendent on the team had the ability to make decisions, build plans, and gather the resources needed to implement those plans. Those teams that remained as a small group of district-level coaches were not able to effectively and efficiently change the overall district system.

Recently, we delivered 3 days of professional development to district-level teams at new districts who were simply interested in learning more about the EBISS model. Some of the teams were enthusiastic and were starting to actively plan for the upcoming year. One small team of three people was engaged and making detailed plans during the first 2 days. They were also feeling a bit frustrated because they didn't know if their plan was really going to go anywhere beyond our conference room. On the third day, the new superintendent attended the training with the team and the smiles of the three team members were hard to ignore. When we asked them at the end of the day how their planning sessions went, they said, "Great! Now that the superintendent is here, we can really get to work and know that it's going to happen!" The superintendent doesn't have to be at every single planning meeting, but that point person will need to be in direct communication with the superintendent for implementation to move smoothly. If the superintendent can stop by at some point during the meetings for a brief period of time or can attend selected meetings per year, the team will be able to work much more efficiently.

### Involve All of Your Stakeholders in the Implementation of MTSS

Many districts have made great gains in the quality of their instruction, the use of academic and social–behavior data sources, and the efficient allocation of resources. One of the last pieces to change is how people are hired. In order to influence how people are hired, the MTSS team must engage the human resources office. The hiring practices of new instructional staff, principals, district-level administrators, and even superintendents should change along with all your building-level practices. For example, many of the districts in EBISS have completely rewritten job descriptions to include data analysis, teaming, and a willingness to be coached. Principals and teachers applying for jobs in districts who have installed EBISS are now being given sample data and asked in the interview to come up with a plan to address the needs demonstrated in the data. Principals are shown videos of instruction and are asked to take notes and model for the hiring committee how they would coach the teacher. Districts that have not changed their hiring practices are stuck in a cycle of needing to retrain new staff every year, or worse, not having the resources to train new staff every year. Therefore, the overall district MTSS loses momentum with every change in leadership.

Leaders in rural settings without a diverse pool of applicants should be aware that they will have to regularly train new cohorts of staff. If staff with the knowledge needed to support MTSS can't be hired, it will be important to have a professional development plan in place to annually train new staff. As long as MTSS is a clear priority and is reflected in policy, it should be easier to hire people who are willing to learn what they don't know in order to support the existing MTSS.

Involving everyone also means including parents, community members, and board of director members. EBISS systems coaches were required to share behavior and literacy data with the school board once per year. Even if the data were not impressive, we asked them to share their outcomes and their action plan to improve them. The D-LIT action plan and goals became the goals of the entire district. Similarly, other districts sent out a press release to their local newspaper at important benchmarks in an effort to involve the community. *For complete systems-level transformation, all stakeholders need to be included in MTSS implementation.*

## Make Sure to Spend Enough Time in the Planning Stages So That MTSS Has the Best Chance of Success

Implementation of MTSS is a marathon. If you were training for a marathon, would you start training the week before? Most likely you would start training months in advance. Planning is an important and often overlooked step in the implementation process. Educational leaders are traditionally efficient and logical people with a long list of action items. Yet before implementing even the most logical steps, make planning and thinking about many features of MTSS a priority.

We all know that sometimes our best plans go astray, so it is perfectly fine to make changes if the system isn't working. We continue to make mistakes along the way. We continue to adjust decision rules, change assessments, or change the frequency with which we meet. The important point is that we continue to use our decision rules consistently, we continue to screen and progress monitor students, and we meet and use the data regularly. It is rarely helpful to worry about the small things. Feel free to make changes along the way to make sure that MTSS benefits everyone. Systemwide transformation takes planning, time, and a team effort. If teams work patiently with each other and the system, in time those teams, teachers, and students will reap the benefits.

# CHAPTER 9

# Florida's Multi-Tiered Support System for Academics and Behavior

## Don Kincaid and George Batsche

## OVERVIEW

Education in the state of Florida has a long history of using data-based problem solving and innovative practices for the delivery of academic and behavior instruction and intervention. These practices, including the use of problem solving as well as systematic implementation of behavior instruction and intervention, date back to the early 1990s. However, such practices were administered and implemented independently through separate organizations (Florida Department of Education) and agencies at the state level and through separate units within the organizational structures of school districts. Therefore, evidence-based practices were being implemented—separately and without benefit of combined effects.

Two significant publications and the passage of two legislative acts by the U.S. Congress at the federal level set the stage for both the integration of the innovative practices in academic and behavior instruction and the delivery of that instruction in a multi-tiered model in Florida. The report of the President's Commission on Excellence in Special Education (PCESE, 2002) and the National Research Council's (2002) *Minority Students in Special and Gifted Education* independently advocated for the two primary components of an MTSS: (1) a structured data-based problem-solving process and (2) a system of supports that delivered instruction and interventions in varying intensities (multi-tiered) to meet the needs of all students. The report of the PCESE, the passage of No Child Left Behind (NCLB, 2001) and the Individuals with Disabilities Education Improvement Act (IDEIA, 2004), and the implementation of regulations for both set in motion the framework for the implementation of an integrated MTSS in Florida.

**Don Kincaid, EdD,** College of Behavioral and Community Sciences, University of South Florida, Tampa, Florida.

**George Batsche, EdD,** College of Education, University of South Florida, Tampa, Florida.

# HISTORY OF IMPLEMENTATION

## *Florida Positive Behavior Support Project*

The Florida Positive Behavior Support (FLPBS) Project was established in 1997 to address the behavioral needs of Florida's students. Initially, the FLPBS Project worked with school teams to develop intensive and specialized supports for the most challenging students in the state. However, in 2001, the FLPBS Project, with assistance from the state, moved to develop and support a multi-tiered approach to school reform. Between 2001 and 2005, the FLPBS Project provided extensive support to establish Tier 1 or schoolwide PBIS as a foundation for an MTSS system starting with "pilot schools" and quickly expanding districtwide in a few districts and into Tier 2 supports. As a result of an increasing emphasis on collaboration with district leadership versus individual pilot schools, the FLPBS Project changed its mission to "increasing the capacity of Florida's school districts to address problem behaviors using Positive Behavior Support" (*http:// flpbs.fmhi.usf.edu/aboutus_projectmission.cfm*). This change in focus reflected the project's emphasis on supporting the district leadership team's shift toward a systems-level collaboration. As a result, in less than 10 years, over 1,400 schools and 82% of Florida's school districts were actively collaborating with the FLPBS Project in a multi-tiered behavior support system.

## *Problem Solving/Response to Intervention Project*

In 1990, the Florida Department of Education funded three statewide projects that led, ultimately, to the statewide Problem Solving/Response to Intervention (PS/RTI) Project in 2006. The three funded statewide projects included the Problem-Solving Project (University of South Florida), the Student Assistance Team Project (Miami–Dade School District), and the Curriculum-Based Measurement Project (Orange County School District). Each of these projects used demonstration districts and schools as exemplars for the implementation of data-based decision making to guide instruction and intervention practices as well as for "incubators" to scale up these practices. However, each of these projects continued their work independently. No plan to integrate these practices was provided. As one might expect, the implementation of these practices was fragmented both within and across districts. Clearly, a better plan was needed.

The Florida Department of Education drew on the work of the previous statewide projects to develop an RTI model for districts in Florida. In 2007, it funded the statewide PS/RTI Project at the University of South Florida, and in 2008, the Florida Statewide Response to Instruction/Intervention (RTI) Implementation Plan was published (*http://florida-rti.org/floridaMTSS/RtI.pdf*). This implementation plan detailed the RTI model, the model of implementation logic, a blueprint with which to create and/or modify existing education laws, rules and policies, and funding considerations. In addition, the responsibilities of the state and districts and the roles of parents and communities were addressed. Finally, the foundation for scaling up the evidence-based practices, the interrelationships within and across state agencies, and the multiyear implementation plan were presented.

In 2007, the PS/RTI Project established demonstration districts in which to collect data to inform the statewide scale-up of RTI. First, extensive data were collected in eight demonstration districts to evaluate every aspect of RTI implementation over a 3-year period of time. Second, statewide professional development and technical assistance were provided over a 3-year period of time for district- and school-based leadership teams. Every district in the state participated in this training and technical assistance.

During this time period, the PS/RTI Project personnel were providing training and technical assistance to the same districts (and many of the same schools) that were receiving training from the statewide FLPBS Project. Some of the personnel in districts who were involved with RTI implementation were also involved with FLPBS implementation. The FLPBS implementation model also used a data-based problem-solving process and a multi-tiered delivery system—and some of the same professional terms. Again, two evidence-based models to improve student performance were being implemented independently in the same places and were causing confusion for district personnel. Some district personnel went so far as to say, "We can no longer implement PBIS because we have to implement RTI," and vice versa. Clearly, there was a better way to approach statewide implementation. Strong evidence was gathering that implementation of an integrated model incorporating both academic and behavior components has a greater positive impact on student performance (Algozzine & Algozzine, 2007; Lassen et al., 2006; McIntosh, Flannery, et al., 2008; Sanford & Horner, 2013).

## RTI and PBIS to MTSS

In 2010, a statewide needs assessment survey was conducted to determine the district priorities for the implementation of RTI. The goal was to provide statewide support to districts based on a multi-tiered service model—that is, identifying supports that *all* (Tier 1) districts shared, supports that *some* (Tier 2) districts needed, and supports that only a *few* (Tier 3) districts needed. The initial intent of the survey was met (stratifying districts into tiers), and additionally, the information that districts shared about their needs for support was so interesting that it set the stage for the development of the integrated MTSS model in Florida. Districts requested support to achieve the following:

1. Integrate the practices of RTI and PBIS to reduce duplication of training and practices.
2. Increase the effective use of personnel and provide greater support for instruction.
3. Provide a "common language/common understanding" regarding the use of data-based problem solving.
4. Build leadership skills to support implementation of MTSS.
5. Provide evaluation models to demonstrate student outcomes.
6. Promote family and community engagement.
7. Align PreK–12 (with a focus on secondary) practices within an MTSS model.
8. Use evidence-based coaching strategies to support implementation.

It was clear that districts needed a model and technical assistance to integrate the academic and behavior supports for students. It also was evident that district leaders needed support to plan and problem-solve the barriers to implementation of an integrated model across all schools in a district.

The PS/RTI and FLPBS Projects were both monitored by the Bureau of Exceptional Education and Student Supports of the Florida Department of Education. District input to the bureau, input from the leadership of the two projects, and the data from the needs assessment surveys all supported a consensus that an integrated (academic and behavior) MTSS model should move forward. The department requested that the two projects combine their leadership and staff activities to create the model for MTSS implementation and provide the infrastructure to support districts in the implementation of the model. In 2010, the blueprint for this integration was developed and initiated, and the two projects began working together to create and implement an integrated MTSS model.

### Systems-Level Impact and Collaboration

Combining two large, successful, statewide training and technical assistance projects with significant independent momentum required mature leadership and "checking egos at the door" attitudes. The directors of the two projects were both fundamentally committed to implementing practices that had positive results for students, parents, and educators. The work of integrating these two projects into an MTSS model would require not only adjustments to the content of the work but also an integration of the infrastructure of the two projects. At one level, creating the infrastructure to integrate the work seemed easier than focusing on modifications to the content. So, that is where we started: Two projects with separate infrastructures needed a single infrastructure to support the combined model.

### Interproject Leadership Team

A single leadership team was needed to guide this combined model. The development of the infrastructure began with the establishment of the interproject leadership team (ILT) and the hiring of an interproject coordinator. The ILT provided the leadership and decision making for all aspects of the combined model. The interproject coordinator was responsible for ensuring open communication and collaboration across projects, ILT agendas, and meeting structures, as well as monitoring the progress of all of the workgroups. The ILT consisted of the senior leadership of each project, including the project directors, the interproject coordinator, and senior staff with responsibilities for project evaluation, professional development and coaching, family and community engagement, and content expertise in academic and behavior areas. The ILT met at least monthly and was responsible for all aspects of implementing the combined model.

A strategic plan was developed to focus and integrate the work of the two projects, based on *combining the areas of strength that each project brought to this effort.* The strategic plan focused initially on the goals, activities, and resource allocation for the first year of the combined effort. The primary goals for the first year were to create a common mission, vision, and definition of MTSS; establish interproject workgroups to create the content for the combined model; create an intraproject professional development plan; convene a statewide conference to launch the MTSS initiative; and create a process that would guide the project's work with districts to support MTSS implementation. An initial (and ongoing) balancing act that each project had to address was the allocation of personnel, time, and funding to the combined project while continuing to engage in the work of the separate projects. The FLPBS Project continued to support the implementation of schoolwide PBIS in districts across the state. The PS/RTI Project continued to implement the activities of that project to support data-based decision making with a particular focus on academic areas. In reality, the addition of the combined project simply added to the workload of each project's staff, because only one additional staff person (the coordinator) was hired.

## Mission: Common Vision and Focus

A few states (e.g., Kansas) had adopted and defined the term *MTSS* for their particular state. Two of the initial tasks of the ILT were to define MTSS for the state of Florida and develop a mission statement for the combined project. The mission statement reflected the common vision of the combined MTSS model by reflecting the strengths of each of the projects separately:

> The collaborative vision of the Florida Problem Solving/Response to Intervention (FL PS/RTI) and the Florida Positive Behavior Support/Response to Intervention for Behavior (FLPBS/RTI:B) Projects is to:
>
> - Enhance the *capacity* of all Florida school districts to successfully implement and sustain a *multi-tiered system* of student supports with *fidelity* in every school;
> - *Accelerate and maximize student academic and social–emotional outcomes* through the application of *data-based problem solving* utilized by *effective leadership* at all levels of the educational system;
> - Inform the *development, implementation, and ongoing evaluation* of an *integrated, aligned,* and *sustainable system of service delivery* that prepares all students for *post-secondary education and/or successful employment within our global society.* (*www. floridarti.usf.edu/floridaproject/connections.html*)

The development of the mission statement helped to create a specific definition of MTSS for the state of Florida that had the following characteristics:

- It defined *MTSS* as a term used to describe an evidence-based model of schooling that uses a data-based problem-solving approach to integrate academic and behavior instruction and intervention.
- It advocated for integrated instruction and intervention delivered to students in varying intensities (multiple tiers) based on student need.
- It advocated a "need-driven" decision-making process to ensure that district resources reach the appropriate students (schools) at the appropriate levels to accelerate the performance of *all* students.

To ensure a common language and understanding of the MTSS model for staff internal to the projects and communicate the critical elements of the combined MTSS model to schools districts (and for their use internally), the ILT developed a document titled "MTSS Implementation Components: Ensuring Common Language and Understanding" (*www.floridarti.usf.edu/ resources/format/pdf/mtss_q_and_a.pdf*).

## Interproject Workgroups

Informed by the statewide needs assessment referenced earlier in this chapter and by evidence-based models of systems change, the ILT established workgroups to guide the development of content and support the work of the combined model. Each workgroup comprised professional staff from both PS/RTI and FLPBS Projects. The initial workgroups were focused on the following areas:

1. Leadership team development: Develop a model of leadership that identifies the critical skills that leaders need to implement MTSS at district and school levels.
2. Integrated program evaluation: Design evaluation tools for monitoring the MTSS team, districts, and schools.
3. Organizational coaching: Develop the model for systems coaching that identifies the district and school skill sets necessary to coach MTSS application.
4. Professional development: Develop our internal capacity to deliver all of the content developed by workgroups with consistency and integrity.
5. Family and community engagement: Develop materials and resources for districts and schools related to involving parents and communities in their MTSS efforts.
6. Data-based problem solving: Identify guiding questions for problem solving across a multi-tiered system and develop a process for teaching districts to gather, analyze, and interpret their academic and behavior data.
7. Early childhood: Explore the application of a MTSS model within our early childhood settings.
8. Interproject alignment and integration: Coordinate the activities of all workgroups to promote integration of materials and ensure a common language and understanding of our approach to MTSS.

Each of these workgroups compiled a set of resources for all staff, including a comprehensive literature review of the content for each area to inform their work, work products to define the scope and content of the work, and content for professional development modules.

## Interproject Professional Development Plan

The professional staff of each project brought years of experience and expertise in either PBIS or PS/RTI to the interproject work. Although the staff of each project was well trained in its particular area, the introduction of this combined model created a strong need for professional development *within* the project to ensure that all of the staff had the training and expertise internally before working with external stakeholders. During the first 2 years of the combined project, professional development activities focused on the content of the workgroups and the development of the combined model. From its inception, professional development has been a *required* activity for all project staff, and participation is monitored for accountability. The professional development activities occur monthly and are presented virtually (Adobe Connect) with all sessions archived for future use. Once or twice each year, face-to-face professional development occurs with all staff.

## Statewide MTSS Conference

In the summer of 2011, the two projects, in collaboration with the Florida Department of Education, held the first MTSS summer conference. The primary stakeholders for this conference were district and state leaders. The conference had two objectives. The first objective was to present the MTSS model that focused on the integration of academic and behavior components for all students. This integration of academic and behavior factors was new, at least to most districts. This model had an impact on staff responsibilities and behaviors, district policies and procedures, and evaluation activities. As the second objective, the conference introduced the professional development and technical assistance available to districts through the combined resources of both projects. Because the projects had combined their work at the state level but districts had not yet combined theirs, the potential for a disconnect existed between how the projects would provide supports and how the district services were organized. It was clear from reviewing the work that had occurred in other states and the literature available that districts would need assistance in planning for this integration and in problem solving to remove barriers to implementation.

## District Action Planning and Problem Solving

### Need for a Process to Support Implementation

Districts engage in strategic planning as a standard way of work, often through planning cycles. Based on the outcomes of those plans (e.g., effects on student progress), districts (and schools) develop improvement plans to address those issues affecting student progress. The implementation of an MTSS involves *both* organizational (district-level organizational patterns, district instructional delivery models) and student outcome factors. Integrating academic and behavior factors into a single model of instruction and instructional delivery often challenges the organizational structure of districts, policies and procedures, staff roles and responsibilities, and expectations for school-level implementation. This large-scale change can be difficult; district strategic plans rarely address many of these issues, and barriers inevitably arise that could prevent the systematic implementation of MTSS districtwide.

In response to these needs, during the first year of the combined project, the ILT and the workgroups developed a systems-level problem-solving protocol to assist districts in this action planning. The MTSS project called this process the *district action planning and problem-solving (DAPPS) process* (see Figure 9.1). The DAPPS process was designed as a district-level process that would involve the primary decision makers in the district. The initial purpose of the DAPPS process was to identify and problem-solve the barriers to the implementation of MTSS that existed in the district organization. The DAPPS process is based on two primary evidence-based procedures: strategic planning and organizational problem solving. It incorporates an eight-step problem-solving process, designed to identify and develop an action plan to reduce or remove barriers to implementation of the MTSS model districtwide (see Figure 9.2).

### Presentation to Districts

During the initial MTSS summer conference, the DAPPS process was presented and explained to districts. In addition, a process through which districts could request DAPPS assistance was presented. At the end of the conference, each district had received professional development on the critical components of the MTSS model, including implications for implementation and a system of technical assistance to support implementation—the DAPPS. The response to the DAPPS process was positive, and its "launch" statewide soon followed.

**FIGURE 9.1.** Overview of the five steps in the DAPPS process.

## Launching the DAPPS Process

The Florida Department of Education has a history of supporting innovative practices that promote positive student outcomes. From the beginning, the state was not only supportive of the MTSS model but an active partner in promoting district support for it. The department understood the need to pilot the DAPPS and review the process and outcomes before expanding the option to other districts. The Florida Department of Education chancellor sent a letter to all superintendents announcing the availability of DAPPS support and the process for requesting that support following the summer conference in 2011. Districts were required to complete an application process that included a wide range of district information, data, district support commitments, and other information that was reviewed by the MTSS leadership to determine the degree to which a district was ready to implement MTSS. Applications were reviewed using a systematic process that included assessment of interrater agreement. The "readiness" to implement and the selection of districts were based, to some degree, on the needs of the district and the resources that the PS/RTI and FLPBS Projects had available. Initially, six districts were selected for immediate DAPPS support, and a number of others received feedback and requests for additional information and were scheduled for future support.

The intraproject professional development process was used to train staff on the steps of the DAPPS, including the eight-step problem-solving process (see Figure 9.2). A comprehensive professional development process (including direct instruction, modeling, practice, the use of video sessions that were evaluated by senior staff members, feedback, and additional training) was used to ensure that staff had the skills to facilitate the DAPPS process with senior district leadership team members. As a result, DAPPS teams consisting of team leaders (the most skilled users), co-leaders, and observers (users in training) were assigned to the districts receiving DAPPS supports.

The ILT created an additional workgroup, the DAPPS integration and evaluation workgroup, to conduct an ongoing evaluation of the effectiveness of the DAPPS support process.

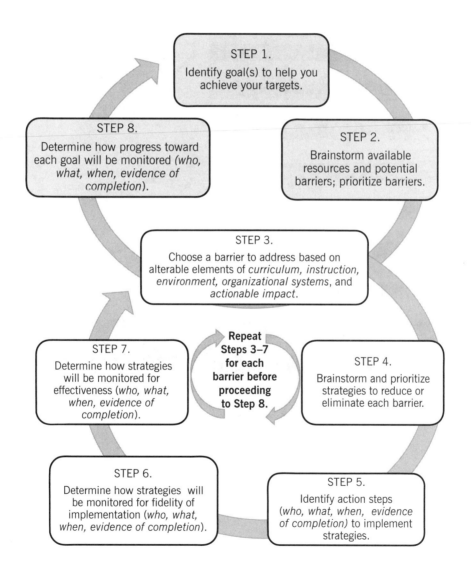

**FIGURE 9.2.** Eight-step problem-solving process used within the DAPPS process. Based on Curtis, Castillo, and Cohen (2008).

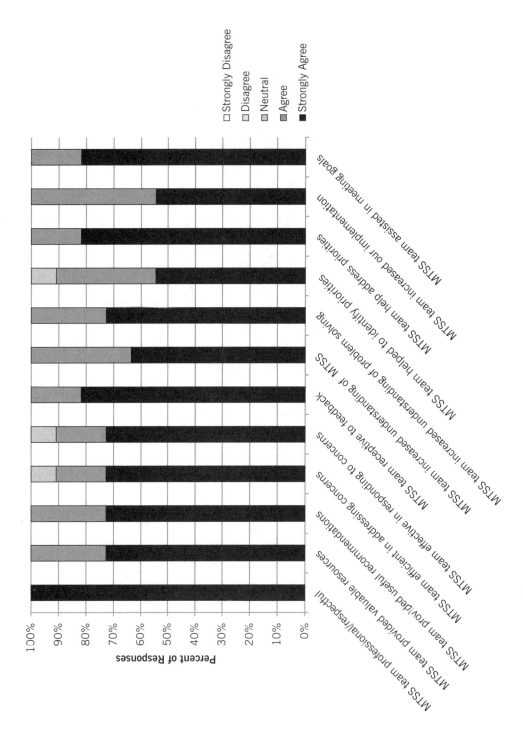

**FIGURE 9.3.** Sample results for the district satisfaction survey for the DAPPS process.

Two surveys were used to evaluate the districts' responses to the DAPPS process. One survey focused on the level of satisfaction that the districts reported each year. Overall, levels of satisfaction with the process were high and provided support for the continued high level of engagement with the process (see Figure 9.3). The second survey focused on the district needs assessment and the degree to which those needs changed as a function of the DAPPS process. The needs assessment survey was designed to assess the specific needs the district identified as critical to the implementation of MTSS. The DAPPS process was designed to assist districts in the development of action plans to meet those needs. Therefore, it was expected that the percent of needs met would increase as the DAPPS process developed. Early feedback from the districts indicated that the needs assessment data at the school level were different for elementary and secondary schools. Therefore, these data were disaggregated to reflect those differences. The needs assessment survey was divided into six broad domains: leadership, communication/collaboration, capacity/infrastructure, data-based problem solving, three-tiered model and data/evaluation system. Each domain contained a number of items. One goal of the DAPPS process was to increase the percent of needs met at the district and school levels. Figures 9.4, 9.5, and 9.6 reflect the change in percent of needs met at the district, elementary, and secondary school levels for one of the original DAPPS districts. The DAPPS process focuses on the *district* team to increase its capacity to support implementation at the school level. These data suggest that the greatest improvement in percent of needs met occurred at the district level—the primary stakeholder in the process. The impact at the elementary level was greater than at the secondary level over the first 2 years of implementation.

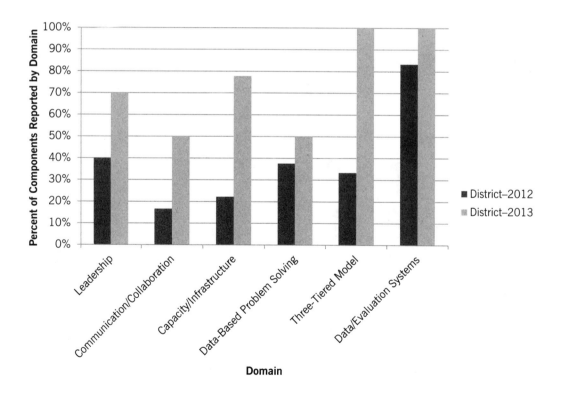

**FIGURE 9.4.** Survey of MTSS implementation needs met at the district level.

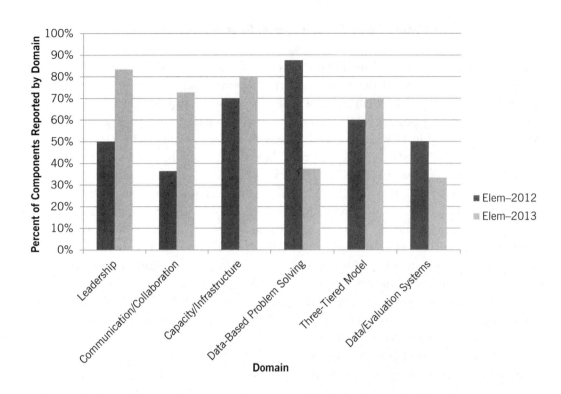

**FIGURE 9.5.** Survey of MTSS implementation needs met at the elementary school level for one district.

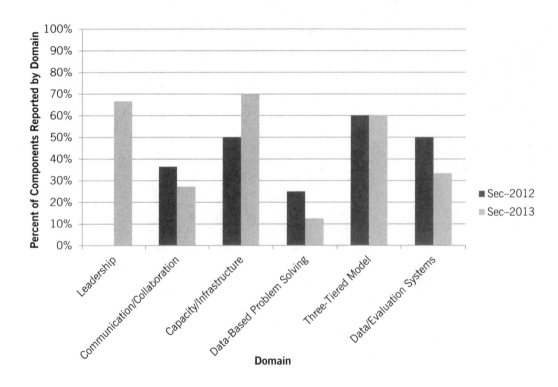

**FIGURE 9.6.** Survey of MTSS implementation needs met at the secondary school level for one district.

A qualitative analysis of the DAPPS process also is included in the evaluation model. Each DAPPS support team completed evaluation protocols after each DAPPS meeting with a district. These protocols were provided to the workgroup, and collaborative interview sessions were held with the DAPPS team members. Through this process, a qualitative and quantitative evaluation of the DAPPS process could be conducted and improvements made in an iterative fashion. From its inception, the MTSS project was committed to using data-based problem solving for both internal and external evaluation purposes.

## CURRENT STATUS

The DAPPS process has been implemented during an interesting time both in Florida and across the United States. The implementation of the Common Core State Standards has taken a central role in Florida. The focus on supports for low-performing schools (*differentiated accountability* in Florida) is a high priority that integrates the MTSS model (both MTSS and the eight-step problem-solving process) and requires significant resources. Districts are facing many challenges and competing priorities for shrinking resources. The DAPPS integration and evaluation workgroup found two important pieces of information through the ongoing evaluation process. Some districts continued to use the DAPPS process to support implementation of MTSS. However, other districts found the DAPPS useful for problem-solving barriers to the implementation of initiatives that were more specific and less encompassing than the implementation of MTSS. As a result, the MTSS project has modified the focus of the DAPPS process to some degree. Currently, the DAPPS process supports teams' focus on the specific goal that a district has identified (e.g., literacy development of ELL students, early warning systems, relationship between behavior variables and academic outcomes) to problem-solve. Clearly, a number of districts continue to use the DAPPS process to support implementation of MTSS districtwide. However, others find that the DAPPS process and its components (e.g., the eight-step problem-solving process) particularly useful in achieving these more specific goals and outcomes. One unanticipated outcome of the MTSS model and the DAPPS process in Florida is the requirement for both MTSS and the use of the eight-step problem-solving process in *all* school improvement plans (SIPs) and district improvement plans (DIPs).

## UNIQUE FEATURES

There are many aspects of our MTSS efforts that may be unique to the context and history of our project activities in Florida. From the beginning, our collaboration on MTSS has focused on enhancing districts' capacities for MTSS problem solving. We agreed that our collaboration would focus on state and district implementation and have only an indirect presence in individual schools. This systems-level perspective and presence have allowed us to promote MTSS strategies at a systems level with a top-down approach that is integrated across multiple state and district initiatives.

As a result of these efforts, Florida's Department of Education has come to understand the foundational importance of MTSS for all of their systems change efforts. Statewide implementation of the Common Core State Standards, school improvement reform, personnel evaluation systems, and other initiatives all reflect the state's appreciation of an MTSS perspective. In turn, this integration provides many opportunities for our project staff to collaborate with and influence the direction of those initiatives. These linkages ensure that consistent messages about MTSS are communicated to state, district, and school personnel and allow us to build awareness-level knowledge that is foundational for our more intensive training and technical assistance activities at the district level. Consistent MTSS messages from our Department of Education collaborators also ensure an understanding that systems may necessitate a redesigning of district and school organizations to nontraditional models. As a result, educational personnel are beginning to appreciate the need to reallocate, to "unsilo," and to reorganize district and school resources to produce meaningful change in student outcomes.

Florida's commitment to building our interproject capacity before we began providing training and technical assistance at the district level was also critical for creating a foundation of highly skilled and collaborative personnel. Initially, there was much work to do to establish a clear mission and vision, redesign our way of working, and develop respect for and trust in the capabilities of our collaborators across both projects, while still providing the siloed, project-specific activities required from our state contracts with the Florida Department of Education. Our ILT moved quickly to establish ongoing professional development for all of our staff so that we operate with the same language and mission, expect high levels of problem-solving and team facilitation skills from all members, and yet respect the unique and complementary skill sets of our colleagues.

This commitment to an internal professional development process has also allowed us to develop and evaluate a wide range of resources, such as materials and tools, which can be shared by staff with our district leadership teams. We have had the capacity to develop well-conceptualized and clear models for coaching, leadership, and data-based problem solving that laid the foundation for our common understanding of our mission and an array of resources for our state. As a result, we have been able to provide intensive training on problem solving that facilitates systems change for our Department of Education, our OSEP-funded discretionary projects, and some of our districts, thus producing a far-reaching impact on our educational system. The collaborations with districts have also resulted in a set of standardized materials and products that consistently meet the needs of all districts, as well as materials that we adapt to fit the unique organization and needs of targeted districts.

Our Florida MTSS efforts also reflect a commitment to collaborative teaming at both state and district levels. Within our interproject work, the multiple workgroups with specific missions and deliverables problem-solve, plan, and produce MTSS content and processes for our work with districts. All of these resources are reviewed and approved by our leadership team and implementation team. At the level of direct support for the districts, Florida has been committed to ensuring that each district MTSS team includes a minimum of one staff member from both the PS/RTI and FLPBS Projects. In addition, each MTSS team has an assigned member from the ILT and the DAPPS integration and evaluation workgroup to provide support with problem-solving issues that arise at the district level.

Florida's MTSS is also committed to a true integration of academic and behavior supports, not to supporting two parallel systems. All shared resources (e.g., leadership, coaching, problem solving, guiding questions) are developed to connect academics and behavior through examples that integrate data from both domains. An MTSS approach that utilizes a universal design for learning presents academic and behavior content in different ways to meet student needs, differentiates ways that students can express that they know behavior and academic expectations, and stimulates interest and motivation for learning. So, not only are behavior skills taught with the same integrity as academic skills, but the academic and behavior pedagogies are integrated.

The DAPPS process was designed to integrate all of the resources, collaborative teaming, and the facilitation, problem-solving, training, and technical assistance capacities of our two projects to meet the needs of all districts in a structured process. Although this process has worked well in some districts, as described earlier, it has met obstacles in other districts. Possible reasons for the lack of impact in some districts are rigidity in application of the DAPSS and an overreliance on the eight-step problem-solving process, both of which might not match the unique needs of the district at any given point in time. As a result, we have developed a more flexible consultation process with clear negotiable and non-negotiable issues, unpacked the components of the DAPPS process to be delivered as separate supports (e.g., trainings, problem solving) based on the needs of the district, and expanded the types of tools and resources beyond the eight-step problem-solving process for use in their activities (e.g., team building, action planning, needs assessment).

Although not unique to Florida, a critical non-negotiable value in our MTSS work at state, district, and school levels is a commitment to the importance of an integrated and effective Tier 1 support system for all students. Although there is more experiential than experimental data regarding the impact of Tier 1 on Tier 2 or 3, we communicate about and advocate for integrity in the implementation of necessary Tier 1 systems changes before considering more intensive and expensive supports for Tiers 2 and 3. If Tier 1 is not implemented effectively and efficiently for academics and behavior within a school, the number of students who need Tiers 2 and 3 supports will quickly overwhelm the temporal, fiscal, and personnel resources of the school and district.

## EVALUATION OF OUTCOMES

After a year of implementing the DAPPS process at the district level, we have six active districts and 14 that are in the initial stages of support. Our outcomes at this early stage have been varied. Our greatest successes have occurred in smaller districts that are able to commit the necessary time and teaming resources to systems change activities. Within these districts, our MTSS teams have successfully addressed barriers related to leadership, teaming, planning, problem solving, MTSS awareness, student attendance, and academic and behavior success. Several difficult systems-level barriers have impacted our success with larger districts (e.g., frequent leadership change, inability to prioritize MTSS for active team participation, competing initiatives) and have resulted in our revising our DAPPS process to deliver a wider range of supports (e.g., team facilitation, problem-solving training, support for data analysis) more flexibly, matched to the expressed needs from the district leadership. Our realization that a single systems change process may not work for every district, given the diversity in districts' sizes, organizations, and ways of functioning, will likely result in continued evaluation and revision of our activities in each district.

Within Florida, our interproject collaboration on MTSS has had a significant impact on multiple state-level initiatives. We have been integral to the state's adoption of the Florida Standards (previously known as *Common Core State Standards*), even providing the initial foundation for conducting needs assessments and problem solving at the district level and for thousands of schools. We are now extending our professional development on the eight-step problem-solving process from our internal staff to develop the knowledge, practice, coaching, and teaching skills of cohorts of related project staff and district personnel. The MTSS efforts have resulted in an instrument (Self-Assessment of MTSS [SAM]; *www.floridarti.usf.edu*) with which schools can self-assess their implementation of the critical components of MTSS. The SAM will be a critical tool for districts and schools to monitor MTSS implementation and will integrate the use of established tools for behavior and academic assessment. Our state's response to low-performing schools is also closely tied to our MTSS efforts with regional teams that have MTTS personnel who collaborate directly with our inter-project staff and utilize many of our resources and approaches (e.g., eight-step problem solving, data review). Our MTSS leadership personnel also facilitate State Performance Plan Indicator Teams, formed by the Florida Department of Education to track and respond to specific national and state indicator data related to special education, including graduation, student success, and discipline. Although much of our state-level emphasis has targeted the establishment of effective Tier 1 academic and behavior systems, our MTSS project staff also lead state efforts to develop or redesign intensive and specialized support systems for students with severe academic and behavior needs (Tier 3). All of these state-level initiatives and activities are essential for promoting the foundation of an integrated academic and behavior MTSS approach for all students.

Because the emphasis of our MTSS work is at the state and district level, we are not easily able to determine the remote and long-term impacts of our collaborative systems change activities on the academic and behavior outcomes of students. Our separate projects do provide school-based training, support, and evaluation, so we have access to academic and behavior outcome data through those projects. Within the context of our collaborative MTSS activities, we are able to measure the following: (1) the degree to which district leadership teams progress through the DAPPS and the eight-step problem solving processes, (2) the status of barriers identified by the DLT within the problem-solving process, (3) the DLT's satisfaction with and perception of the impact of the DAPPS process, and (4) an annual needs assessment process that examines district academic and behavior data and surveys the DLT about the district structures that facilitate or inhibit MTSS progress. At the individual school level, the development of the progress monitoring tool will allow schools and districts to assess how well each school is progressing in establishing the critical components of an MTSS system by measuring the school's leadership, infrastructure for implementation, capacity for communication and collaboration, data-based problem solving, three-tiered instruction and intervention, and data evaluation.

## LESSONS LEARNED

In summary, the lessons learned from our nearly 3-year collaboration include the following areas:

1. All members of the collaborative MTSS team must develop and communicate a common language and understanding of the MTSS mission, definition, and critical components. Not only is it important to have whole-staff approval of concrete, written products that communicate

consistent messages, but also the process of developing a shared vision, mission, and language is essential for building respect, trust, and collaboration.

2. The core sets of skills for systems-level coaching (professional development, leadership, consultation, and content knowledge) are diverse and will require significant commitment to internal professional development. We have been approached by MTSS project staff members in other states who indicate that they plan to "just throw academic RTI and PBIS staff together in some districts and they can work out the process on the fly." Our belief is that there are plenty of opportunities to apply good consultation and coaching skills at the district level, but your internal staff should share common language, protocols, and ways of working before initiating district work. Districts appreciate competent and complementary staff and will quickly disengage from consultation that is not planned, effective, and efficient.

3. The internal professional development activities are useful not only for building collaborative teaming among all staff but also as an effective process for developing, evaluating, and revising all materials, products, and tools before they are utilized by districts and schools.

4. Finding the balance between a consultation model that is too rigidly tied to a protocol and one that has no clear process and thus no capacity to assess implementation fidelity is difficult. Our initial consultation efforts were perhaps too inflexible, but they did allow us to evaluate the components of the model that worked or needed revision. Allowing flexibility within consultation guidelines should provide our staff with an acknowledgment of their excellent coaching skills and support districts that present with very diverse structures and needs for assistance.

5. Although all work in education systems change is driven by student outcomes, those outcomes are often less than immediately apparent. As we work with districts to implement MTSS, measures of project, district, and school implementation fidelity are also critical for understanding student success or lack of RTI.

6. Integration of separate project activities was difficult to produce and maintain, as each project was already contractually committed to a wide range of specific academic and behavior deliverables. Our simultaneous operation in both a segregated and integrated fashion has been, at times, overwhelming, confusing, and challenging for our staff. In retrospect, it might have been easier to start an entirely new integrated MTSS program rather than maintain and integrate concurrent programs, but the process has resulted in our combined staff developing a deeper understanding of MTSS and expanded skill sets for work at the district level.

7. The implementation of MTSS is not a linear process. School districts have strategic plans that guide the allocation of resources and priorities. It became clear to us that, although some districts wanted support to implement MTSS, other districts wanted support (e.g., DAPPS) to reduce or remove barriers as they implemented MTSS. As a result, the work with those districts was more focused. District leadership will not suddenly change course just because resources are available to implement a reform process that is not a priority.

The evolution of a multi-tiered *system* of supports in Florida has brought together two well-developed, independent initiatives, both of which enjoyed high levels of implementation and acceptance as *separate* projects. We learned that the development of the new MTSS model could not be an *additive* process—one that simply took the components of each approach and added them together—but had to be an *integrated* process. Each of the two approaches shared basic foundations: the use of a problem-solving process (although somewhat different between them) and a delivery system that used a multi-tiered approach. On the surface, it appeared that bringing these two approaches together would not be that difficult. However, it became clear that each approach had its own lexicon, its own place in the organizational structure of school districts, personnel with diverse educational and experiential backgrounds, and its own unique mission. The decision was made early on to create a *new* vision and mission statement, develop a common language and common understanding of the model, lexicon, and implementation science. The professional staff from each project received intensive and ongoing professional development regarding common content, and we adopted a common approach to systems change and organizational problem solving.

In essence, instead of moving into one or the other's existing home, we decided to build a new home with a blueprint that was shared from the beginning. As we begin our third year of the *integrated* MTSS model of schooling, we have learned that the process takes time, continuous professional development, and a common vision and way of work that our stakeholders view as *one* model, rather than two.

**CHAPTER 10**

# Michigan's Integrated Behavior and Learning Support Initiative

## *A Statewide System of Support for MTSS*

### Christine Russell and Anna Harms

## OVERVIEW

Michigan's Integrated Behavior and Learning Support Initiative (MiBLSi) is a statewide system of support for intermediate school districts (ISDs) and local school districts as they implement an integrated multi-tiered system of support (MTSS) for reading and behavior. The mission of MiBLSi is to "scale-up a statewide structure to create local capacity to implement an integrated behavior and reading MTSS with fidelity, that endures over time and utilizes data-based decision making at all levels of implementation support" (Goodman, 2013b). The project aims to support schools in implementing MTSS by developing the capacity of ISDs and districts to provide the necessary leadership functions: a host environment that makes the MTSS work easy for staff to carry out, and supports to develop staff competency. These aims reflect a shift from the earlier work of MiBLSi, which emphasized the provision of direct implementation supports to individual schools. Visibility, funding, and political support are provided by the Michigan Department of Education (MDE) and the federal Office of Special Education Programs (OSEP). MiBLSi is one of 8 grant-funded initiatives in Michigan and has also been the recipient of two state personnel development grants from OSEP.

MiBLSi's model is grounded in the following evidence bases: (1) PBIS, developed from the scientific research base of applied behavior analysis (Horner et al., 2009); (2) research-based reading practices developed from the findings of the National Reading Panel Report (National

**Christine Russell, EdD,** Research and Evaluation Specialist, Michigan's Integrated Behavior and Learning Support Initiative, Michigan Department of Education, Lansing, Michigan.

**Anna Harms, PhD,** Evaluation and Research Coordinator, Michigan's Integrated Behavior and Learning Support Initiative, Michigan Department of Education, Lansing, Michigan.

**305**

Reading Panel, 2000); (3) the National Research Council and the Institute for Educational Science Practice Guides (e.g., Gersten et al., 2008); (4) evidence-based problem solving, linking gathering and studying of data to clear action plans based on research (Elliott & Fuchs, 1997); and (5) implementation science, guiding the creation and sustainability of systems that support continuous improvement (Blase, Van Dyke & Fixsen, 2009; Sugai, Horner, Fixsen, et al., 2010; Fixsen et al., 2005).

## HISTORY OF IMPLEMENTATION

MiBLSi has evolved over time from a small model demonstration project to a statewide initiative with a national presence. The evolution has been shaped by needs within the state, resources and funding opportunities, individuals in leadership positions, and the political landscape. Despite the evolution of several aspects of the project, some key factors have remained constant since day one. MiBLSi has maintained a focus on improving outcomes for students. Despite shifts over time to support higher levels within the state's organizational structure, the end prize has always been to have a positive impact on students' academic achievement and behavior. MiBLSi has also demonstrated an unwavering commitment to support implementation fidelity as a means to impact students. Training, coaching, technical assistance, and evaluation have emphasized implementation fidelity and provision of the information, resources, and feedback that teams need to implement with fidelity. Finally, MiBLSi began as an integrated model of academics and behavior, recognizing the interaction of academic and behavior skills, needs, and instructional supports.

The project began small. In 2000, a team of five practitioners and university faculty in the southwest region of Michigan applied for and received a federally funded model demonstration grant to develop and implement a replicable model for data-driven problem solving in schools that focused dually on behavior and reading (Ervin, Schaughency, Goodman, McGlinchey, & Matthews, 2007). They provided training and coaching support for five elementary schools. At the time, few schools in Michigan were implementing RTI or had staff with training in this framework. In many schools in Michigan, data were less readily available, and decisions were often made based on opinion, convenience, or previous experience. MiBLSi's work with those first five schools yielded promising results for reducing problem behaviors and improving students' reading skills (Ervin et al., 2006).

At the time, Michigan's state Director of the Office of Special Education saw RTI as a cutting-edge practice worthy of political and financial support. MiBLSi received support as a mandated activities project designed to address multiple indicators in the State Performance Plan. In 2007, the Michigan Department of Education was awarded an OSEP State Personnel Development Grant (SPDG) to scale up implementation of MTSS. This grant allowed MiBLSi to hire additional technical assistance partners with the goals of regionalizing support and scaling school-level implementation across the state.

### Origins

From 2004 to 2013, 521 elementary and middle schools (see Table 10.1) participated with MiBLSi, including a formal application process, selection as project partners, and completion of a 3-year professional development series. The professional development series included training and coaching supports on implementing an integrated model of MTSS (see Table 10.2). The primary audience for MiBLSi professional development was self-selected school leadership teams, consisting of four to seven school staff, including the principal, teachers, and at least one systems coach, whose role was to support the school leadership team to implement an integrated model of MTSS. Coaches held a variety of job titles within schools, but they were most often school psychologists, school social workers, and reading specialists. Trainings were organized regionally across the state to allow schools to participate as a cohort of schools from the same geographic region and start year. At the time, MiBLSi staff served as the primary trainers for school leadership teams. The project also worked to develop a cadre of over 100 local trainers across the state. These trainers included consultants, principals, teachers, and retired educators. Developing a cadre of local trainers was one way that MiBLSi began increasing capacity across the state to sustain implementation of MTSS.

## Professional Development Sequence

Year 1 of professional development focused on implementation of Tier 1, universal supports for both reading and behavior. Eleven full days of training were spread across the school year (see Table 10.2). Teams were introduced to the data, practices, and systems that comprise school-wide PBIS and a schoolwide reading model, and they were successively introduced to new content throughout the year and asked to implement specific components between each training session. Coaching meetings were held approximately three times per year to help coaches prepare for next steps and get support to address implementation barriers. Year 1 culminated with data review trainings that supported teams to systematically apply a problem-solving process using the implementation fidelity and student outcome data they had been collecting throughout the year. Data review trainings were designed to align with Michigan's Continuous School Improvement Framework and help teams develop fluency with analyzing data to identify suc-

**TABLE 10.1. Number of Schools Participating with MiBLSi between 2004 and 2013 That Implemented an Integrated MTSS Model**

| MiBLSi cohort | Training years | Elementary schools | Middle schools | Total |
|---|---|---|---|---|
| Model demonstration schools | 2000–2003 | 5 | 0 | 5 |
| 1 | 2004–2007 | 14 | 0 | 14 |
| 2 | 2005–2008 | 26 | 0 | 26 |
| 3 | 2006–2009 | 49 | 2 | 51 |
| 4 | 2007–2010 | 103 | 14 | 117 |
| 5 | 2008–2011 | 70 | 14 | 84 |
| 6 | 2009–2012 | 86 | 15 | 101 |
| 7 | 2010–2013 | 87 | 41 | 128 |
| All cohorts | | 440 | 86 | 526 |

**TABLE 10.2.  Professional Development Sequence for Cohorts 1–7 (More information and training topic materials can be downloaded at *http://miblsi.org*)**

| Sequence | | |
|---|---|---|
| Year | Approximate timing of training | Training topic |
| 1 | Fall | Leadership Launch: *Deepen administrators' and coaches' leadership and coaching capacity, skills, and knowledge so they can better lead and facilitate the building leadership team in developing a sustainable system for MTSS implementation.* |
| | | Schoolwide PBIS Day 1: *Overview and introduction to PBIS concepts, tools, and assessments. Begin the work of identifying and defining behavior expectations.* |
| | | Schoolwide PBIS Day 2: *Develop systems for teaching and monitoring behavior expectations, acknowledgment, and behavior tracking (SWIS).* |
| | | Schoolwide PBIS Day 3: *Develop systems for correction to effectively respond to problem behaviors, define major versus minor problem behaviors, and support PBIS-based classroom management.* |
| | Winter | Schoolwide Reading Day 1: *Provide training and support in a reading universal screener (DIBELS or AIMSweb).* |
| | | Schoolwide Reading Day 2: *Link reading universal screening data to instructional priorities, address the needs of diverse learners by maximizing classroom instruction, and strengthen the use of explicit instruction.* |
| | | Schoolwide Reading Day 3: *Continue the focus on maximizing student learning during the protected reading block and use of a fidelity of implementation measure (PET) to evaluate the existing schoolwide reading model.* |
| | Spring | Systems Review: *Work with principals and coaches to review the implementation of schoolwide behavior and reading supports in their school. Begin the process of using data to plan for further work in MTSS implementation.* |
| | | Spring Data Review: *Review status of implementation and student outcomes with the building leadership team. Identify successes to celebrate and problem-solve any areas of need or barriers to implementation. Discuss action plan for the coming year.* |
| 2 | Fall | Leadership Launch Year 2: *Work with principals and coaches to prepare for upcoming trainings focused on Tier 2 supports. Identify, prevent, and repair common implementation errors. Discuss current implementation status.* |
| | | Targeted Behavior Systems: *Learn about and begin to develop systems necessary to support the implementation of targeted behavior supports. Introduce a targeted behavior intervention (check-in/check-out) and use of data to support Tier 2 process evaluation (BAT).* |
| | | Strategic Reading Systems: *Review current status of Tier 1 reading implementation. Learn how to use universal screening data to make instructional decisions.* |

*(continued)*

**TABLE 10.2.** *(continued)*

| Year | Approximate timing of training | Training topic |
|---|---|---|
| | | **Sequence** |

| Year | Approximate timing of training | Training topic |
|---|---|---|
| | Winter | Intensive Reading Systems: *Enhance or establish the process for identifying, supporting, and accelerating the learning of students in need of intensive reading instruction through data-based decision making.* |
| | | Intensive Behavior Systems: *Learn about and begin to develop systems necessary to support the implementation of intensive behavior interventions. Introduce the team to FBA and behavior intervention planning and use of data to support Tier 3 fidelity evaluation (BAT).* |
| | Spring | Spring Data Review: *Review the role of the building leadership team in sustaining MTSS implementation efforts. Provide time and direction in reviewing schoolwide data for the purpose of decision making, celebrating, action planning, and connecting the MTSS work to the school improvement plan.* |
| 3 | Fall | Leadership Launch Year 3: *Work with principals and coaches to prepare for upcoming trainings with a focus on maintaining the momentum of implementation and on implementing a durable and sustainable MTSS model.* |
| | | Fall Data Review: *Review the status of the Tier 1, 2, and 3 supports through data analysis. Act upon data to improve behavior and reading outcomes. Identify areas to celebrate success and prep for continued yearlong implementation and scale up of practices across the building.* |
| | Winter | Winter Data Review: *Continue with data review and action planning activities.* |
| | Spring | Spring Data Review: *Continue with data review and action planning activities.* |

cesses and determine the next steps that would be most likely to yield improved implementation and student outcomes.

In the second year of professional development, schools continued implementing and enhancing Tier 1 implementation while also layering on systems, data, and practices for reading and behavior at Tiers 2 and 3. This support included 8 days of training, as well as coaching meetings and training on specific intervention programs. Year 3 provided additional support for schools to strengthen their systems at Tiers 1, 2, and 3. The number of formal training days was faded to just three data review sessions. More information about the 3-year training series for Cohorts 1–7 can be found on the MiBLSi website (*http://miblsi.org/MiBLSiModel/ProfessionalDevelopment/BuildingTrainingScopeandSequence.aspx*).

Within this model, schools and districts across Michigan embedded MTSS data, practices, and systems within their school improvement plans. Schools modified discipline policies to align with PBIS and best practices for keeping students in the classroom and engaged in effective instruction, and therefore learning. Schools and districts also began taking best practices for intervention and data collection and generalizing their systems-level work to writing and math. Steady increases in implementation fidelity and student outcomes have been seen for both reading and behavior over time. Another indicator that this process was valuable was revealed when schools began modifying teacher and administrator selection procedures to prioritize experience with MiBLSi MTSS implementation as a qualification for being hired. Many schools that participated with MiBLSi, even in early years of the project, have been able to sustain implementation and have continued to improve student outcomes. These successes will be discussed more fully in the section on Evaluation of Outcomes.

## CURRENT STATUS

A commitment to continuous improvement in MTSS implementation efforts has been essential as MiBLSi has moved from supporting the first 50 schools, to the next 500 schools, to the current scale-up demand across the state as MTSS becomes the standard practice of how educational systems function in Michigan. With scaling up in mind, in 2009 MiBLSi, along with the Michigan Department of Education, entered into a partnership with the OSEP Center on State Implementation and Scaling Up of Evidence-Based Practices (SISEP) to take formal steps to apply implementation science to MTSS. This partnership, coupled with the demand to have a larger and more sustainable impact across the state, has greatly influenced the way MiBLSi is structured and how outcomes of MiBLSi are measured. Rather than solely focusing on increasing the number of educators across the state "doing MiBLSi," the focus is on how to develop an MTSS framework within educational systems that will endure through time with a focus on fidelity across stages of implementation.

### Scaling Up a Statewide Project While Continuing to Influence Student Outcomes

To be able to affect a high percentage of the state's schools, a building-by-building approach is neither feasible nor practical. Fixsen, Blase, Horner, and Sugai (2008) described the process of scaling up as the "development of organizational capacity to move from exemplars sustained by extraordinary supports, to typical application with organizations and systems that are designed to make full, effective, and sustained use of innovations" (p. 2). A different approach and focus of support was needed within the state of Michigan to move MTSS implementation beyond those educators deeply interested and committed to MTSS to a scalable framework across the state that could endure over time.

Although MiBLSi's work through the school cohort model proved supportive to school structures and staff, there were some areas of need not covered within that approach. Schools were not always able to implement with full fidelity by the end of the 3 years of MiBLSi professional development. Although most schools within the project made improvements, many schools did not reach full implementation with strong fidelity when MiBLSi supports were provided directly to schools.

Another concern centered on difficulty maintaining school implementation efforts without the support of district leadership. Within the school cohort model, 3 years of support and funding were provided directly to the schools. Often, schools were unable to develop their own training, coaching, and resource allocation to MTSS efforts once the MiBLSi professional development sequence ended. One clear example was found in the data on SWIS accounts across the state. SWIS has been the behavior data tracking system used by MiBLSi partnering schools throughout the project's history. Although Michigan data showed a high number of new school accounts opening each year, SWIS accounts were closed after an average of 3.4 years. These data highlight the clear issues of sustainability of practices put in place through school-level implementation. The project team hypothesized that developing district leadership support and allocation of resources through a district cohort model could create a better host environment for long-term sustainability.

In 2011, MDE and MiBLSi applied for a second SPDG from OSEP. This grant was sought to extend the project to focus on developing local capacity and sustainability. As part of that grant, a landmark shift occurred in the MiBLSi support structure. A new district cohort model was conceptualized, whereby the MiBLSi partnerships shifted from individual schools to intermediate school districts (ISDs) and local school districts to increase shared ownership and accountability. Within Michigan, ISDs are educational support structures organized at the county or multiple-county level to serve as intermediate mechanisms between the state and local districts. The ISD assists local school districts in providing programs and services such as special education services, general education consultation services, career and technical education, professional development, and some financial services. MiBLSi's shift to working at the ISD level has moved the project from working with individual schools to the larger role of providing an educational framework that can go to scale across the state.

When focused on implementation at the school level during the first 9 years, MiBLSi was able to partner with 521 schools across Michigan. In contrast, within the first 3 years of partnering with ISDs, the long-term potential number of schools that could be reached is exponentially higher (see Figure 10.1). Since 2011, three cohorts of ISDs and districts have been supported under the district cohort model. Currently, MiBLSi is directly supporting 22 ISDs and 2 local school districts (Detroit Public Schools and Portage Community Schools), which in turn have the potential to support 282 local school districts, charters, and public school academies; 1,412 public schools; and 601,412 students across the state of Michigan. Across time, additional ISDs will be added, with each partnership increasing the potential districts and schools that will be affected by MiBLSi MTSS practices and support.

## Structuring MTSS Support

To better understand how MiBLSi's MTSS supports flow across Michigan's educational structure, Figure 10.2 illustrates the cascading model of educational support, as well as how the support is provided. This stairstep depiction of a cascading system illustrates that units within educational systems build upon each other. Each unit is connected in a variety of ways, such as through policy development, funding, and coordination of services. Each unit is dependent on the systems above it in the cascade to support its work. In addition, each educational body across the cascade is connected through communication and feedback regarding needs, supports, and progress. This figure shows how much the success of MTSS is dependent on the flow of services and communication through the cascade.

In the initial years of MiBLSi, within the school cohort model the regional support for MTSS implementation directly targeted the school leadership team. What has been evident in

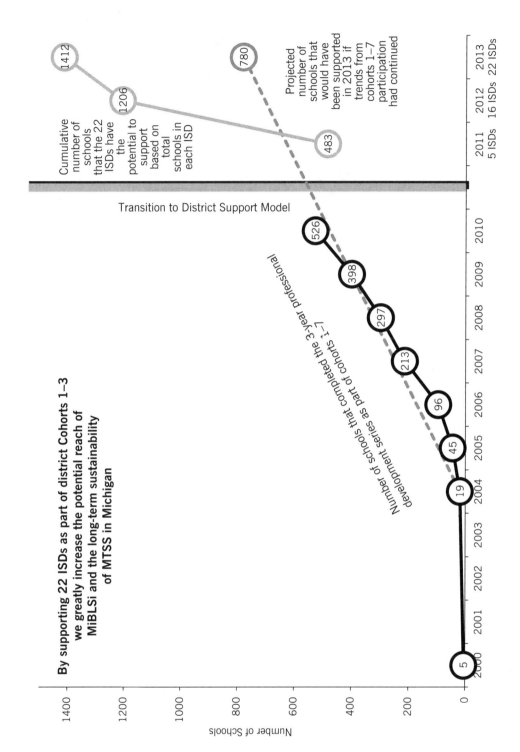

**FIGURE 10.1.** Increasing support by investing support in intermediate school districts.

By supporting 22 ISDs as part of district Cohorts 1–3 we greatly increase the potential reach of MiBLSi and the long-term sustainability of MTSS in Michigan

Cumulative number of schools that the 22 ISDs have the potential to support based on total schools in each ISD

Projected number of schools that would have been supported in 2013 if trends from cohorts 1–7 participation had continued

Transition to District Support Model

Number of schools that completed the 3-year professional development series as part of cohorts 1–7

Number of Schools

2000 2001 2002 2003 2004 2005 2006 2007 2008 2009 2010 2011 2012 2013
                                                          5 ISDs 16 ISDs 22 ISDs

312

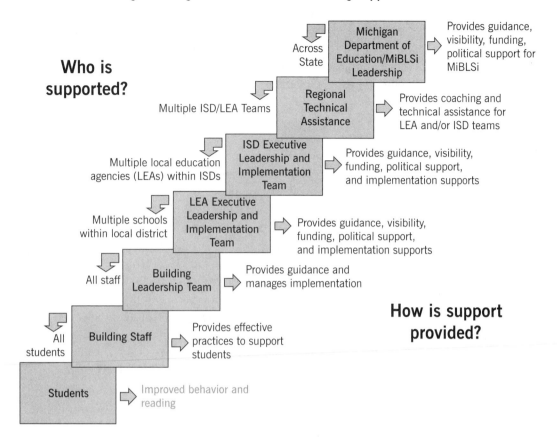

**FIGURE 10.2.** Michigan's statewide cascading model of educational support. *Note.* This figure is designed to be viewed starting at the bottom left corner, then following the cascade up and to the right, ending at the top right corner with the Michigan Department of Education.

the long-term work within the schools supported by the initial model is that school leadership teams repeatedly came up against barriers related to vision, policy, funding, and resource allocation. Destabilizing events, such as school leadership turnover, cuts in funding, or competing initiatives, can quickly overturn MTSS work that had been successful at the school level for years.

The shift to the district cohort model in 2011 has allowed MiBLSi's support to flow more systematically across the cascade throughout Michigan. This new support structure directly addressed the need to intentionally focus on leadership at all levels of the system to ensure durable and sustainable implementation. Rather than a classroom teacher contemplating universal screening data alone and independently determining how to move all students to mastery both academically and behaviorally, that teacher has access to a host of intentional research-based supports that are layered and aligned along the cascade. The ISD provides structured coaching and training supports so that all educators within the system are better equipped with the knowledge and skills needed to interpret data, match students to interventions, and support all students across the continuum of needs. The district has a vision of supporting all needs throughout the district through allocation of resources to both preventive practices and supplemental interventions that have sound research and empirical evidence. The school personnel understand the vision of the district and ISD and have received training, coaching, and evaluation support to enhance their work with students. Everyone across the system knows that it is a community of practice effort that will move students toward both academic and behavior success, regardless of their entry level of readiness.

## *Sustainable Infrastructure*

A key piece to understanding the current MiBLSi support model is a recognition that the core of MTSS implementation takes place at the school level. Communication regarding school outcomes, action plans, and needs drive districtwide plans. Intentional work must be done to enhance the quality and flow of information across the levels of support. Communication plans and use of data in decision making help to maintain a collaborative atmosphere and keep the efforts of MTSS from becoming a top-down approach. For each school to receive sustainable and effective support, ISD and district personnel must provide leadership and organizational and competency supports to focus educational efforts in a way that meets the needs and action plans of their schools. MTSS is threatened when it is managed solely by a principal and the school leadership team. The work is vastly strengthened when principals and their school-level teams are provided training, support, and resources through their district and ISD plans.

MiBLSi supports implementation efforts at many steps of the cascade; however, the goal is to further the capacity of educators to continue and sustain the efforts independently. To achieve this goal, MiBLSi initially works with the ISD and district implementation teams to set up the organizational structures necessary to support MTSS. Next, side-by-side support is provided at the school level through initial implementation to ensure that all are well supported at the onset of their work. This intensity of project support helps to maintain implementation fidelity for the districts and schools but also provides a model for those who will be long-term supports for those within the district and school. The long-term vision is to invest time in deepening the knowledge and skills of the professionals who work directly with the local systems so they are fully prepared to carry on implementation independently after working with MiBLSi for a period of time. The goal is that an ISD will continue to move forward with its other districts and schools to the point of supporting—at minimum—a critical mass of their districts and schools with the implementation of MTSS with a high degree of fidelity.

As ISDs branch out to working with their local districts, there is an expectation that the ISD and district will work together with a shared vision of implementation. Districts are supported in their MTSS endeavors through stages of implementation, including adoption/exploration, program installation, initial implementation, elaboration, and then moving into continuous improvement/sustainability of the practice (Fixsen et al., 2005). However, implementation is not always linear; indeed, it is often recursive. In light of this fact, teams are guided through the stages of implementation based on assessments that indicate readiness for implementation and current success. In other words, rather than sending districts and schools through a predetermined training sequence, MiBLSi ISDs determine training content and sequences based on need, fit, resources, evidence, readiness, and capacity (Blase, Kiser, et al., 2013). The standard scope and sequence of our original cohort model did not account for school-level context, which can lead to varying lengths of time needed to progress through each stage of implementation. With the current district cohort MiBLSi structure that invests in ISDs and districts, schools are able to implement MTSS practices within an infrastructure that supports continuous improvement, fidelity of implementation, and long-term sustainability.

## UNIQUE FEATURES

### *Investing in Leadership and Existing Structures*

A defining feature of MiBLSi MTSS implementation is leaving structures in place that facilitate implementation and maintenance of MTSS long after MiBLSi supports are first provided. A key belief is that our educational systems will be able to achieve a sustainable and durable three-tier model of MTSS when the conceptual framework of the three-tier triangle of supports is complemented with principles of organizational change. Outcomes can be enhanced when the systems focus on the development of internal capacity to implement practices at the three tiers. Although implementation of MTSS takes place at the school level, structural organization at the ISD and district levels will lead to the most dramatic shifts in student outcomes. These enhancements to, and restructuring of, the host environment to make room for MTSS are also essential to creating durable and sustainable improvement.

To provide support across the cascade, MiBLSi is developing and offering coaching for the use of a district management structure to support implementation (see Figure 10.3). The focus of this structure is to embed MTSS implementation into standard practice so that the work is a part of the fabric of the district. With the levels of support intact, MTSS implementation should withstand the test of time, administration turnover, the addition of new initiatives, and other common destabilizing events that, without this structure, commonly compromise the work.

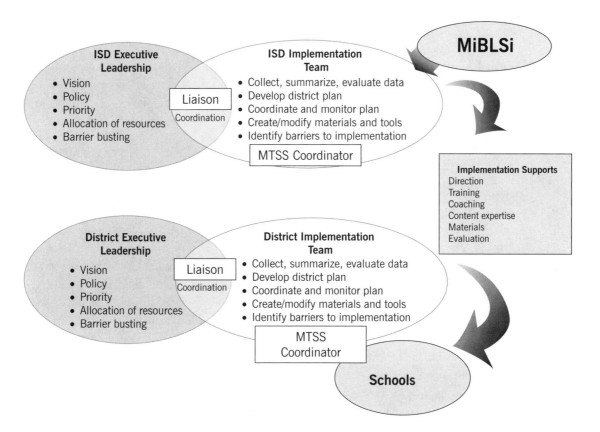

**FIGURE 10.3.** Intermediate school district and local school district management structure.

### District Management Structure

This district management structure relies on two separate teams at each ISD and district. The first step in creating an enhanced organizational environment is to determine who serves the function of executive leadership for ISDs and districts. This layer of support allocates resources, helps to eliminate barriers to MTSS implementation, and manages the finances of the educational body. Rather than creating a new group, implementers should look to an existing group of central office administrators who are key decision makers and therefore already fulfill this function. These executive teams set the vision, control resources, and can bust implementation barriers, but due to the high work demands on administrators, they are unable to be the worker bees of implementation. An additional team, the implementation team, comprises those who are knowledgeable of MTSS practices but also hold a systemwide lens when decision making is necessary. The group is focused on data-based decision making, looking across ISD/districtwide datasets, and triangulating information in a way that leads to using multiple data sources to better understand the strengths, needs, and priorities of the districts or schools that they serve. This group creates and modifies tools, policies, and practices that help make MTSS implementation easier at the school level.

The MiBLSi approach acknowledges that there are rarely new funds available to create the structures necessary for full implementation. This fact makes it even more critical to use existing structures to support the work. Reallocating existing staff and organizing this work in an efficient way—while paying attention to decreasing other inefficiencies across the system—makes room for effective systems reorganization. Utilizing committees and groups that already serve the defined functions, such as a district improvement team, helps to embed the work into existing structures rather than creating redundancies or, conversely, silos across committees.

This management structure should be organized, developed, and given appropriate authority at both the ISD and district levels. This replication of leadership support systems through the cascade leads to the flow of supports, resources, training, coaching, and evaluation to make MTSS implementation possible, feasible, and sustainable. The ultimate goal of each step in the cascade is to make it easier for MTSS to be implemented well at the school and classroom level.

### MTSS Coordination

Within each district and ISD, implementation is guided by MTSS coordinators. As seen in Figure 10.3, those who serve in the role of MTSS coordinators act as a part of the implementation team but are also as a conduit between the system in which they reside and the educational body they are working to support. For example, an MTSS coordinator at the district level supports the ISD implementation team but also is a key player in providing coaching to schools engaged in MTSS implementation. Although some districts have created full-time MTSS coordinator positions, typically those serving in this role continue to hold positions and job responsibilities such consultants, school psychologists, social workers, or academic coordinators. Most often, the function is fulfilled through the reallocation of existing personnel to provide time for management of the work.

Along with developing the capacity to train and coach MTSS systems and practice, MTSS coordinators guide problem solving using data-based decision making as well as ensure that all involved are working to deepen their own personal knowledge of MTSS data, practices, and systems. To be able to effectively accomplish the work, MTSS coordinators must have effective communication skills and be able to set up strong two-way communication throughout the systems that they are navigating. They also serve the function of evaluating the effectiveness and efficiency of implementation through a continuous improvement cycle at all levels. MTSS coordinators are the main communication source for training from MiBLSi to the systems in which they serve and also are critical in the feedback loop to MiBLSi regarding supports and work.

MTSS coordinators within the MiBLSi model have been described as indispensable to the process. Without strong local MTSS coordination efforts by the ISD and local school district, MTSS implementation will not be able to move at an efficient and effective pace. In general, MTSS coordinators develop and support local implementation capacity while ensuring implementation fidelity. An MTSS coordinator helps to move the work forward as intended while also developing the skills of others within the system to train, coach, and support MTSS across the educational system.

## Braiding with Current Statewide and District Initiatives

The vision and outlook of MiBLSi is that through the utilization of existing structures in place within Michigan's education system, implementation will be more feasible, streamlined, and efficient. Integrating national information and research into school-level professional development is just one component of the value added in partnering with MiBLSi MTSS. An additional critical piece in making the work easier for our partners is ensuring that our materials and support align with state and federal priorities that are required for schools, districts, and ISDs. Increasingly, schools are asked to be more effective at producing successful student outcomes while facing decreasing resources. In an effort to help ISDs and districts understand that MTSS is not an add-on, MiBLSi stresses its connections to the multiple programs, initiatives, and policies at the state level that relate to MTSS. This information on intentional integration can help those ISDs and districts that are contemplating adopting MiBLSi. MiBLSi's professional development materials, resources, and technical assistance align with critical state mandates and policies, such as Michigan's Continuous School Improvement Framework, Michigan's State Board of Education Policy on Positive Behavior Interventions and Supports, Matt's Safe School Law (bullying prevention), State Board of Education Policy on Seclusion and Restraint, and state initiatives to reduce racial/ethnic disproportionality in school discipline.

## MiBLSi Project Structure

The MiBLSi project originated with three co-directors supported by one part-time secretary. Over time, the leadership of MiBLSi has been able to justify the hiring of additional staff by demonstrating the need to build internal capacity to keep pace with the demands of a model that is going to scale. MiBLSi currently employs 40 staff who are a combination of full-time employees, part-time consultants, and regional support staff to support ISD and district partners. Project staff is located throughout the state at 10 different ISDs. Advances in technology have also allowed a few project staff to work remotely from other states while maintaining high levels of communication and collaboration. It is rare for state projects to have such a large number of staff to support the work. The project has been fortunate to have such a large number of staff members who are highly skilled and extremely passionate about supporting MTSS.

Figure 10.4 provides MiBLSi's current organizational chart. All 40 staff members contribute to the overall project while also providing unique contributions based on their unit, spe-

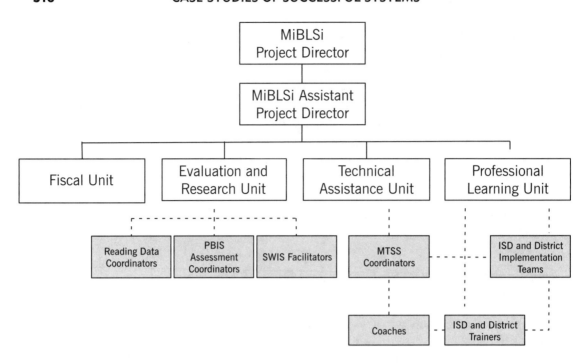

**FIGURE 10.4.** MiBLSi organizational chart.

cific job responsibilities, and skill sets. Underneath the MiBLSi director and assistant director, staff members are organized into four units, each with distinct internal and external functions: technical assistance, professional learning, evaluation and research, and finance. The technical assistance unit works directly with the MTSS coordinators and the implementation teams across the state providing guidance, problem solving, and feedback on organizational infrastructure and capacity to support implementation of MTSS. Staff members within this unit help educators understand and implement the MiBLSi MTSS model while adapting the model to regional contexts. The professional learning unit provides skill and knowledge through information and materials to support individuals within the local setting to develop and deepen their competencies in the implementation of MTSS. The evaluation and research unit has the mission of investigating project activities, trainings, and support in a way that is focused on improving the efficiencies of our work as well as enhancing our project outcomes. This unit also assists with the content and materials needed for each level of the cascade (e.g., ISD, district, school, grade level) to evaluate their practices. The fiscal unit ensures that the allocation and dissemination of funds enhance MTSS implementation. The organizational structures of MiBLSi are regularly enhanced or modified to align with the framework that we are helping ISDs, districts, and schools to establish. These changes include addressing our capacity in the areas of leadership, organizational environment, and structures to develop staff competency.

In addition to MiBLSi's four distinct units, there are critical MTSS roles that the project is actively supporting and developing within each partnering ISD and district, shown in the shaded boxes in Figure 10.4 in gray. The purpose of including these local roles on the MiBLSi organizational chart is to illustrate to whom the MiBLSi supports are provided. Additionally, creating the chart in this way makes it clear that MiBLSi is actively working to cultivate the same types of MTSS supports at the ISD and district levels. Including the crucial district staff within the organizational chart helps to keep at the forefront the long-range plan of the project: to change and enhance the ISD and district systems so that they are better poised to support the schools, teachers, and students that they serve.

## EVALUATION OF OUTCOMES

An innovation is more likely to endure when there is evidence that it is making a positive difference for students and when stakeholders have access to that evidence. Improved student achievement is the ultimate goal, the unwavering target upon which we set our sights. The way we aim to hit this target is by using data to make decisions that will yield improved support at each level of the cascade, ultimately leading to high levels of implementation fidelity and student achievement. This approach contrasts with evaluation for the sole purpose of demonstrating how successful we are as a project. Our project success is inextricably connected to our problem-solving process for evaluation and continuous improvement. The same is true for how districts and schools might measure their success. MiBLSi's evaluation model includes three levels of evaluation: organizational, process, and worker. The remainder of this section focuses on the organizational level of evaluation, as the other two levels function primarily for internal decision making. The organizational level of evaluation focuses on two primary questions:

1. Is the support provided by MiBLSi resulting in improved infrastructures, implementation fidelity, and student outcomes at a local level?
2. What is the perceived quality of MiBLSi's support to participating ISDs, local districts, and schools?

MiBLSi supports data collection for multiple purposes. The first and most important purpose of data collection has been for local teams to have access to the information necessary for data-driven decision making to improve systems and practices that will positively impact student outcomes. A secondary purpose of gathering data from participating schools, districts, and ISDs has been for the project to monitor implementation and outcomes to continuously improve the support it provides. Historically, MiBLSi's evaluation efforts focused primarily at the school level. Over time, with the shifts in the model of support, the scope of evaluation has also widened to include additional levels of the cascade. Table 10.3 provides an overview of the primary evaluation questions and corresponding data sources at the school, district, ISD, and project levels. Outcomes at lower levels of the cascade are one way to measure the impact of the supports provided higher up the cascade. For example, the impact of district supports can be evaluated by examining school-level outcomes. Impact of ISD supports can be evaluated by examining district-level outcomes. The impact of MiBLSi supports can be evaluated by examining ISD-level outcomes.

Given that the desired focus of implementation is at the school level and students are the end receivers of MiBLSi's support, it makes sense to start evaluating MiBLSi outcomes by examining impact at the school level before discussing how MiBLSi influences districts and ISDs. As has been previously discussed, data from the 521 schools that completed MiBLSi's school-level professional development sequence demonstrated that MiBLSi positively influenced school outcomes and at the same time revealed challenges with the original model. At the school level, data are collected on implementation fidelity and student outcomes for

**TABLE 10.3. Evaluation Questions and Data Sources**

| Question | Data Source |
| --- | --- |
| *School level*<br><br>What number and proportion of schools are implementing an integrated model of MTSS with fidelity?<br><br>What number and proportion of schools are improving student outcomes in (1) reading and (2) behavior? | • BoQ<br>• PET for effective schoolwide reading programs<br>• Secondary schoolwide PET<br>• R-TFI<br>• DIBELS or AIMSweb<br>• ODRs |
| *District level*<br><br>What number and proportion of districts have developed the internal capacity to support districtwide implementation of MTSS? | • District MTSS Capacity Assessment |
| *ISD level*<br><br>What number and proportion of ISDs have developed the internal capacity to support ISD-wide implementation of MTSS? | • Intermediate Unit Capacity Assessment |
| *Project level*<br><br>Is the support provided by MiBLSi resulting in improved infrastructures, implementation fidelity, and student outcomes at a local level?<br><br>What is the perceived quality of MiBLSi's support to participating ISDs, local districts, and schools? | • Impact data from the ISD, district, and school levels<br>• Annual Consumer Feedback Survey<br>• Evaluation data from professional development sessions<br>• Informal feedback |

*Note.* BoQ, Benchmarks of Quality; DIBELS, Dynamic Indicators of Basic Early Literacy Skills; ODRs, office discipline referrals; PET, Planning and Evaluation Tool; R-TFI, Reading Tiered Fidelity Inventory.

both reading and behavior. Sample results from Cohort 7 are provided to illustrate patterns in school outcomes with the most recent group of schools (see Figure 10.5). The majority of participating schools have successfully implemented an integrated model of MTSS. Implementation fidelity is indicated by scores at or above 70% on the BoQ (Kincaid et al., 2005) and total scores at or above 80% on the PET-R (Kame'enui & Simmons, 2002). Data also show that as implementation fidelity improves, so do student outcomes. As the median BoQ score increased throughout the 3 years of participation for Cohort 7 schools, the median rate of ODRs decreased. Likewise, as the median PET-R total score increased, the median percent of students scoring at or above the spring DIBELS Next benchmark score also increased. When looking at reading and behavioral data simultaneously, as reading scores increased over time, rates of ODRs decreased.

For schools to implement with fidelity and improve student outcomes successfully and in a sustained way, local school districts and ISDs must provide the support necessary. Through a partnership with the OSEP Center on SISEP, MiBLSi has recently developed measures that will help a district or ISD implementation team to self-assess the extent to which they have the implementation drivers (e.g., leadership, organizational environment, staff competency) in place for MTSS. These tools fill a large gap in available assessments for ISDs and districts to guide their work. The ISD-level tool is called the *Regional Capacity Assessment* (RCA; St. Martin, Ward, Fixsen, Harms & Russell, 2015), and the district-level tool is called the *District Capacity Assessment* (DCA; Ward et al., 2015). Both measures were developed based on active implementation frameworks, have recently been piloted, and are undergoing standard steps for constructing measures, including expert feedback, cognitive interviewing, field testing, and analyses of technical adequacy. Initial feedback on the capacity assessments has been positive:

> "The [RCA] helped us to refine and operationalize our goals and align our work to school improvement. It helped us prioritize where to start in honing our ISD-level infrastructures. We came away with a great action plan."
>
> —MTSS Coordinator, District Cohort 1

> "We have long needed a way to collect process data at the ISD level, so were very excited to have the tool. It really brought to light just how complex this work is that we're doing. This will help us to create the action plan we are so in need of at the ISD level."
>
> —MTSS Coordinator, District Cohort 2

Although the second project-level evaluation question does not reflect our ultimate goal of impacting student outcomes, it provides a necessary first gate for interpreting subsequent layers of data. Because MiBLSi staff no longer provides direct services to school-level staff and students, evaluation structures must take into account the immediate impact of our work and the successively more distal impact on other steps of the cascade. Data used to answer the first evaluation question include (1) retrospective self-assessment and feedback gathered at the end

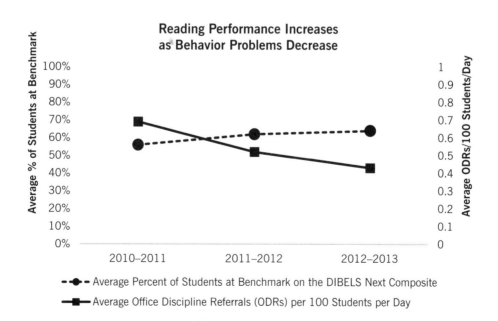

**FIGURE 10.5.** Student reading and behavior outcomes in Cohort 7.

of every professional development session provided by MiBLSi, (2) consumer feedback gathered through an annual survey sent to all project participants, and (3) informal feedback from project participants. For the past 2 years, 96% of MiBLSi Consumer Feedback Survey respondents have either agreed or strongly agreed with the statement, "Overall, I am satisfied with the supports provided by MiBLSi and believe partnership with this project is beneficial." Retrospective self-assessment data from training sessions consistently show that participants perceive improvements in their knowledge and skills from the beginning to the end of training sessions.

General feedback from training sessions also consistently demonstrates high levels of satisfaction with the experience. For example, we consistently hit a target of 80% of participants who agree or strongly agree that the goals were clearly defined; the content matched the priorities of their school, district, and ISD; they were leaving with the necessary information, tools, and resources to develop an action plan; and the day was valuable and worth their time. These data are all initial indicators that MiBLSi is meeting participant needs. Without high levels of immediate satisfaction, ISD, district and school staff would be less likely to see the value in translating information from training into practice. The MTSS coordinators receiving MiBLSi support and professional development report that the work they are doing with MiBLSi has immediate positive effects on their work:

> "It allows us to have access to research and structure in getting the work done in a sustainable manner. It's also access to a network of people doing similar work, so we can learn from other people's challenges and successes."
>
> —MTSS Coordinator, District Cohort 2

> "MiBLSi helps us plan strategically and work in congruence with the latest research. MiBLSi is always thinking ahead and developing useful tools and resources to guide our work and our support to districts, which frees up our time to support our local districts."
>
> —MTSS Coordinator, District Cohort 1

## Future Directions

This section was introduced with the suggestion that an innovation is more sustainable when there is evidence to support it and stakeholders have access to that evidence. MiBLSi has demonstrated a history of making a difference for students, and the project is making every effort to ensure that those changes are widespread and sustained. We continue to work on methods for ensuring that all stakeholders have easy access to the evidence or evaluation findings. Our approach to accomplishing this aim in the future is multipronged. First, we intend to open up our project database and reporting system to all of our partnering ISDs, districts, and schools. This move will streamline our process for gathering impact data and will ensure that there is immediate access to data across the cascade, using a common format for data entry and reporting. Second, we are developing templates for formally reporting on context, input, fidelity, and outcomes on an annual basis. Our hope is that these reports will be able to be used for a variety of stakeholders for the purposes of communication, consistent messaging, generating interest in MiBLSi, and supporting buy-in. Finally, we plan to embed all of these resources into our project website (*http://miblsi.org*), to be accessed by project staff, MiBLSi participants, other stakeholder groups, and the general public.

MiBLSi is currently funded as a professional development grant. Therefore, the collection and analysis of data are primarily for program evaluation and improvement purposes and may be best categorized as action research. Recognizing our limited internal capacity to conduct research, MiBLSi has established partnerships with several faculty from five of the largest state universities in Michigan. These mutually beneficial partnerships allow for more in-depth analyses of specific features of MiBLSi. Current projects include (1) the systematic examination of the value added by technical assistance providers, (2) the analysis of how an organization like MiBLSi enacts large-scale systems change, (3) how MiBLSi's support to ISDs and districts is translated into action by teachers in schools, and (4) the role of MTSS coordination within an ISD and district management structure for MTSS.

## LESSONS LEARNED

There are three key lessons that we have learned through the MiBLSi implementation process: (1) Start small and use learning to scale up, (2) change is required at every level of the system to establish sustainable MTSS practices in schools, and (3) use evaluation for continuous improvement. It is through learning these three lessons that MiBLSi has been able to expand its reach and deliver quality outcomes.

### Start Small and Use Learning to Scale Up

As MiBLSi has shifted its direct support from schools to ISDs and districts, project staff frequently field questions from other projects or initiatives that are currently small in scale or are working primarily at the school level. These colleagues express concerns that they are starting too small or perhaps making a mistake by not beginning their work at a district or regional level. On the contrary, MiBLSi's history and successful scaling over time should help to illustrate that it is important to try out the integrated behavior and reading model in demonstration sites. By starting with just five pilot schools and gradually replicating success, MiBLSi has been able to learn lessons with lower risk and gradually accumulate evidence and experiences that over time have shaped the scope, priorities, and structure of the current initiative. If successful outcomes cannot be produced in the model demonstrations with an adequate investment of resources, it is hard to justify replicating implementation efforts in other settings. Long-term success by MiBLSi has been grounded in taking time to understand what it takes to make the model work, first on a small scale, and then applying this learning to modify program supports with more schools. As the program is improved, additional schools are added to see if the program can work in different settings with different populations.

### Sustainable Change

From the beginning, the MiBLSi team has made a conscious effort to promote, encourage, and support the use of effective interventions in the application of MTSS. Additionally, it has become clear over time that intentional implementation of those interventions at the local level will lead to long-term academic and behavior gains. By supporting the implementation of evidence-based interventions across the stages of implementation and through reorganization of the educational environment in which the interventions will be implemented, the project can better support the allocation of ISD and district funds to activities that have a high probability of producing successful student outcomes. Additionally, schools have limited resources. The focus on implementing in a more concentrated and intentional way is resonating with leadership across all levels of the cascade.

Ongoing supports are critical for implementation fidelity and durability. With training and coaching, schools are able to meet criteria on implementation fidelity. However, after initial training has been completed and coaching fades, implementation fidelity of MTSS may begin to decline, resulting in deteriorating student outcomes. Implementation supports include professional development, coaching, technical assistance, materials, and feedback. It is through implementation supports that we develop "host environments" within the school to make it easy to apply the MTSS practices with fidelity that will endure over time (Kame'enui et al., 2000). An essential component of our implementation supports includes embedding MTSS into current initiatives and priorities.

## *Continuous Improvement through Use of Data*

Formative and summative evaluation is necessary to adjust the MTSS program based on current needs and changes that occur over time as students and educators react to MTSS. We use data at all levels for continuous improvement (e.g., student outcomes, implementation fidelity, system quality). There are currently many sophisticated programs and systems available for storing and summarizing data, which can make data-driven decision making more efficient. However, lack of a sophisticated system need not be an initial barrier to engaging in evaluation of an integrated model of MTSS. What is essential is that there is an initial and ongoing emphasis on data-driven decision making across the cascade. This emphasis means supporting evaluation and problem solving with leadership and implementation teams within the MiBLSi project, ISDs, local school districts, schools, and classrooms, as well as continuing that support through all stages of implementation to the point where they are continuously regenerating evaluation practices within an effective and integrated multi-tiered system of supports.

## KEY POINTS FROM THE CASE STUDIES

The authors of the case studies in Chapters 8–10 have provided excellent examples of integrating academic and behavior systems into a single MTSS. As can be seen, there are many differences in how the leaders structured their initiatives, as well as the paths taken to arrive at their present condition. Yet there are also many common features across each of these examples. Beyond the obvious similarities of a strong focus on the main concepts on integrated MTSS models described in this book, there were other commonalities. First, each project started with a small group of individuals, but that group made a concerted effort to bring others into the fold after initial successes. Second, each group invested in structures to support school personnel in their implementation efforts, especially as they went to scale and found the need to work more systematically. Finally, each group sought to integrate their work into new initiatives and opportunities at the state level when they arose. As such, even these highly articulated initiatives are constantly evolving to enhance the effectiveness, expansion, and durability of their integrated MTSS models.

# PART IV

# LOOKING BACK,
# LOOKING FORWARD

## CHAPTER 11

# Conclusion

As you've no doubt experienced, academic and behavior supports are most often implemented in parallel systems that typically work independently of each other. We have shown that academic RTI and PBIS can be integrated and that doing so can optimize systems and improve student outcomes. However, we do not want to simply force *full* integration without considering whether it will produce better outcomes than parallel systems. Instead, we believe that the best outcomes can be achieved by strategically considering what to integrate and how best to do it, based on each school and district's unique context. This viewpoint has been strengthened for us over the course of writing this book. This final chapter summarizes lessons we've learned along the way and what lies ahead for integration in the future.

## KEY LESSONS IN INTEGRATING SYSTEMS

We have focused on identifying the key features of integrated MTSS models and their efficient and effective implementation, while understanding that variations are needed depending on priorities, resources, and local capacity. There are many excellent resources that describe academic RTI and PBIS separately. At every turn, we have pushed each other to go beyond simply describing both systems in the same book and calling that integration. Instead, we have tried to explore what true integration really means and what that would look like from the individual student level to the district level. In the process of getting it all down on paper, six key lessons that we have learned about integrated MTSS models have become clear.

### Lesson 1: Integrate Strategically

The first lesson is the notion that an integrated approach is best accomplished strategically. Although maintaining parallel systems is less efficient and can add to conflict and confusion about priorities and responsibilities, we need to make sure that integration adds real value. In theory, full integration improves effectiveness, efficiency, and ease of use, but we can't afford to add more complexity to educational systems that are already stressed. Strategic integration is thus a viable middle road between parallel systems and full integration. In strategic integration, we look for the easiest and most logical aspects to integrate before taking on more painful change. In our experience, it is easier to start by integrating systems at Tiers 2 and 3 than at Tier 1. Because of the importance of considering individual needs of the whole child when planning support, we do better when we have the same team looking at both types of data, with more options for intervention. Using this planful, sequential, and systematic approach can avoid an undue burden on teachers and educational systems.

## Lesson 2: Function Is More Important Than Form

As we have discussed in the case study chapters, schools and districts implement integrated MTSS models in different ways. In our experience, it is more important to focus on implementing critical features and addressing key functions than trying to replicate the exact form of these examples. The case studies illustrate a wide range of how different districts and states integrate systems, and each study is based on its particular context, including policy, priority, and capacity. We acknowledge and have come to appreciate that integration takes place in different forms. Instead of stipulating one way to do it, it is probably better to identify how the various elements described in this book could fit with the local school or district context and then be open to the shape that develops.

## Lesson 3: Lead with a Team

We have learned that any initiative is better supported by a team working as a unit than by a single, motivated leader or a group of individuals working separately. The number and makeup of teams will vary from school to school and district to district, but the critical features underlying integrated MTSS models are the *use of teams* and *effective teaming processes*. It is unreasonable and unfair to rely on teachers' heroic individual performances every single day. Although the bottom line of education is to provide the individual student with high-quality instruction by the educator, we know that this outcome is more attainable and sustainable through a collaborative schoolwide approach guided by school leadership teams, which are supported in their implementation by district teams.

## Lesson 4: Focus on Doing a Few Things Well

An important lesson is that we should not only choose the most effective practices, but also create the systems needed to support implementation of the practices with fidelity. Whenever we choose to implement a practice, we should do it with as much commitment to ensuring fidelity as possible. With current levels of educational funding, we do not have the resources to implement every good idea or everything that that we would like to do. This acknowledgment means that we are better off implementing fewer initiatives well than more initiatives poorly. It also highlights the importance of increasing the support provided to educators, embedding MTSS into existing structures and key initiatives, and removing barriers to implementation.

### Lesson 5: Integration Is Hard Work

Integration has at least a few things going for it. Both academic RTI and PBIS share common features that make them easier to integrate (e.g., team approach, focus on effective instructional practices, data-based decision making). In addition, for most schools, integration will be viewed as building on previous successes. However, all change is difficult, even when we know that this change will lead to improvement in outcomes we value. There are so many tasks competing for our time, focus, and energy. Integration requires new learning and negotiating new roles in collaboration. There is always resistance to doing things differently, as well as turf wars when budgets are merged. At times, we may need to seek support from administrators with the level of authority to force us to work together for the benefit of students. At times, it may seem easier to go back to the status quo of having separate systems. George Batsche uses the analogy that an integrated MTSS model is like a blended family: At the end of the day, somebody's couch is going to end up on the curb. Any change is hard, but it is even more difficult to give up or share ownership of systems that have produced such great student outcomes. It is important not to gloss over this very real challenge to integration.

### Lesson 6: Integration Is Worth the Effort

Given the hard work involved in integration, it is easy to overlook what is gained from it. Yet there are so many advantages to taking on the challenge. An integrated MTSS model holds amazing promise for improving student outcomes and developing more efficient, effective, and sustainable systems. As we discussed in Chapter 2, research supports the effectiveness of an integrated MTSS approach over parallel systems. If we return to George Batsche's metaphor of a blended family, when we integrate, we might lose a couch but gain a nice big-screen TV. During times of uncertainty about integration, we need to help people focus on what is gained rather than only on what could be lost in the process.

## WHAT WE STILL NEED TO KNOW

Although we've learned much about an integrated approach over the past few years, this understanding is still emerging, and we all still need to know more about refining the process and implementation roles for key individuals, such as teachers and administrators. Many more questions remain. As we've described, integrated models have considerable promise, and they will have even more potential once the following important questions are answered.

### Data

We probably know more about the collection and use of data than we know about any other feature of an integrated MTSS model. There are established tools for assessing student outcomes and fidelity of implementation across domains and content areas, and the analysis process and decision rules generalize fairly well. In addition, it is clear that having integrated data warehouses to store and access the different data sources would be incredibly helpful for teams. However, there are many obstacles to making this vision a reality. Data systems are typically created to collect, store, and summarize specific sources of data; however, they are often incompatible with other data systems. These systems do not typically interact effectively with one another. Moreover, technologies for making data systems compatible across systems and third-party vendors (i.e., technology companies) are always shifting, and thus there is currently no standard for integration. In some cases, there is a disincentive for vendors to allow integration because of the cost of updating software code, as well as their interest in marketing their own products. We need to learn how to encourage a concerted effort from districts and states to demand that vendors allow and facilitate integration across different data systems.

## Practices

When discussing integrated MTSS models, it is fairly easy to consider behavior and literacy together in the elementary grades, but straying too far from these content areas and age groups (particularly in academics) highlights how much we need to know about effective interventions across the spectrum of domains and school types. Although the same principles of effective instruction apply, it appears that there are enough differences between literacy and other content areas that we need to vary our practices. However, we can build on our experiences implementing systems in literacy and behavior to help us when we implement in less familiar ground. Yet moving from elementary to middle and high schools presents challenges to our fundamental ideas about prevention and what interventions are feasible in complex systems (Flannery, Sugai, & Anderson, 2009; Vaughn et al., 2010). We need to know more about what adaptations are needed to implement RTI systems with adolescents. The organizational structures and the focus of high schools on content-rich courses require more attention to building an array of effective practices geared to secondary students.

## Teaming

Along with other researchers and practitioners, we note that a team approach is absolutely essential for implementing any kind of educational systems change. We also recommend that schools and districts take advantage of existing teaming structures instead of creating new teams solely for the purpose of implementing integrated MTSS. However, there are times when adding too many items to one team's agenda prevents the team from addressing any item fully. Can a school leadership team that works effectively on Tier 1 literacy also add behavior support and still function well? What about adding mathematics? Written expression? Tier 2? Tier 3? We don't have the evidence base to tell us the perfect configuration or the right balance between effectiveness and efficiency. Future research in integrated MTSS models may not identify one optimal teaming structure for every school (or even most schools), but hopefully at least some empirical guidance will emerge.

## Integration

A great deal of time and effort go into the process of implementing integrated MTSS models. We can suggest how to begin this process based on our own experiences, but these suggestions represent our best guess, without research indicating the most empirically supported approach. Is it best to invest in an individual domain first before integration? If so, is it better to start with behavior or academics? Or do we invest in an integrated MTSS model from the start rather than building on successes from individual systems? These are large questions that need large-scale research to answer. However, we may very well find that each answer depends on the context. In many cases, thoughtful teams can make wise decisions about the particulars of integration when they have the right data.

## NEW DIRECTIONS FOR INTEGRATED MTSS MODELS

As this work on integration is emerging, it will become increasingly important to expand the general concept of integration beyond literacy and behavior, furthering the work into numeracy, writing, and content-area instruction. We feel that the future will include work in both integration and alignment in areas that cut across special and general education systems in education and other fields. By *integration*, we mean that each system's actual components are blended to create a functional single system. By *alignment*, we mean that the core features of systems are systematically compared, adjusted, and coordinated for effective and efficient parallel performance without friction, all within an overall system with the same overarching goals. We mention alignment here because when we move beyond systems within education, state and federal laws or structures may not allow true integration across social service agencies. There are two main areas that we suggest for future MTSS work: (1) integrating vertically and horizontally to form comprehensive educational systems and (2) expanding beyond educational systems to social service agencies and public health services.

### Integrating to Form Comprehensive Educational Systems

In this book, the primary unit of implementation has been the school level, and the primary unit of support has been the district level. This focus is a perfectly reasonable starting point (especially for school personnel), but at some point, mature initiatives would strongly benefit from integrating and aligning at regional, state, and federal levels (McIntosh, Mercer, et al., in press). There are many serious challenges in education that cannot be tackled sustainably without a broad systems approach, which often means coordination with policymakers. For example, we should take the opportunity to learn how to best embed an integrated MTSS model within new state curriculum and college and career readiness standards to clarify how MTSS connects with these standards. Another example of integrating comprehensive systems involves linking MTSS with teacher evaluation schemes. Instead of simply viewing evaluation as a dubious way to identify and remove underperforming teachers, districts and states can link evaluation criteria to objective MTSS competencies and then identify professional development activities that will enhance effectiveness.

### Expanding beyond Educational Systems

At the federal level, there has been a recent emphasis on collaborating across agencies to improve outcomes for students even further. For example, the U.S. Departments of Education and Justice have collaborated on the Supportive School Discipline Initiative (U.S. Department of Justice, 2011) and Nondiscriminatory Provision of School Discipline (U.S. Departments of

Education and Justice, 2014). The knowledge gained through implementing integrated MTSS systems within a school setting may contribute to leveraging integration with systems that exist outside of education but also serve students and their families. The *interconnected systems framework* (Barrett et al., 2013) shows how school teams using a PBIS approach can work collaboratively with community-based mental health providers and other social services. Some social problems (e.g., homelessness, poverty, community violence, and substance abuse) clearly affect student learning but are so enormous that they require more resources and approaches than can be addressed through education alone. However, working in an integrated approach with other agencies has significant potential to improve outcomes on a societal level. Although such cross-agency integration and alignment makes good sense, it will require new approaches to addressing barriers to integration, such as constraints in how funds are utilized.

## FINAL THOUGHTS

Regardless of what we still need to know and the enormity of these new directions, we are thoroughly optimistic about education and the role of integrated MTSS models in it. When looking back at the history of systems in schools shared in Chapter 1, we see that previous challenges included agreeing on what constitutes valid measures and effective practices. Although these debates are not fully settled, the tools and strategies available to today's educators are more advanced than ever before. In the same way, we have made progress in terms of developing systems for implementing academic and behavior models that have been shown to improve student outcomes. Academic RTI and PBIS represent true sea changes in education. We also better understand the systems required to ensure that effective practices can be implemented with fidelity and durability. This work is difficult, but it has advanced from simply developing effective practices and accurate measures, to developing these systems for effective implementation of practices and data, and now to the challenge of integrating them for even more effectiveness and efficiency. Although any single content area or instructional strategy is important, we know that it is the combination of each and all of these that defines a comprehensive and quality education. This blending of our work is one of the key promises of integration. There are many paths to integrated MTSS models and improved student outcomes, and we hope that this book is useful as a roadmap for the work ahead.

# References

Adams, M. J. (1990). *Beginning to read: Thinking and learning about print.* Cambridge, MA: MIT Press.

Adelman, H. S., & Taylor, L. (2003). On sustainability of project innovations as systemic change. *Journal of Educational and Psychological Consultation, 14,* 1–25.

Albin, R. W., Lucyshyn, J. M., Horner, R. H., & Flannery, K. B. (1996). Contextual fit for behavioral support plans: A model for "goodness of fit." In L. K. Koegel, R. L. Koegel, & G. Dunlap (Eds.), *Positive behavioral support: Including people with difficult behavior in the community* (pp. 81–98). Baltimore, MD: Brookes.

Albin, R. W., & Todd, A. W. (2015). Application of a multielement positive behavior interventions and supports plan for Alie, an elementary student with intellectual disabilities. In F. Brown, J. Anderson, & R. L. DePry (Eds.), *Individual positive behavior supports: A standards-based guide to practices in school and community-based settings* (pp. 463–480). Baltimore, MD: Brookes.

Algozzine, K. M., & Algozzine, B. (2007). Classroom instructional ecology and school-wide positive behavior support. *Journal of Applied School Psychology, 24,* 29–47.

Algozzine, R. F., & Algozzine, K. M. (2009). Facilitating academic achievement through schoolwide positive behavior support. In W. Sailor, G. Dunlap, G. Sugai, & R. H. Horner (Eds.), *Handbook of positive behavior support* (pp. 521–550). New York: Springer.

Algozzine, R. F., Barrett, S., Eber, L., George, H., Horner, R. H., Lewis, T. J., . . . Sugai, G. (2014). *PBIS Tiered Fidelity Inventory.* Eugene, OR: OSEP Technical Assistance Center on Positive Behavioral Interventions and Supports. Available at *www.pbis.org.*

Algozzine, R. F., Horner, R. H., Sugai, G., Barrett, S., Dickey, C. R., Eber, L., . . . Tobin, T. (2010). *Evaluation blueprint for school-wide positive behavior support* (2nd ed.). Eugene, OR: National Technical Assistance Center on Positive Behavior Interventions and Support. Retrieved from *www.pbis.org.*

Algozzine, R. F., Wang, C., & Violette, A. S. (2011). Reexamining the relationship between academic achievement and social behavior. *Journal of Positive Behavior Interventions, 13,* 3–16.

Allen, S. J., & Blackston, A. R. (2003). Training preservice teachers in collaborative problem solving: An investigation of the impact on teacher and student behavior change in real-world settings. *School Psychology Quarterly, 18,* 22–51.

Anderson, C. M., Childs, K., Kincaid, D., Horner, R. H., George, H., Todd, A. W., . . . Spaulding, S. A. (2012). *Benchmarks for advanced tiers.* Unpublished instrument, Educational and Community Supports, University of Oregon & University of South Florida.

Andreou, T. E., McIntosh, K., Ross, S. W., & Kahn, J. D. (2015). Critical incidents in the sustainability of school-wide positive behavioral interventions and supports. *Journal of Special Education, 49,* 157–167.

Archer, A. L., & Gleason, M. M. (1990). *Skills for school success.* North Billerica, MA: Curriculum Associates.

Archer, A. L., Gleason, M. M., & Vachon, V. (2006). *REWARDS (Reading Excellence, Word Attack, and Rate Development Strategies)* (2nd ed.). Longmont, CO: Sopris West Educational Services.

Archer, A. L., & Hughes, C. A. (2011). *Explicit instruction: Effective and efficient teaching.* New York: Guilford Press.

Arnold, E. M., Goldston, D. B., Walsh, A. K., Reboussin, B. A., Daniel, S. S., Hickman, E., & Wood, F. B. (2005). Severity of emotional and behavioral problems among poor and typical readers. *Journal of Abnormal Child Psychology, 33,* 205–217.

Ayllon, T., Layman, D., & Burke, S. (1972). Disruptive behavior and reinforcement of academic performance. *The Psychological Record, 22,* 315–323.

Ayllon, T., & Roberts, M. D. (1974). Eliminating discipline problems by strengthening academic performance. *Journal of Applied Behavior Analysis, 7,* 71–76.

Baker, S. K., Fien, H., & Baker, D. L. (2010). Robust reading instruction in the early grades: Conceptual and practical issues in the integration and evaluation of Tier 1 and Tier 2 instructional supports. *Focus on Exceptional Children, 42*(9), 1–20.

Baker, S. K., Gersten, R., Dimino, J. A., & Griffiths, R. (2004). The sustained use of research-based instructional practice: A case study of peer-assisted learning strategies in mathematics. *Remedial and Special Education, 25,* 5–24.

Barrett, P. (2004). *FRIENDS for life: Group leader's manual for children.* Bowen Hills, Queensland, Australia: Academic Press.

Barrett, S., Eber, L., & Weist, M. (Eds.). (2013). *Advancing education effectiveness: Interconnecting school mental health and school-wide positive behavior support.* Eugene, OR: OSEP Center for Positive Behavioral Interventions and Supports.

Barrish, H. H., Saunders, M., & Wolf, M. M. (1969). Good Behavior Game: Effects of individual contingencies for group consequences on disruptive behavior in a classroom. *Journal of Applied Behavior Analysis, 2,* 119–124.

Barton-Arwood, S. M., Wehby, J. H., & Falk, K. B. (2005). Reading instruction for elementary-age students with emotional and behavioral disorders: Academic and behavioral outcomes. *Exceptional Children, 72,* 7–27.

Bear, G. G., Gaskins, C., Blank, J., & Chen, F. F. (2011). Delaware School Climate Survey—Student: Its factor structure, concurrent validity, and reliability. *Journal of School Psychology, 49,* 157–174.

Bearman, S. K., Ugueto, A., Alleyne, A., & Weisz, J. R. (2010). Adapting cognitive-behavioral therapy for depression to fit diverse youths and contexts: Applying the deployment-focused model of treatment development and testing. In A. E. Kazdin & J. R. Weisz (Eds.), *Evidence-based psychotherapies for children and adolescents* (2nd ed., pp. 466–481). New York: Guilford Press.

Becker, W. C., & Engelmann, S. (1978). Systems for basic instruction: Theory and applications. In A. Catania & T. Brigham (Eds.), *Handbook of applied behavior analysis: Social and instructional processes* (pp. 57–92). Chicago: Science Research Associates.

Benner, G. J., Nelson, J. R., Sanders, E. A., & Ralston, N. C. (2012). Behavior intervention for students with externalizing behavior problems: Primary-level standard protocol. *Exceptional Children, 78,* 181–198.

Bennett, K. J., Brown, K. S., Boyle, M., Racine, Y., & Offord, D. (2003). Does low reading achievement at school entry cause conduct problems? *Social Science and Medicine, 56,* 2443–2448.

Blase, K. A., Fixsen, D. L., Naoom, S. F., & Wallace, F. (2005). *Operationalizing implementation: Strate-*

*gies and methods.* Tampa, FL: University of South Florida, Louis de la Parte Florida Mental Health Institute.

Blase, K. A., Kiser, L., & Van Dyke, M. (2013). The hexagon tool: Exploring context. Chapel Hill, NC: National Implementation Research Network, FPG Child Development Institute, University of North Carolina.

Blase, K. A., Van Dyke, M., & Fixsen, D. (2009). Evidence-based programming in the context of practice and policy. *Social Policy Report, 23,* 13–14.

Blase, K. A., Van Dyke, M., & Fixsen, D. L. (2013). *Implementation drivers: Assessing best practices.* Chapel Hill, NC: University of North Carolina.

Bohanon, H., Goodman, S., & McIntosh, K. (2009). Integrating behavior and academic supports within RtI framework: General overview. Retrieved July 2, 2015, from *www.rtinetwork.org/learn/behavior-supports/integrating-behavior-and-academic-supports-general-overview.*

Boneshefski, M. J., & Runge, T. J. (2014). Addressing disproportionate discipline practices within a school-wide positive behavioral interventions and supports framework: A practical guide for calculating and using disproportionality rates. *Journal of Positive Behavior Interventions, 16,* 149–158.

Boyd, R. J., & Anderson, C. M. (2013). Breaks are Better: A Tier II social behavior intervention. *Journal of Behavioral Education, 22,* 348–365.

Bradley, R., Danielson, L., & Hallahan, D. P. (Eds.). (2002). *Identification of learning disabilities: Research to practice.* Mahwah, NJ: Erlbaum.

Bradshaw, C. P., Koth, C. W., Thornton, L. A., & Leaf, P. J. (2009). Altering school climate through school-wide positive behavioral interventions and supports: Findings from a group-randomized effectiveness trial. *Prevention Science, 10,* 100–115.

Bradshaw, C. P., Mitchell, M. M., & Leaf, P. J. (2010). Examining the effects of schoolwide positive behavioral interventions and supports on student outcomes: Results from a randomized controlled effectiveness trial in elementary schools. *Journal of Positive Behavior Interventions, 12,* 133–148.

Bradshaw, C. P., & Pas, E. T. (2011). A state-wide scale-up of positive behavioral interventions and supports (PBIS): A description of the development of systems of support and analysis of adoption and implementation. *School Psychology Review, 40,* 530–548.

Bradshaw, C. P., Waasdorp, T. E., & Leaf, P. J. (2012). Effects of school-wide positive behavioral interventions and supports on child behavior problems and adjustment. *Pediatrics,* e1136–e1145.

Brophy, J. (1988). Educating teachers about managing classrooms and students. *Teaching and Teacher Education, 4,* 1–18.

Brown-Chidsey, R., Bronaugh, L., & McGraw, K. (2009). *RTI in the classroom: Guidelines and recipes for success.* New York: Guilford Press.

Brown-Chidsey, R., & Steege, M. W. (2010). *Response to intervention: Principles and strategies for effective practice* (2nd ed.). New York: Guilford Press.

Bruhn, A. L., & Watt, S. (2012). Improving behavior by using multi-component self-monitoring within a targeted reading intervention. *Behavioral Disorders, 38,* 3–17.

Burke, M. D., Davis, J. L., Lee, Y., Hagan-Burke, S., Kwok, O., & Sugai, G. (2012). Universal screening for behavioral risk in elementary schools using SWPBS expectations. *Journal of Emotional and Behavioral Disorders, 20,* 38–54.

Burns, M. K., Riley-Tillman, T. C., & VanDerHeyden, A. M. (2012). *RTI applications: Vol. 1. Academic and behavioral interventions.* New York: Guilford Press.

Campbell, A. L., & Anderson, C. M. (2011). Check-in/check-out: A systematic evaluation and component analysis. *Journal of Applied Behavior Analysis, 44,* 315–326.

Caplan, G., & Grunebaum, H. (1967). Perspectives on primary prevention. *Archives of General Psychiatry, 17,* 331–346.

Carnine, D. W., Silbert, J., Kame'enui, E. J., Tarver, S. G., & Jungjohann, K. (2006). *Teaching struggling and at-risk readers: A direct instruction approach*. Columbus, OH: Pearson.

Carr, E. G. (1977). The motivation of self-injurious behavior: A review of some hypotheses. *Psychological Bulletin, 84*, 800–816.

Carroll, J. M., Maughan, B., Goodman, R., & Meltzer, H. (2005). Literacy difficulties and psychiatric disorders: Evidence for comorbidity. *Journal of Child Psychology and Psychiatry, 46*, 524–532.

Chaparro, E. A., Nese, R. N. T., & McIntosh, K. (2015). *Examples of engaging instruction to increase equity in education*. Eugene, OR: Center on Positive Behavioral Interventions and Supports. University of Oregon.

Chaparro, E. A., Park, H., Baker, S. K., & Ryan-Jackson, K. M. (2011). *District system support plan: A district level self-assessment tool* (Report No. 1102). Eugene, OR: Center on Teaching and Learning, University of Oregon.

Chaparro, E. A., Smolkowski, K., Baker, S. K., Hanson, N., & Ryan-Jackson, K. M. (2012). A model for system-wide collaboration to support integrated social behavior and literacy evidence-based practices. *Psychology in the Schools, 49*, 465–482.

Chard, D. J., & Harn, B. A. (2008). Project CIRCUITS: Center for Improving Reading Competence Using Intensive Treatments Schoolwide. In C. R. Greenwood, T. R. Kratochwill, & M. Clements (Eds.), *Schoolwide prevention models: Lessons learned in elementary schools* (pp. 143–172). New York: Guilford Press.

Childs, K. E., Kincaid, D., George, H. P., & Gage, N. A. (2016). The relationship between school-wide implementation of positive behavior intervention and supports and student discipline outcomes. *Journal of Positive Behavior Interventions, 18*, 89–99.

Christenson, S. L., Reschly, A. L., Appleton, J. J., Berman-Young, S., Spanjers, D. M., & Varro, P. (2008). Best practices in fostering student engagement. In A. Thomas & J. P. Grimes (Eds.), *Best practices in school psychology V* (pp. 1099–1119). Bethesda, MD: National Association of School Psychologists.

Coburn, C. E. (2003). Rethinking scale: Moving beyond numbers to deep and lasting change. *Educational Researcher, 32*(6), 3–12.

Coffey, J., & Horner, R. H. (2012). The sustainability of school-wide positive behavioral interventions and supports. *Exceptional Children, 78*, 407–422.

Coie, J. D., & Krehbiel, G. (1984). Effects of academic tutoring on the social status of low achieving, socially rejected children. *Child Development, 55*, 1465–1478.

Collaborative for Academic Social and Emotional Learning. (2003). *Safe and sound: An educational leader's guide to evidence-based social and emotional learning programs*. Chicago: Author.

Committee for Children. (1997). *Second Step: A violence prevention curriculum* Seattle, WA: Author.

Cook, B. G., & Odom, S. L. (2013). Evidence-based practices and implementation science in special education. *Exceptional Children, 79*, 135–144.

Cook, C. R., Dart, E., Collins, T., Restori, A., Daikos, C., & Delport, J. (2012). Prelimiary study of the confined, collateral, and combined effects of reading and behavioral interventions: Evidence for a transactional relationship. *Behavioral Disorders, 38*, 38–56.

Cornell, D. G. (2006). *School violence: Fears vs. facts*. Mahwah, NJ: Erlbaum.

Coyne, M. D., Kame'enui, E. J., & Carnine, D. (2007). *Effective teaching strategies that accommodate diverse learners* (3rd ed.). Bloomington, MN: Pearson.

Cronbach, L. J. (1957). The two disciplines of scientific psychology. *American Psychologist, 12*, 671–684.

Cronbach, L. J. (1975). Beyond the two disciplines of scientific psychology. *American Psychologist, 30*, 116–127.

Crone, D. A., Hawken, L. S., & Horner, R. H. (2010). *Responding to problem behavior in schools: The Behavior Education Program* (2nd ed.). New York: Guilford Press.

Crone, D. A., Hawken, L. S., & Horner, R. H. (2015). *Building positive behavior support systems in schools: Functional behavioral assessment* (2nd ed.). New York: Guilford Press.

Cummings, J. G., Pepler, D. J., Mishna, F., & Craig, W. M. (2006). Bullying and victimization among students with exceptionalities. *Exceptionality Education Canada, 16,* 193–222.

Curtis, M. J., Castillo, J. M., & Cohen, R. (2008). Best practices in system-level change. In A. Thomas & J. P. Grimes (Eds.), *Best practices in school psychology V* (pp. 887–901). Bethesda, MD: National Association of School Psychologists.

Daly, E. J., Neugebauer, S., Chafouleas, S. M., & Skinner, C. H. (2015). *Interventions for reading problems: Designing and evaluating effective strategies* (2nd ed.). New York: Guilford Press.

Darch, C. B., & Kame'enui, E. J. (2003). *Instructional classroom management: A proactive approach to behavior management* (2nd ed.). Upper Saddle River, NJ: Prentice Hall.

Darney, D., Reinke, W. M., Herman, K. C., Stormont, M., & Ialongo, N. S. (2013). Children with co-occurring academic and behavior problems in first grade: Distal outcomes in twelfth grade. *Journal of School Psychology, 51,* 117–128.

Dawson, P., & Guare, R. (2010). *Executive skills in children and adolescents: A practical guide to assessment and intervention* (2nd ed.). New York: Guilford Press.

Deno, S. L. (1989). Curriculum-based measurement and special education services: A fundamental and direct relationship. In M. R. Shinn (Ed.), *Curriculum-based measurement: Assessing special children* (pp. 1–17). New York: Guilford Press.

Deno, S. L. (1995). School psychologist as problem solver. In A. Thomas & J. P. Grimes (Eds.), *Best practices in school psychology III* (pp. 471–484). Bethesda, MD: National Association of School Psychologists.

Deno, S. L., & Mirkin, P. K. (1977). *Data-based program modification: A manual.* Reston, VA: Council for Exceptional Children.

DiPerna, J. C., Volpe, R. J., & Elliott, S. N. (2002). A model of academic and elementary reading/language arts achievement. *School Psychology Review, 31,* 298–312.

Dishion, T. J., French, D. C., & Patterson, G. R. (1995). The development and ecology of antisocial behavior. In D. Cicchetti & D. J. Cohen (Eds.), *Developmental psychopathology: Vol. 2. Risk, disorder, and adaptation* (pp. 421–471). New York: Wiley.

Dishion, T. J., & Snyder, J. (Eds.). (2016). *Handbook of coercive relationship dynamics: Basic mechanisms, developmental processes, and intervention applications.* New York: Oxford University Press.

Dixon, R., & Carnine, D. W. (1994). Ideologies, practices, and their implications for special education. *Journal of Special Education, 28,* 356–367.

Drummond, T. (1994). *The Student Risk Screening Scale (SRSS).* Grants Pass, OR: Josephine County Mental Health Program.

Duda, M. A., Ingram-West, K., Tadesco, M., Putnam, D., Buenerostro, M., Chaparro, E. A., & Horner, R. H. (2012). *District Capacity Assessment.* Unpublished instrument. Chapel Hill, NC: University of North Carolina.

Duncan, G. J., Dowsett, C. J., Claessens, A., Magnuson, K., Huston, A. C., Klebanov, P., . . . Brooks-Gunn, J. (2007). School readiness and later achievement. *Developmental Psychology, 43,* 1428–1446.

Durlak, J. A., Weissburg, R. P., Dymnicki, A. B., Taylor, R. D., & Schellinger, K. B. (2011). The impact of enhancing students' social and emotional learning: A meta-analysis of school-based universal interventions. *Child Development, 82,* 405–432.

Dweck, C. S. (1975). The role of expectations and attributions in the alleviation of learned helplessness. *Journal of Personality and Social Psychology, 31,* 674–685.

Eaker, R., Dufour, R., & Dufour, R. (2002). *Getting started: Reculturing schools to become professional learning communities.* Bloomington, IN: Solution Tree.

Eber, L., Hyde, K., & Suter, J. C. (2011). Integrating wraparound into a schoolwide system of positive behavior supports. *Journal of Child and Family Studies, 20,* 782–790.

Elliott, S. N., & Fuchs, L. S. (1997). The utility of curriculum-based measurement and performance assessment as alternatives to traditional intelligence and achievement tests. *School Psychology Review, 26,* 224–233.

Embry, D. D., & Biglan, A. (2008). Evidence-based kernels: Fundamental units of behavioral influence. *Clinical Child and Family Psychology Review, 11,* 75–113.

Ervin, R. A., Schaughency, E., Goodman, S. D., McGlinchey, M. T., & Matthews, A. (2006). Merging research and practice agendas to address reading and behavior school-wide. *School Psychology Review, 35,* 198–223.

Ervin, R. A., Schaughency, E., Goodman, S. D., McGlinchey, M. T., & Matthews, A. (2007). Moving from a model demonstration project to a statewide initiative in Michigan: Lessons learned from merging research–practice agendas to address reading and behavior. In S. R. Jimerson, M. K. Burns, & A. M. VanDerHeyden (Eds.), *Handbook of response to intervention: The science and practice of assessment and intervention* (pp. 354–377). New York: Springer.

Fairbanks, S., Simonsen, B., & Sugai, G. (2008). Classwide secondary and tertiary tier practices and systems. *Teaching Exceptional Children, 40*(6), 44–54.

Feuerborn, L., Wallace, C., & Tyre, A. D. (2013). Gaining staff support for schoolwide positive behavior supports: A guide for teams. *Beyond Behavior, 22*(2), 27–34.

Filter, K. J., & Horner, R. H. (2009). Function-based academic interventions for problem behavior. *Education and Treatment of Children, 32,* 1–19.

Fisher, A. V., Godwin, K. E., & Seltman, H. (2014). Visual environment, attention allocation, and learning in young children: When too much of a good thing may be bad. *Psychological Science, 25,* 1362–1370.

Fisher, C. W., Berliner, D. C., Filby, N. N., Marliave, R., Cahen, L. S., & Dishaw, M. M. (1981). Teaching behaviors, academic learning time, and student achievement: An overview. *Journal of Classroom Interaction, 17,* 2–15.

Fixsen, D. L., Blase, K., Horner, R., & Sugai, G. (2008). *Developing the capacity for scaling up the effective use of evidence-based programs in state departments of education.* Chapel Hill, NC: University of North Carolina.

Fixsen, D. L., Blase, K. A., Horner, R. H., & Sugai, G. (2009a). *Scaling up brief.* Chapel Hill, NC: University of North Carolina.

Fixsen, D. L., Blase, K. A., Horner, R. H., & Sugai, G. (2009b, February). *Intensive technical assistance: Scaling up brief #2.* Chapel Hill, NC: University of North Carolina.

Fixsen, D., Blase, K., Metz, A., & Van Dyke, M. (2013). Statewide implementation of evidence-based programs. *Exceptional Children, 79,* 213–230.

Fixsen, D. L., Naoom, S. F., Blase, K. A., Friedman, R. M., & Wallace, F. (2005). *Implementation research: Synthesis of the literature.* Tampa, FL: University of South Florida, Louis de la Parte Florida Mental Health Institute, National Implementation Research Network (FMHI Publication #231).

Flannery, K. B., Sugai, G., & Anderson, C. M. (2009). School-wide positive behavior support in high school: Early lessons learned. *Journal of Positive Behavior Interventions, 11,* 177–185.

Flay, B. R., Biglan, A., Boruch, R. F., Castro, F. G., Gottfredson, D., Kellam, S., . . . Ji, P. (2005). Standards of evidence: Criteria for efficacy, effectiveness, and dissemination. *Prevention Science, 6,* 151–175.

Fleming, C. B., Harachi, T. W., Cortes, R. C., Abbott, R. D., & Catalano, R. F. (2004). Level and change in reading scores and attention problems during elementary school as predictors of problem behavior in middle school. *Journal of Emotional and Behavioral Disorders, 12,* 130–144.

Florida Statewide Response to Instruction/Intervention Implementation Plan. (2008). Retrieved August 1, 2013, from *http://florida-rti.org/floridaMTSS/RtI.pdf.*

Florida's MTSS. (2013). *Self-assessment of MTSS implementation.* Unpublished instrument. Tampa, FL: University of South Florida.

Florida's Positive Behavior Support Project. (2004). *Children's literature: Tools for teaching school-wide expectations and rules.* Tampa, FL: University of South Florida.

Fuchs, D., Fuchs, L. S., Mathes, P. G., & Martinez, E. A. (2002). Preliminary evidence on the social standing of students with learning disabilities in PALS and no-PALS classrooms. *Learning Disabilities Research and Practice, 17,* 205–215.

Fuchs, D., Mock, D., Morgan, P. L., & Young, C. L. (2003). Responsiveness-to-intervention: Definitions, evidence, and implications for the learning disabilities construct. *Learning Disabilities Research and Practice, 18,* 157–171.

Fuchs, L. S. (1995). *Curriculum-based measurement and eligibility decision making: An emphasis on treatment validity and growth* [Commissioned paper]. Washington, DC: National Academy of Sciences.

Fuchs, L. S., & Fuchs, D. (1998). Treatment validity: A unifying concept for reconceptualizing the identification of learning disabilities. *Learning Disabilities Research and Practice, 13,* 204–219.

Fuchs, L. S., Fuchs, D., Yazdian, L., & Powell, S. R. (2002). Enhancing first-grade children's mathematical development with peer-assisted learning strategies. *School Psychology Review, 31,* 569–583.

Furey, J., & Stoner, G. (2015). *Multi-tiered systems of support needs assessment* [Excel workbook for use by school personnel]. Unpublished instrument. Retrieved from *https://sites.google.com/site/mtssneedsassessment.*

Garbacz, S. A., McIntosh, K., Eagle, J., Dowd-Eagle, S., Hirano, K., & Ruppert, T. (2016). Family engagement within School-wide Positive Behavioral Interventions and Supports. *Preventing School Failure,* 60–69.

George, H. P., & Kincaid, D. K. (2008). Building district-level capacity for positive behavior support. *Journal of Positive Behavior Interventions, 10,* 20–32.

Gersten, R. (2013, March). *A candid look at RTI mathematics.* Invited keynote presentation at MiBLSi State Implementer's Conference, Lansing, MI.

Gersten, R., Chard, D. J., & Baker, S. (2000). Factors enhancing sustained use of research-based instructional practices. *Journal of Learning Disabilities, 33,* 445–457.

Gersten, R., Compton, D., Connor, D., Dimino, J., Santoro, L., Linan-Thompson, S., & Tilly, W. D. (2008). *Assisting students struggling with reading: Response to intervention and multi-tier intervention in the primary grades. A practice guide.* (NCEE 2009-4045). Washington, DC: National Center for Education Evaluation and Regional Assistance, Institute of Education Sciences, U.S. Department of Education. Retrieved from *http://ies.ed.gov/ncee/wwc/publications/practiceguides.*

Gersten, R., Fuchs, L. S., Compton, D., Coyne, M., Greenwood, C., & Innocenti, M. S. (2005). Quality indicators for group experimental and quasi-experimental research in special education. *Exceptional Children, 71,* 149–165.

Gietz, C., & McIntosh, K. (2014). Relations between student perceptions of their school environment and academic achievement. *Canadian Journal of School Psychology, 29,* 161–176.

Gilbert, T. F. (1978). *Human competence: Engineering worthy performance.* New York: McGraw-Hill. (Tribute Edition published in 1996 by HRD Press and ISPI Publications, Washington, DC.)

Gladwell, M. (2006). *The tipping point: How little things can make a big difference.* New York: Little, Brown.

GlobalScholar. (2011). *Response to intervention (RTI) adoption survey 2011.* Bellevue, WA: GlobalScholar/Spectrum K12.

Good, C., McIntosh, K., & Gietz, C. (2011). Integrating bullying prevention into school-wide positive behavior support. *Teaching Exceptional Children, 44*(1), 48–56.

Good, R. H., Gruba, J., & Kaminski, R. A. (2002). Best practices in using Dynamic Indicators of Basic Early Literacy Skills (DIBELS) in an outcomes-driven model. In A. Thomas & J. P. Grimes (Eds.), *Best practices in school psychology IV* (pp. 699–720). Bethesda, MD: National Association of School Psychologists.

Good, R. H., & Kaminski, R. A. (Eds.). (2010). *Dynamic Indicators of Basic Early Literacy Skills* (7th ed.). Eugene, OR: Dynamic Measurement Group. Available at *http://dibels.org.*

Goodman, S. (2005, October). *Implementation of reading and behavior support at the state level.* Paper presented at the PBIS Forum, Chicago.

Goodman, S. D. (2013a). Implementation of a district-wide multi-tiered system of supports (MTSS) initiative through stages of implementation. *Utah Special Educator, 35,* 20–21.

Goodman, S. D. (2013b). About MiBLSi. *Michigan's integrated behavior and learning support initiative.* Retrieved November 1, 2013, from *http://miblsi.org/About.aspx.*

Gordon, R. S. (1983). An operational classification of disease prevention. *Public Health Reports, 98,* 107–109.

Gottman, J. M., Coan, J., Carrere, S., & Swanson, C. (1998). Predicting marital happiness and stability from newlywed interactions. *Journal of Marriage and the Family, 60,* 5–22.

Gray, S. A. O., Carter, A. S., Briggs-Gowan, M. J., Jones, S. M., & Wagmiller, R. L. (2014). Growth trajectories of early aggression, overactivity, and inattention: Relations to second-grade reading. *Developmental Psychology, 50,* 2255–2263.

Greenberg, M. T., Weissburg, R. P., & O'Brien, M. E. (2003). Enhancing school-based prevention and youth development through coordinated social, emotional, and academic learning. *American Psychologist, 58,* 466–474.

Greenwood, C. R., Horton, B. T., & Utley, C. A. (2002). Academic engagement: Current perspectives on research and practice. *School Psychology Review, 31,* 328–349.

Gregory, A., Skiba, R. J., & Noguera, P. A. (2010). The achievement gap and the discipline gap: Two sides of the same coin? *Educational Researcher, 39,* 59–68.

Gresham, F. M. (1989). Assessment of treatment integrity in school consultation and prereferral intervention. *School Psychology Review, 18,* 37–50.

Gresham, F. M. (1991). Conceptualizing behavior disorders in terms of resistance to intervention. *School Psychology Review, 20,* 23–36.

Gunn, B., Biglan, A., Smolkowski, K., & Ary, D. (2000). The efficacy of supplemental instruction in decoding skills for Hispanic and non-Hispanic students in early elementary school. *Journal of Special Education, 34,* 90–103.

Hall, T. E., Meyer, A., & Rose, D. H. (2012). *Universal design for learning in the classroom: Practical applications.* New York: Guilford Press.

Harry, B., & Klingner, J. K. (2014). *Why are so many minority students in special education?: Understanding race & disability in schools* (2nd ed.). New York: Teachers College Press.

Hattie, J. (2009). *Visible learning: A synthesis of over 800 meta-analyses relating to achievement.* Oxford, UK: Routledge.

Hayes, S. C., Wilson, K. G., Gifford, E. V., Follette, V. M., & Strosahl, K. (1996). Experiential avoidance and behavioral disorders: A functional dimensional approach to diagnosis and treatment. *Journal of Consulting and Clinical Psychology, 64,* 1152–1168.

Heath, S. B. (1980). The functions and uses of literacy. *Journal of Communication, 30,* 123–133.

Heifetz, R. A., Grashow, A., & Linksy, M. (2009). *The practice of adaptive leadership: Tools and tactics for changing your organization and the world.* Cambridge, MA: Harvard Business Press.

Herman, K. C., Lambert, S. F., Reinke, W. M., & Ialongo, N. S. (2008). Low academic competence in first grade as a risk factor for depressive cognitions and symptoms in middle school. *Journal of Counseling Psychology, 55,* 400–410.

Hinshaw, S. P. (1992). Externalizing behavior problems and academic underachievement in childhood and adolescence: Causal relationships and underlying mechanisms. *Psychological Bulletin, 111,* 127–155.

Horner, R. H., Carr, E. G., Halle, J., McGee, G., Odom, S., & Wolery, M. (2005). The use of single-subject research to identify evidence-based practice in special education. *Exceptional Children, 71,* 165–180.

Horner, R. H., McDonnell, J. J., & Bellamy, G. T. (1985). Teaching generalized behaviors: General case instruction in simulation and community settings. In R. H. Horner, L. H. Meyer, & H. D. Fredericks (Eds.), *Education of learners with severe handicaps: Exemplary service strategies* (pp. 289–315). Baltimore, MD: Brookes.

Horner, R. H., & McIntosh, K. (2016). Reducing coercion in schools: The impact of School-wide Positive Behavioral Interventions and Supports. In T. Dishion & J. Snyder (Eds.), *Handbook of coercive relationship dynamics: Basic mechanisms, developmental processes, and intervention applications* (pp. 330–340). New York: Oxford University Press.

Horner, R. H., Sampson, N. K., Anderson, C. M., Todd, A. W., & Eliason, B. M. (2013). *Monitoring advanced tiers tool.* Unpublished instrument, Educational and Community Supports, University of Oregon.

Horner, R. H., & Sugai, G. (2006). *Policy brief: Scaling up effective educational innovation.* Policy brief prepared at the request of the U.S. Department of Education, Office of Special Education Programs, Washington, DC.

Horner, R. H., Sugai, G., & Anderson, C. M. (2010). Examining the evidence base for school-wide positive behavior support. *Focus on Exceptional Children, 42*(8), 1–14.

Horner, R. H., Sugai, G., Smolkowski, K., Eber, L., Nakasato, J., Todd, A. W., & Esparanza, J. (2009). A randomized, wait-list controlled effectiveness trial assessing school-wide positive behavior support in elementary schools. *Journal of Positive Behavior Interventions, 11,* 133–144.

Horner, R. H., Sugai, G., & Todd, A. W. (2001). "Data" need not be a four-letter word: Using data to improve schoolwide discipline. *Beyond Behavior, 11*(1), 20–26.

Horner, R. H., Sugai, G., Todd, A. W., & Lewis-Palmer, T. (2005). Schoolwide positive behavior support: An alternative approach to discipline in schools. In L. M. Bambara & L. Kern (Eds.), *Individualized supports for students with problem behaviors: Designing positive behavior plans* (pp. 359–390). New York: Guilford Press.

Horner, R. H., & Todd, A. W. (2002). *Targeted interventions: A reference guide for function-based support options.* Eugene, OR: Educational and Community Supports, University of Oregon.

Hosp, M. K., Hosp, J. L., & Howell, K. W. (2016). *The ABCs of CBM: A practical guide to curriculum-based measurement* (2nd ed.). New York: Guilford Press.

Ialongo, N. S., Werthamer, L., Kellam, S. G., Brown, C. H., Wang, S., & Lin, Y. (1999). Proximal impact of two first-grade preventive interventions on the early risk behaviors for later substance abuse, depression, and antisocial behavior. *American Journal of Community Psychology, 27,* 599–641.

Individuals with Disabilities Education Improvement Act, 20 U.S.C. § 1400 P.L. 108-446 (2004).

Intervention Planning and Assessment System. (2008) [Software and training materials]. Tigard–Tualatin, OR: Tigard–Tualatin School District. Retrieved from *www.oregonrti.org/node/174.*

Jerald, C. D. (2006). *Identifying potential dropouts: Key lessons for building an early warning data system.* New York: Carnegie Corp.

Jitendra, A. (2002). Teaching students math problem-solving through graphic representations. *Teaching Exceptional Children, 34*(4), 34–38.

Joyce, B. R., & Showers, B. (2002). *Student achievement through staff development* (3rd ed.). Alexandria, VA: ASCD.

Jussim, L. (2013). Teachers' expectations. In J. Hattie & E. Anderman (Eds.), *International guide to student achievement* (pp. 243–246). New York: Routledge.

Kalberg, J. R., Lane, K. L., & Menzies, H. M. (2010). Using systematic screening procedures to identify students who are nonresponsive to primary prevention efforts: Integrating academic and behavioral measures. *Education and Treatment of Children, 33,* 561–584.

Kame'enui, E. J., & Simmons, D. C. (2002). *Planning and Evaluation Tool for Effective Schoolwide Reading Programs—Revised (PET-R)*. Eugene, OR: Institute for the Development of Educational Achievement.

Kame'enui, E. J., Simmons, D. C., & Coyne, M. D. (2000). Schools as host environments: Toward a school-wide reading improvement model. *Annals of Dyslexia, 50,* 31–51.

Kamphaus, R. W., & Reynolds, C. R. (2007). *Behavioral and emotional screening system.* Bloomington, MN: Pearson.

Kansas MTSS Project. (2012). Timeline to Kansas multi-tier system of supports. Topeka, KS: Kansas State Department of Education.

Kellam, S. G., Mayer, L. S., Rebok, G. W., & Hawkins, W. E. (1998). Effects of improving achievement on aggressive behavior and of improving aggressive behavior on achievement through two preventive interventions: An investigation of causal paths. In B. P. Dohrenwend (Ed.), *Adversity, stress, and psychopathology* (pp. 486–505). London: Oxford University Press.

Kelm, J. L., & McIntosh, K. (2012). Effects of school-wide positive behavior support on teacher self-efficacy. *Psychology in the Schools, 49,* 137–147.

Kelm, J. L., McIntosh, K., & Cooley, S. (2014). Effects of implementing school-wide positive behaviour interventions and supports on problem behaviour and academic achievement in a Canadian elementary school. *Canadian Journal of School Psychology, 29,* 195–212.

Kincaid, D., Childs, K., & George, H. (2005). *School-wide benchmarks of quality.* Unpublished instrument, University of South Florida, Tampa, FL.

Kratochwill, T. R., & Shernoff, E. S. (2004). Evidence-based practice: Promoting evidence-based interventions in school psychology. *School Psychology Review, 33,* 34–48.

Kratochwill, T. R., & Stoiber, K. C. (2002). Evidence-based interventions in school psychology: Conceptual foundations of the Procedural and Coding Manual of Division 16 and the Society for the Study of School Psychology Task Force. *School Psychology Quarterly, 17,* 341–389.

Kusché, C., & Greenberg, M. T. (1994). *The PATHS curriculum: Instructor's manual.* South Deerfield, MA: Channing Bete.

Lane, K. L. (1999). Young students at risk for antisocial behavior: The utility of academic and social skills interventions. *Journal of Emotional and Behavioral Disorders, 7,* 211–223.

Lane, K. L., & Menzies, H. M. (2005). Teacher-identified students with and without academic and behavioral concerns: Characteristics and responsiveness. *Behavioral Disorders, 31,* 65–83.

Lane, K. L., Menzies, H. M., Oakes, W. P., & Kalberg, J. R. (2012). *Systematic screenings of behavior to support instruction: From preschool to high school.* New York: Guilford Press.

Lane, K. L., O'Shaughnessy, T. E., Lambros, K. M., Gresham, F. M., & Beebe-Frankenberger, M. E. (2001). The efficacy of phonological awareness training with first-grade students who have behavior problems and reading difficulties. *Journal of Emotional and Behavioral Disorders, 9,* 219–232.

Lane, K. L., Wehby, J. H., Menzies, H. M., Gregg, R. M., Doukas, G. L., & Munton, S. M. (2002). Early literacy instruction for first-grade students at-risk for antisocial behavior. *Education and Treatment of Children, 25,* 438–458.

Layne, A. E., Bernstein, G. A., & March, J. S. (2006). Teacher awareness of anxiety symptoms in children. *Child Psychiatry and Human Development, 36,* 383–392.

Lassen, S. R., Steele, M. M., & Sailor, W. (2006). The relationship of school-wide positive behavior support to academic achievement in an urban middle school. *Psychology in the Schools, 43,* 701–712.

Latham, G. (1988). The birth and death cycles of educational innovations. *Principal, 68,* 41–43.

Lee, J. (2002). Racial and ethnic achievement gap trends: Reversing the progress toward equity? *Educational Researcher, 31,* 3–12.

Lee, Y., Sugai, G., & Horner, R. H. (1999). Using an instructional intervention to reduce problem and off-task behaviors. *Journal of Positive Behavior Interventions, 1,* 195–204.

Legters, N., & Balfanz, R. (2010). Do we have what it takes to put all students on the graduation path? *New Directions for Youth Development, 127,* 11–24.

Levy, S., & Chard, D. J. (2001). Research on reading instruction for students with emotional and behavioural disorders. *International Journal of Disability, Development and Education, 48,* 429–444.

Lewis, T. J., Barrett, S., Sugai, G., & Horner, R. H. (2010). *Blueprint for school-wide positive behavior support training and professional development* (2nd ed.). Eugene, OR: National Technical Assistance Center on Positive Behavioral Interventions and Support. Retrieved from *www.pbis.org.*

Lewis-Palmer, T., Bounds, M., & Sugai, G. (2004). Districtwide system for providing individual student support. *Assessment for Effective Intervention, 30,* 53–65.

Lewis-Palmer, T., Todd, A. W., Horner, R. H., Sugai, G., & Sampson, N. K. (2003). *Individual Student Systems Evaluation Tool (ISSET).* Eugene, OR: Educational and Community Supports.

Lin, Y., Morgan, P. L., Hillemeier, M., Cook, M., Maczuga, S., & Farkas, G. (2013). Reading, mathematics, and behavioral difficulties interrelate: Evidence from a cross-lagged panel design and population-based sample of U.S. upper elementary students. *Behavioral Disorders, 38,* 212–227.

Locke, W. R., & Fuchs, L. S. (1995). Effects of peer-mediated reading instruction on the on-task behavior and social interaction of children with behavior disorders. *Journal of Emotional and Behavioral Disorders, 3,* 92–99.

Lohrmann, S., Forman, S., Martin, S., & Palmieri, M. (2008). Understanding school personnel's resistance to adopting schoolwide positive behavior support at a universal level of intervention. *Journal of Positive Behavior Interventions, 10,* 256–269.

Loman, S., Strickland-Cohen, M. K., Borgmeier, C., & Horner, R. H. (2013). *Basic FBA to BSP trainer's manual.* Eugene, OR: University of Oregon, Educational and Community Supports.

Lorhmann, S., & Davis, B. (2014, May). *Examples of implementing PBIS in urban settings.* Paper presented at the Northeast PBIS Conference, Mystic, CT.

Losen, D. J., Hodson, C., Keith, M. A., Morrison, K., & Belway, S. (2015). *Are we closing the school discipline gap?* Los Angeles, CA: Center for Civil Rights Remedies at The Civil Rights Project at UCLA.

Luiselli, J. K., Putnam, R. F., Handler, M. W., & Feinberg, A. B. (2005). Whole-school positive behaviour support: Effects on student discipline problems and academic performance. *Educational Psychology, 25,* 183–198.

MacKay, L., Andreou, T., & Ervin, R. A. (2009). Peer-mediated intervention strategies. In G. Gimpel Peacock, R. A. Ervin, E. J. Daly & K. W. Merrell (Eds.), *The practical handbook of school psychology: Effective practices for the 21st century* (pp. 319–336). New York: Guilford Press.

March, R. E., Horner, R. H., Lewis-Palmer, T., Brown, D., Crone, D., Todd, A. W., & Carr, E. G. (2000). *Functional Assessment Checklist: Teachers and Staff (FACTS).* Eugene, OR: Educational and Community Supports. Available at *www.pbis.org/tools.htm.*

Mathews, S., McIntosh, K., Frank, J. L., & May, S. L. (2014). Critical features predicting sustained implementation of school-wide positive behavior support. *Journal of Positive Behavior Interventions, 16,* 168–178.

Mattison, R. E., & Blader, J. C. (2013). What affects academic functioning in secondary special education students with serious emotional and/or behavioral problems? *Behavioral Disorders, 38,* 201–211.

McCart, A., Wolf, N., Sweeney, H. M., & Choi, J. H. (2009). The application of a family-based multi-tiered system of support. *NHSA DIALOG, 12,* 122–132.

McGlinchey, M., Goodman, S., & Schallmo, K. (2005, February). *Michigan's Integrated Behavior and Learning Support Initiative.* Paper presented at the DIBELS Summit, Albuquerque, NM.

McIntosh, K. (2007, June). *Sustaining school-wide reading and positive behavior support through collaboration.* Keynote paper presented at the Southwest Ohio SERRC Conference, Columbus, OH.

McIntosh, K., Barnes, A., Morris, K., & Eliason, B. M. (2014). *Using discipline data within SWPBIS to identify and address disproportionality: A guide for school teams.* Eugene, OR: Center on Positive Behavioral Interventions and Supports, University of Oregon.

McIntosh, K., Borgmeier, C., Anderson, C. M., Horner, R. H., Rodriguez, B. J., & Tobin, T. J. (2008). Technical adequacy of the Functional Assessment Checklist—Teachers and Staff (FACTS) FBA interview measure. *Journal of Positive Behavior Interventions, 10,* 33–45.

McIntosh, K., Campbell, A. L., Carter, D. R., & Dickey, C. R. (2009). Differential effects of a Tier Two behavior intervention based on function of problem behavior. *Journal of Positive Behavior Interventions, 11,* 82–93.

McIntosh, K., Campbell, A. L., Carter, D. R., & Zumbo, B. D. (2009). Concurrent validity of office discipline referrals and cut points used in schoolwide positive behavior support. *Behavioral Disorders, 34,* 100–113.

McIntosh, K., Chard, D. J., Boland, J. B., & Horner, R. H. (2006). Demonstration of combined efforts in school-wide academic and behavioral systems and incidence of reading and behavior challenges in early elementary grades. *Journal of Positive Behavior Interventions, 8,* 146–154.

McIntosh, K., Eliason, B. M., Horner, R. H., & May, S. L. (2014). Have schools increased their use of the SWIS school ethnicity report? *PBIS Evaluation Brief.* Eugene, OR: Educational and Community Supports.

McIntosh, K., Filter, K. J., Bennett, J. L., Ryan, C., & Sugai, G. (2010). Principles of sustainable prevention: Designing scale-up of school-wide positive behavior support to promote durable systems. *Psychology in the Schools, 47,* 5–21.

McIntosh, K., Flannery, K. B., Sugai, G., Braun, D., & Cochrane, K. L. (2008). Relationships between academics and problem behavior in the transition from middle school to high school. *Journal of Positive Behavior Interventions, 10,* 243–255.

McIntosh, K., Frank, J. L., & Spaulding, S. A. (2010). Establishing research-based trajectories of office discipline referrals for individual students. *School Psychology Review, 39,* 380–394.

McIntosh, K., Girvan, E. J., Horner, R. H., & Smolkowski, K. (2014). Education not incarceration: A conceptual model for reducing racial and ethnic disproportionality in school discipline. *Journal of Applied Research on Children, 5*(2), 1–22.

McIntosh, K., Goodman, S., & Bohanon, H. (2010). Toward true integration of academic and behavior support. *NASP Communique, 39*(2), *1,* 14–16.

McIntosh, K., Herman, K., Sanford, A., McGraw, K., & Florence, K. (2004). Teaching transitions: Techniques for promoting success between lessons. *Teaching Exceptional Children, 37*(1), 32–38.

McIntosh, K., Horner, R. H., Chard, D. J., Boland, J. B., & Good, R. H. (2006). The use of reading and behavior screening measures to predict non-response to school-wide positive behavior support: A longitudinal analysis. *School Psychology Review, 35,* 275–291.

McIntosh, K., Horner, R. H., Chard, D. J., Dickey, C. R., & Braun, D. H. (2008). Reading skills and function of problem behavior in typical school settings. *Journal of Special Education, 42,* 131–147.

McIntosh, K., Horner, R. H., & Sugai, G. (2009). Sustainability of systems-level evidence-based practices in schools: Current knowledge and future directions. In W. Sailor, G. Dunlap, G. Sugai, & R. H. Horner (Eds.), *Handbook of positive behavior support* (pp. 327–352). New York: Springer.

McIntosh, K., Kelm, J. L., & Canizal Delabra, A. (2016). In search of how principals change: A qualitative study of events that help and hinder administrator support for school-wide PBIS. *Journal of Positive Behavior Interventions, 18,* 100–110.

McIntosh, K., Lucyshyn, J. M., Strickland-Cohen, M. K., & Horner, R. H. (2014). Building supportive environments: Toward a technology for enhancing fidelity of implementation. In F. Brown, J. Anderson, & R. L. DePry (Eds.), *Individual positive behavior supports: A standards-based guide to practices in school and community-based settings* (pp. 413–428). Baltimore, MD: Brookes.

McIntosh, K., MacKay, L. D., Andreou, T., Brown, J. A., Mathews, S., Gietz, C., & Bennett, J. L. (2011). Response to intervention in Canada: Definitions, the evidence base, and future directions. *Canadian Journal of School Psychology, 26,* 18–43.

McIntosh, K., Massar, M., Algozzine, R. F., George, H. P., Horner, R. H., Lewis, T. J., & Swain-Bradway,

J. (in press). Technical adequacy of the SWPBIS Tiered Fidelity Inventory. *Journal of Positive Behavior Interventions.*

McIntosh, K., Mercer, S. H., Hume, A. E., Frank, J. L., Turri, M. G., & Mathews, S. (2013). Factors related to sustained implementation of schoolwide positive behavior support. *Exceptional Children, 79,* 293–311.

McIntosh, K., Mercer, S. H., Nese, R. N. T., Strickland-Cohen, M. K., & Hoselton, R. (2016). Predictors of sustained implementation of school-wide PBIS at 3 and 5 years after initial implementation. *Journal of Positive Behavior Interventions.*

McIntosh, K., Predy, L. K., Upreti, G., Hume, A. E., Turri, M. G., & Mathews, S. (2014). Perceptions of contextual features related to implementation and sustainability of school-wide positive behavior support. *Journal of Positive Behavior Interventions, 16,* 29–41.

McIntosh, K., Reinke, W. M., & Herman, K. E. (2009). Schoolwide analysis of data for social behavior problems: Assessing outcomes, selecting targets for intervention, and identifying need for support. In G. Gimpel Peacock, R. A. Ervin, E. J. Daly, & K. W. Merrell (Eds.), *The practical handbook of school psychology: Effective practices for the 21st century* (pp. 135–156). New York: Guilford Press.

McIntosh, K., Sadler, C., & Brown, J. A. (2012). Kindergarten reading skill level and change as risk factors for chronic problem behavior. *Journal of Positive Behavior Interventions, 14,* 17–28.

McIntosh, K., Ty, S. V., Horner, R. H., & Sugai, G. (2013). School-wide positive behavior interventions and supports and academic achievement. In J. Hattie & E. Anderman (Eds.), *International guide to student achievement* (pp. 146–148). New York: Routledge.

McIntosh, K., Ty, S. V., & Miller, L. D. (2014). Effects of school-wide positive behavior support on internalizing problems: Current evidence and future directions. *Journal of Positive Behavior Interventions, 16,* 209–218.

McLaughlin, M. W., & Mitra, D. (2001). Theory-based change and change-based theory: Going deeper, going broader. *Journal of Educational Change, 2,* 301–323.

Mercer, S. H., McIntosh, K., Strickland-Cohen, M. K., & Horner, R. H. (2014). Measurement invariance of an instrument assessing sustainability of school-based universal behavior practices. *School Psychology Quarterly, 29,* 125–137.

Merrell, K. W., & Gueldner, B. A. (2010). *Social and emotional learning in the classroom: Promoting mental health and academic success.* New York: Guilford Press.

Merton, R. K. (1968). *Social theory and social structure.* New York: Free Press.

Metcalfe, L. A., Harvey, E. A., & Laws, H. B. (2013). The longitudinal relation between academic/cognitive skills and externalizing behavior problems in preschool children. *Journal of Educational Psychology, 105,* 881–894.

Miller, D., & Goodman, S. (2012, October). *A district model for integrated RtI systems.* Paper presented at the 2012 PBIS Implementers Forum, Chicago.

Morgan, P. L., Farkas, G., Tufis, P. A., & Sperling, R. A. (2008). Are reading and behavior problems risk factors for each other? *Journal of Learning Disabilities, 41,* 417–436.

Morgan, P. L., Farkas, G., & Wu, Q. (2012). Do poor readers feel angry, sad, and unpopular? *Scientific Studies of Reading, 16,* 360–381.

Morrison, G. M., Anthony, S., Storino, M., & Dillon, C. (2001). An examination of the disciplinary histories and the individual and educational characteristics of students who participate in an in-school suspension program. *Education and Treatment of Children, 24,* 276–293.

National Reading Panel. (2000). *Report of the National Reading Panel: An evidence-based assessment of the scientific research literature on reading and its implications for reading instruction.* Bethesda, MD: National Institute of Child Health and Human Development.

National Research Council. (2002). *Minority students in special and gifted education.* Washington, DC: National Academies Press.

Nelson, J. R. (1996). Designing schools to meet the needs of students who exhibit disruptive behavior. *Journal of Emotional and Behavioral Disorders, 4*, 147–161.

Nelson, J. R., Benner, G. J., Lane, K. L., & Smith, B. W. (2004). Academic achievement of K–12 students with emotional and behavioral disorders. *Exceptional Children, 71*, 59–73.

Nelson, J. R., Benner, G. J., Reid, R. C., Epstein, M. H., & Currin, D. (2002). The convergent validity of office discipline referrals with the CBCL-TRF. *Journal of Emotional and Behavioral Disorders, 10*, 181–188.

Nelson, J. R., & Carr, B. A. (2000). *The Think Time strategy for schools.* Longmont, CO: Sopris West.

Nelson, J. R., Lane, K. L., Benner, G. J., & Kim, O. (2011). A best evidence synthesis of literacy instruction on the social adjustment of students with or at-risk for behavior disorders. *Education and Treatment of Children, 34*, 141–162.

Nelson, J. R., Martella, R. M., & Marchand-Martella, N. (2002). Maximizing student learning: The effects of a comprehensive school-based program for preventing problem behaviors. *Journal of Emotional and Behavioral Disorders, 10*, 136–148.

Nese, R. N. T., Horner, R. H., Dickey, C. R., Stiller, B., & Tomlanovich, A. (2014). Decreasing bullying behaviors in middle school: Expect Respect. *School Psychology Quarterly, 29*, 272–286.

Nese, R. N. T., McIntosh, K., Mercer, S. H., Bloom, J., Johnson, N. W., Phillips, D., . . . & Hoselton, R. (2016). *Predicting abandonment of School-wide PBIS.* Manuscript submitted for publication.

Newton, J. S., Horner, R. H., Algozzine, B., Todd, A. W., & Algozzine, K. (2012). A randomized wait-list controlled analysis of the implementation integrity of team-initiated problem solving processes. *Journal of School Psychology, 50*, 421–441.

Newton, J. S., Todd, A. W., Algozzine, B., Algozzine, K., Horner, R. H., & Cusumano, D. L. (2014). Supporting team problem solving in inclusive schools. In J. McLeskey, N. L. Waldron, F. Spooner, & B. Algozzine (Eds.), *Handbook of research and practice for inclusive schools* (pp. 275–291). New York: Routledge.

No Child Left Behind Act of 2001, 20 U.S.C. 70 § 6301 *et seq.*

O'Neill, R. E., Albin, R. W., Storey, K., Horner, R. H., & Sprague, J. R. (2015). *Functional assessment and program development for problem behavior: A practical handbook* (3rd ed.). Pacific Grove, CA: Brooks/Cole.

Oregon Coach Task Force. (2011). *Systems coach manual.* Center on Teaching and Learning, University of Oregon, Eugene, OR. Retrieved from *http://ctl.uoregon.edu/node/613#coach_manuals.*

Oregon Department of Education, (2007). *Oregon RTI Technical Assistant to School Districts: Identification of Students with Learning Disabilities under IDEA 2004.* Retrieved from *www.ode.state.or.us.*

Oregon State Archives. (2011, February 14). Public education in Oregon. Retrieved from http://bluebook.state.or.us/education/.

Osher, D., Bear, G. G., Sprague, J. R., & Doyle, W. (2010). How can we improve school discipline? *Educational Researcher, 39*, 48–58.

Paine, S. C., Radicchi, J., Rosellini, L. C., Deutchman, L., & Darch, C. B. (1983). *Structuring your classroom for academic success.* Champaign, IL: Research Press.

Preciado, J. A., Horner, R. H., & Baker, S. K. (2009). Using a function-based approach to decrease problem behavior and increase reading academic engagement for Latino English language learners. *Journal of Special Education, 42*, 227–240.

Predy, L. K., McIntosh, K., & Frank, J. L. (2014). Utility of number and type of office discipline referrals in predicting chronic problem behavior in middle schools. *School Psychology Review, 43*, 472–489.

President's Commission on Excellence in Special Education. (2002). A new era: Revitalizing special education for children and their families. Retrieved August 1, 2013, from *www.ufttc.org/index.php?s=49643ae017a5447b784bbad32970df68&act=attach&type=post&id=119.*

Rasplica, C., McIntosh, K., & Hoselton, R. (2016). *Concurrent validity among fidelity of implementation of SWPBIS during initial implementation.* Manuscript submitted for publication.

Rathvon, N. (2004). *Early reading assessment: A practitioner's handbook.* New York: Guilford Press.

Rathvon, N. (2008). *Effective school interventions: Evidence-based strategies for improving student outcomes* (2nd ed.). New York: Guilford Press.

Reschly, D. J. (1988). Special education reform: School psychology revolution. *School Psychology Review, 17,* 459–475.

Reschly, D. J. (1995). Psychological practice in the schools: System change in the heartland. In R. C. Talley & R. J. Short (Eds.), *Creating a new vision of school psychology: Emerging models of psychological practice in the schools* (pp. 23–27). Washington, DC: American Psychological Association.

Reynolds, M. C., Wang, M. C., & Walberg, H. J. (1987). The necessary restructuring of special and regular education. *Exceptional Children, 53,* 391–198.

Riley-Tillman, T. C., & Burns, M. K. (2010). *Evaluating educational interventions: Single-case design for measuring response to intervention.* New York: Guilford Press.

Riley-Tillman, T. C., Burns, M. K., & Gibbons, K. (2013). *RTI applications: Vol. 2. Assessment, analysis, and decision making.* New York: Guilford Press.

Roeser, R. W., & Eccles, J. S. (2000). Schooling and mental health. In A. J. Sameroff, M. Lewis, & S. M. Miller (Eds.), *Handbook of developmental psychopathology* (2nd ed., pp. 135–156). New York: Kluwer Academic/Plenum.

Rogers, E. (2003). *Diffusion of innovations* (5th ed.). New York: Free Press.

Ross, S. W., & Horner, R. H. (2009). Bully prevention in positive behavior support. *Journal of Applied Behavior Analysis, 42,* 747–759.

Sadler, C. (2000). Effective behavior support implementation at the district level: Tigard–Tualatin school district. *Journal of Positive Behavior Interventions, 2,* 241–243.

Sadler, C. (2003, March). *EBIS: Effective behavior and instructional support.* Paper presented at the first annual EBIS statewide conference, Corvallis, OR.

Sadler, C., & Sugai, G. (2009). Effective behavior and instructional support: A district model for early identification and prevention of reading and behavior problems. *Journal of Positive Behavior Interventions, 11,* 35–46.

Sanche, B. (1976, October). *Implementing the SEECC model of special education service delivery in rural Saskatchewan.* Paper presented at the National Congress of the Council for Exceptional Children, Saskatoon, Saskatchewan, Canada.

Sanford, A. K., & Horner, R. H. (2013). Effects of matching instruction difficulty to reading level for students with escape-maintained problem behavior. *Journal of Positive Behavior Interventions, 15,* 79–89.

Schaper, A., McIntosh, K., & Hoselton, R. (2016). Within-year growth in implementation fidelity of SWPIS during installation and initial implementation. *School Psychology Quarterly, 31,* 358–368.

Scott, T. M., Anderson, C. M., & Alter, P. (2012). *Managing classroom behavior using positive behavior supports.* Upper Saddle River, NJ: Pearson.

Scott, T. M., & Barrett, S. B. (2004). Using staff and student time engaged in disciplinary procedures to evaluate the impact of school-wide PBS. *Journal of Positive Behavior Interventions, 6,* 21–27.

Seligman, M. E. P. (1972). Learned helplessness. *Annual Review of Medicine, 23,* 407–412.

Seligman, M. E. P. (2002). Positive psychology, positive prevention, and positive therapy. In C. R. Cnyder & S. J. Lopez (Eds.), *Handbook of positive psychology* (pp. 3–9). New York: Oxford University Press.

Severson, H. H., Walker, H. M., Hope-Doolittle, J., Kratochwill, T. R., & Gresham, F. M. (2007). Proactive, early screening to detect behaviorally at-risk students: Issues, approaches, emerging innovations, and professional practices. *Journal of School Psychology, 45,* 193–223.

Shapiro, E. S. (2010). *Academic skills problems: Direct assessment and intervention* (4th ed.). New York: Guilford Press.

Shaywitz, B. A., Shaywitz, S. E., Blachman, B. A., Pugh, K. R., Fulbright, R. K., Skudlarski, P., . . . Marchione, K. E. (2004). Development of left occipitotemporal systems for skilled reading in children after a phonologically-based intervention. *Biological Psychiatry, 55*, 926–933.

Shinn, M. R. (2008). Best practices in using curriculum-based measurement in a problem-solving model. In A. Thomas & J. P. Grimes (Eds.), *Best practices in school psychology V* (pp. 243–261). Bethesda, MD: National Association of School Psychologists.

Sideridis, G. D., Antoniou, F., Stamovlasis, D., & Morgan, P. L. (2013). The relationship between victimization at school and achievement: The cusp catastrophe model for reading performance. *Behavioral Disorders, 38*, 228–242.

Sindelar, P. T., Shearer, D. K., Yendol-Hoppey, D., & Liebert, T. W. (2006). The sustainability of inclusive school reform. *Exceptional Children, 72*, 317–331.

Singleton, G. E., & Linton, C. (2005). *Courageous conversations about race: A field guide for achieving equity in schools.* Thousand Oaks, CA: Corwin Press.

Skiba, R. J., Horner, R. H., Chung, C., Rausch, M. K., May, S. L., & Tobin, T. (2011). Race is not neutral: A national investigation of African American and Latino disproportionality in school discipline. *School Psychology Review, 40*, 85–107.

Skiba, R. J., Simmons, A. B., Ritter, S., Gibb, A. C., Rausch, M. K., Cuadrado, J., & Chung, C. (2008). Achieving equity in special education: History, status, and current challenges. *Exceptional Children, 74*, 264–288.

Skinner, B. F. (1953). *Science and human behavior.* New York: Macmillan.

Simeonsson, R. J. (Ed.). (1994). *Risk, resilience and prevention: Promoting the well-being of all children.* Baltimore, MD: Brooks.

Simmons, D. C., Kame'enui, E. J., Good, R. H., Harn, B. A., Cole, C., & Braun, D. (2002). Building, implementing, and sustaining a beginning reading model: Lessons learned school by school. In M. R. Shinn, H. M. Walker, & G. Stoner (Eds.), *Interventions for academic and behavioral problems II: Preventive and remedial approaches* (pp. 403–432). Bethesda, MD: National Association of School Psychologists.

Social and Character Development Research Consortium. (2010). *Efficacy of schoolwide programs to promote social and character development and reduce problem behavior in elementary school children.* (NCER 2011-2001). Washington, DC: National Center for Education Research, Institute of Education Sciences, U.S. Department of Education.

Sprague, J. R., Colvin, G., & Irvin, L. K. (2002). *The school safety survey* (2nd ed.). Eugene, OR: Institute on Violence and Destructive Behavior.

Spira, E. G., Bracken, S. S., & Fischel, J. E. (2005). Predicting improvement after first-grade reading difficulties: The effects of oral language, emergent literacy, and behavior skills. *Developmental Psychology, 41*, 225–234.

Sprick, R. (2009). *CHAMPS: A proactive and positive approach to classroom management.* (2nd Ed.) Eugene, OR: Pacific Northwest Publishing.

Sprick, R., Knight, J., Reinke, W. M., & McKale, T. (2006). *Coaching for positive classrooms: Supporting teachers with classroom management.* Eugene, OR: Pacific Northwest Publishing.

Stewart, R. M., Benner, G. J., Martella, R. C., & Marchand-Martella, N. E. (2007). Three-tier models of reading and behavior: A research review. *Journal of Positive Behavior Interventions, 9*, 239–253.

St. Martin, K. A., Huth, E., & Harms, A. (2015). *Reading Tiered Fidelity Inventory Comprehensive Edition.* Lansing, MI: Michigan's Integrated Behavior and Learning Support Initiative, Michigan Department of Education.

St. Martin, K. A., Nantais, M., & Harms, A., Huth, E. (2015). *Reading Tiered Fidelity Inventory (Elementary-Level Edition).* Lansing, MI: Michigan Department of Education, Michigan's Integrated Behavior and Learning Support Initiative.

St. Martin, K. A., Nantais, M., & Harms, A. (2015). *Reading Tiered Fidelity Inventory (Secondary-Level Edition).* Lansing, MI: Michigan Department of Education, Michigan's Integrated Behavior and Learning Support Initiative.

St. Martin, K. A., Ward, C., Fixsen, D., Harms, A., & Russell, C. (2015). Regional Capacity Assessment. Unpublished instrument, University of North Carolina at Chapel Hill.

Stoll, L., Bolam, R., McMahon, A., Wallace, M., & Thomas, S. (2006). Professional learning communities: A review of the literature. *Journal of Educational Change, 7,* 221–258.

Stollar, S. A., Poth, R. L., Curtis, M. J., & Cohen, R. M. (2006). Collaborative strategic planning as illustration of the principles of systems change. *School Psychology Review, 35,* 181–197.

Stormont, M., Reinke, W. M., Herman, K. C., & Lembke, E. S. (2012). *Academic and behavior supports for at-risk students: Tier 2 interventions.* New York: Guilford Press.

Stormshak, E. A., Fosco, G. M., & Dishion, T. J. (2010). Implementing interventions with families in schools to increase youth school engagement: The family check-up model. *School Mental Health, 2,* 82–92.

Strickland-Cohen, M. K., McIntosh, K., & Horner, R. H. (2014). Sustaining effective practices in the face of principal turnover. *Teaching Exceptional Children, 46*(3), 18–24.

Sugai, G. (2010). *Committee/group self-assessment and action planning (working smarter matrix).* Eugene, OR: Center on Positive Behavioral Interventions and Supports, University of Oregon.

Sugai, G., & Horner, R. H. (2009a). Defining and describing schoolwide positive behavior support. In W. Sailor, G. Dunlap, G. Sugai, & R. H. Horner (Eds.), *Handbook of positive behavior support* (pp. 307–326). New York: Springer.

Sugai, G., & Horner, R. H. (2009b). Responsiveness-to-intervention and school-wide positive behavior supports: Integration of multi-tiered system approaches. *Exceptionality, 17,* 223–237.

Sugai, G., Horner, R. H., Algozzine, R., Barrett, S., Lewis, T., Anderson, C., . . . Simonsen, B. (2010). *School-wide positive behavior support: Implementation blueprint and self-assessment* (2nd ed.). Eugene, OR: University of Oregon. Available at *http://pbis.org/resource/216.*

Sugai, G., Horner, R., Fixsen, D., & Blase, K. (2010). Developing systems-level capacity for RTI implementation: Current efforts and future directions. In T. A. Glover & S. Vaughn (Eds.), *The promise of response to intervention: Evaluating current science and practice* (pp. 286–309). New York: Guilford Press.

Sugai, G., Horner, R. H., & Lewis-Palmer, T. L. (2001). *Team Implementation Checklist (TIC).* Eugene, OR: Educational and Community Supports. Available at *www.pbis.org.*

Sugai, G., Horner, R. H., & Todd, A. W. (2000). *PBIS Self-Assessment Survey 2.0.* Eugene, OR: Educational and Community Supports. Available at *www.pbisapps.org.*

Sugai, G., Kame'enui, E. J., Horner, R. H., & Simmons, D. C. (2002). *Effective instructional and behavioral support systems: A school-wide approach to discipline and early literacy.* Washington, DC: U.S. Office of Special Education Programs.

Sugai, G., Lewis-Palmer, T. L., Todd, A. W., & Horner, R. H. (2001). *School-wide Evaluation Tool (SET).* Eugene, OR: Educational and Community Supports. Available at *www.pbis.org.*

Sugai, G., Sprague, J. R., Horner, R. H., & Walker, H. M. (2000). Preventing school violence: The use of office discipline referrals to assess and monitor school-wide discipline interventions. *Journal of Emotional and Behavioral Disorders, 8,* 94–101.

Sugai, G., & Todd, A. W. (2004). *Conducting leadership team meetings* (2nd ed.). Eugene, OR: Center on Positive Behavioral Interventions and Supports, University of Oregon.

Sugai, G., & Todd, A. W. (2006). *Coaching introduction and readiness self-assessment* (2nd ed.). Eugene, OR: Center on Positive Behavioral Interventions and Supports, University of Oregon.

Sullivan, E., & Daily, J. (2013, March). *Family school and community partnerships within a multi-tiered system of supports.* Paper presented at the International APBS Conference, San Diego, CA.

Sutherland, K. S., & Snyder, A. (2007). Effects of reciprocal peer tutoring and self-graphing on reading fluency and classroom behavior of middle school students with emotional or behavioral disorders. *Journal of Emotional and Behavioral Disorders, 15,* 103–118.

Tilly, W. D., Reschly, D. J., & Grimes, J. P. (1998). Disability determination in problem solving systems: Conceptual foundations and critical components. In D. J. Reschly, W. D. Tilly, & J. P. Grimes (Eds.), *Functional and noncategorical identification and intervention in special education* (pp. 285–300). Des Moines, IA: State of Iowa Department of Education.

Tobin, T. J., & Vincent, C. G. (2011). Strategies for preventing disproportionate exclusions of African American students. *Preventing School Failure, 55,* 192–201.

Todd, A. W., Horner, R. H., Berry, D., Sanders, C., Bugni, M., Currier, A., . . . Algozzine, K. (2012). A case study of team-initiated problem solving addressing student behavior in one elementary school. *Journal of Special Education Leadership, 25,* 81–89.

Todd, A. W., Horner, R. H., Newton, J. S., Algozzine, R. F., Algozzine, K. M., & Frank, J. L. (2011). Effects of team initiated problem solving on meeting practices of schoolwide behavior support teams. *Journal of Applied School Psychology, 27,* 42–59.

Todd, A. W., Horner, R. H., Sugai, G., & Colvin, G. (1999). Individualizing school-wide discipline for students with chronic problem behaviors: A team approach. *Effective School Practices, 17,* 72–82.

Todd, A. W., Sampson, N. K., & Horner, R. H. (2005). Data-based decision making using office discipline referral data from the School-Wide Information System (SWIS). *Association for Positive Behavior Support Newsletter, 2*(2), 3.

Torgesen, J. K. (2006). *A comprehensive K–3 reading assessment plan: Guidance for school leaders.* Portsmouth, NH: RMC Research Corporation, Center on Instruction.

Trzesniewski, K. H., Moffitt, T. E., Caspi, A., Taylor, A., & Maughan, B. (2006). Revisiting the association between reading achievement and antisocial behavior: New evidence of an environmental explanation from a twin study. *Child Development, 77,* 72–88.

Turri, M. G., Mercer, S. H., McIntosh, K., Nese, R. N. T., & Hoselton, R. (in press). Assessing barriers to sustainability of school-based interventions and effects on fidelity of implementation. *Assessment for Effective Intervention.*

Tyack, D. B., & Cuban, L. (1995). *Tinkering toward utopia: A century of public school reform.* Cambridge, MA: Harvard University Press.

University of Oregon, Center on Teaching and Learning. (2007). *EBISS District Systems Support Plan.* Unpublished instrument. University of Oregon, Center on Teaching and Learning.

U.S. Census Bureau, (2013). *2013 Population Estimates.* Retrieved from *http://quickfacts.census.gov.*

U.S. Department of Justice. (2011). Attorney General Holder, Secretary Duncan announce effort to respond to school-to-prison pipeline by supporting good discipline practices [Press release]. Retrieved from *www.justice.gov/opa/pr/2011/July/11-ag-951.html.*

U.S. Departments of Education and Justice. (2014). Dear Colleague letter: Nondiscriminatory administration of school discipline. Retrieved from *www2.ed.gov/about/offices/list/ocr/letters/colleague-201401-title-vi.html.*

Valli, L., & Buese, D. (2007). The changing roles of teachers in an era of high-stakes accountability. *American Educational Research Journal, 44,* 519–588.

VanDerHeyden, A. M., & Witt, J. C. (2008). Best practices in can't do/won't do assessment. In A. Thomas & J. P. Grimes (Eds.), *Best practices in school psychology V* (pp. 131–139). Bethesda, MD: National Association of School Psychologists.

VanDerHeyden, A. M., Witt, J. C., & Gilbertson, D. (2007). A multi-year evaluation of the effects of a response to intervention (RTI) model on identification of children for special education. *Journal of School Psychology, 45,* 225–256.

Vaughn, S., Cirino, P. T., Wanzek, J., Wexler, J., Fletcher, J. M., Denton, C. D., & Barth, A. (2010). Response to intervention for middle school students with reading difficulties: Effects of a primary and secondary intervention. *School Psychology Review, 39,* 3–21.

Vaughn, S., Linan-Thompson, S., & Hickman, P. (2003). Response to instruction as a means of identifying students with reading/learning disabilities. *Exceptional Children, 69,* 391–409.

Vellutino, F. R., Scanlon, D. M., Sipay, E. R., Small, S. G., Pratt, S., Chen, R., & Denckla, M. B. (1996). Cognitive profiles of difficult-to-remediate and readily remediated poor readers: Early intervention as a vehicle for distinguishing between cognitive and experiential deficits as basic causes of specific reading disability. *Journal of Educational Psychology, 88,* 601–638.

Vincent, C. G., Swain-Bradway, J., Tobin, T. J., & May, S. (2011). Disciplinary referrals for culturally and linguistically diverse students with and without disabilities: Patterns resulting from school-wide positive behavior support. *Exceptionality, 19,* 175–190.

Volpe, R. J., DuPaul, G. J., DiPerna, J. C., Jitendra, A., Lutz, J. G., Tresco, K., & Junod, R. V. (2006). Attention deficit hyperactivity disorder and scholastic achievement: A model of mediation via academic enablers. *School Psychology Review, 35,* 47–61.

Volpe, R. J., & Fabiano, A. (2013). *Daily behavior report cards: An evidence-based system of assessment and intervention.* New York: Guilford Press.

Waasdorp, T. E., Bradshaw, C. P., & Leaf, P. J. (2012). The impact of schoolwide positive behavioral interventions and supports on bullying and peer rejection. *Archives of Pediatrics and Adolescent Medicine, 166,* 149–156.

Walker, B., & Cheney, D. (2012). *The SAPR-PBIS manual: A team-based approach to implementing effective schoolwide positive behavior interventions and supports.* Baltimore, MD: Brookes.

Walker, H. M., Horner, R. H., Sugai, G., Bullis, M., Sprague, J. R., Bricker, D., & Kaufman, M. J. (1996). Integrated approaches to preventing antisocial behavior patterns among school-age children and youth. *Journal of Emotional and Behavioral Disorders, 4,* 194–209.

Walker, H. M., & Severson, H. (1992). *Systematic screening for behavior disorders* (2nd ed.). Longmont, CO: Sopris West.

Wang, M. C., Haertel, G. D., & Walberg, H. J. (1997). Learning influences. In H. J. Walberg & G. D. Haertel (Eds.), *Psychology and educational practice* (pp. 199–211). Berkeley, CA: McCutchan.

Wanzek, J., Al Otaiba, S., & Petscher, Y. (2013). Oral reading fluency development for children with emotional disturbance or learning disabilities. *Exceptional Children, 80,* 187–204.

Wanzek, J., Vaughn, S., Kim, A., & Cavanaugh, C. L. (2006). The effects of reading interventions on social outcomes for elementary students with reading difficulties: A synthesis. *Reading & Writing Quarterly, 22,* 121–138.

Ward, C., St. Martin, K., Horner, R., Duda, M., Ingram-West, K., Tedesco, M., . . . Chaparro, E. (2015). District Capacity Assessment. Unpublished instrument, University of North Carolina at Chapel Hill.

Wehby, J. H., Falk, K. B., Barton-Arwood, S., Lane, K. L., & Cooley, C. (2003). The impact of comprehensive reading instruction on the academic and social behavior of students with emotional and behavioral disorders. *Journal of Emotional and Behavioral Disorders, 11,* 225–238.

Wehby, J. H., Lane, K. L., & Falk, K. B. (2003). Academic instruction of students with emotional and behavioral disorders. *Journal of Emotional and Behavioral Disorders, 11,* 194–197.

Westen, D., & Morrison, K. (2001). A multidimensional meta-analysis of treatments for depression, panic, and generalized anxiety disorder: An empirical examination of the status of empirically supported therapies. *Journal of Consulting and Clinical Psychology, 69,* 875–899.

Wickstrom, K. F., Jones, K. M., LaFleur, L. H., & Witt, J. C. (1996). An analysis of treatment integrity in school-based behavioral consultation. *School Psychology Quarterly, 13,* 141–154.

Witt, J. C., Daly, E. J., & Noell, G. H. (2000). *Functional assessments: A step-by-step guide to solving academic and behavior problems.* Longmont, CO: Sopris West.

Wong, H. K., Wong, R. T., & Seroyer, C. (1998). *The first days of school: How to be an effective teacher.* Mountain View, CA: Harry K. Wong.

Yong, M., & Cheney, D. A. (2013). Essential features of tier 2 social–behavioral interventions. *Psychology in the Schools, 50,* 844–861.

Young, E. L., Caldarella, P., Richardson, M. J., & Young, K. R. (2012). *Positive behavior support in secondary schools: A practical guide.* New York: Guilford Press.

# Index

Note. Page numbers in italics indicate a figure or a table.

Academic achievement, office discipline
referrals and, 24
Academic benchmarking, 46–47
Academic challenges
inadequate response to leads to
behavior problems, 23, 26–28
leading to social challenges, 23, 25–26
Academic enablers, 133
Academic facilitators, 133
Academic interventions
fidelity assessment, 40–41, 43
problem behavior created by
inadequate response to, 23,
26–28
research on crossover effects, 29–30
Academic problems/needs
progress monitoring, 58
screening for, 46
Tier 2 integrated practices, 128, 129,
131, 132–133
Academic response to intervention (RTI)
choosing first in a staggered approach
to integration, 239
conceptual origins, 11–13
defined, 6
foundational resources, 18
integrated approaches in, 9
in integrated entire systems (see
Integrated entire systems)
integration into MTSS, 5
prevalence and efficacy, 4–5
rationale for integrating with PBIS,
9–11
similarities and differences with PBIS,
5–8
Academics
choosing first in a staggered approach
to integration, 239
diagnostic assessment, 50
general outcomes measurement, 60
(see also Outcomes)
Academic skills and behavior
big ideas about the relationship
between, 31–32
crossover effects, 21, 28–31

intervention research on the
relationship between, 28–31
multiple pathways to combined
academic and behavior
challenges, 22–28
Adaptive problems, in implementation,
206
Annual timetables, 183, 184
Assessment
EBISS Systems Coach Self-
Assessment, 228–233
evaluation of outcomes
Florida's integrated MTSS model,
301–302
Michigan's Integrated Behavior
and Learning Support Initiative,
319–323
Oregon's Effective Behavioral and
Instructional Support system,
278–283
of implementation drivers, 214
similarities and differences between
academic RTI and PBIS, 8
two-step process for identifying
assessment needs, 63
Assessment plans, 64, 65
Assessment tools
diagnostic assessment, 47–56
fidelity assessment, 39–44
general outcomes measurement, 59–61
progress monitoring, 57–59
purpose of, an overview, 38–39
quality of, 62
screening tools, 44–47
selecting, 62–63
Attention deficits, 23, 24–25

Behavior
challenges created by attention deficits,
23, 24–25
choosing first in a staggered approach
to integration, 239–240
classwide behavior expectations
matrix, 120
connection to literacy, 22

crossover effects, 21, 28–31
diagnostic assessment, 48–50
expectations for MTSS team members,
173, 174
general outcomes measurement, 60
(see also Outcomes)
problem behavior reduces access to
instruction, 22, 23, 24
problems created by inadequate
response to academic
intervention, 23, 26–28
progress monitoring, 57–58
screening tools, 45–46
Tier 2 integrated practices, 128–133
See also Academic skills and behavior
Behavioral and Emotional Screening
System (BESS), 45
Behavior education program, 130
See also Check-in/check-out
Behavior interventions
fidelity assessment, 40, 42–43
research on crossover effects, 30–31
Benchmarks for Advanced Tiers (BAT),
40, 42
Benchmarks of Quality (BoQ), 281
Big ideas, 114–115, 116, 118–119
Breadth professional development, 273
Breaks are Better, 132–133
Building leadership implementation team
(B-LIT), 277
Bullying, 25–26
children's literature for teaching, 125

Cabinet team, 214–215, 216, 217–218
Check-in/check-out, 130, 132–133
Children's literature, for teaching
schoolwide expectations and
rules, 123, 124–127
Classroom management practices,
119–120
Classroom routines, 120–121
Classroom teams, 163–164, 170
Classwide behavior expectations matrix,
120
Classwide peer tutoring, 122

Coaching
  as a competency driver, *208, 213–214*
  differentiated, *221–224*
  systems coaching in the Oregon EBISS system, *271, 275*
  training and coaching providers, *215, 216–217, 218*
Collaboration
  collaborative professional development in the Oregon EBISS system, *277–278*
  expanding MTSS beyond educational systems, *331–332*
Collaborative for Academic, Social, and Emotional Learning (CASEL), *115*
Comma separated files (CSVs), *69–70*
Common Core State Standards, *299, 301*
Competency drivers, *208, 211–214*
Competing pathways
  analysis of behavior, *136*
  integrated approach to Tier 3 interventions, *137–139*
Comprehensive educational systems, *331*
Conspicuous strategies, *115, 116, 119*
Contexture drivers, *207–208, 210–211*
Continuous regeneration stage, in implementation, *240, 252–254*
Core, strategic, and intensive (CSI) map, *145*
Courageous Conversations about Race, *274*
Crossover effects
  of academic interventions on behavior, *29–30*
  ambiguous research evidence for, *28*
  defined, *21*
Curriculum-based measurement (CBM), *46, 58*

Daily behavior report cards, *57–58*
DAPPS. *See* District Action Planning and Problem Solving
Data
  concerns and solutions about the collection, interpretation, and use of, *36–38*
  importance to academic RTI and PBIS, *6–7*
  information as a contexture driver, *210*
  key areas for future research, *329–330*
  *See also* Integrated data
Data-based decision rules, *189*
Data dashboards, *69*
Data-driven education, *36–38*
Data entry, *68–69*
Data warehousing, *68*
Decision-making, integrated, *183, 185–189*
Decision rules, data-based, *189*
Depth professional development, *273*
Diagnostic assessment
  common tools for, *48–50*
  integrated, *51*
  overview, *47–48*
  typical processes for, *50*
  vignette, *51–56*
DIBELS. *See* Dynamic Indicators of Basic Early Literacy
Differentiated coaching, *221–224*
Differentiated MTSS training, *220–221*
Display boards, *151, 152*

District Action Planning and Problem Solving (DAPPS)
  current status, *299, 301*
  evaluation of, *302*
  formation of, *293*
  integration and evaluation workgroup, *295, 300*
  launching of, *294–299*
  presentation to districts, *293*
District Capacity Assessment (DCA), *214, 321*
District evaluation plans, *66–67*
District leadership implementation team (D-LIT), *275, 277, 286*
District leadership team(s), *167–168, 170, 302*
District-level EBISS systems, *281, 283*
District-level Team Checklists
  for Integrating Data, *73*
  for Integrating District support, *226*
  for Integrating Entire Systems, *262–263*
  for Integrating Practices, *154*
  for Integrating Teams, *190*
District level teams, *167–169, 170*
District size, variations in district support based on, *218–220*
District student support teams, *168–169, 170*
District support
  additional structures for, *219–220*
  drivers of, *204–214 (see also* Implementation drivers)
  effective, *204, 205*
  to individual schools in implementing MTSS, *203–204*
  model for organizing, *214–218*
  overview and significance of, *202–203*
  team checklists, *224–226*
  variations in
    based on district size, *218–220*
    based on need, *220–224*
D-LIT. *See* District leadership implementation team
Domains, integrating teams across, *171*
DSSP. *See* EBISS District Systems Support Plan
Dynamic Indicators of Basic Early Literacy (DIBELS), *46, 51, 54, 55, 56*

EBISS. *See* Oregon's Effective Behavioral and Instructional Support Systems initiative
EBISS District Systems Support Plan (DSSP), *277, 281, 283*
EBISS Systems Coach Self-Assessment, *228–233*
EBISS teaming framework, *275–277*
Educational innovation, cycles of and initiative fatigue, *3–4*
Effective classroom management practices, *119–120*
Effective practices
  in district support to individual schools in implementing MTSS, *203–204, 205*
  key areas for future research, *330*
Elaboration stage, in implementation, *240, 251–252*
Evaluation plans, *64–67*
Evidence-based practices
  defined, *140–141*
  selecting, *139–141*
Executive function deficits, *23, 24–25*
Experiential avoidance, *37*

Exploration/adoption stage, in implementation, *240, 241–246*

Facilitative administration, as a leadership driver, *207, 209–210*
Fairness, children's literature for teaching, *125*
Family members, on school leadership teams, *165*
FBAs. *See* Functional behavior assessments
Fidelity assessment
  common tools for, *39–41, 42–43*
  integrated, *44*
  overview, *39*
  typical processes for, *41*
Florida Positive Behavior Support (FLPBS) Project
  children's literature for teaching schoolwide expectations and rules, *123, 124–127*
  integration into Florida's integrated MTSS model, *288–299, 300*
  overview, *288, 289*
Florida's integrated MTSS model
  current status, *299*
  District Action Planning and Problem Solving, *293–299*
  evaluation of outcomes, *301–302*
  history of implementation, *288–299*
  lessons learned, *302–304*
  overview, *287*
  unique features, *299–301*
Florida Standards, *301*
Florida Statewide Response to Instruction/Intervention Implementation Plan, *288*
Focused coaching support, *223–224*
FRIENDS for Life program, *9*
Functional academic assessment, *49*
Functional Assessment Checklist for Teachers and Staff (FACTS), *50*
Functional Assessment Interview, *50*
Functional behavior assessments (FBAs), *48–50, 135, 167*

Gap analysis, *141*
General case instruction, *220*
General outcomes measurement, *59–61*
General social and emotional competencies, children's literature for teaching, *124*
Good Behavior Game, *30, 31*
Grade-level Team Postbenchmarking Meeting Agenda, *199–201*
Grade-level teams, *164, 170*

Harassment, *25–26*
Hexagon tool, for exploration and adoption decisions, *242, 243–244*
History instruction, including social and emotional content at Tier 1, *123–127*
Honesty, children's literature for teaching, *126*

IEP teams, *163*
ILT. *See* Interproject leadership teams
Implementation
  of Florida's integrated MTSS model, *288–299*
  of fully integrated MTSS models, *237–238*

Implementation *(cont.)*
  importance of involving stakeholders, 285–286
  of Michigan's Integrated Behavior and Learning Support Initiative, 306–310
  of Oregon's Effective Behavioral and Instructional Support Systems initiative, 268–272
Implementation drivers
  assessment of, 214
  common activities for installation, 207–208
  competency drivers, *208*, 211–214
  contexture drivers, *207–208*, 210–211
  leadership drivers, *207*, 208–210
  overview and description of, 204–208
  technical or adaptive problems, 206
Implementation science, 240
Implementation stages
  continuous regeneration stage, 252–254
  elaboration stage, 251–252
  exploration/adoption stage, 241–246
  initial implementation, 249–251
  installation stage, 246–249
  overview, 240–241
Implementation support team, 215, 216, 217–218
Index cards, 146
Individual progress monitoring graph, integrated, 72
Individual Student Information System— School Wide Information System (ISIS-SWIS), 41, *43*
Individual Student Systems Evaluation Tool (ISSET), 40
Individual student teams, 163, *170*
Individual support plans, 41
Individuals with Disabilities Education Act (IDEA), 11
Information, as a contexture driver, *207*, 210
Initial implementation, *240*, 249–251
Initiative fatigue, 3–4
Installation stage, in implementation, *240*, 246–249
Instructional time, 119
Integrated Academic Behavior Request for Assistance Form, 106–108
Integrated data
  assessment plans, 64, *65*
  assessment tools
    diagnostic assessment, 47–56
    fidelity assessment, 39–44
    general outcomes measurement, 59–61
    progress monitoring, 57–59
    purpose of, an overview, 38–39
    screening tools, 44–47
    selecting, 62–63
  concerns and solutions about data-driven education, 36–38
  efficiency and effectiveness of, 35–36
  evaluation plans, 64–67
  importance to and purpose in MTSS, 35, 36
  integrated data analysis, 71–72
  team checklists, 72–74
Integrated data systems
  importance of, 67–68
  integrated data analysis, 71–72
  necessary components for effective integration, 68–70

Integrated entire systems
  compared to parallel systems, 237
  concerns regarding and possible solutions, 254–259
  implementation stages
    continuous regeneration stage, 252–254
    elaboration stage, 251–252
    exploration/adoption stage, 241–246
    initial implementation, 249–251
    installation stage, 246–249
    overview, 240–241
  key areas for future research, 329–331
  key lessons in integrating systems, 327–329
  overview, 236–237
  pathways to integrated MTSS models, 237–240
  team checklists, 259–263
  *See also* Integrated MTSS models
Integrated individual progress monitoring graph, 72
Integrated instructional plans, 145–146, *147–150*, 157
Integrated Instruction Plan: Literacy and Behavior, *147–150*, 157
Integrated models, history of, 16–17
Integrated MTSS Implementation Readiness Application, 234–235
Integrated MTSS models
  concerns regarding and possible solutions, 254–259
  implementation stages
    continuous regeneration stage, 252–254
    elaboration stage, 251–252
    exploration/adoption stage, 241–246
    initial implementation, 249–251
    installation stage, 246–249
    overview, 240–241
  key areas for future research, 329–331
  key lessons in integrating systems, 327–329
  new directions, 331–332
  pathways to, 237–240
  *See also* Florida's integrated MTSS model; Michigan's Integrated Behavior and Learning Support Initiative; Oregon's Effective Behavioral and Instructional Support Systems initiative
Integrated MTSS training, differentiated, 220–221
Integrated practices
  guidance in selecting
    overview, 139
    selecting evidence-based practices, 139–141
    selecting practices by assessing practices already in place, 141–152
  overview, 113
  smart integrated thinking, 113–114
  team checklists, 152–154
  Tier 1 universal supports, 114–127
  Tier 2 secondary supports, 127–133
  Tier 3 tertiary supports, 133–139
Integrated problem solving, 183, 185–189

Integrated screening scatterplot, 71
Integrated student request for assistance process, 187–189
Integrated teaming
  effective strategies for (*see* Teaming strategies)
  MTSS teams
    district level teams, 167–169, *170*
    nesting structure, *163*
    overview, 162
    school level teams, 163–167, *170*
    recommendations for strategic integration, 169, 171–172
    team approach, 161–162
    team checklists, 189–191
  *See also* Teams/Teaming
Interconnected systems framework, 332
Intermediate school districts. *See* Michigan's Integrated Behavior and Learning Support Initiative
Interproject leadership teams (ILT), 290, 291–292, 293, 300
Intervention Planning and Assessment System (IPAS), 272
Intervention tracking tools, 66
Inventory for Identifying MTSS Assessment Needs, 109–110

Judicious review, *117*, 118

Kindness, children's literature for teaching, *126*

Large urban districts, district support and, 218–219
Leadership
  importance to success of the Oregon EBISS initiative, 283–284
  in Michigan's Integrated Behavior and Learning Support Initiative, 315
Leadership drivers, *207*, 208–210
Leadership implementation teams, 285
Leadership teams, in the Oregon EBIS system, 274
Learned helplessness, 26
Learning Disability Summit of 2001, 12
Literacy, connection to problem behavior, 22
Literacy instruction, including social and emotional content at Tier 1, 123–127
Literacy systems, fidelity assessment, 40–41, *43*

Management and coordination, as a leadership driver, *207*, 209
Master display boards, 146, *151*, 152
Mediated scaffolding, 115, *116*, 119
Meeting agendas. *See* Structured meeting agendas
Michigan's Integrated Behavior and Learning Support Initiative (MiBLSi)
  current status, 310–314
  evaluation of outcomes, 319–323
  history of implementation, 306–310
  integrated data system, 68–70
  lessons learned, 323–324
  overview, 305–306
  project structure, 317–319
  unique features, 315–319

Mission statements, 173, 291
Monitoring Advanced Tiers Tool (MATT), 40, *43*
MTSS. *See* Multi-tiered system of support
MTSS conferences, in Florida, 292–293
MTSS Initiative Alignment Worksheet, 247, 258–259, 264
MTSS Quick Audit, 142, *143*, 155, 246
MTSS teams
  district level teams, 167–169, *170*
  nesting structure, *163*
  overview, 162
  recommendations for strategic integration, 169, 171–172
  school level teams, 163–167, *170*
  strategies for effective teaming (*see* Teaming strategies)
Multiple-gate screening systems, 45–46
Multi-tiered systems of support (MTSS)
  broad conceptualization of, 8–9
  components of academic RTI and PBIS, 5–8
  conceptual origins, 11–17
  dangers of "parallel play," 17
  defined, 5, *6*
  foundational resources, *18–19*
  implementation (*see* Implementation)
  integrated data (*see* Integrated data)
  prevalence and efficacy of academic and behavior response-to-intervention systems, 4–5
  rationale for integrating academic RTI and PBIS, 9–11
  recent prominence of, 4
  relationship between academic skills and behavior, 21–32
  teams (*see* MTSS teams; Teams/Teaming)
  *See also* Integrated MTSS models
Multi-tiered systems
  conceptual origins, 13–15
  misrules and myths, 15–16
Multi-tiered Systems of Support Needs Assessment
  Elementary Version, 89–97
  Secondary Version, 98–105

National Research Council, 11
NWPBIS Network, 277

OAKS. *See* Oregon Assessment of Knowledge and Skills
Office discipline referrals (ODRs), 24, 45, 57
Opportunities to respond, increasing in Tier 1, 121–122
Oregon Assessment of Knowledge and Skills (OAKS), 278, *280*
Oregon Coach Task Force, 275
Oregon Response to Intervention (OrRTI), 270, 272
Oregon's Effective Behavioral and Instructional Support Systems (EBISS) initiative
  current status, 272–273
  district-level and stat- level overview, 267–269
  evaluation of outcomes, 278–283
  history of implementation, 268–272
  lessons learned, 283–286
  unique features, 273–278

Outcomes
  evaluation of
    Florida's integrated MTSS model, 301–302
    Michigan's Integrated Behavior and Learning Support Initiative, 319–323
    Oregon's Effective Behavioral and Instructional Support Systems, 278–283
  general outcomes measurement, 59–61

PALS. *See* Peer-assisted learning strategies
"Parallel play," 17
Parallel systems, 237
Patience, children's literature for teaching, *127*
PBIS. *See* Positive behavioral interventions and supports
PBIS Self-Assessment Survey (SAS), 40, *42*
Peer-assisted learning strategies (PALS), 122–123, 145
Peer-mediated instruction, 122–123
Performance feedback, as a contexture driver, *207*, 210–211
Planning and Evaluation Tool for Effective School-wide Reading Programs (PET-R), 40–41, *43*
Pocket charts, 146
Positive behavioral interventions and supports (PBIS)
  as an evidence-based practice, 141
  choosing first in a staggered approach to integration, 239–240
  conspicuous strategies, 115, *116*
  defined, *6*
  fidelity assessment, 40, *42–43*
  foundational resources, *19*
  integrated approaches in, 9
  in integrated entire systems (*see* Integrated entire systems)
  integration into MTSS, 5
    Florida's integrated MTSS model, 288–290
  judicious review, *117*, 118
  mediated scaffolding, 115, *116*
  prevalence and efficacy, 4–5
  rationale for integrating with academic RTI, 9–11
  research on crossover effects, 30–31
  similarities and differences with academic RTI, 5–8
Positive Behavior Support, 288
  *See also* Florida Positive Behavior Support Project
Primed background knowledge, *117*, 118
Problem solving
  integrated, 183, 185–189
  team-initiated, 172–173, 176
Problem Solving/Response to Intervention (PS/RTI) Project, 288–299, *300*
Professional development
  depth and breadth, 273
  in Florida's integrated MTSS model, 292, 295, 303
  in Michigan's Integrated Behavior and Learning Support Initiative, 307–310

in the Oregon EBISS initiative, 271–272, 273, 277–278
  *See also* Training
Progress monitoring, 57–59
Project CIRCUITS, 145
Promoting Alternative Thinking Strategies (PATHS), 9
Punctuality, children's literature for teaching, *127*
Purpose statements, 173

Racial/ethnic disproportionality, general outcomes measurement, 60–61
Reading Tiered Fidelity Inventory
  Comprehensive Edition, 41, *43*, 81–88
  Elementary-Level Edition, 75–77
  Secondary-Level Edition, 78–80
Read Naturally program, 132
Referral process, 187–189
Regional Capacity Assessment, 321
Relational database programs, 68
Relationship skills, children's literature for teaching, *125*
Reliability, 62
Reports, 69
Research-based practices, 140, 141
Resource mapping
  additional approaches, 146, *151*, 152
  integrated instructional plans, 145–146, *147–150*
  MTSS Quick Audit, 142, *143*, 155
  overview, 141
  Tier 2 resource maps, 142, 144–145
Resources, as a contexture driver, *208*, 211
Response to intervention (RTI)
  conceptual origins, 11–13
  integration into Florida's integrated MTSS model, 288–290
  *See also* Academic response to intervention
Responsible decision making, children's literature for teaching, *125*
REWARDS, 130
RTI. *See* Response to intervention

Scaffolding, mediated, 115, *116*, 119
School-based teams, 166–167
School evaluation plans, 65–66
School improvement teams, 165
School Leadership Team Meeting Agenda, *177–179*, 192–194
School leadership teams
  annual timetable for, *184*
  description of, 164–165, *170*
  problem-solving process, *186*
  structured meeting agenda, 176–179, 192–194
School-level EBISS systems, in Oregon, 281, *282*
School-level Team Checklists
  for Integrating Data, 73
  for Integrating District Support, 225
  for Integrating Entire Systems, 260–261
  for Integrating Practices, 153
  for Integrating Teams, 190
School level teams, 163–167, *170*
Schools
  district support to individual schools in implementing MTSS, 203–204
  variations in district support

Schools *(cont.)*
  based on district size, 218–220
  based on need, 220–224
Schoolwide assessment plans, 64, 65
School-wide Benchmarks of Quality
  (BoQ), 40, 42
School-wide Evaluation Tool (SET), 40,
  42, 278, 279, 281
School-Wide Information System (SWIS),
  45, 51, 52, 53
School-wide reading model (SWRM),
  270
Screening
  common tools for, 44–46
  integrated, 47
  overview, 44
  typical processes for, 46–47
Screening data
  using in diagnostic assessment, 48
  using to measure general outcomes,
  59–60
Screening scatterplot, integrated, 71
Second Step: A Violence Prevention
  Curriculum, 132
Selection, as a competency driver, 208,
  212
Self-assessments
  EBISS Systems Coach Self-
  Assessment, 228–233
  of fidelity, 40
  Self-Assessment of MTSS, 302
Self-awareness and self-management,
  children's literature for teaching,
  124
SET. *See* School-wide Evaluation Tool
Short-run empiricism, 12
Siloed approach, to Tier 3 interventions,
  136–137
Siloed systems, 237
Skills for School Success program, 133
Small school districts, district support
  and, 219
Social and emotional learning programs,
  30
Social awareness, children's literature for
  teaching, 124
Social behavior systems, fidelity
  assessment, 40, 42–43
Social rejection, 23, 25–26
Social studies instruction, including
  social and emotional content at
  Tier 1, 123–127
Special education eligibility, 274
Staggered approach to integration
  choosing academics or behavior first,
  239–240
  description of, 238–239
Stand-alone districts, district support
  and, 219
Standard coaching support, 221–222
Strategic integration, 117, 118
Structured meeting agendas
  description of, 176–182
  Grade-level Team Postbenchmarking
  Meeting Agenda, 199–201

School Leadership Team Meeting
  Agenda, 177–179, 192–194
Student Support Team Meeting
  Agenda, 180–182, 195–198
Student assistance teams, 166–167
Student-Directed Functional Assessment
  Interview, 50
Student request for assistance process,
  integrated, 187–189
Student Risk Screening Scale (SRSS), 45
Students, on school leadership teams, 165
Student study teams, 166–167
Student Support Team Meeting Agenda,
  180–182, 195–198
Student support teams
  description of, 166–167, 170
  problem-solving process, 186–187
  structured meeting agenda, 179,
  180–182, 195–198
Supplemental coaching support, 222–223
Sustainability. *See* Continuous
  regeneration stage
SWIS. *See* School-Wide Information
  System
SWPBIS Tiered Fidelity Inventory, 40,
  43, 177-179, 180-182, 230, 233
Systematic behavior screeners, 45–46
Systematic Screening for Behavior
  Disorders (SSBD), 45–46
Systems coaching, in the Oregon EBISS
  system, 271, 275

Team approach, 161–162
Team checklists
  for integrated district support, 224–226
  for integrating data, 72–74
  for integrating entire systems, 259–263
  for integrating practices, 152–154
  for integrating teams, 189–191
Team Implementation Checklist (TIC),
  40, 42
Teaming strategies
  effective teaming structures, 172–183,
  184
  integrated problem-solving and
  decision-making processes, 183,
  185–189
Teaming structures
  agreements and norms, 173, 174
  annual timetable for agenda items,
  183, 184
  mission and purpose statements, 173
  overview, 172–173
  specified meeting roles, 173–175
  structured agendas, 176–182
Team-initiated problem solving (TIPS),
  172–173, 176
Teams/Teaming
  EBISS teaming framework in Oregon,
  275–277
  effective strategies for *(see* Teaming
  strategies)
  importance and benefits of, 162
  importance to academic RTI and
  PBIS, 7

integrating systems and, 328
key areas for future research, 330
similarities and differences between
  academic RTI and PBIS, 8
  *See also* Integrated teaming; MTSS
  teams
Technical problems, in implementation,
  206
Think Time, 31
Three-tiered model
  conceptual origins, 13–15
  integrating teams across, 171–172
Tier 1
  conceptual overview, 13, 14
  importance of integrated academic and
  behavior support, 32
  integrated strategies, 118–127
  overview of integrated practices, 114
  six principles of effect academic and
  behavior instruction, 114–118
  Tier 2 practices and, 127–128
Tier 2
  conceptual overview, 13, 14
  function of behavior as the key to
  integrated support, 32
  integrated interventions, 129–133
  Intervention Tracking Tool, 111–112
  overview of integrated practices, 127–128
Tier 2 Function-Based Intervention and
  Resource Mapping Worksheet,
  142, 144, 156
Tier 2 resource maps, 142, 144–145
Tier 3
  conceptual overview, 14, 15
  example of integrated support,
  135–139
  function of behavior as the key to
  integrated support, 32
  importance of FBAs in developing
  support plans, 135
  Intervention Tracking Tool, 111–112
  overview of integrated practices, 133
  resources for developing support plans,
  134–135
  Tiered Fidelity Inventory (TFI).
  See SWPBIS Tiered Fidelity
  Inventory.
Tigard-Tualatin School District, 267–286
  *See also* Oregon's Effective Behavioral
  and Instructional Support
  Systems initiative
Training
  as a competency driver, 208, 212
  differentiated MTSS training, 220–221
  training and coaching providers, 215,
  216–217, 218
  *See also* Professional development

Universal design for learning, 123
Unsupported practices, 140

Validity, 62
Vision, as a leadership driver, 207, 209

Wait-to-fail approach, 11